Community Justice

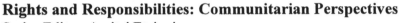

Rights and Responsibilities: Communitarian Perspectives
Series Editor: Amitai Etzioni

National Parks: Rights and the Common Good
    by Francis N. Lovett

Community Justice: An Emerging Field
    by David R. Karp

Community Justice

An Emerging Field

Edited by
David R. Karp

ROWMAN & LITTLEFIELD PUBLISHERS, INC.
Lanham • Boulder • New York • Oxford

ROWMAN & LITTLEFIELD PUBLISHERS, INC.

Published in the United States of America
by Rowman & Littlefield Publishers, Inc.
4720 Boston Way, Lanham, Maryland 20706

12 Hid's Copse Road
Cumnor Hill, Oxford OX2 9JJ, England

British Library Cataloguing in Publication Information Available

Library of Congress Cataloging-in-Publication Data

Community justice : an emerging field / edited by David R. Karp.
     p.   cm. — (Rights and responsibilities)
   Includes bibliographical references and index.
   ISBN 0-8476-9084-9 (pbk. : alk. paper). — ISBN 0-8476-9083-0 (cloth :
alk. paper)
   1. Community policing—United States. 2. Neighborhood justice centers—United
States. 3. Community organizations—United States. 4. Community-based corrections
—United States. 5. Citizens' advisory committees—United States. I. Carp, David R.,
1964– . II. Series: Rights and responsibilities (Lanham, Md.)
HV7936.C8C64   1998
363.2'3'0973—dc21   98-20870

Printed in the United States of America

♾ ™ The paper used in this publication meets the minimum requirements of American
National Standard for Information Sciences—Permanence of Paper for Printed Library
Materials, ANSI Z39.48–1984.

Contents

Preface   vii

I. INTRODUCTION

1. The Community Justice Movement   3
   Todd R. Clear and David R. Karp

II. COMMUNITY ACTION

2. Community Organizations and Crime   31
   Susan F. Bennett

3. The Takoma Orange Hats: Fighting Crime and
   Building Community in Washington, D.C.   47
   Suzanne Goldsmith-Hirsch

4. Building Community Capacity to Prevent
   Violence through Coalitions and Partnerships   81
   David M. Chavis

III. RACE AND CLASS

5. Toward a Theory of Race, Crime, and Urban
   Inequality   97
   Robert J. Sampson and William Julius Wilson

6. Crime and the Racial Fears of White Americans   119
   Wesley G. Skogan

IV. COMMUNITY POLICING

7. A Tale of Two Targets: Limitations of
Community Anticrime Actions 137
Michael E. Buerger

8. "Angels in Marble": Problems in Stimulating
Community Involvement in Community Policing 167
Randolph M. Grinc

9. Civil Liberties and Aggressive Enforcement:
Balancing the Rights of Individuals and Society
in the Drug War 203
Dennis P. Rosenbaum

10. Disorder and the Court 233
George L. Kelling and Catherine M. Coles

V. COMMUNITY PROSECUTION AND SANCTIONING

11. Community Prosecution: Portland's Experience 253
Barbara Boland

12. Conditions of Successful Reintegration
Ceremonies: Dealing with Juvenile Offenders 279
John Braithwaite and Stephen Mugford

13. The "Community" in Community Justice:
Issues, Themes, and Questions for the
New Neighborhood Sanctioning Models 327
Gordon Bazemore

VI. CONCLUSION

14. Community Justice in a Communitarian Perspective 373
Amitai Etzioni

Index 379

About the Contributors 385

Preface

Community justice is a phenomenon of growing interest among academics, policymakers, and criminal justice practitioners. The term is commonly used to reflect the increasing collaboration between criminal justice agencies and communities in the joint pursuit of public safety and a less tangible, but no less significant, pursuit of justice for victims, offenders, and all community members affected by crime. Nevertheless, the concept of community justice has not yet been well developed; it is not the bold header of textbook chapters or literature reviews. The chapters of this volume suggest a field of research is emerging that can fall under the community justice banner.

Community justice encompasses a gamut of criminal justice agency initiatives; the "community" prefix is ubiquitous—community crime prevention, community policing, community prosecution, community defense, community courts, community corrections. The emerging model is not simply a matter of organizational change within the justice system. It also reflects a changing philosophy about the role of the community in American society. Some of this is seen in liberal-communitarian debates about the role of individuals in democratic society, whether their rights trump social responsibilities or vice versa, or if the two need be conceptualized in opposition. The emerging model is also concerned with the nature and organization of community life and the role community organizations and institutions play in socializing and enforcing behavioral standards. At a higher level of analysis, community justice is also concerned with the dynamic relations between communities, particularly in how such interdependencies affect the quality of community life at the neighborhood level.

This book is evidence of the growing concern about community justice among academics. Though only a few of the chapters specifically use the term "community justice," all address central questions of this emerging field. It is my hope that the reader will observe common themes across the chapters and will gain an understanding of the scope and depth of a community justice perspective.

The chapters of this volume are not summaries of quantitative analyses, though a few do report some results. Most address the broad questions of community justice, and a few provide some rich description of community justice processes based on qualitative studies. The intended audience of this book is the general reader who wants a thoughtful consideration of conceptual issues.

In addition to an introductory chapter by myself and Todd Clear which provides a synthetic overview of the community justice movement, and a concluding chapter by Amitai Etzioni which places the chapters in broader perspective, the volume is divided into four sections. The first section, "Community Action," emphasizes the role of community organizations in crime prevention. These chapters identify the vital role of community organizations as autonomous actors and as partners with the criminal justice system. The second section, "Race and Class," speaks to the structural and cultural issues underlying the concentration of race, poverty, and crime. The third section, "Community Policing," is a selection from a now quite large literature on community policing. In this book, the emphasis is on the challenge and promise of this approach. The final section, "Community Prosecution and Sanctioning," speaks to the emerging priorities of community justice in response to criminal incidents. It is especially concerned with the debate about retributive and restorative justice.

I. Introduction

1

The Community Justice Movement

Todd R. Clear and David R. Karp

In recent years, there has been a rapid growth in justice approaches that turn their attention toward the community. There are literally hundreds of examples of this trend, from offender-victim reconciliation projects in Vermont and Minneapolis to "beat probation" in Madison, Wisconsin; from neighborhood-based prosecution centers in Portland, Oregon, and New York City, to community probation in Massachusetts. Of course, the most well-known version of community justice is community policing, but localized projects involving all components of the justice system have been widely promoted (see National Institute of Justice 1996).

The community-oriented models of criminal justice are also becoming emphasized in other countries. Family group conferencing for juvenile offenders is a prominent method in New Zealand and Australia—juvenile offenders and their families meet in conferences with community members and discuss strategies for victim restitution and personal interventions to prevent further delinquency (Alder and Wundersitz 1994). Native American groups in Canada use sentencing circles—tribal members meet together with the offender and the victim to discuss a resolution to the criminal conduct (Stuart 1996).

All indications are that we are in the early stages of a Western movement to make the criminal justice system more responsive to the community. The initiatives that accompany this trend are idiosyncratic, too varied to be characterized in a simple manner. They have come about not as a part of a grand plan, but as a disjointed product of local problem-solving efforts. However diverse, these initiatives all have in common (to some degree or another) a new perspective on crime and justice. They share an ideal that the justice system ought to be made relevant (or, perhaps, more relevant) to the quality of community life, and that it ought to make better use of a community's individual and institutional resources in dealing with crime.

At first blush, this seems a simple, unremarkable concept: "community justice." There also seems to be little to find disturbing in the idea—who could object to a call for our justice system to more actively improve community life? A deeper investigation of the idea reveals considerable complexity and no small degree of controversy: What exactly *is* "community"? How can the justice system be made relevant to all the various communities out there; indeed, should it? What is the relationship between the ideal of "equal protection under the law" and the movement toward innovation and variation at the community level? These and other questions illustrate that a community justice program, for all its apparent appeal, is a potentially profound shift away from traditional conceptions of criminal justice.

Recently, a working group at the Department of Justice began to clarify the underpinnings of the wide variety of "community justice" programs. In one of the working group's early drafts, it listed as "principles" the following:

- The community is the ultimate customer and the full partner of the system.
- The primary goal is harmony of system components and the community.
- Community-based sanctions are worthy responses to the problem of crime.
- Work efforts must focus on the underlying causes of *crime* rather than only responding to *criminal behavior*. (Working Group on Restorative Justice 1996)

These principles are offered as more than glib public relations sentiments; they are meant to guide the design and implementation of community justice initiatives. They help define a new approach to the establishment of justice that makes the community and its members figure prominently. What is suggested by these changes is what we refer to as a "community justice ideal." This is the vision of a justice system that links its actions to the quality and safety of community life. It redefines the justice objectives away from traditional, disinterested law enforcement toward an activist, involved system that treats crime as a community problem to be unraveled. In short, *the ideal of community justice is that the agents of criminal justice should tailor their work so that its main purpose is to enhance community living, especially through reducing the paralysis of fear, the indignities of disorder, and the agony of criminal victimization.*

Recent Innovations

Without making explicit claims, the new interest in community embraces, to at least some degree, the community justice ideal. These initiatives shift the focus of the justice process from the accused and convicted to the resident and the neighbor. While there are many examples of this new interest in the community, it is helpful to review a few to illustrate how traditional criminal justice functions of policing, adjudication, and correcting are being reinterpreted to embrace a community emphasis by innovations currently under way. Our purpose in this initial review is not a comprehensive critique of community justice or its antecedent programs, but rather to show how community-driven changes are redefining the work of the main, traditional justice functions.

Policing

The push for community justice in many ways derives from the community-oriented and problem-solving policing experience. In a very short time, policing has shifted from a detached professional model to an involved community model. Because *community policing* has gained widespread popularity across the nation (for example, Peak and Glensor [1996, p. 68] report that the majority of America's police departments have adopted a community policing approach), there has been much variation to both the definition and practice of community policing. Underlying the various approaches are the dual strategies of problem-solving and community involvement (Goldstein 1990; Skogan 1997; Skolnick and Bayley 1986; Sparrow et al. 1990; Trojanwicz and Bucqueroux 1990).

Problem-solving is a conceptual shift that focuses on the identification and resolution of underlying causes to criminal incidents rather than on quick reaction to a particular incident. This has not been an easy reassignment of priorities. There is a certain tension between the dedication of resources to 911 calls for service and the commitment of officers to a variety of in-depth problem-solving efforts. The hypothesis guiding community policing is that prevention efforts will better address the inadequacies of "911 policing" than more aggressive cops, more sophisticated 911 technology, or shorter response times. The shift in focus has necessitated wide-ranging organizational changes in police departments from new recruitment policies that seek well-educated self-starters to greater autonomy and authority for line officers. The paradigmatic shift is best reflected in the seeming common sense of everyday activities that characterize the approach:

> In Aurora, Colorado, on the eastern edge of Denver, a popular bar catering to hordes of young people was hit with a rash of purse thefts from customers' cars. Community police officers working with the bar owner and patrons determined that young women left their purses in their cars because they liked to dance and feared their purses would be stolen off tables while they danced. Police got the bar owner to install lockers where women could lock their purses; the incidents went from hundreds per month to virtually none. (Peak and Glensor 1996, p. 332)

In addition to problem-solving, community policing is typified by a concern for community involvement. At minimum, this involves a sincere effort to identify and address community concerns. One major outcome of this effort has been an increased emphasis on addressing social disorder—public drinking, panhandling, graffiti, prostitution, and so on—because of widespread community concern over these problems (Kelling and Coles 1996; Skogan 1990). More profoundly, community involvement means sharing the responsibility for social control with community members. Rather than being simply the "eyes and ears" of the police, the community is the more powerful agent of social control, if for no other reason than the fact that parents, teachers, or neighbors provide a level of surveillance that can never be matched by the police (at least in a free, democratic society).

Community involvement can encompass a broad range of activities. Efforts range from police participation in community anticrime campaigns through citizen patrols (Davis and Lurigio 1996) to the creation of police "mini-stations" in local areas that foster greater police-community contact and long-term relationships (Skolnick and Bayley 1986).

There is now a broad experience with these policing initiatives, though only a small evaluation record exists to support the experience. A few patterns seem to emerge from studies to date (Police Executive Research Forum 1995). First, community policing strategies encounter significant resistance from line workers, especially in initial stages. Line workers define police work as crime-fighting labor, and they are often tempted to see the community/problem strategies as "soft," giving up hard-won authority for uncertain gains. Second, no standard, proven procedure exists for the design and implementation of the idea; rather, effective community policing appears to be a product of idiosyncratic efforts to mobilize the community. Because the mobilization objective has to do with quality-of-life issues, the techniques police often use are "problem-solving" in nature. Third, the move to community policing is a long-term effort that cannot be fully accomplished in a few months—or even a year or two. Fourth, the long-term relationship between the community approaches and serious crime is unclear, though promising reductions in some forms of "street" crime have occurred in some cities (Bratton 1995; Kelling and Coles 1996).

Community strategies are redefining police work. Line officers are less and less seen as bureaucrats caught in autocratic organizations; they are more and more seen as innovators whose knowledge of the world at the line level gives them a special expertise in problem-solving. Arrest rates and 911 calls are decreasingly used as indicators of success; they are being replaced by citizen satisfaction with police services and direct solutions to citizen-articulated problems—and even reductions in victimizations based on victim surveys. Police are learning to divest themselves of the "we-they" syndrome that dominates the "thin blue line" tradition and instead to see residents as potential partners in making localities better places to live.

Adjudicating

There are five examples of the community movement in case adjudication: victim impact statements, victim-offender mediation, neighborhood defense, community prosecution, and community courts.

The victims' movement has called for ways to give the victim "a voice" in the criminal justice system, for the state to provide services such as legal advice, therapeutic counseling, and security enhancement assistance, and for offenders to receive tougher punishments and/or to make restitution. With regard to the victim's role, the movement to date has been rather circumscribed. At formal decision points, such as sentencing or parole, the system's officials provide an opportunity through *victim impact statements* for victims to speak about the crime's impact and voice an opinion as to the most appropriate decision. Almost nobody disputes the value of allowing victims to voice their feelings about crime and justice, but some critics of the victims' movement point out that this is a very narrow type of involvement (Elias 1983).

The victim's role in the justice process is much expanded in *victim-offender mediation* (Van Ness and Strong 1997). Many victim-offender mediation programs exist as diversionary programs: if offenders agree to participate, they can avoid going to trial (and, obviously, jail). Here, the victim is given the opportunity to meet with the specific offender with questions or statements about the impact of the crime and may negotiate terms for restitution or other community-based sanctions. These programs allow for a more intensive involvement of victims in the adjudication process. Studies show that victim-offender meetings often lead to a stronger sense of satisfaction with the justice process for both victims and offenders (Quinn 1996; Umbreit 1994).

Community defense represents both a shift in approach among public defenders and a continuity of their concerns for the protection of rights and safety of their clients. The shift is found in new priorities for serving a wider array of needs of both clients and their neighbors. The most important example of community defense is the Neighborhood Defender Service of Harlem (Stone 1996). One unique feature of this program is its location outside the court and inside the neighborhood it serves. Another feature is its active outreach in the community, fostering ongoing relationships with residents rather than performing as an impersonal default referral service of the court. A third feature of the program is that each client is assigned to a team that includes attorneys and community workers, which helps shift priorities from court activities to problem-solving efforts on the street. Perhaps the most important aspect of community defense is its central concern for the experience clients have when in contact with the justice system: it prioritizes fair and respectful treatment in a system that often drives a wedge between troubled residents and the community.

Prosecutors have also become more involved in the community. One of the best examples of *community prosecution* is provided in Portland, Oregon, as described by Barbara Boland in this volume. There, District Attorney Michael Schrunk, troubled about crime complaints in one of the local areas in Portland, moved one of his central offices out to the district to provide a more localized, relevant prosecution of crime. Local prosecutors soon learned that residents were not only concerned about serious crimes, but they were concerned about disorder, petty disturbance, and overall quality of neighborhood life.

In Portland, citizen input into the prosecutor's function called forth changes mirroring those of the police in problem-solving mode: crime-fighting became less central to the activities of the office. Instead, prosecutors (adopting a name change to "neighborhood district attorneys") took on the role of legal advisors to local police and community members who were dealing with crime problems. Instead of automatically invoking the adversarial system, neighborhood DAs found they were often called upon to resolve disputes, restore orderly relations, and intervene into problem situations. Their role shifted from the prosecution of specific cases to the solving of crime and disorder problems.

Community courts represent a fifth community approach to the adjudication process. Variations of the community court model, such as teen courts, drug courts, and family violence courts, specialize in particular issues in order to develop more comprehensive solutions. The underlying assumption of community courts is that communities are deeply affected by the sentencing process yet are rarely consulted and involved in judicial outcomes. One important example is Manhattan's Midtown Community Court that specializes in misdemeanor offenses (Rottman 1996). Contained in one building, the Midtown Community Court makes concrete use of a social services center, a community service program, community mediation services, and a sophisticated information network which tracks and relays cases as they travel between departments. The central message of the court exemplifies the community orientation:

> Take the defendants one by one and hold them immediately accountable with swift, real sanctions. Beyond that, pay attention to who they are and address the issues underlying the charges that brought them in. Above all, keep the emphasis on quality-of-life crimes, those pervasive low-level offenses that undermine a whole community's morale. (Anderson 1996, p. 3)

This experience hints at a general point about community justice: what communities seek are often not traditional images of crime fighting. Instead, residents want quality of living; that is often not a direct product of the adversarial, war-on-crime model. The adjudication apparatus is at its most restricted in terms of the actions that can be taken when it seeks to prosecute, convict, and punish. When the legal system sets out to solve local problems and address the concerns of crime victims, it has available a much wider set of choices. A community-oriented adjudication model can become tailored to local issues and concerns more easily if it does not keep the adversarial as its ideal.

Correcting

One whole faction of corrections comes under the title *community corrections*, so it would seem an active community-oriented correctional function would have a long tradition in corrections. This is not entirely the case. While it is true that for most of this century the number of offenders under active supervision in the community has well outnumbered those in prison, at times by multipliers, that still does not amount to a community corrections. Merely because some offenders happen to reside in the community does not mean that a corrections exists that considers itself a community function. For the most part, community corrections refers to mechanisms for dealing with convicted offenders who happen to reside in the community. Corrections enters the community, but the community never makes it into corrections.

But there is extraordinary promise for community corrections from the point of view of community development. It is known that previously active offenders contribute disproportionately to the amount of crime in a community (Wolfgang et al. 1972); it is also believed that nearly all offenders removed from a community for incarceration will return—usually to that same community. It would seem that substantial benefits would occur if corrections could make its priority improving community life through effective offender reintegration.

Some new projects have emerged. In Vermont, a series of "consumer studies"—focus group interviews with citizen groups—led to a major overhaul of the relationship between correctional practice and the community. Community advisory boards now play an active role in the process of restoring offenders to community life after having been sanctioned for their offenses (Dooley 1995). They are charged with the task of making the offender fully aware of the damage caused by the crime, for negotiating a sanction with the offender that will make up for this damage, and for charting a course for the offender to become better integrated into the community. This strategy is not used exclusively by rural Vermonters; a similar approach is taken by the district attorney's office in Philadelphia for juvenile offenders (DiIulio and Palubinsky 1997). In countless other community corrections systems, citizens are called upon to serve as volunteers, advisors, paraprofessionals, and the like. A recent publication highlights nearly twenty examples of community/citizen partnerships with correctional agencies (American Probation and Parole Association 1996). These range in focus from offenders to victims to coalitions oriented toward neighborhood problems.

Yet in contrast to policing and prosecution, the community movement in corrections is nascent—perhaps in part because the term "community" gives false comfort that the issues of local residents are already taken into account. In reality, most community corrections agencies act as though they are somehow afraid of the residents who live in the areas they serve. Historically, many local leaders, far from being supportive of community corrections, have been hostile to the agency that manages what many citizens consider to be a threat: the former offender who lives among them.

The isolated examples in which correctional leaders have reached out to community members reveal a different potential reality. Citizens can learn to understand and support the necessity—even appropriateness—of the correctional worker's job. Local leaders can take responsible roles in assisting in the supervision and reintegration of convicted offenders.

Yet it seems so much more should be possible. A major impediment to offender readjustment is the suspicion and hostility of community members. A community yearning for public safety is an opportunity for justice professionals to help offenders and reduce public fears by creating supportive and supervisory links between community members and offenders. The point is not to dismiss or diminish public fears in the absence of other changes; it is to forge realistic links to community members and institutions when facing the problem of reducing risk through effective reintegration. The community agenda, as it moves into the correctional realm, will increasingly find itself concerned with these questions.

There is, of course, one area where the community has entered the correctional world—the victims' movement. Correctional personnel, from probation officers to parole boards, are increasingly called upon to consider the implications of the victim's needs and experiences for day-to-day correctional work. For the most part to date, this has been seen as a problem of "managing" victims and their input, but the promise of a much more active concern for victims and offenders both remains on the horizon (Galaway and Hudson 1996; Van Ness and Strong 1997). Incarcerated offenders may engage in community service and, more radically, volunteer community boards may orchestrate reparative agreements between victims (often broadly conceived) and offenders (Dooley 1995). Such approaches combine formal social control with informal control by forcing offenders to confront the consequences of their behaviors before their community peers and assume responsibility by writing letters of apology, making restitution, and performing community service. A number of other innovative approaches now call for offenders to repair the damage of their criminal acts and to otherwise demonstrate why fellow citizens ought to have enough faith in the possibility of a crime-free life that former offenders may reclaim their status as citizens.

Beyond the Criminal Justice System

Community justice is not the exclusive domain of the criminal justice system. When the focus shifts from crime control to the quality of community life, the antecedents of crime become central: the activities of community justice become oriented toward prevention in complement to crime response. Broadly, community justice may be concerned with neighborhood stability, the quality and nature of community social networks, and the community's institutional capacity from families to schools to housing to churches and other voluntary organizations. A community-building orientation blurs the boundaries that have traditionally compartmentalized various social welfare and public safety functions.

A recent approach, particularly among private foundations, that is consistent with the community justice perspective is to support *comprehensive community initiatives* (Connell et al. 1995; Kennedy 1996; Schorr 1997). These initiatives try to address multiple problems of a neighborhood at once, focusing as much on coordination and collaboration as on individual program development. Projects that focus on social or economic conditions of a neighborhood often intersect with criminal justice concerns. For example, projects with a central focus on improving public housing must also consider the criminal activities almost endemic to large, urban public housing projects (Chavis et al. 1997; Sampson 1995).

Community justice activities are also reflected in various efforts taken by communities to prevent crime that do not formally involve the criminal justice system. One example of this is the assortment of practices that fall under the heading *situational crime prevention* (Clarke 1995; Ekblom 1995; Taylor and Harrell 1996). Private security, burglar alarms, street lighting, steering wheel locks, surveillance cameras, and so on are all direct efforts to reduce crime by private citizens, businesses, and municipal governments. Another recent trend has been the mobilization of the business community to form *business improvement districts* (BIDs). Such entities levy their own taxes to fund crime prevention and disorder reduction activities to enhance community conditions for the protections of both employees and customers (MacDonald 1996).

Summary

In many respects, the community justice movement reflects a radical departure from the past of criminal justice activity. Localized, dynamic, variable strategies replace the centralized, standardized, expert model that has been the object of most professional development of recent years. The new frontier of community justice is thus a cutting edge in the way it uses information, organizes staff, plans its activities, and is accountable to its environment. These are the outer boundaries of community justice; what now exists may be thought of as interim stages of the general shift toward a more community-relevant justice strategy.

Taken collectively, current innovations reflect a sporadic, uncoordinated movement toward the community by the justice system. The experience with these changes has been promising. Justice officials involved in these programs report that they successfully transform the justice worker into much more of a community worker. Satisfaction with these new approaches is based upon a sense of greater citizen involvement and, as a consequence, support of the justice work.

But it is important to emphasize that these changes are something of a spontaneous adaptation of the system to its lack of credibility and effectiveness, undertaken by some elements of the justice system, often in isolation from others. What has not occurred is a systematic, overarching conceptualization of the potential of community justice and its design and implementation. Until an encompassing notion of community justice is established, the piecemeal and idiosyncratic manner of these changes will continue to predominate. It is our aim to contribute to community justice by providing a broader, more encompassing conceptualization of its meaning and value—a "community justice ideal." We begin with a listing of the basic elements of community justice practice.

Elements of Community Justice

These recent innovations are widely varied versions of the effort to move justice into the community. In some ways, they are appropriately seen as essentially unrelated initiatives. But the surface dissimilarities obscure a foundational set of corresponding assumptions and tactics that place these initiatives within a loosely articulated common framework of the community justice ideal.

Definition

Community justice broadly refers to all variants of crime prevention and justice activities that explicitly include the community in their processes and set the enhancement of community quality of life as an explicit goal. Community justice is rooted in the actions that citizens, community organizations, and the criminal justice system can take to control crime and social disorder. Its central focus is community-level outcomes, shifting the emphasis from individual incidents to systemic patterns, from individual conscience to social mores, and from individual goods to the common good. Typically, community justice is conceived as a partnership between the formal criminal justice system and the community, but often communities autonomously engage in activities that directly or indirectly address crime.

Community justice is an emerging perspective that is gaining attention partly as a result of setbacks in other arenas and partly on the promise of the community concept. It is not yet a coherent practice, a systematic theory, nor is it grounded in a particular tradition of cumulative empirical research. As we look at the various trends in crime prevention and criminal justice, we see common concerns across spheres, common goals being articulated, and common strategies amid the experiments.

Community justice may be identified by four core elements that distinguish the emerging community justice activities from prior policies and practices. These characteristic elements are not disclosed on the basis of abstract theory. Rather, they seem to be born of the frustrations of implementation, the practical necessities of attempts to improve community life by reducing disorder and crime, and by a desire to increase the public trust.

First, there is an explicit attention to the coordination of activities at the *neighborhood level.* The meaning of the term "community" in community justice requires some extended consideration, but without doubt one of its core features is the sense of belonging that a neighborhood provides. This membership in a place-based community is grounded in the important set of relationships and institutions that help create standards and expectations of behavior. Community justice relies in large part on these local institutions. Second, explicit attention is given to both short- and long-term *problem-solving.* Community justice activities are proactive, based on identified problems. This is a conceptual shift from traditional reactive approaches that address incidents as they occur, without attention to underlying causes. Third, community justice practices require *decentralization of authority and accountability* that empowers communities and local agencies. In the criminal justice system, organizational changes are necessary to give line workers more decision-making autonomy and facilitate collaboration across law enforcement and social service agencies. Fourth, *citizen participation* is central. Not only do citizens participate to ensure local concerns are addressed, but such participation is strategic for building community capacity so that informal mechanisms of control can gradually share or even replace much of the formal justice apparatus. Below we describe these four elements and illustrate their importance in existing programs.

Community Justice Operates at the Neighborhood Level

Community justice is experienced by members of a community. Recently, James Q. Wilson observed, in the introduction to Kelling and Coles' (1996) book, *Fixing Broken Windows,* that judges view a crime quite differently than does a community. Where judges see an isolated incident, as a snapshot to use his metaphor, the community views the event as one frame in a filmed documentary of community life. The crime takes place in real time and space, in a context of local relationships and institutions. Community justice takes this moving-picture view of crime, attempting to expand the partial traditional outlook to a holistic community perspective. To do so requires consideration of natural areas and indigenous definitions of community boundaries instead of relying on jurisdictional or political boundaries.

Criminal law jurisdictions are defined by political boundaries—states, municipalities, and governments—but from the point of view of community life, these legal perimeters are often without meaning. Both Lubbock and El Paso implement Texas criminal law, but the nature of community life in these towns, hundreds of miles apart, is quite different when it comes to crime and its control. Indeed, within Lubbock and El Paso, there will be local variations that have a major impact on the way crime is addressed in those areas. Differences among communities are the facts that lead to a desire for greater community-level justice, but it is the disjointed relationship between legal categories and neighborhoods that poses the biggest problem for community justice ideals. Some way must be found to identify and mobilize more geographically confined versions of justice system activities. Operationally, this means thinking in terms of *blocks* of space, not cities, counties, or states. Under a community justice ideal, criminal justice activities will be tied to these delimited localities and will be free to adapt to particular manifestations of community life there.

New York City is experimenting with this conceptual shift in its creation of the Midtown Community Court (Anderson 1996). Unlike other courts which tend to represent much larger geographic areas, the

Midtown Court is located in the center of a well-defined neighborhood—Times Square, Clinton, and Chelsea—in this case, a highly commercial area and bordering residential neighborhoods well known for their high levels of disorder (prostitution, panhandling, illegal vending, graffiti, shoplifting, fare-beating, vandalism, etc.). The neighborhood focus is not simply a matter of relocation or redrawing boundaries. The purpose is to respond to specific problems in a comprehensive, context-specific manner. The Midtown Court does this by coordinating justice activities so that efforts are supported and multiplied. It works with police in disorder enforcement strategies. It works with local residents, businesses, and social service agencies to forge creative, collaborative solutions to quality-of-life issues. It develops individualized sanctions for offenders that bring restitution to victims, community service to the neighborhood, and education and treatment programs for offenders.[1]

The focus of community justice is not individuals or individual criminal incidents. Nor is the focus on a citywide, statewide, or nationwide crime problem. Community justice is explicitly concerned with a pattern of relations and institutions that effectively operate at the neighborhood level. These loom large enough to affect crime and disorder rates over time (why, for example, does a particular neighborhood remain criminogenic long after a cohort of delinquents has moved on or passed away?), but also small enough to be relevant to the behavior of particular individuals. At the same time, community justice is not myopic with regard to neighborhood boundaries. Neighborhoods are understood in the context of larger economic, political, and social systems, subject to forces beyond neighborhood control. Thus community justice begins with a focus on solving neighborhood problems, first by drawing on local resources and initiatives, but additionally by bolstering them with extra-local resources often necessary to create viable local institutions and practices.

Community Justice Is Problem-Solving

In the public discourse about crime, "war" terminology dominates. Offenders are talked about as "them," victims are "us." Policy to deal with crime is described in terms of "combating" crime, and strategies are thought to be effective when they make the offender, thought to be an unusual miscreant, into an "enemy" of the people. This type of imagery distorts the reality of criminality and victimization. Young males are predominately the offenders brought into the system, and they are also overrepresented among victims. Almost a third of all males will experience a felony arrest (Wolfgang et al. 1972) and self-report studies show that most citizens have both committed an offense and been victim of one (Dunford and Elliott 1984; Huizinga and Elliot 1987). In short, domestic tranquillity is not a problem of warfare; it is a general problem of citizenship.

The war metaphor is inadequate in another way. It seeks to attack an external foe, but in crime there is seldom an external threat; usually the offender is a fellow citizen. Combat enemies can be "vanquished," whereas offenders who are arrested and convicted may be removed from the community for a period, but they nearly always return to their neighborhoods.

An alternative to the "war" metaphor is to treat crime as a societal problem. Under this approach, the people affected by crime—offenders, victims and their families, and neighbors—are seen as afflicted by the precursors and consequences of crime. Each of these factors can be defined not as an "enemy" to be conquered, but as posing problems to be solved. In community justice, a much greater emphasis is placed on both the priority of public safety problems that need to be solved in order to improve community life and on the potential consequences of the means taken to solve those problems.

Problem-solving approaches are different from the conflict paradigm in that they rely upon information, deliberation, and mutual interest for a resolution. The belief is that citizens share a set of values and concerns, and with proper information and order, a way out of the problem can be found. When crime is approached as a problem, solutions can take various forms, from rearranging public space to providing oversight of youths. Prosecution and punishment need not be the only ways to approach a crime problem. Indeed, the search for a creative solution derived from community members' own ideas is one of the hallmarks of community justice approaches.

Information is a key to solving problems. Local areas conduct crime analyses to determine the type and nature of public safety problems that residents want to establish as a priority. The uniqueness of these crime problems to the specific area will set the substantive foundation for the community justice initiatives. Actual strategies will emanate from interactions between citizens and justice system officials as they try to determine the most productive means to solve crime problems.

Kelling and Coles (1996) describe an excellent example of the problem-solving approach. The New York subway system was once well known for its high levels of disorder—one manifestation being the graffiti that covered train cars from top to bottom, inside and out. Today,

the more than 5,000 train cars are virtually graffiti-free. Critical components of the successful strategy involved interviews with subway
passengers, transit officials, and graffiti artists. It was discovered that a
major motivation behind the graffiti was the knowledge that others
would see the artists' "tags." The strategy called for entering the trains,
one by one, into a program that required each car be completely cleaned
and returned to service. If graffiti appeared on a "clean car," it was
immediately taken out of service and cleaned again. In time, the graffiti
artists stopped their tagging because their motivation was taken away:
they never saw their tags. The end result of this and other efforts was a
reduction in disorder and crime and a renewed public trust in the safety
of the subways.

Information is used in three ways. First, geo-specific information
organizes places into priorities (Taylor and Harrell 1996). High crime
locations receive greater attention, greater investment of local resources,
for not only is the problem more difficult, but the potential payoff in
improved quality of life is greater. Second, resident concerns and desires
are a source of program information. They tell the justice system actors
what factors residents see as most closely tied to quality of community
life problems (Kelling 1992). Third, information translates into targets
that can be used to evaluate the successfulness of a given strategy for
confronting crime (Sherman et al. 1997).

The new age of community justice is made possible by the power of
information. Using geo-coded data, crime control services are organized
around locations of crime events, offenders, and victims. Data, both
official data about crimes and offenders and qualitative data that come
from interaction with offenders, victims, and neighborhood residents,
drive problem-solving and action. Information will also provide evaluative feedback about the successes of strategies. The imaginative use (and
production) of information is one of the factors that sets aggressive
community safety strategies apart from the more mundane concept of the
local constable.

Community Justice Decentralizes Authority and Accountability

Moving toward community justice requires a rethinking of the line-
authority relations within criminal justice organizations. Traditionally,
criminal justice management is hierarchical: at each level of the organization, a worker reports to an immediate superior, who in turn reports to
the next level. All positions have one "boss," and each manager has a
span of control. Under community justice, this traditional manner of

organizing is complicated by the advent of community involvement, and agencies are experimenting with ways to formalize the relationship between residents and the professional justice workers.

Community justice approaches have nontraditional organizational alignments. Staff may report to citizen groups in addition to professional superiors. Managers in one organization (say, policing) may be "matrixed" with managers of another (say, probation or prosecution) in order to improve coordination and increase cross-fertilization of ideas and action. For example, in Wisconsin, "Beat Probation" links probation officers to police officers with shared, localized workloads involving offenders on probation. In Boston, "Operation Night Light" (Corbett et al. 1996) uses a similar teaming approach with the police and probation officers to facilitate monitoring and supervision of offenders in their neighborhoods, particularly at night. In each of these illustrations, multiple lines of authority exist and some involve roles played by nonemployees such as volunteer mentors.

The communication channels under such inventive organizational structures are complicated. Lateral information sharing and short-term, ad hoc problem-solving groups may be a dominant mode of work. Community justice approaches have dynamic organizational models that shift and are reconstituted, based upon the problem being encountered. Community justice calls for more authority and accountability at lower organizational levels as well as for community members and community organizations.

The decentralization of authority and accountability encourages innovative problem-solving. Processes of change are based on a foundation of interaction with citizens in which new ideas are valued and new solutions encouraged. In order to be effective, new methods and strategies have to replace the old. Since the new ideas are grounded in the problem-solving process, they tend to be creative and reflect the particular experiences and priorities of the locality. The spirit of innovation requires a transformation of the justice profession from hidebound antagonisms among citizens and across agencies to interconnected processes of problem identification, information gathering, intervention design, and evaluation.

This innovation is not only a transformation for staff, many of whom are used to a traditional "command" model of their profession, it is also a remarkably different way of identifying accountability criteria. Instead of accountability for operational standards of practice (as is the case today for most criminal justice workers) accountability operates at the strategic level, requiring of staff the implementation of a vision more so than

concrete preordained actions. Moving away from the comfort of operational standards is one of the major challenges of community justice
approaches, since workers tend to be more comfortable being accountable for their actions but not for the impact of those actions on broader
measures of public safety.

The point, of course, is not to reduce or diffuse responsibility, but to
enable stakeholders to deliver on promises to solve problems even when
they fall outside the traditional purview of the particular stakeholder. For
example, new line authority in community policing often enables the cop
on the beat to do much more than exercise enforcement powers. He or
she is often able to organize community anticrime campaigns, mediate
ongoing disputes, and coordinate the solution to problems by collaborat-
ing with workers from other agencies. Whether a social worker places an
at-risk youth in a drug treatment program or a transportation planner
alters traffic flow through a highly visible drug market or "bazaar," the
solution to any particular public safety problem will nearly always
require inter-organizational integration.

Community Justice Involves Citizens in the Justice Process

A variety of roles exist for citizens in community justice initiatives,
but every role involves the capacity of the citizen to influence the local
practice of justice. The least involved role may influence practices by
attending and participating in meetings in which issues of crime and
order are discussed. Others may volunteer their time to work on particular projects, provide support to victims, assist offenders in their reintegration back into the community, and carry out community crime
prevention activities. Still others will take more formal roles as member
of advisory boards, providing more structured input into community
justice practices.

In the traditional model, the system of justice performs as a professional service system of state agents who work in response to criminal
events. This model can be detached and impersonal. It is accountable for
a set of professional standards that apply uniformly to all who are
engaged in the practice of justice. While this helps create a set of
universal ideals, it often mitigates responsiveness at the neighborhood-
level. By contrast, the community model involves professionals who
work in response to problems articulated by citizens. The worker is
accountable to those citizens for the types of service responses taken to
correct problems. Because of the heavy dosage of citizen input and
activity in the latter model, professional effort tends to be judged on the

basis of citizen satisfaction with justice services.

Even though this is a seemingly minor shift—criminal justice professionals will say they were *always* concerned with public satisfaction—the shift from professional to community accountability is a profound difference for the justice system. The participation of local residents in justice shifts priorities toward local problems and refocuses the attention of justice officials to take on more of the viewpoints of local residents.

The shift toward citizen participation is grounded in two important insights. First, formal social control by police and the courts is a thin layer in a much thicker foundation of institutions and cultural practices that produce social order. The "thin blue line" is buttressed by the important work of families, schools, churches, civic organizations, and so on in the creation of law-abiding citizens and safe public spaces. Community justice is an attempt to recognize, support, and expand the partnership between the community and the criminal justice system in their shared common goal of improving community life. Second, the shift toward citizen participation is grounded in the basic recognition that community members are citizens in a democratic society. Each community member is to be treated with dignity and respect and provided with the autonomy necessary for creating competent, self-reliant, civically oriented selves. This commitment to individuals extends to crime victims as well as to offenders. At the same time, it is assumed that citizens in a democracy must actively work toward the welfare of the whole society and not just look out for themselves. Thus, they are morally obligated to fulfill whatever tasks are necessary to sustain a good society. Our past failures, in part, result from a false assumption that the onus of public safety falls entirely on the criminal justice system.

Questions About Community Justice

There are considerable problems in realizing a community justice ideal. The illustrations in this chapter provide an intriguing glimpse of what might occur if community justice were the dominant paradigm rather than traditional criminal justice. But it must be stressed that these programs currently operate within the existing adversarial model, and in some ways they strain against that model in order to be responsive to the community. When a citizen advises a law enforcement official about priorities, it changes the accountability pattern of this function; when local residential preferences for social control help to determine allocation of time and other resources, requirements of practice become different from one area of a city to the next. Shifts such as these raise fundamental questions about the rationale and practicality of community justice ideals under traditional criminal law. Because the movement toward community justice has been haphazard, some of these questions have not surfaced very clearly. But any attempt to systematically embrace the community justice ideal will inevitably raise these issues to a visible and controversial reality.

What About Community Justice and Individual Rights?

If community justice takes the improvement of community life as its central aim, we must quickly wonder how much consensus exists over what constitutes improvement. While we would expect nearly universal agreement that a reduction of crime is desirable, we can also expect much disagreement over the price. For some, to obtain a high level of security, it would be permissible to build high walls to separate those who pose some risk from those who pose little. They will not only willingly sacrifice the rights of others to ensure their protection, but even many of their own rights—encouraging universal curfews, drug-tests, identification cards; enhancing the surveillance of public spaces, work-place computers, and private bank accounts; creating and toughening punishments for a wider array of nonconforming behaviors; legislating new regulations on permissible practices in the manufacture and sale of goods. For others, these are all signs of Orwellian state tyranny and if the price of freedom must be a high level of social disorder, then the bargain may be tragic, but tolerable.

We argue that the Hobbesian exchange of freedom for security is a mischaracterization of the problem. First of all, the contest is not merely between the individual and state, much of civil society stands between the two. As such, we see that freedom is made possible not only by the protections from state power, but also by the cultivation of cultural conditions that enable and encourage the growth of competent individuals who can make positive contributions both to their own lives and to the general welfare. Second, it is not clear that only increases in social order reduce freedom. It is also the case that movements toward disorder do the same. City air may make men (and women) free, but it also paralyzes many behind dead-bolted doors. Individuals need a substantial baseline of security in order to pursue their own happiness.

In a democratic community justice model, there may be variation in the way different communities adjudicate between twin desires for social order and individual autonomy. For example, if localities are allowed to determine justice (and crime) priorities, then it follows that services such as policing and prosecution may operate with differences in resource allocation and even practical action, even though they operate under identical criminal codes. How far may these differences be taken before they are deemed to violate our belief in equality under the law? To what extent may a locality exert its unique vision of social control without infringing upon freedoms of "deviant" members who are in the minority? Will a neighborhood justice movement take on some characteristics of vigilantism; if not, what is to stop it in the future?

As citizens become more active in various aspects of the justice process, the state's role in presiding over that process can be undercut. The adversarial ideal assumes that the state accuses a citizen and brings to bear evidence that supports the accusation. The dispute is between the state and the accused. Inserting other citizens—neighbors and residents—into that arrangement muddies the water by creating a third party to the dispute. It is unclear precisely what that third party's role ought to be—it could be observational, participatory, advisory, or even advocacy—but the presence of that party means that the state and its adversary can no longer be concerned only about each other. The concern for rights protections extends beyond those of the accused: to the rights of victims and to indirectly affected community members.

While it seems natural for the state and the accused to seek full vindication—a declaration of guilt or innocence—as an outcome of a contest, a third party interest may press for alternative outcomes. For instance, the community may want assurance of future protection, some restoration of the victim, assurance that the accused family will not suffer from punishments, and so forth. Creative resolutions of the dispute reshape the contest as well, suggesting that it is less about blaming and more about restoring peace in the community.

We must be uneasy about the implications of any developments that undermine the protection of rights. Perhaps the finest contribution of Western civilization to modern civil life is the idea of the sanctity and dignity of the individual. This idea is given life in the form of legal rights, in which citizens stand equal to one another as well as to the state. Any movement toward community justice taken at the expense of this priceless heritage would impose a cultural cost of profound dimensions. Community justice ideals *will* alter established practices of substantive and procedural criminal law. The test will be to devise the changes in ways that protect precious civil liberties.

What About Community Justice and Social Inequality?

Neighborhoods not only differ in their crime control priorities, they differ in their capacities, resources, and resilience in meeting crime problems. The same inequality that characterizes America at the individual level plays out as a community dynamic. The justice system operates really as two different systems, one for people with financial resources and another for the poor. Is there any assurance that the same kind of inequality will not come to characterize community justice?

This is not a small concern. Research shows that poor communities, particularly those hit hard by crime, tend also to lack resources to regulate neighborhood problems and pursue social control (Bursik and Grasmick 1993). These communities do not come together to solve problems, and they have low rates of citizen participation in official business. One of the lessons of community policing has been that in troubled neighborhoods, it is often difficult to get citizens to take responsible action in response to their crime problems (Rosenbaum 1988; Skogan 1990).

More prosperous localities will also have disproportionate political influence in many city and county governments. They will be better at organizing to influence the crime priorities, directing the funding decisions, and protecting their residents from negative impacts of change. A community justice model that enables localities to pursue interests and preferences will inevitably raise the potential for these more successful communities to strengthen their position in relation to other localities. The community justice ideal, therefore, cannot treat all communities as of equal importance or as independent from one another. Communities exist within larger social and political systems and local problems and public policies to address them must be understood within this broader context.

Inequality breeds crime. It would be a dismal irony if community justice, advanced to help places deal more effectively with their crime problems, contributed to the very dynamics that make those problems worse. If the problem of inequality is to be avoided, some local areas will likely require differential resource investment in order to take advantage of the promise of community justice.

What About Community Justice and the Increasing Costs of Criminal Justice?

We spend nearly $100 billion on official criminal justice in America every year (Bureau of Justice Statistics 1995).[2] The cost of justice is increasing, and the burden it places on the resources of local areas (through tax revenues) interferes with the capacity to fund schools, provide child health care, and maintain basic services. A community justice model calls for criminal justice organizations to augment current services. How will these be paid for?

The disparity between community resources and crime rates means that local revenues cannot be the basis for funding community justice capacity. As indicated above, the very communities that suffer most from crime are least able to pay to combat it. Some mechanism for moving financial support of community justice from affluent communities to impoverished ones will be needed. This will obviously raise sensitive political issues—American taxpayers are leery of spending for services from which they do not directly benefit.

Moreover, some way of shifting costs *within* the existing justice budget will be needed. New money for new programs is scarce, and a proposal to greatly increase funding of justice work will be met with skepticism. Instead, community justice needs to be based upon a shifting of resources within existing justice functions. The overall dollar costs of justice cannot be expected to rise too much; what can occur is a change in the allocation of justice dollars to provide support for new activities in place of previous functions no longer supported by the same level of revenues. Community justice advocates for collaboration between criminal justice agencies and other governmental and community social welfare agencies and services. Coordinated efforts will enhance effectiveness by combining the resources of different agencies using similar strategies to obtain different ends. For example, while one agency's objective may be increasing employment within a neighborhood, this goal may also reduce criminal activity.

Will Community Justice Improve Community Life in America?

The principles outlined above and the illustrations of them in today's justice practices represent responses to changes in crime and community life. They are a call for a justice system that is more attuned to the need to improve the quality of community life in America. They also contain the seeds of safer communities and more responsible community members. The vision promoted by these changes is of an increasingly relevant, increasingly purposeful set of justice practices carried out in close cooperation with citizens affected by those practices.

This is of course an attractive vision. A justice apparatus that had as its aim the sustaining of community would indeed be precious. But the potential perils are also important: community justice must also protect individual rights and autonomy, reduce social inequalities, and be cost-effective.

Notes

This chapter originally appeared in *Community Justice: Preventing Crime and Achieving Justice,* a report to the National Institute of Justice, November 1997. This work was supported by Grant No. 97-IJ-CX-0032 awarded by the National Institute of Justice, Office of Justice Programs, U.S. Department of Justice. Points of view in this document are those of the authors and do not necessarily represent the official position or policies of the U.S. Department of Justice. It is reprinted here with permission.

1. We note in passing that many of the offenders in the Midtown Court are not local residents since the court serves a largely commercial area. This makes for a unique version of community adjudication and sets the Midtown Court apart from more prototypical community justice, as we would define the term.

2. Another $52 billion is spent on private security annually (Cunningham et al. 1991).

References

Alder, Christine, and Joy Wundersitz, eds. 1994. *Family Conferencing and Juvenile Justice.* Canberra: Australian Institute of Criminology.

American Probation and Parole Association. 1996. "Restoring Hope through Community Partnerships: The Real Deal in Crime Control." *Perspectives* 20: 40-42.

Anderson, David C. 1996. "In New York City, a 'Community Court' and a New Legal Culture." *National Institute of Justice Program Focus.* Washington, DC: U.S. Department of Justice.

Bratton, William J. 1995. "Explaining the Drop in Urban Crime." Paper presented at the American Society of Criminology Annual Meeting. Boston.

Bureau of Justice Statistics. 1995. "Justice Expenditure and Employment Extracts: 1992." Washington, DC: U.S. Department of Justice.

Bursik, Robert J., and Harold G. Grasmick. 1993. *Neighborhoods and Crime: The Dimensions of Effective Community Control.* New York: Lexington Books.

Chavis, David M., Kien Lee, and Suzanne Merchlinsky. 1997. *National Cross-Site Evaluation of the Community Building Initiative.* Bethesda, MD: Cosmos, Inc.

Clarke, Ronald V. 1995. "Situational Crime Prevention." In *Building a Safer*

Society: Strategic Approaches to Crime Prevention, edited by Michael Tonry and David P. Farrington, 91-150. Chicago: University of Chicago Press.

Connell, James P., Anne C. Kubisch, Lisbeth B. Schorr, and Carol H. Weiss, eds. 1995. *New Approaches to Evaluating Community Initiatives*. Washington, DC: Aspen Institute.

Corbctt, Ronald P., Bernard L. Fitzgerald, and James Jordan. 1996. "Operation Night Light: An Emerging Model for Police-Probation Partnership." In *Invitation to Change: Better Government Competition on Public Safety*, edited by Linda Brown and Kathryn Ciffolillo, 105-15. Boston: Pioneer Institute for Public Policy Research.

Cunningham, William C., John J. Strauchs, and Clifford W. Van Meter. 1991. "Private Security: Patterns and Trends." Washington, DC: U.S. Department of Justice.

Davis, Robert C., and Arthur J. Lurigio. 1996. *Fighting Back: Neighborhood Antidrug Strategies*. Thousand Oaks, CA: Sage Publications.

DiIulio, John J., and Beth Z. Palubinsky. 1997. "How Philadelphia Salvages Teen Criminals." *City Journal* (Summer): 29-40.

Dooley, Michael. 1995. "Restorative Justice in Vermont: A Work in Progress." In *Topics in Community Corrections*, 31-36. Louisville, CO: LIS, Inc.

Dunford, Franklyn W., and Delbert S. Elliott. 1984. "Identifying Career Offenders Using Self-Reported Data." *Journal of Research in Crime and Delinquency* 21: 57-82.

Ekblom, Paul. 1995. "Less Crime, by Design." *Annals of the American Academy of Political and Social Science* 539: 114-29.

Elias, Robert. 1983. *Victims of the System*. New Brunswick, NJ: Transaction.

Galaway, Burt, and Joe Hudson, eds. 1996. *Restorative Justice: International Perspectives*. Monsey, NY: Criminal Justice Press.

Goldstein, Herman. 1990. *Problem-Oriented Policing*. New York: McGraw-Hill.

Huizinga, David, and Delbert S. Elliott. 1987. "Juvenile Offenders: Prevalence, Offender Incidence, and Arrest Rates by Race." *Crime and Delinquency* 33: 208-10.

Kelling, George. 1992. "Measuring What Matters: A New Way of Thinking About Crime and Public Order." *City Journal* (Spring): 21-33.

Kelling, George L., and Catherine M. Coles. 1996. *Fixing Broken Windows*. New York: Free Press.

Kennedy, David M. 1996. "Neighborhood Revitalization: Lessons from Savannah and Baltimore." *National Institute of Justice Journal* (August): 13-17.

MacDonald, Heather. 1996. "BIDs Really Work." *City Journal* (Spring): 29-42.

National Institute of Justice. 1996. *National Institute of Justice Journal* (August). Washington DC: U.S. Department of Justice.

Peak, Kenneth J., and Ronald W. Glensor. 1996. *Community Policing and*

Problem Solving. Upper Saddle River, NJ: Prentice Hall.

Police Executive Research Forum. 1995. "Community Policing." Washington, DC: Department of Justice.

Quinn, Thomas. 1996. "Restorative Justice." Presentation to the National Institute of Justice. Washington, DC.

Rosenbaum, Dennis P. 1988. "Community Crime Prevention: A Review and Synthesis of the Literature." *Justice Quarterly* 5: 323-95.

Rottman, David B. 1996. "Community Courts: Prospects and Limits." *National Institute of Justice Journal* (August): 46-51.

Sampson, Robert J. 1995. "The Community." In *Crime,* edited by James Q. Wilson and Joan Petersilia, 193-216. San Francisco, CA: Institute for Contemporary Studies.

Schorr, Lisbeth B. 1997. *Common Purpose: Strengthening Families and Neighborhoods to Rebuild America.* New York: Doubleday.

Sherman, Lawrence W., Denise Gottfredson, Doris MacKenzie, John Eck, Peter Reuter, and Shawn Bushway. 1997. *Preventing Crime: What Works, What Doesn't, What's Promising: A Report to the United States Congress.* Washington, DC: Department of Justice.

Skogan, Wesley G. 1990. *Disorder and Decline: Crime and the Spiral of Decay in American Neighborhoods.* New York: Free Press.

———. 1997. *Community Policing, Chicago Style.* New York: Oxford University Press.

Skolnick, Jerome H., and David H. Bayley. 1986. *The New Blue Line: Police Innovation in Six American Cities.* New York: Free Press.

Sparrow, Malcolm K., Mark H. Moore, and David M. Kennedy. 1990. *Beyond 911: A New Era for Policing.* New York: Basic Books.

Stone, Christopher. 1996. "Community Defense and the Challenge of Community Justice." *National Institute of Justice Journal* (August): 41-45.

Stuart, Barry. 1996. "Circle Sentencing: Turning Swords into Ploughshares." In *Restorative Justice: International Perspectives,* edited by Burt Galaway and Joe Hudson, 193-206. Monsey, NY: Criminal Justice Press.

Taylor, Ralph B., and Adele V. Harrell. 1996. "Physical Environment and Crime." National Institute of Justice.

Trojanowicz, Robert, and Bonnie Bucqueroux. 1990. *Community Policing: A Contemporary Perspective.* Cincinnati, OH: Anderson.

Umbreit, Mark S. 1994. *Victim Meets Offender: The Impact of Restorative Justice and Mediation.* Monsey, NY: Criminal Justice Press.

Van Ness, Daniel, and Karen Heetderks Strong. 1997. *Restoring Justice.* Cincinnati, OH: Anderson.

Wolfgang, Marvin E., Robert M. Figlio, and Thorsten Sellin. 1972. *Delinquency in a Birth Cohort.* Chicago: University of Chicago Press.

Working Group on Restorative Justice. 1996. "Community Justice Principles: Report of the Working Group." Washington, DC: U.S. Department of Justice.

II. Community Action

2

Community Organizations and Crime

Susan F. Bennett

It is commonplace to see news reports of residents marching down community streets with signs protesting the presence of drug dealers, picketing in front of a building used by drug dealers, or holding prayer vigils on street corners used by drug dealers. In response to illegal drug dealing, residents and community organizations plan activities to "take back" their communities from drug dealers and criminals, even if such events are only temporary reclamations of the community's public areas. In most cases, the press and civic leaders applaud the communities' resumption of responsibility for what happens in the community and their determination to create safer communities through their own actions.

This support for community-based action against crime is based on several assumptions: police alone cannot create safe communities; communities are an appropriate arena for crime prevention efforts; and police are more effective when they act *with residents* to "co-produce" safe communities (Lavrakas 1985; Skogan 1988). However, evaluations have raised questions about the efficacy of community-based crime prevention programs; reports of these studies provide an overview of the effectiveness and limitations of community organizations' role and address potential problems arising from their involvement (Rosenbaum 1987; Skogan 1988, 1990). This article focuses on the strengths that community organizations can bring to crime prevention efforts and the limitations of the usual evaluation approach for assessing their efficacy.

Community Organizations in Crime Prevention

A variety of community organizations engage in crime prevention: block clubs, community associations, umbrella organizations of community groups, and community development corporations. Their programs have been equally varied: reducing the opportunities for crime through target hardening, better surveillance of the neighborhood, and changes in the physical design of the neighborhood; reducing the causes of crime, usually through youth programs that provide tutoring, recreational activities, employment opportunities, and similar activities; helping victims through victim-witness programs; and strengthening law enforcement efforts. Often police departments, other city agencies, and social service organizations sponsor similar programs. Community organizations, however, are particularly suited to fulfill several functions needed for community crime prevention programs: generating participation, developing an understanding of community problems, addressing the broader social causes of crime, and developing the residential side of the partnership for community policing.

Generating Participation

Studies of community activism and crime prevention programs indicate that relatively few individuals begin participating because they are concerned about crime or other community problems. More generally, individuals are recruited through face-to-face encounters with acquaintances who are members or a community organizer (McCourt 1977; Perkins et al. 1990; Prestby and Wandersman 1985). And residential turnover means that recruitment in this fashion is an ongoing process. Community organizations are better suited to maintain face-to-face contacts with community residents than police departments or other city agencies. In some communities where the police (and possibly other government authorities) are mistrusted, residents are more likely to respond to local leaders and organizations.

Sustaining participation in community activities is also a challenge, and crime prevention activities present their own difficulties. In fact, several evaluations have noted that generating and maintaining participation is one of the major implementation difficulties for community crime prevention programs (Lavrakas and Bennett 1988; Rosenbaum 1986). Although community organizations have no magic wands for this problem, community crime prevention programs that are run by community organizations appear to last longer than those established by police departments or other city agencies (Lindsay 1988). In part, their greater success is due to their multi-issue agenda; groups focused only on crime prevention experience considerable difficulties maintaining participation and often fade rather quickly (Bursik and Grasmick 1993; Skogan 1988).

Generating Understanding of Community Problems

Many studies of community participation evoke images of a solitary individual concerned about a problem and deciding rationally on the best course of action to obtain maximum (individual) benefits for minimal (individual) costs (Olson 1965; Orbell and Uno 1972). Individuals, however, are frequently unaware that the problems they are experiencing are shared with many others and can or should be addressed through collective rather than individual action. Participation in community organizations may play an important role in helping individuals to define their political interests and concerns (Mansbridge 1985; Offe and Wiesenthal 1980). Some theorists argue that participatory democratic organizations are more likely to generate definitions of interests that are based on a collective good, rather than an aggregation of individual preferences (Barber 1984; Mill 1975; Pateman 1970). Through participation, individuals develop as "public citizens" who take into account factors beyond their own self-interests and develop genuinely "public" or collective policies. To the extent that community organizations facilitate the development of a collectively defined good, they provide a valuable function, particularly for communities with heterogeneous populations facing diverse problems with potentially conflicting solutions.

This potential advantage remains speculative, as there is little evidence about the ability of democratic organizations to go beyond the aggregation of individual preferences in defining goals. In fact, some activists and researchers have expressed concern about the extent to which crime is a divisive issue, and that crime prevention programs may be used by some groups to "protect" themselves against others (Skogan 1990). Indeed, stories of how "those people" (often youths or minority groups) are the problem in the neighborhood are common in community crime meetings. Yet, as programs develop, one begins to hear other stories as well. As a community policing participant, a young mother recruited neighbors to hang out in the park during the evenings to deter the youth who generally occupied it. The youths were noisy and intimidated other residents, who were unsure if the young people were gang members or drug dealers. During the co-occupation, the youth and adults began to discuss their contentions over the use of the park. The mother reported the youth's concerns about their limited options in the community and started to question the group's frequent assumption that young people are the problem. This small example occurred in an area where crime is particularly likely to be divisive: a very heterogeneous community, where racial differences are intensified by socioeconomic differences. This and similar incidents suggest that when given opportunities for collective actions and decision making, residents can broaden problem definitions to be more inclusive and reflect collective goods of the community.

Addressing Broader Social Causes of Crime

Community organizations usually address a broad range of local issues, including improving the physical environment (e.g., housing rehabilitation), developing the community's economic structure (e.g., attracting new businesses or providing support services to existing businesses), and enhancing the social environment (e.g., providing youth services). Many of these programs are aimed at problems that are considered to be underlying causes of crime, or that residents link to crime (e.g., panhandlers and teenagers hanging out on the corner) but are not effectively dealt with by usual law enforcement activities. Although community policing programs are expanding the role of police in responding to community problems, their ability to work on long-term solutions to complex community problems is uncertain at this point. Community organizations, assuming adequate support, have a structure better suited to attacking these problems. Their multi-issue focus is better suited to dealing with the intertwined problems of housing, economic development, families, schools, and crime than a single city agency which generally has responsibility for only a small part of the factors that make a community a safer and better place to live. And their continued recruitment and contact with residents ensures not only community participation but also community "ownership" of the problem-solving process. "[T]hus, [community organizations] may represent the most promising approach to urban crime prevention" (Perkins et al. 1990, p. 90; see also Lindsay 1988).

Forming Partnerships in Community Policing

The adoption of a community policing model by many departments further emphasizes the role of community organizations in crime prevention and control efforts. Community policing, though variously defined, relies heavily on a proactive stance to community problems and problem-solving activities through partnership with community residents. A partnership implies a sharing of responsibilities and decision making, and a joint contribution to problem-solving. In many instances, however, police treat residents more as clients than partners. Residents are consulted about community problems, but they are *not* engaged in the process of identifying problems and solutions for the community. In this model, the police retain the status of "experts" who develop appropriate solutions and implement them.

If residents and communities are to be partners rather than clients, they need sufficient resources to assume the role of partner. One critical resource is some level of collective organization: individual residents cannot function as "partners" with a police station or department, given the imbalance of expertise, resources, experience, and so forth. Residents need opportunities for collective consultation and decision making about problems and their solutions, often without police involvement. If such interactions only occur within a police setting, many residents are likely to be intimidated or overwhelmed by police officers' expertise and less likely to think outside of a criminal justice framework when exploring problems and their solutions.

Little consideration has been given to the community's involvement in this new policing model. Although not a panacea, community organizations are well situated to facilitate the development of the residential side of the community-police partnership, for many of the same reasons that they are good sponsors of crime prevention programs.

The Efficacy of Community Crime Prevention Programs

Bursik and Grasmick (1993, p. 149) noted that "crime prevention programs are notoriously hard to implement and evaluate, especially when they are instituted at the neighborhood level." Many evaluations of crime prevention programs have used inadequate research designs to test the programs' effectiveness (Greenberg et al. 1985; Lurigio and Rosenbaum

1986). Evaluations that used more rigorous methodologies generally concluded that the effectiveness of community organizations in implementing crime prevention programs and reducing local crime programs has been limited (Bennett and Lavrakas 1989; Bursik and Grasmick 1993; Rosenbaum 1986, 1987; Skogan 1990). Our knowledge of community organizations' role in crime prevention, however, may underestimate their role because of the means used to assess their accomplishments, misunderstandings (or misspecifications) of their goals, and the use of a limited impact model. The remainder of this chapter reviews possible limitations in the ways researchers have examined the roles of community organizations in crime prevention.

Political Planning

The planning of social programs is usually assumed to follow a "rational" or "analytical" process, in which "the collection and analysis of objective data and information (usually quantitative) forms the basis for assessing alternatives and making decisions" (McPherson and Silloway 1981, p. 150). The result is a program with clearly delineated goals, objectives, and tasks, which remain basically stable during program implementation. Planners using this approach generally give little consideration to how residents perceive local problems or the solutions they prefer for those problems. Attempts to provide communities with these predesigned crime prevention programs may be rejected, not because residents are unconcerned about crime, but because they oppose the solutions being offered for the problem (or the definition of the problem). Community-based planning, therefore, is more likely to focus on a political form of planning: the emphasis is on forming a consensus on the problems to be addressed and the strategies for doing so rather than developing a detailed work plan based on objective data (Brower 1986; McPherson and Silloway 1981; Podolefsky 1985).

Political planning has several consequences that make it more difficult to evaluate the resulting programs. One consequence is that the need to maintain a consensus on group goals and activities may result in goals that are less clearly stated. Another consequence is that the program is more flexible, perhaps opportunistic, in its functioning than would be expected for a "rationally planned" program. Residents' concerns change, influenced by numerous, often mundane factors. One community organization, for instance, originally targeted underage drinking in local parks in their antidrug work plan. By the time the work plan was approved and the program started, fall had arrived and residents were no longer concerned about drinking in the parks. This issue was replaced with others of more immediate importance and by the next spring, residents' concerns about youth activities had evolved beyond park drinking. Community organizations need to respond to residents' current interests in order to recruit and maintain members. Stricter adherence to a work plan may decrease participation. In other situations, community organizations' plans are disrupted by the need to respond to initiatives from city agencies or other organizations.

In short, political planning by community organizations may result in generally worded goals and in frequent changes in program objectives and activities. The former makes it difficult to ascertain the extent to which groups have achieved their goals. The latter may give the impression that the group is inconsistent in maintaining program activity, despite continued efforts to involve residents in relevant community activities, and this decreases the likelihood of finding a measurable change in community conditions through usual evaluation methodologies.

Focus on Process versus Product

The tension between organizing to represent and press for common concerns effectively and organizing to provide political experience and development for individual members has become an important concern of contemporary community activists (Menefee-Libey 1985). The former emphasizes the ability of community organizations to create tangible products for the community; the latter emphasizes the process of leadership development. Although many organizations choose to stress one of these goals, existing knowledge of community organizations suggests that no organization can afford to ignore either. Unfortunately, efforts to maximize one often seems to come at the expense of accomplishing the other.

Offe and Wiesenthal (1980, p. 82) note the need for community organizations to "maintain a precarious balance between mobilization of resources and mobilization of activity, . . . between bureaucracy (which allows them to *accumulate* power) and internal democracy (which allows them to *exercise* power)." To produce community goods, community organizations generally need to work collaboratively with other organizations or agencies and to mobilize additional resources beyond those of their members. Often to facilitate networking with other agencies (generally bureaucracies) and to generate resources from external funders, community organizations adopt bureaucratic structures or processes (such as strategic plans). Such solutions to producing community goods, however, reduce the likelihood of continuing participatory forms of organization and change the relationship between the organization and its members (Milofsky 1988). One community organization, for example, needed to develop collaborative relationships with city and state agencies to work on its goals of increasing employment and housing opportunities. This focus reduced its contacts within the neighborhoods, alienating at least some of the members and reducing attendance at the organization's annual meeting (Rosenbaum et al. 1993). If community organizations lose their grass-roots membership base, however, they lose legitimacy both within the community and with external agencies.

This need to balance the two goals of product and process make it difficult to study community organizations, because "the products of [their] activities cannot be easily measured and may not be related to any immediate activities. . . the patterns are related to a logic of voluntarism and to processual aspects of organization, and they require a longitudinal view" (Milofsky 1988, p. 195).

Many community organizations consciously emphasize the development of community participation and leadership (process) over the attainment of specific program goals. For these groups, the primary goal is the process, and they design organizational programs and activities to maximize participation, not to maximize specific community goods. As one staff member explained, "[Our] process involves listening to needs, being responsive to needs, and developing leadership and a constituency around the problem. The process is the most important; the work plan is just a by-product" (Rosenbaum et al. 1993, p. 72). Traditional impact evaluations that focus on clearly defined programmatic goals (e.g., reduction in citizens' fear of crime) misrepresent the purpose of the organization's activities and are likely to underestimate the organization's accomplishments.

Social Learning Process

Community organizations that decide to implement a crime prevention or antidrug program, or to engage in problem-solving in a community policing program, must develop the skills and knowledge needed for the task. Other researchers have referred to this skill and knowledge development as a social learning process (Brower 1986; Korten 1980; McLaughlin 1985). The social learning that occurs during program planning and implementation is a critical factor to success, as "implementation is a complex, multistage process of institutional and individual learning" (McLaughlin 1985, p. 100). For community organizations that operate with small staffs and rely primarily on community volunteers to maintain programs, the learning process is particularly important. At least three different forms of social learning are discernible in these community programs.

One aspect of the learning process includes developing effective ways to act collectively. At a basic level, some residents and newer organizations may need to develop skills of collective decision making. More experienced groups may find that the need to include previously uninvolved segments of the community requires new ways of interacting that are more inclusive. Or, the nature of the issue being addressed may require new techniques for old tasks. Organizations working on antidrug programs often find that residents' fear of opposing local drug dealers requires them to develop new techniques for recruiting participants, ones that reduced their sense of vulnerability (Rosenbaum et al. 1993).

Second, social learning may focus on developing cooperative relationships with other organizations or agencies. Thomas (1986, pp. 97-100) noted that the development of cooperative relationships between city agencies and community councils in Cincinnati required a lengthy learning process by both sides.

Finally, social learning also occurs in the policy areas on which the program focuses. As residents work to reduce crime or drug selling in their community, they become more knowledgeable about the problem, possible solutions to it, and the likely consequences of those solutions. With their increased knowledge, they often develop new strategies, or even new problem definitions, and the focus of the program changes.

The capacity of residents and community organizations to engage in a social learning process and incorporate it into their collective activities is central to successful program implementation. A traditionally designed impact evaluation may hinder the effective development of programs by pressuring community organizations to focus on substantive program goals early in the program, rather than on the social learning process. "A demand for detailed preplanning and subsequent adherence to . . . project plans and implementation schedules would immediately pre-empt the learning process by imposing the demand that leadership of the incipient effort act as if it knew what it was doing before there was an opportunity for learning to occur" (Korten 1980, p. 502).

Limitations of the Usual Impact Model

Discussions of community crime prevention have focused on community organizations' role in strengthening informal social control. The model that is usually advanced in support of this role assumes the following steps. First, the program mobilizes residents to participate. Through participation, residents' interactions increase and they assume more responsibility for community conditions. In turn, these behaviors lead to a stronger sense of community and more exercise of informal social control. The result is a decrease in community crime and in residents' fear of crime. As changes in crime are long-term effects and are difficult to measure, many evaluations use measures of social interaction among neighbors, the exchange of mutual favors, and their sense of community as their "intermediate" outcomes expected from the program. Measures of social control generally focus on residents' perceptions that neighbors will intervene if inappropriate or criminal behavior is observed.

Yet social disorganization theory, upon which the impact model is based, stresses *institutional* instability and the isolation of community institutions as causes of the community's inability to exert social control. If the community institutions provide the organizational network within which residents develop social ties, shared values, and a sense of neighborhood, then trying to increase social cohesion through resident interaction at small block meetings seems to focus on an intervention point that lacks the needed institutional base to be successful. Furthermore, the usual measures of social control reflect only a portion of the concept as outlined in social disorganization theory: "the extent to which a community structure is effective in articulating and realizing the common values of its residents and solving common problems" (Simcha-Fagan and Schwartz 1986, p. 669). The impact model underlying most crime prevention evaluations has two major shortcomings: first, it assumes that all communities use the same mechanisms for achieving collective goals; and second, it pays scant attention to institutional and political questions.

Existing research demonstrates that communities vary in the means they use to deal with problems. A survey of Seattle residents, for example, found that communities tended to rely *either* on formally organized community groups *or* on neighbors and the existing authority structure (Guest and Oropesa 1984). Several studies concluded that residents in communities with looser-knit ties (fewer primary relationships in the community) are more likely to know of and join community organizations and more likely to rely on formal social controls (Ahlbrandt 1986; Crenson 1978; McCourt 1977). Reliance on authority structures (or formal social control) may also vary in part by the racial composition of the community: an earlier study found that black residents were more likely to rely on police than were white residents (Boggs 1971).

Hunter and Staggenborg, in fact, argue that such variations follow logically from research by Chicago sociologists demonstrating that the effects of social disorganization vary across community areas, depending upon their social and economic characteristics. Similarly, "one could advance the corollary that the types of social *organization* and *collective action* among different classes would also take different forms and have different foci of activity" (Hunter and Staggenborg 1988, p. 247). Evaluations of community crime prevention programs, then, should not consider social interaction and social cohesion as the only possible path to safer communities.

Crenson's detailed study of six Baltimore neighborhoods demonstrates that the social and organizational (political) networks of a community are distinct, though related. Although organizations in loose-knit communities were better at mobilizing community residents and representing their interests, even organizations whose residents had primarily external ties "performed at least moderately well on all tests of political capacity" (Crenson 1983, p. 593). And Crenson's definition of the political life of a neighborhood clearly overlaps with broader definitions of social control: "a capacity (extemporaneous or otherwise) to aggregate and articulate the interests of neighborhood residents and an 'executive power' of sorts capable of producing public goods or alleviating public harms" (p. 579).

Crenson (1983) emphasizes the importance of neighborhood identity in creating a neighborhood political life and, like other researchers, concludes that a sense of neighborhood identity is based not on social interactions among residents, but on the presence of shared institutions and the nature of the community area. He contrasts the *political* nature of problem-solving activities with the more typical image of strong communities as arenas of dense social and interpersonal networks:

The survey results again reflect the distinctly political pre-dispositions that lie behind city residents' ideas of neighborhood. Those who can identify their neighborhood are inclined to use them as forums in which to discuss neighborhood concerns. They show no special tendency to employ their neighborhoods as personal havens in which to exchange sympathy and advice about personal matters. In general, the survey results have shown that the personal ties that may bind neighbors together are not responsible for sustaining neighborhood identity or neighborhood discourse, nor do they contribute to the relationship between these two aspects of the neighborhood polity. (Crenson 1978, pp. 147-48)

The delineation between the social and political aspects of community life, combined with the emphasis on institutional capacities in the social disorganization theory, suggests that evaluations of community crime prevention need to expand the impact model to include alternate means of creating community safety. The political capacity of a community may be a critical factor, particularly for those communities that have fewer internal resources and need to increase their access to external resources.

Like social cohesion, community organizations are not evenly distributed across the urban landscape. They are more common in communities that are racially and ethnically homogeneous, have higher median incomes, and have a more stable population. Generating participation in communities without existing organizations or identifiable leaders has proven difficult. Available research, however, uncovers a more complex situation than the summary statement suggests. Communities with more serious crime problems and residents who think they receive inadequate police services are *more* likely to be organized, alleviating the class bias generally present in community organizations (Skogan 1989). Other research has related economic status and stability with participation at the individual level but *not* the block level, suggesting that "poor and residentially unstable communities *can* develop a level of participation equal to other communities, but . . . *within* a given community, those with more resources and a greater vested interest in property are still more likely to participate" (Perkins et al. 1990, p. 106). Finally, public policies can be used to influence the social and political context of communities and the ability of residents to mobilize themselves, through zoning and investment policies that maintain smaller neighborhoods and slow down processes of change and through provision of formal structures for citizen participation in city decision making (Haeberle 1986; Hope and Foster 1992; Hutcheson and Prather 1988).

Conclusion

Community organizations offer neither a universal nor a single solution to community crime problems. The role of community organizations in crime prevention can be questioned in several ways: many organizations' reluctance to include crime on their agenda because of its "unwinnable" nature as a problem; the questionable viability of community organizations compared to more bureaucratic organizations; the possible inequities in services resulting from differential strengths of communities and their organizations; and the potential for the programs to be used for racist or other divisive purposes. Despite these unresolved differences, community organizations have particular strengths that make them a useful, even necessary, component in a multiprong effort to reduce community crime. Available evaluation results probably underestimate the effects of community organizations' efforts at crime reduction. Further attempts to assess their efficacy should take into account the fluid and flexible processes by which community organizations function, the importance of process in their functioning, and the multiple means by which various communities may work to create safer and better communities.

Note

This chapter originally appeared in *The Annals of the American Academy of Political and Social Science*, Volume 539, 1995, pp. 72-84. It is reprinted with permission.

References

Ahlbrandt, Roger, Jr. 1986. "Using Research to Build Stronger Neighborhoods." In *Urban Neighborhoods: Research and Policy*, edited by Ralph B. Taylor, 285-309. New York: Praeger.

Barber, Benjamin. 1984. *Strong Democracy: Participatory Politics for a New Age*. Berkeley: University of California Press.

Bennett, Susan F., and Paul J. Lavrakas. 1989. "Community-Based Crime Prevention: An Assessment of the Eisenhower Foundation's Neighborhood Program." *Crime and Delinquency* 35: 345-64.

Boggs, Sarah L. 1971. "Formal and Informal Crime Controls." *Sociological Quarterly* 12: 312-27.

Brower, Sidney. 1986. "Planners in the Neighborhood: A Cautionary Tale." In *Urban Neighborhoods: Research and Policy,* edited by Ralph B. Taylor, 181-214. New York: Praeger.

Bursik, Robert J., Jr., and Harold G. Grasmick. 1993. *Neighborhoods and Crime: The Dimensions of Effective Community Control.* New York: Lexington Books.

Crenson, Matthew. 1983. *Neighborhood Politics.* Cambridge: Harvard University Press.

———. 1978. "Social Networks and Political Processes in Urban Neighborhoods." *American Journal of Political Science* 223: 578-94.

Greenberg, Stephanie W., William M. Rohe, and Jay R. Williams. 1985. *Informal Citizen Action and Crime Prevention at the Neighborhood Level.* Washington, DC: National Institute of Justice.

Guest, Avery, and R. S. Oropesa. 1984. "Problem-Solving Strategies of Local Areas in the Metropolis." *American Sociological Review* 49: 828-40.

Haeberle, Steven. 1986. "Good Neighbors and Good Neighborhoods." *State and Local Government Review* 18: 109-16.

Hope, Timothy, and Janet Foster. 1992. "Conflicting Forces: Changing the Dynamics of Crime and Community on a 'Problem' Estate." *British Journal of Criminology* 224: 488-504.

Hunter, Albert, and Suzanne Staggenborg. 1988. "Local Communities and Organized Action." In *Community Organizations: Studies in Resource Mobilization and Exchange*, edited by Carl Milofsky. New York: Oxford University Press.

Hutcheson, John, Jr., and James Prather. 1988. "Community Mobilization and Participation in the Zoning Process." *Urban Affairs Quarterly* 233: 346-68.

Korten, David D. 1980. "Community Organization and Rural Development: a Learning Process Approach." *Public Administration Review* (September/October): 480-511.

Lavrakas, Paul J. 1985. "Citizen Self-Help and Neighborhood Crime Prevention Policy." In *American Violence and Public Policy*, edited by Lynn A. Curtis, 87-115. New Haven, CT: Yale University Press.

Lavrakas, Paul J., and Susan F. Bennett. 1988. "Thinking about the Implementation of Citizen and Community Anti-Crime Measures." In *Communities and Crime Reduction*, edited by Tim Hope and Margaret Shaw, 221-32. London: Her Majesty's Stationery Office.

Lindsay, Betsy. 1988. "Community-Based Versus Police-based Models of Problem Definition and Organizing." Paper presented at the annual meeting of the American Society of Criminology. Chicago.

Lurigio, Arthur J., and Dennis P. Rosenbaum. 1986. "Evaluation Research in Community Crime Prevention: A Critical Look at the Field." In *Community Crime Prevention*, edited by Dennis P. Rosenbaum, 19-44. Beverly

Hills: Sage.

Mansbridge, Jane J. 1985. "Measuring the Effect of Direct Democracy." Paper presented at the annual meeting of the International Political Science Association. Paris, France.

McCourt, Kathleen. 1977. *Working Class Women and Grass-roots Politics.* Bloomington: Indiana University Press.

McLaughlin, Milbray Wallin. 1985. "Implementation Realities and Evaluation Design." In *Social Science and Social Policy,* edited by R. Lance Shotland and Melvin M. Mark, 96-120. Beverly Hills: Sage.

McPherson, Marlys, and Glenn Silloway. 1981. "Planning to Prevent Crime." In *Reactions to Crime,* edited by Dan A. Lewis. Beverly Hills: Sage Publications.

Menefee-Libey, David. 1985. "The State of Community Organizing in Chicago." Planning Paper #1. Chicago: Community Renewal Society.

Mill, John Stuart. [1861]1975. *Three Essays: On Liberty; Representative Government; The Subjection of Women.* Oxford: Oxford University Press.

Milosfky, Carl. 1988. "Structure and Process in Community Self-Help Organizations." In *Community Organizations: Studies in Resource Mobilization and Exchange,* edited by Carl Milofsky, 193-211. New York: Oxford University Press.

Offe, Claus, and Helmut Wiesenthal. 1980. "Two Logics of Collective Action: Theoretical Notes on Social Class and Organizational Form." *Political Power and Social Theory* 1: 67-115.

Olson, Mancur. 1965. *The Logic of Collective Action.* Cambridge: Harvard University Press.

Orbell, John M., and Toru Uno. 1972. "A Theory of Neighborhood Problem Solving." *The American Political Science Review* 66: 471-89.

Pateman, Carole. 1970. *Participation and Democratic Theory.* Cambridge: Cambridge University Press.

Perkins, Douglas, Paul Florin, Richard C. Rich, Abraham Wandersman, and David M. Chavis. 1990. "Participation and the Social and Physical Environment of Residential Blocks." *American Journal of Community Psychology* 18: 83-115.

Podolefsky, Aaron M. 1985. "Rejecting Crime Prevention Programs: The Dynamics of Program Implementation in High Need Communities." *Human Organization* 44: 33-40.

Prestby, John E., and Abraham Wandersman. 1985. "An Empirical Exploration of a Framework of Organizational Viability." *The Journal of Behavioral Sciences,* 21: 287-305.

Rosenbaum, Dennis P. 1987. "The Theory and Research behind Neighborhood Watch." *Crime and Delinquency* 33: 103-34.

———, ed. 1986. *Community Crime Prevention.* Beverly Hills: Sage Publications.

Rosenbaum, Dennis P., Susan F. Bennett, Betsy Linsday, Deanna Wilkinson, Breanda Davis, Chet Taranowski, and Paul J. Lavrakas. 1993. *Cross-site Comparisons and Conclusions: The Community Responses to Drug Abuse National Demonstraton Program Final Process Evaluation Report*, Volume 1. Chicago: University of Illinois at Chicago.

Simcha-Fagan, Ora, and Joseph Schwartz. 1986. "Neighborhood and Delinquency: An Assessment of Contextual Effects." *Criminology* 244: 667-703.

Skogan, Wesley G. 1988. "Community Organizations and Crime." In *Crime and Justice: A Review of Research*, vol. 10, edited by Michael Tonry and Norval Morris, 39-78. Chicago: University of Chicago Press.

———. 1989. "Communities, Crime, and Neighborhood Organization." *Crime and Delinquency* 353: 437-57.

———. 1990. *Disorder and Decline: Crime and the Spiral of Decay in American Neighborhoods.* New York: Free Press.

Thomas, John Clayton. 1986. *Between Citizen and City.* Lawrence: University Press of Kansas.

3

The Takoma Orange Hats:
Fighting Crime and Building Community
in Washington, D.C.

Suzanne Goldsmith-Hirsch

A Quiet Contest at Georgia and Aspen

It's 9:30 on a cold December Saturday night in northwest Washington, D.C. and something suspicious is happening—or trying to happen—near the corner of Aspen Street and Georgia Avenue. A young man in his late twenties or early thirties is standing at the curb in front of a brick apartment complex, checking his watch and glaring uneasily at a small cluster of people across the street. He leans out to look up and down Georgia Avenue, then turns and paces for a few moments. He looks again at the group. There are eight of them, mostly middle-aged men and women, some white, some black, all wearing bright orange baseball caps. A woman in the group stares back at the man; others glance at him more discreetly. The young man checks his watch again, then disappears into the apartment building. A few minutes later, he is back at the curb, nearly a block away.

"What's he up to?" asks one woman, the one who stared, with an edge of irritation in her voice.

"We saw him last week," says one of her companions. "Remember? He kept walking up and down, up and down."

"Come on—Thunderbird, Sergeant Major," says the first woman. "Let's check out the mail detail." Four of the group walk down to the corner of Georgia and Whittier—site of a public mailbox—where they can have a better view. Along the way, they encounter a woman staggering up Georgia, reeking of perfume and booze. Although it is well below freezing, her legs and her midriff are bare. Her face is covered with scars, and she is missing several teeth.

"How can I get me one of those orange hats?" she calls out.

"Walk with us," answers one of the men. The group moves on up the street, as the prostitute stands watching.

The Takoma Coalition

At Whittier and Georgia, the group continues watching the man across the street. After twenty minutes more of pacing, watch-checking, looking up and down the street and glaring at the group, he disappears again. This time he doesn't return.

The orange-hatted citizens who keep watch at the southeast corner of Aspen Street and Georgia Avenue are not auxiliary police officers. They carry no weapons and little equipment. Some are retirees, well into their sixties, while others are younger people, with full-time day jobs. They are men and women, married and single, black, white, and Hispanic. They are not paid, they operate with little institutional support, and they incur almost no costs. All they really have in common is the neighborhood they live in and a desire to keep it safe. For more than four years, they have walked the streets at night, facing down drug dealers and prostitutes, keeping the streets they live on from open drug selling and prostitution—and from the violence, theft, and disorder that accompany such illicit markets.

This group, the Takoma Coalition, is one of more than two hundred citizen antidrug patrol groups in Washington, D.C. On the Saturday night described above, the young man who glared at them from across the street was the only person the group encountered who may have been a drug dealer; the drunken woman was the only likely prostitute who crossed their path. But it wasn't always that way. Five years ago, the spot where they meet at the corner of Aspen and Georgia was headquarters for a quite different group: young men in dark clothes and hooded sweatshirts who flagged down cars and sold drugs directly from the street. The pay phone on the corner was in constant use as drivers stopped at the curb and placed calls to drug sellers in the apartment building across the street. Women in outlandish and provocative attire strolled up and down the block—even, in one case, beckoning from a street-level window—calling and whispering to potential customers. The parking lot and lobby of a hotel on the corner were the site of great activity—with drivers of cars with license plates from as far away as New York and New Jersey stopping and going in for just a few minutes before returning to their cars and driving away.

The sudden appearance in the late 1980s of a drug and prostitution market on a formerly quiet stretch of Georgia Avenue was like an infection in the middle of what had long been a stable, working- and middle-class neighborhood of black and white homeowners along the side streets feeding into Georgia Avenue. Burglaries, vandalism, and car break-ins sharply increased. Litter was everywhere. People were afraid to walk their dogs and took to driving the two or three blocks to the local Safeway for groceries. Casual curbside conversation became a rarity as residents chose to spend as little time as possible outside the protection of their homes.

The story of how a small group of determined citizens succeeded—peacefully—in reclaiming the streets of their neighborhood from a criminal occupation and restoring the sense of safety and civility that is a necessary condition for community life demonstrates the potential power of citizen action in the face of seemingly intransigent problems. It is a story about citizens taking risks to fight for a sense of dignity and ownership in the place where they live. Their efforts succeeded not only in driving drug dealers from the neighborhood, but also in providing a model for other groups and spawning a host of other community-building activities in surrounding neighborhoods.

What's more, members of the Takoma Coalition and other neighborhood groups inspired by their example say that their efforts to combat crime have helped them begin to realize the promise of their diverse neighborhood by developing friendships they say would not have otherwise come to be, friendships that cut across barriers of race and age, friendships that make them feel more secure and welcome in their own community.

Tudor Homes and Trimmed Hedges

Takoma Park, which straddles the dividing line between the District of Columbia and Maryland, was developed in the 1880s at the end of the streetcar line as a "healthful retreat" from a swampy, malaria-ridden city.

Advertising brochures proclaimed it as a haven for middle-class people: bankers, lawyers, even shop clerks. "All you need is a moderate income," claimed the developer. When the proliferation of automobiles increased access to farther suburbs with more space and fancier homes— the houses in Takoma Park are generously proportioned but plain—some of the houses became rental properties and the residents became more economically diverse. It has always been, however, in the main, a community of working- and professional-class homeowners.

The corner of Georgia and Aspen is a relatively quiet spot. There are no shops or other businesses at this intersection except for a hotel—the Walter Reed Convenience Motor Inn—which flies a tattered banner advertising a special winter rate of $34.95 a night and an all-you-can-eat lunch for $4.95.

East of Georgia Avenue, a central business artery of northwest Washington, the streets become narrow, quiet, and residential. The large, single-family homes along Aspen have generous front porches and small side and rear yards, many of which have carefully trimmed hedges and are in the main well kept. So are the small apartment buildings on Butternut and the somewhat grand, tudor-style houses on 8th and 9th Streets, roads that run parallel to Georgia. Whittier Street, while a little scruffier, still has the look of a neighborhood populated by striving homeowners.

On the west side of Georgia, the Aspen Court apartment complex, with seven buildings connected by paths, is not fancy but not run-down either, and in the morning grounds workers can often be seen picking up trash in the bushes and grass around the buildings. Just to the north on Georgia looms the enormous Walter Reed Army Medical Center complex.

This is not a neighborhood in which a daytime pedestrian would be fearful. But even today, a close observer can see signs of the neighborhood's recent troubles. The pay phone on the corner has been vandalized, and its metal cord hangs limply down, receiverless. Outside the Motor Inn, on a waist-high brick ledge are mounted two rows of short metal spikes, designed to keep loafers—or worse—from sitting there. A small house on Aspen has a big sign over the door: NO LOITERING. At the corner of Georgia and Whittier, an abandoned house stands boarded up and peeling, a weathered FOR SALE sign in the yard. And inside the Motor Inn, the cashier sits quietly, looking bored, behind a wall of bulletproof glass.

There's no more blatant drug dealing at the corner of Georgia and Aspen. But signs are everywhere of how close this neighborhood stands to criminal threats and disarray.

A Sudden Occupation

"It wasn't like what you read about in some of these other areas," says longtime Aspen Street resident Don Young, 63,[1] describing the problems he began to notice in the neighborhood in the mid- to late 1980s. "We didn't have any major or organized drug dealing. It wasn't a major crime problem—but it was developing into one."

Aspen Street neighbor Thomas Green first noticed the change when he was out walking his dog early in the mornings. "We could not prove . . . that this person or that person was pushing drugs. But it was obvious that these people were up to no good, they're out there at all hours of the night, cars are stopping by, they're chatting with the cars. . . . You go out there 6:30 in the morning and they're going back and forth on the street. You know they're not out there for their health."

Why did drug dealers choose this area for their illegal activities? No single factor is to blame. Police point out that stretches of Georgia Avenue to the north and south were already troubled and that this quiet residential enclave was simply getting some of the overflow activity. Residents blame the hotel, which each year seemed to have a new manager, all of whom turned a blind eye to suspicious activity in the parking lot and lobby. For a time, neglectful management of the Aspen Apartments across the street was also a problem, they say; tenants who engaged in illegal activity were not evicted, the grounds were not kept up, and the maze of paths between the buildings offered many places to consummate transactions initiated at curbside.

Young and Green—and their wives, Mary Young and Sarah Green—are good friends who have lived in the neighborhood almost three decades and have raised their children there. At 63, Don Young recently retired from the federal government police. Prior to that, he put in twenty years in the Marines, where he attained the rank of sergeant major. He and Mary, a former hospital technician, raised five children on Aspen Street; now they care for Mary's ailing mother, who lives with them, and for an infant grandchild that their daughter drops off each morning on the way to work.

The Greens are both in their fifties and still working. Thomas Green is a personnel and staffing specialist with the Defense Department, and Sarah teaches third grade. Their daughter is away at veterinary school; their son, an artist, lives at home and is studying for a graduate degree. The Greens came to Aspen Street in 1967 and have been deeply involved in the neighborhood ever since.

The Youngs and the Greens have seen many changes along Aspen Street and in the surrounding area since they arrived in 1963 and 1967, respectively. They were among the earliest black families to move to Aspen. Both couples, however, say they always felt at home in the neighborhood and did not feel excluded because of their race. As older white residents passed away or sold their homes and retired to other places, the balance shifted and the neighborhood became predominantly black. In the 1980s, young white couples began moving to the neighborhood, creating a mix that seems to have stabilized, at least for the moment.

Longtime residents like the current mix, but they remember with nostalgia a time when there was less mobility, when everyone in the neighborhood knew one another and kept an eye on each other's children.

"It was a nice neighborhood," says Don Young. "The kids would go out and talk and play together. They were in the boy scouts, all those activities. We knew all our neighbors."

"I knew everybody from here to Georgia Avenue because I used to collect for the Heart Association," says Sarah Green. "Between here and Sixth Street also. . . . We knew just about everybody in these square blocks. We knew when somebody was here who didn't belong here. I would usually go out and greet whoever moved in and introduce our children to each other. I'm just that type of person. I don't need any strangers around."

Both couples played a leadership role in neighborhood activities, which through the decades have reflected the changing concerns of urban residents. In the 1970s, Thomas Green organized a petition drive to have signs posted on the street preventing employees and visitors to nearby Walter Reed Hospital from monopolizing the parking spaces. There were other traffic-related activities over the years, including a successful effort to have a stoplight installed at Georgia and Aspen.

In the early 1980s, residents of Aspen formed a Neighborhood Watch group with help from the police department. The goal was to prevent burglaries and other crime on the street by reporting all suspicious activities to the police. Thomas Green became a block captain.

Keeping an eye on the neighborhood is second nature to these longtime homeowners. Don Young often sits on his porch in the evenings and keeps watch, taking special care to keep an eye on the houses of neighbors who have let him know they are out of town. The Greens and the Youngs have keys to one another's homes and those of other neighbors as well. During an afternoon interview with the Greens, they got up more than once to check the source of noises in the street and when a fire engine pulled up in front of a neighbor's home they got on the phone to find out what was happening and if there was anything they could do to help.

When the Youngs and the Greens discovered that open drug selling was taking place on Georgia Avenue within sight of their homes, however, they decided some action would be needed beyond the Neighborhood Watch approach of asking neighbors to "keep an eye out." Although Washington, D.C. has the highest ratio of police personnel to population in the country, the murder rate in 1991 was 81 deaths per 100,000 residents, compared with 31 per 100,000 in New York City.[2] Washington residents know what drug markets can lead to. Much of the violence in the city springs from drug market turf wars—and innocent citizens can easily get caught in the crossfire.

In 1989, shootings were not yet a part of life in the Aspen Street area, but a quarter-mile to the north on Georgia Avenue gunfire was heard on a weekly basis. The Greens, Youngs, and others began a series of informal meetings to talk about the growing crime problem.

"The meetings weren't frequent in the beginning," says Don Young. "We would just discuss what was going on. Discuss the change in the neighborhood, the problems with prostitutes up in the hotel on the corner. . . . And then a month or two later, some other neighbors would become concerned, that may not even have been at that first meeting. They would meet and discuss what was going on. And a few months later, the same thing would happen."

For a while, the meetings were simple information-sharing sessions. A representative of the local police district's community relations office attended at least one of the meetings and gave the concerned residents what they considered "lip service" about increased attention to problems in the neighborhood. If police were targeting the area for enforcement, it wasn't working; there was no change.

One day, someone saw an article in the paper about citizen antidrug patrols and decided to invite organizer James Foreman to come to one of their gatherings.

Enter "Knee Cap"

James Foreman is a former union organizer and high school basketball coach who works days in the customer service department of a Washington department store. His nights, however, he spends spreading the gospel of citizen patrolling. He and his neighbors in the Fairlawn section of Anacostia started the city's first citizen antidrug patrol in response to the encroachment of drug sellers in their quiet neighborhood, which had for many years been an oasis of peace in troubled southeast Washington. Wearing signature orange hats, the group set out to patrol their own streets at night—and, with some help from a local police officer who supported their efforts, they succeeded in driving away the drug dealers and the disorder the dealers had brought. Along the way, they refined the techniques that have become central to "orange hatting."

The group is still active, but Foreman—who goes by the street name "Knee Cap"—carved a new mission for himself: showing others in the city how to follow Fairlawn's lead. He formed the Metro Orange Coalition and began visiting other community groups and exhorting them to start their own citizen patrol groups. With donated funds he bought a few pieces of equipment to lend to new groups when they were starting up. Foreman even began wearing a beeper so that groups who needed help and advice could contact him quickly. The police department agreed to support his efforts by referring him to groups that needed his assistance, and by committing itself to work with those groups.

Today, Foreman—who is not paid for this work—spends nearly every night on the streets or in the living rooms of Washington residents, meeting with people to explain how citizen patrols work, walking with new groups to help them get started, or simply driving around, checking in with the groups that are on the street. Of the more than two hundred Orange Hat patrols currently active in D.C., every one got started with the help of James Foreman.

Police Captain Claude J. Beheler, once an officer in Foreman's home district who helped the Fairlawn Coalition get started and now commander of the Traffic Enforcement Branch, is an enthusiastic supporter of the Orange Hats. "This is something that costs nothing," he told the *Washington Times*. "It was just people getting together and participating with police. It's amazing how something so penniless, cost-wise, could grow to be something so big."

Most of the members of the Takoma Park Coalition remember their first meeting with Knee Cap. Foreman was "a charismatic speaker," according to George Stern, who lives two doors down from the Greens on Aspen. "He can really get people on their feet."

Foreman made a rousing speech to the group that ignited their ambition and increased their fears. He told the gathered neighbors that they could stop the drug dealing in their neighborhood; and he said that if they did not, their problems would soon be much worse than having to take alternate routes to the supermarket. He talked about drive-by shootings. About young children recruited into the drug trade. About what it is like to visit one's own children—or grandchildren—in the graveyard.

How It Works

Foreman described how an Orange Hat patrol works. Its purpose, he said, is not to frighten or confront drug dealers and prostitutes, but to scare away their market. A citizen patrol can make a neighborhood an inhospitable place for selling drugs simply by letting skittish buyers know they are being watched.

Police tend to focus on catching drug dealers, which is helpful but ultimately ineffective in breaking up a drug market. If the location is lucrative—that is, if buyers come there looking for drugs—there always seem to be more dealers to take the place of those who have been arrested. On the other hand, if buyers are afraid they will be exposed or arrested if they go to buy drugs in a particular spot, they quickly choose to buy their supply elsewhere, and the drug dealers are forced to move on.

By acting—or simply by appearing to act—in concert with the police, a citizen patrol can reduce the viability of a location for drug dealers by scaring away their customers. It does not stop drug dealing, Foreman emphasizes, but drives it elsewhere—or forces dealers to switch to an underground referral market, which is not accompanied by the same degree of street crime and violence.

Foreman gave a quick primer in the tools and the tricks of the trade. Neon orange hats give the groups visibility, unity and a quasi-official look. Some groups also wear orange T-shirts or jackets. Two-way radios allow them to communicate with one another for safety—or with a person who remains at home near the phone to call for help if needed. Radios also create the perception that the group is in constant communication with the police. This is especially true if a police officer walks with the group from time to time and stops to visit them regularly.

Good relations with police are important, said Foreman, because their presence—even if it is only occasional—gives the group credibility in the eyes of dealers and buyers. Patrollers can also assist police by giving them information. They carry pads and pens and write down the license plate numbers of cars they believe are in the neighborhood for the purpose of buying or selling drugs or hiring prostitutes. They pass these numbers to the police, who can use the information in investigations. More importantly, drug buyers who see them writing down tag numbers are frightened away.

Orange Hat members also bring video cameras, still cameras, and binoculars and train them on the suspected drug dealers. It doesn't matter, says Foreman, whether there is tape in the recorder or film in the camera. What is important is giving the impression that they are conducting official surveillance.

For their own safety and the security of their homes and families, Foreman instructs Orange Hat group members to use pseudonyms or "street names" to protect their identities when patrolling. But as long as members do not confront drug dealers directly, he says, they do not need to be too worried about their safety. To his knowledge, there has never been a serious incident of retributive violence against a member of an Orange Hat patrol.

"Guys who deal drugs are more afraid of the people than the people are of them," says Foreman. "They will never, never defend their turf. . . . We have never had a member of an Orange Hat group even get in a fight."

Foreman only attended one living-room meeting with the Takoma Park residents. Next time they got together, he told them, it should be on the street. They decided to get right to work.

What About Privacy?

Is all this prying legal? According to community antidrug strategy expert Roger Conner, there is no constitutional barrier to any of the activities conducted by groups like the Takoma Coalition. Conner is director of the American Alliance for Rights & Responsibilities, a public-interest law group, and co-author of a book outlining practical strategies for fighting drugs called *The Winnable War: A Community Guide to Eradicating Street Drug Markets*. Conner also lives five blocks from Aspen Street and started his own Orange Hat group with help from Knee Cap and members of the neighboring Takoma Park Coalition.

The right to privacy, says Conner, exists only to protect citizens from the government, not from one another. Citizens who publish information about drug activity observed on the street may be open to libel actions—

but only if the information they publish is not true. "Truth is always a defense to libel," says Conner.

Furthermore, Conner points out, any and all information gleaned on the street may legally be passed to police, who may not act on that information if it is not supported by their own investigation.

"As far as picture taking," says Conner, "the issue is, do you have a reasonable expectation of privacy? You do not have a reasonable expectation of privacy if you carry on a transaction on a public street, on the public pavement, or in any place that can be seen from a public place. So I can take a picture of it, I can write it down, I can use my binoculars. If it can be seen from the sidewalk, you have no reasonable expectation of privacy."

Getting Started

No group is ever ready. Because the fear is in there. But if they get 10, 12 people, we can go with that. We know it'll grow. —Knee Cap

"That first night, I was scared, I must admit," says Sarah Green, remembering the October night in 1990 when the group first took to the street. "I don't know how Thomas felt, but I was afraid. The unknown is always fearful. But we got out there, and we had about 40 people out there. . . . Knee Cap was there and he brought other Orange Hat groups out with us to help us get a feeling of belonging to something and that helped a lot when I saw all those people.

"It tapered off, but that first night it was inspiring to see all those people come out to help."

The group was also joined that night, and on many succeeding nights, by police officer Mark Marshall. Marshall didn't make arrests that night; he simply walked with the group. But he was enthusiastic about their efforts, and his presence showed the drug dealers and others on the street that this group was working with the police.

Knee Cap had brought two video cameras and tripods, which they set up at Georgia and Aspen, and he had also brought them walkie-talkies. The radios crackled dramatically as they walked in groups of four or five around the neighborhood, reporting their location to one another as they went. For safety, they called each other by the street names they had chosen before setting out. Thomas and Sarah Green were Fisherman and Pisces, after his passion and her zodiac sign; Don Young called himself Sergeant Major.

Others who were there that first night included George and Elise Stern, a white couple in their forties who had recently moved to the neighborhood and who worked out of their Aspen Street home as a builder and a writer; they called themselves Gonzo and Deep Freeze. Jaime Velez, an assistant high school principal who was born in Argentina and lived on Butternut Street took the name Termite; and Patty Walker, a single white woman in her fifties who worked for the Army Corps of Engineers was Twinkletoes, a nickname she had been given in childhood when the plantar's warts on her heels made her walk on her toes. Others in the group took names that were exotic or that reflected their jobs and personalities: Thunderbird and Queen Firebird, Roadhog and Roadmap, Chalkdust, Bunny Rabbit. The names added a special thrill and a sense of unity—a secret shared only within the group.

The area they patrolled encompassed nine blocks, extending from Butternut in the north to Whittier in the south, and from Georgia Avenue west to Piney Branch east. Occasionally they stopped and stood in front of a house on Whittier they suspected was being used to sell drugs.

As they walked around the neighborhood, they saw that they were noticed. Cars with out-of-state tags and cardboard temporary plates (which are often used by criminals because they are easily stolen and hard to trace) would slow down to check out the patrollers as they cruised by. Some would drive around the block and come back once or twice—and then disappear. Out on Georgia Avenue, group members wrote down the tag numbers of the cars that headed into the hotel parking lot and then, quickly, back out again. A group went to stand on the same corner as a cluster of young men who had congregated there; after a long, chilly silence, the young men moved on to stand somewhere else, out of sight.

Sarah Green says that the immediate response to the patrol group energized her that night, and still motivates her, four and a half years later. "It's kind of like the rush that I get when I sit down to work a crossword puzzle," she says, with an excitement that could only be appreciated by another avid puzzler. "I can't wait to get into that crossword. . . . It's something that comes over me that I can't describe the feeling. And that's how I feel when I get out on the street. I don't care how tired we are. When it's time to go out, the adrenaline starts flowing."

That first night, the group stayed out from seven until midnight. And, euphoric with the sense of their own strength and potential power, they came out again the following night. There had been no violent incidents; their presence seemed to have an effect; and they enjoyed the excitement and the camaraderie. They came out every night that week, and the next week, and the next.

Toughing It Out

In a way it's kind of a battle. Whose street is it, ours or theirs? And if we're not there, it's gonna be theirs. —Patty Walker

The novelty wore off quickly, however. Few in the group realized what they were getting themselves into when they first agreed to join the patrol. George Stern—the builder who lives on Aspen with his wife and his parents-in-law—chuckles, remembering: "We said we were willing to participate once a month," he says. But while results were quick in coming—after only a few weeks it appeared to them that drugs and prostitution on the street were dramatically reduced, and the number of out-of-town cars passing through the hotel parking lot was way down—it was also clear that these positive results were limited to the time when they were patrolling. After they went home, activity resumed.

It was obvious that to create an environment that was truly inhospitable to illegal activity, the Orange Hats would have to be out on the street every night. Those whose commitment was less than total quickly fell out.

"A lot of people, they got nervous," says Don Young. "And they just stopped. But we maintained a good nucleus of about 20-some-odd people who would come out regularly. As long as the drug dealers were there, we stayed there. . . . We stayed out till well after midnight. As long as they stayed out on the corner, we stayed. This went on for at least two years. Every night. Come rain, snow, sleet, what-have-you."

Not every member of the group came out every night, but many of them came out five or six nights a week. They established a telephone tree to facilitate communications. And they let each other know when they could and could not come, to ensure that a critical mass was present on the street each night. It was important not to let up the pressure—and as it became clear to the dealers that the group was serious, they answered with their own kind of pressure.

"There were some incidents," says George Stern. "A rock-throwing incident, a push and shove type of thing, there were lots of those."

Often the group would point out troublemakers to police, and when they acted on the information, hostility increased. "The police would challenge them: frisk them; harass them," explains Don Young. "The drug dealers, they knew we were pointing them out. They knew. The next night they would come by and make a comment. 'You put the police on us. You better watch it.'"

"I was down there one night," says Henry Stevens, Stern's father-in-law, "and a guy came by and talked about getting a shotgun and blowing us all off the corner."

Young men on the street flipped the finger and shouted names. "Pumpkin Heads," they sneered. Groups in cars would shout obscenities as they whizzed by. A woman lifted up her dress and "mooned" them. Don Young's son came home agitated from school one day, reporting that another boy had instructed him to tell his father to "watch out."

One night, a rock was thrown from a moving car. It didn't hit anyone; rather, it smashed the window of a car parked at the curb.

Some in the group were frightened, and the threatening incidents drove away the "dabblers" who patrolled only occasionally. Those who stayed with it took the risks seriously but felt protected by their numbers.

"I never wear my [orange] hat on my way to the corner," says Jaime Velez, the assistant high school principal from Butternut Street. "One person can be a victim very easily. But there's a strength in numbers. Not physically, but the eyes and ears."

To discourage physical attacks, the group adopts a staunchly non-confrontational stance.

"When you look for trouble," says Thomas Green, "you will find trouble. We emphasize the importance of not challenging them. We don't want any confrontation. We don't want to argue with people who come by and curse us out, we just stand and listen. If they compliment us, fine, if they don't, no big thing."

"Sometimes you gotta eat crow," says Velez, who once had a hot drink knocked out of his hand by the enraged owner of a car whose license plate number he was writing down. He calmly handed over the sheet of paper, avoiding a fight. "They want to intimidate you. Taunt you. And you don't know what they got in the car. They could blow you away. . . .

"But this is a bunch of unarmed people with a hat on. There is a strength about that. If that gets broken, and you plant this fear factor, the whole thing may crumble. I'm glad that nothing has happened."

George Stern describes one occasion when he felt physically threatened. That night he had brought out a still camera. He was using the telephoto lens to watch a suspected dealer across the street.

The man he was watching suddenly ran across the street and began threatening Stern directly, spitting the words into his face. Stern felt sure he would have to fight and wondered if the man was armed. The group circled around them, however, and his challenger backed down and stalked away.

"I've been out there for three years," he says, "and never had a response like that. People have hollered, there are times when you feel a sense of vulnerability, watching every car that goes by, watching everybody's hands, making sure their hands stay on the wheel, but I never felt like that before."

He adds, "I don't think there was anything more provocative that any of us did than bringing that still camera down. The video camera was a little more neutral because the camera was set up on a tripod; it was there passively."

Even now, after four years of patrolling and a radical decrease in the amount of criminal activity on the street, the Takoma Coalition Orange Hats still sometimes feel vulnerable. I watched one night as a group member ducked behind a public mailbox, pretending to take cover from a hostile-looking dealer. They take precautions: they walk one another home; and on each occasion that I patrolled with the group, they remained on the corner after breaking up for the night, watching me until I was safely inside my car.

They combat their fear—and disarm their adversaries—by being unwaveringly friendly and polite. Whether a pedestrian stops to say hello, reels by in a stupor, or stalks by haughtily, they are careful to part their circle and make room on the sidewalk and to greet each person who passes, usually by name. Often they hold long, cordial conversations with young men whom they know to be dealers, inquiring about families and jobs, exchanging pleasantries.

In four years of patrolling, no member of the Takoma Coalition has ever been harmed.

Obstacles—and a Frustrating Lack of Support

Officer Marshall, the police officer who spent so much time walking with the Takoma Orange Hats when they were starting out, was eventually reassigned to another beat, and the group found that the response of other police officers to their efforts was far less encouraging.

Thomas Green expresses frustration at trying to get police to enforce standards of decency he considered central to maintaining a civil neighborhood. He describes the police reaction to his complaint one night that a man had urinated on the street in full view of the group, which included women. When an officer stopped by shortly afterward, Green asked him to admonish the man. The officer refused, claiming there was nothing he could do, as he had not observed the act. "Can't you at least say something to him?" Green asked. "If I do that," the officer replied, "I'll probably have to shoot him."

"Now, urinating in public is not something that we accept," says Green. "But that was the kind of support that we got from some of the officers. They just didn't seem to care. They didn't seem to have much of an interest in the community."

Some citizen patrols report that their presence on the street encourages police to take a greater interest in their neighborhood. One police officer that I spoke with when he stopped to visit with the Orange Hats at Aspen and Georgia said he pays more attention to that area because of the Takoma Coalition. "They live here," he said. "They know who belongs and who don't belong. I'm not here every day. They heightened my attention to this area." Indeed, police officers generally stop to talk with the group once or twice a night when they are patrolling. Still, most in the group feel that the police have done little to help them in their mission.

"We kept giving them these lists of tag numbers and gradually we came to realize that nothing was being done with them," says Patty Walker.

D.C. Police Sergeant James Miller commands Sector Two of the Fourth Police District, which includes this neighborhood. Miller says it is true that sometimes police do not follow up on information provided by citizens, pointing out that tracing out-of-state licenses is time consuming, and requires the cooperation of the Department's vice squad. "With the officers, [working with the Orange Hats] is a pain in the butt. Totally. They don't want to be there. . . . Some do. And there are some that have a great working relationship. But as a majority attitude, I'd say it's a negative one."

Still, Miller keeps the Takoma Coalition's patrol schedule pinned to the wall by his desk and tells officers to check in regularly with the group when they are out. Such communication is, in fact, required as part of the D.C. Police Department's "community empowerment policing" policy.

Thomas Green points out that it is important not only for police to pay attention to street-level drug dealing, but to attend to a wide range of violations that, if unchallenged, broadcast a sense of disorder within a community. "Officers Marshall and Gross were the best," he says. "If they saw people violating a law, they just didn't look the other way. If they were illegally parked, they would approach them about that. If they were disturbing the peace, they would approach them about that. Some of the other officers would look the other way. They just didn't seem to be that concerned about the fact that people were in violation of the law. They didn't seem to realize that those are things that lead up to greater violations. If they can double park in areas up there and no one will say anything to them about it, well, the next time they are going to do something worse than double park. One thing leads to another. One violation leads to another."

In the end, however, group members are resigned to the low level of assistance they get from police. "You can't have enough cops," says Jaime Velez. "People just have to get involved. There's nothing better than people in an area to know what's going on."

It's Nine O'Clock— Do You Know Where Your Neighbors Are?

Getting more people in the neighborhood to help out, however, has been an ongoing challenge for the group. They are encouraged by the friendly waves, the words of support, the tooting horns as neighbors drive by them on the corner. But getting people to put on an orange hat and stand with them is something else entirely. They are keenly aware that at fifteen active members and a total roster of about forty, they represent a tiny percentage of the residents in their nine-block area.

"A lot of people relate to us that they are glad to see us out there," says Don Young. "They tell us now they can go to the Safeway without having their purses snatched. . . . And sometimes we would ask them, well, why don't you come out? But they just say, 'no way.'" He throws back his head and laughs.

Jaime Velez is angrier about his neighbors' failure to help out. He is the only person on Butternut Street who participates. He describes bitterly how some people, taken with a romantic image of neighborhood vigilantism, come out once or twice and never return. "One lady down on the corner expressed a lot of interest," he says. "She called everybody. She came out with the group a couple times, bought an orange hat and never was seen again. So we think when she goes for a drink with her social group she can show her hat and . . . I don't know. It was a very quick flame. We never saw her again."

Another woman—one who had never walked with the group—confronted Velez on the street one day after she had been mugged outside her home. "Where were you?" she demanded. "Where were you when I was mugged? I thought your group was out every night!"

"Where were you?" he rejoined, stunned. "Do you think I am out there working for you?"

"Some people, they think we just have a lot of free time," he says. "They think that this is an adventure, that this is what we get high on. Meanwhile, she's now trying to sell her house. . . . People have a lot of excuses. I'm not passing judgment. I think it's very difficult to show up. It's unusual—to stand on the corner on watch."

"At first, we kept trying to get more people out," says Patty Walker. "We put flyers in doors. We went door to door, talking to people, wearing our orange hats, trying to get them to come out."

Once the group was approached by a resident of the Aspen Court Apartments—the buildings on Georgia Avenue where many of the drug dealers lived—who wanted to know more about getting involved. Filled with enthusiasm, a delegation went to visit her in her apartment, bearing flyers and instructions on how to start a citizen patrol, as well as invitations to join their own group. She thanked them, and they never heard from her again. "I think what she wanted was for us to patrol her building," says Walker.

"Finally I guess we just realized that we had all the participation we were gonna get—the rest of them weren't gonna come out no matter what we did. So in the last year and a half, two years, we haven't had any meetings, campaigns, anything, we've just stuck with the group we have, and kept going out. And every once in a while we get to feeling like, gee, you know, there are other people that are benefiting from all this and they're doing nothing. But we're the ones who want it done, so we're the ones who are going to do it."

Rage and Responsibility

What drove these people to undertake such a dangerous, time-consuming, and sometimes tedious activity? Each person has a different answer.

For Jaime Velez, the emotion that drives him is simple and strong. "Rage," he says. "How dare you? A block from my house. How dare you sell drugs? Or urinate in public or deface my neighborhood? How dare you? So it's anger. You get upset. And you realize police can't do it all. You can't go blaming them. So you take steps.

"It's also having a sense of pride in your own environment. Protecting the environment physically, aesthetically. Who's on the corner? What are they doing? Is it healthy? Someone is trying to inject a hypodermic needle right in the alley behind your house? It's not because you own a house, it's because you want to be able to step out and not see that."

For George Stern, joining at the start did not require any soul-searching. "Who wants to live down the street from a drug market?" he asks. And as far as staying with it, "Everybody knows if I don't go down there, this whole thing will collapse," he says. "And those who have put in a lot of time want to see it go on."

Elise Stern's father and mother came to live with the couple two years ago when her mother became ill and needed their care. Her father, Henry Stevens, says he joined the patrol to fulfill a family responsibility.

"I've never been as civic-minded as they are," he says. "I'm not an activist. But sometimes I see that George and Elise don't go because they are too overloaded with trying to help us, and I just feel that I should represent the house and the family. That's my way of contributing to the family."

For Patty Walker, it was a matter of ownership. Not real estate, but community ownership. "I wanted to do whatever we could do as citizens to keep the neighborhood from belonging—that's how I would put it—to these people who were hanging around in the streets, selling drugs or whatever they were doing. They were just kind of taking over the place, and I certainly didn't want that to happen."

Many in the group struggle to answer the question, "Why did you want to get involved in this?" They never really considered not getting involved. They point out that because they started their patrol before the neighborhood had been destroyed by crime, there was still something to save. It was their community. They felt they had no choice.

The Death of a Neighbor

Three months after the group began patrolling, a young man who lived in the Aspen Court Apartments was shot to death, execution style—his body was found in an alley, riddled with bullets—just a few blocks north on Georgia Avenue. Group members read about the murder in the paper on a Sunday morning; several of them remembered talking to the young man the night before, just hours before he was killed. Sarah Green knew him from way back; she had been his teacher back in the third grade. All of the group members believed he was a leader in the drug trade in their neighborhood.

They had a theory about why he was shot. His business having been disrupted by their patrol, they thought, he had gone to try and sell drugs on another section of Georgia Avenue and had been killed for poaching on another dealer's turf.

This violent murder was, to everyone in the group, a turning point, a moment of revelation. The shooting saddened and shocked them, but it also confronted them, more intimately than many of them had been confronted before, with the violence of the drug trade, its seductive power, and with their own potential impact as a group.

"I feel bad that a kid got shot," says Patty Walker. "I feel bad that anybody would get shot. But I think it did take a negative influence out of the neighborhood. And I also had the feeling that perhaps if we had not been standing on the corner perhaps he would not have got shot."

Finding Common Ground

From an outsider's perspective, there is much that would seem to divide this group: they are black, white, Hispanic, married, single, working, retired, professional, blue collar, middle aged, and old (no one seems to be younger than forty). And yet it is obvious that they relish each other's company. Out on the corner, they spend most of their time talking not about drugs and violence but about children and grandchildren, vacations, newspaper articles and hobbies, and gossiping in friendly fashion about the neighbors. Conversations are free-flowing and casual, moving seamlessly from group discussions that involve everyone to intimate tête-à-têtes and back again. Night after night, they find things to talk about.

"We enjoy it," says Patty Walker. "We may complain, oh it's cold out here or hot out here or I'm bored or I'd rather be doing something else, but I do think that we enjoy it. You talk, you see what's going on. In the course of all these years you've gotten to find out names and locations of everyone's children or grandchildren, how they're doing in school, where they're going to school. Things like that. So there's always, 'how's so and so doing?' 'Well, such and such.' Which I think is a good thing."

"Our group is made up of people who . . . genuinely like each other," says Don Young. "That's why we don't mind going out. It's something that just really developed. We have a lot in common: people that really enjoy fishing, people who do a lot of traveling.

"It took time for it to develop for everyone to become as close as we are. The first year or so, we were really business. But even at that, there was still a closeness; we were beginning to build a bond. And as time went on, that bond just became stronger and stronger. Now we go out there more or less just to meet!" At this, Young sits back in his chair and laughs.

I ask him whether there is any awareness of racial differences within the group. He laughs again. "No. I can say that unequivocally. There is none whatsoever."

Others in the group respond the same way to questions about race relations within the group. They are surprised at the question; they have been connected to one another as neighbors and Orange Hat colleagues for so long that they have almost ceased to see one another as members of different racial groups. To them, race simply does not matter. "We are all equal on the corner," says Sarah Green.

One person who addresses the issue of race directly is Henry Stevens. An elderly but spry white man who lived in all-white neighborhoods before coming to live with his daughter and son-in-law in Washington, he says orange hatting has given him his first chance to become friends with black people. "I haven't, myself, spent a lot of time with the other races," he says, "and consequently it's been a new experience for me. Everyone in the neighborhood is fine, educated people and all-around good citizens." He launches into a story about a fishing trip he took with Thomas Green—"the Fisherman." He has also attended baseball games with the Greens and the Youngs. Membership in the Orange Hats gave him access to a diverse social network that has helped him to feel at home in his new city.

Jaime Velez says he has had friends of diverse racial backgrounds all his life, but still was surprised at how easily members of the Takoma Coalition got along, right from the start. He says it is because people have come together not to focus on race but on issues that they all share. "I was amazed. Because it's a very integrated group. I mean, I'm the only Latino there, but it's mixed, black, white, and everybody's different, but there are certain things we have in common. A very strong sense of respect. I think it helps in feeling that you belong."

Velez finds in that feeling a source of strength. "It's liberating to go out and meet people and to know that your neighborhood is more than your house. That people are different, but that they have so much in common. That they are friends. And that would never happen if it wasn't for this. That's what makes me go."

The Secrets of Their Success

Even with such strongly committed members, one might wonder how the group has managed to sustain itself over more than four years, especially in the face of widespread apathy from others in the neighborhood. Part of the reason may be found in the group's unique culture and a set of un-written rules that work to prevent conflict and burnout and to boost the enjoyment that group members take from patrolling. The following fac-tors emerged as common themes in interviews with members and from observation on the street:

No guilt. Many in the group say that one reason they continue to come out is that they know the others would not make them feel guilty if they did not. Nobody acts as if this were a desperate, life-or-death en-deavor or as if a failure to appear is somehow a betrayal of the group.

"We always remind each other that you don't have to come out," says Don Young. "If you've got something to do, do it. Because you have a life outside of standing on the corner."

"No one is criticized for not coming," says Patty Walker. "And the reason is because we feel that the group has held together pretty well throughout this time. And we don't want to endanger that by picking on people who don't show up. And I think it works.

"I've missed now for two or three weeks. But I don't have to go out there feeling guilty. If I knew that I was going to face a lot of harassment the first night out there, I might not."

No hierarchy. "We're not organized, we're closely knit," says Don Young. In fact, the Takoma Coalition has no officers, nor even any ac-knowledged leaders. The lack of hierarchy is typical of Orange Hat groups. With hierarchy comes jealousy, power struggles, and resentment.

"One of the keys to our success," says George Stern, "is that no-body's ever said, I'm the premier or the pope or whatever. We maintain a healthy disrespect."

Without a formal leadership structure, petty jealousies are less likely to develop, and all group members feel an equal personal investment. The Takoma Coalition sees no need for leaders.

Lack of hierarchy does not, however, mean there is a lack of struc-ture. When the group makes a decision—usually by consensus, not by vote—systems are in place for notifying members who are not present. All it takes is for one person—any person—to make two phone calls to activate the telephone chain and keep open the flow of communication that is critical to the survival of any Orange Hat group.

No publicity. Unlike many citizen action groups, the Takoma Coalition doesn't go in for a lot of fanfare and publicity. They shun the media, and although Foreman's citywide coalition often holds rallies and other events to allow people from different Orange Hat groups to meet and to draw attention to their successes, this group rarely participates. Members keep to themselves in a way that would appear clannish if they weren't also so welcoming to outsiders who seek to join with them. The group was slightly suspicious of this case study, and some members were reluctant to be interviewed—but they always welcomed my efforts to patrol with them at night.

Part of the group's desire to keep a low profile stems from their suspicion of politicians. They tell stories about candidates who came by to walk with them for a night, accompanied by reporters and TV cameras, and never returned or acknowledged them again. One politician who was running for reelection came to patrol with the group one night and passed out brand new, better quality radios. They experienced a momentary thrill: the city was finally helping them out with some new equipment! But as soon as the city councillor left, her staff took the radios back. The group was left with a lingering resentment.

"It doesn't take much to turn us against you," says Thomas Green. "An official who comes by at election time, it must be for publicity. Don't use us to get into office. That's not what we're about."

"And they do come out of the woodwork at election time," Sarah Green chimes in.

Apart from their jaded attitude toward politicians who would capitalize on their efforts, the group has a practical reason for keeping a low profile.

"We rarely participate [in citywide Orange Hat meetings,]" says Patty Walker. "And the reason is, people think, if I've got another night to devote to this cause, I'll go to the street. We don't have any other spare time to go to the meetings or do this thing or the other."

Keep it simple. This is one group that does not have grand aspirations. Its goal—keeping drugs and prostitution out of their neighborhood—has never changed or expanded. Neither has its territory. Members don't proselytize, and they have never tried to expand their mission beyond keeping their few blocks of Washington, D.C. free of blatant drug selling and prostitution. They set a goal, and they stuck with it.

Neither does the group hold meetings, take votes, hold forums, or do anything else that would take time away from the street. "We figure what time we can spare we give to patrolling on the street," says Patty Walker. "And so we don't have meetings. If anything needs to be discussed or taken care of we do it on the street."

A habitable spot. The corner of Aspen and Georgia is not a truly comfortable spot. The sidewalk is narrow, and there are no benches or other amenities. But there is a streetlight there, as well as a stoplight, and these days foot traffic is light. It doesn't feel like a dangerous spot. Its landscape—the disabled pay phone, a newspaper dispensing box, a trash can installed by the city after two years of letters from the group—these are the furnishings of what has become, for the Takoma Coalition, a kind of community living room.

When the group circles up on the corner of Georgia and Aspen, group members tend to stand in the same spots from one night to the next: Thomas Green with his back to the light pole and the newspaper box, Don Young with his back to the phone. Sarah Green puts her bag with Styrofoam cups, a thermos of hot water and instant hot chocolate for everybody on top of the pay phone and when it's time to serve it up they all step over to a ledge on the side of the hotel that acts as a serving counter. This corner is a place they have come to feel at home.

Bonding rituals and traditions. While the group has no formal rituals, over time they have developed patterns, habits, and ways of relating to one another that seem to reinforce their sense of inclusion and cohesion.

Group members often use one another's street names even in casual conversation. Some whose friendships dated to before the group started to refer to one another by real names—but in many cases they had to struggle to remember the real names of those they knew from the street corner. Like a secret handshake or a password, these alternative names seemed to add a sense of belonging to something special. On occasion, the street names may even have served to blunt cultural differences. "If Termite called me up and said, 'Hey, Sarah, this is Jaime,' I don't think I'd know who it was at first," says Sarah Green. "I can't even pronounce it! But when he calls me, he says, 'Pisces? Termite.' Then I know who I'm talking to."

They have nicknames, as well, for some of the people and the places they encounter in their patrols—the "mail detail," for instance. One nighttime denizen of Georgia Avenue they call "Million Dollar Walk"; another is called "Camouflage," after her customary attire.

The group also looks forward to its annual backyard party. It's usually a potluck, although sometimes members do a fish fry—with those group members who like to fish providing the main course. Neighbors who do not participate in the patrol are also invited to attend, and there is usually a good turnout. Don Young speculates that coming to the annual party is one way others in the neighborhood seek to show their support for the Orange Hats and give them an emotional boost.

Even the small rituals of their nighttime forays play a role in fostering the group's sense of membership: mixing up the hot chocolate, walking one another home, etc. These expected, predictable, and shared moments and habits make the activity pleasantly familiar, enhance people's sense of comfort with one another, define the boundaries of their activities, and give them a sense of inclusion and comfort. What's more, they provide a shared context that is a necessary condition for building friendships, friendships that serve to sustain the group.

Stay with what's possible. Finally, the Takoma Coalition recognized that people cannot keep patrolling every night for five hours for the rest of their lives. In the second year, they reduced their hours to two a night (from 8:00 to 10:00) and stopped patrolling on Sundays. The third year, they cut back to four nights a week. Today, they patrol from 8:30 to 10:00, two to three nights a week. There has been some rise in illegal activity on the nights that they are not out, but they feel they have reached a comfortable compromise between the perfect and the possible.

Beyond Fighting Drugs

> Success breeds more success. They usually go on to other things. Things they should have been doing in the community. Once they win a battle against what they thought was the baddest, meanest people in the world, people no one could stop, they feel unstoppable. —James Foreman

Is all of this activity only about fighting drugs? Across the city, Orange Hat groups report that what starts as an antidrug patrol often leads to other activities—some targeted at reducing crime, others at addressing other neighborhood issues. From beautification to human needs like homework assistance and escorts for the elderly, Orange Hat groups tend to acquire other interests. The Takoma Coalition is no exception.

Two Saturdays a year it sponsors a neighborhood cleanup. It was Thomas Green's idea. "He just said, 'You know, this neighborhood really has been looking raggedy—I think we oughta get out,'" remembers George Stern. "'Everybody bring a shovel and a rake. Weed whack-ers.' So we set a date, and we did a spit-shine. It became a tradition."

"We get out there early Saturday morning with our rakes and wheel-barrows and cutters and we literally clean this entire area, including the alleys," says Thomas Green. "And we cut grass and rake leaves," adds Sarah. "And some of those in the community who are too old to partici-pate come out and bring us things to drink. One lady gives us money to buy hot chocolate. One guy came by and gave us a box of donuts. Most people come out and if they don't clean anything but just in front of their house—we usually have pretty good participation from people who are non-orange hatters."

Every season more people participate in the cleanup day. It's fun, and some feel it does more than simply create a short-term improvement. Rather, it sets a standard for residents to live up to. The cleaning fever is contagious.

"I've noticed that if there's a cleanup scheduled for Saturday the 15th, many of us will go out and make sure our space is clean a week beforehand," says Patty Walker.

"We even have some folks who refused to participate in the cleanup day but who I have seen since then get out and rake leaves—folks who never raked leaves before," remarks Sarah Green. "They cut grass, they clean up the strip. They are doing more cleaning lately than they have been the whole time they lived here."

"I feel when you do things like that," says Thomas Green, "when you maintain your property or to the point where you are cleaning other areas of the neighborhood—that other people get the hint and say, this is good for the community, I'm going to do more. There are people who will cut the grass and will not even do anything to the strip out front of the house. The alley the same way. They say, well, that's the city's re-sponsibility. But now rather than leave the trash in the alley and wait for the city, I go ahead and clean our alley. We try and encourage others to do the same, because the city just isn't able to do those things. They just don't have the manpower, the resources."

Green conducts a personal campaign to get neighbors to keep their porch lights on at night to deter crime, and most of his Aspen Street neighbors now comply.

Are other neighbors not involved in the Orange Hat patrol more vigilant as a result of the Orange Hats' success? "I think now more so than before we got started," says Green. "People are more apt to get in-volved. If they see something that looks rather suspicious, they're going to check it out. They're not just going to look at it and say, 'Well, that's what's happening,' and just close the doors and forget about it. I think now they will check out situations more than they would have."

Inspiring Others

Just as James Foreman and members of other Orange Hat patrols helped the Takoma Coalition get started, they have reached out a helping hand to other fledgling groups, offering advice, support, and inspiration. Just to the north of their area along Georgia Avenue, they assisted in the formation of the GFEDDs group (named for the streets in its membership area: Georgia, Fern, Elder, Dahlia, and Dogwood). The history of GFEDDs, which started with patrolling but quickly moved on to a range of other activities, shows that orange hatting, defined broadly, can address a range of neighborhood concerns and can be adapted to meet the needs and utilize the strengths of varied communities.

Roger Conner lives on Elder Street, just east of Georgia and five blocks to the north of Aspen. For his book on fighting drugs, Conner had already done a good deal of research on citizen antidrug patrols and other grassroots strategies for fighting drug markets, when he became aware sometime in 1990 that drug dealing was a problem in his own neighborhood. The sound of gunfire on weekend nights was becoming a common occurrence. Conner and a neighbor decided to hold a meeting. A neighbor who owned a restaurant on Georgia Avenue opened up the shop on a Saturday afternoon, and Conner invited Knee Cap to attend.

"So we went to the meeting and I was delighted because there were like 11 people," says Conner, describing the meeting, "and I thought, 'man, this is great.' But once we got started it turned out that eight of them were from the Takoma Coalition. They were wearing these orange hats, and it seemed like a cult. . . . Foreman said, we need to have a walk. We'll start tomorrow night. And I said, 'Don't you think we ought to have a meeting, get people together first?' And he said 'No, no meetings. We go out on the street.' And all the Takoma folks said, 'That's right, we did it. We went out every night and we got rid of the drug dealing.'

"We got swept along by their commitment and their clarity that this was the thing to do. Among all the bewildering array of options that might have been put in front of us, somebody put a simple, clear thing in front of us.

"So they gave us a flyer that they had used, and I modified it and made copies and started knocking on doors the next day. I found the first three people that first Sunday afternoon." With Conner and his fiancée, Margaret Blair, the group numbered five.

"Some of the Takoma people came up that first night to swell our numbers and give us some reassurance that there was going to be more of us than there was of them. And when you're first doing it it seems hopelessly quixotic and exotic and dangerous. But having these other people with you who've already done it—you're joking and talking and feeling a little strange, you're all neighbors but you're just meeting for the first time, and you're thinking, what are we doing out here? Are we included or excluded? And is this a group? What's happening here? Having them around that first night was very important. Even doing the research for the book and with everything else that I knew, I don't believe that I would have started—I would not have walked out there that first night without them."

After that first night, the Takoma Coalition never walked with the GFEDDs group, but the groups communicated on their radios each night. For five months, the GFEDDs walked every night. Conner was out six nights a week. The core was small—just three or four residents—but many people came out and walked occasionally. Like the Takoma Coalition, they were thrilled at their own success. Where gunfire had become a weekly occurrence, there was now almost none, and the large groups of teenagers that had congregated on the corner of Georgia and Fern had dispersed. Unlike the Takoma Coalition, the GFEDDs stopped patrolling after about five months.

Drug activity did not immediately return to its earlier level, but without the nightly patrol, the dealers and the problems they brought with them slowly began to return. Conner points to two factors that made it difficult for GFEDDs to sustain energy for patrolling. First, he notes, the group never found a comfortable spot—like Georgia and Aspen—in which to congregate and remain. The trouble spot in their neighborhood was the corner of Fern and Georgia, near a bar and restaurant called the Hummingbird that had a dangerous clientele. Neighbors suspected open drug dealing was tolerated inside the club, and before the patrol began there were gun battles outside the Hummingbird almost every weekend. Standing on that corner, the small band of GFEDDs patrollers felt threatened and exposed and so rather than try to occupy the corner they walked through the neighborhood, which spread their influence but made them less effective at driving away the drug buyers who came to the Hummingbird and, at the same time, made socializing within the group more difficult.

Second, says Conner, the group was simply not as social as the Takoma group. "We didn't have someone who wanted to be the life of the party to make it into a social event, the way the Takoma group does, in addition to being a quasi-law enforcement vigilante event. I think that's the key transition for one of these groups that's going to stay on—the patrol has to become a social event that people feel attracted to coming. It has to fill human needs to be part of a group."

The GFEDDs did not disappear, however. Instead, they took legal action against the Hummingbird, initiating a civil suit claiming that the club violated the terms of its liquor license. In order to file the suit, it had to collect signatures from over half the registered voters in the immediate vicinity of the bar, which proved to be a Herculean task. The litigation dragged out for three years but was ultimately successful. The restaurant lost its liquor license, and the problems of drug selling and violence seemed to abate. After a year, the restaurant closed.

The GFEDDs turned to other activities as well. The group formed a neighborhood association that met monthly. Aware that children and elderly people had not been able to participate in the nighttime patrols, they now mount periodic daylight patrols on Saturday afternoons, a community-building and visibility gesture that draws as many as twenty-five people, many of them children. They have held neighborhood parties and a couple of alley cleanup days. And last Halloween, they organized a neighborhood Halloween party in which parent volunteers accompanied groups of children to designated participating homes to collect candy and then back to a party where children received GFEDDs Halloween posters with maps of the neighborhood and materials to paste on the posters, including Polaroid photos of themselves in costume. More than sixty children participated, many of them children who had never been allowed to go "trick-or-treating" before.

Recently, new violence erupted in the neighborhood with the arrival of a gang occupying the alley between Elder and Fern Streets. Gang insignia were scrawled on garages and young men dressed in black prowled the alley each night. An emergency meeting at Conner's home drew more than thirty residents. The next morning, Conner found his tires slashed. He activated the Orange Hat phone chain, and neighbors responded immediately with a flood of telephone calls to city councillors, police, local neighborhood commissioners, and the mayor of DC. Within days, police responded to this "squeaky wheel" by sending an undercover vice squad to arrest the drug dealers in the alley, and followed up by assigning a foot patrolman and two bicycle cops to the area. The owners of two dilapidated garages the gang members had been ducking into for shelter responded—the first by sealing his garage and the second by destroying his. The gang disappeared.

"Orange hatting is like Johnson grass," says Conner. "Where I grew up, Johnson grass, the roots were always there. And when the environmental conditions are right, the plant comes up. And you can't kill it. It's always there.

"What happens is that people meet each other—just the simple act of asking who each other are and exchanging a phone number. So that you can call them. Getting to know each other, getting to know who's good and who's bad and who lives in which house, and which kids belong to which parents, and what the phone numbers are and what your history is, that is the building block of the capacity of a community to respond to any threat."

Alpha McPherson is one of those who has been with the group from the first night out. McPherson wrote a paper about the group's early experiences for a college course he was taking. In his paper he acknowledged that the group had been successful only in reclaiming the streets from the drug dealers for the time slot during which they patrolled; when they were not there the dealers returned. However, he found many other benefits in the experience.

"We have begun to foster good relations with the decent people in the community," he wrote. "People walk up to us and tell us what a good job we are doing. Some come out and walk with us for a while during our patrol. We've had whole families join us for an evening. A mother and daughter walked with us. Husbands and wives stopped and spent time with us. People who own businesses near our area joined us for an evening too. Roger always has extra orange caps for our frequent honorary patrollers. We have a spirit now of turning to one another instead of on one another."

McPherson and Conner, while not elected leaders, are the linchpins of the group. McPherson is black; Conner is white. Both speak compellingly of the contribution the group has made to fostering good relations in their diverse neighborhood.

Without groups that give people an opportunity to build trust in one another, says Conner, it is very difficult to overcome a sense of alienation between racial groups, even when people live on the same block. "The barrier is that you don't know what the rules are. You don't know what conduct is appropriate . . . and what you can complain about."

Conner cites as an example an extremely loud summer daytime party that some of his black neighbors were holding. A newcomer to the community, he was irritated by the noise, but was uncertain whether it would be appropriate to complain. He was uncertain of the norms in this predominantly black neighborhood. "Is that what black people do? Is that behavior that is just acceptable in my neighborhood and it's the dominant culture and I'm just supposed to live with it? Or can I call the cops and have the cops come and tell them to turn the music down without having somebody laugh at me and be mad at me? I don't know."

Because of his Orange Hat-instigated friendship with McPherson, Conner felt comfortable asking him about the party. McPherson told him it was generally tolerated because it occurred only once a year. Having someone he could ask made Conner feel much more at ease.

"In a diverse neighborhood," he says, "you don't know what the rules are. And what's worse, you don't have a way to find out. Especially when you tend to retreat from the public space because you don't know what the rules are. People need to decide how to go about a diverse group of people living in a common space. Normally, you just have no way of doing this. But I feel I can ask Alpha or a dozen people in my neighborhood. I can be up front and honest with them and ask them a question like this without any fear that they're going to judge me to be a bad person for having raised that question."

In his paper, McPherson attributes the sense of mutual respect between all members of the group, black and white alike, to the enormity of the challenge they face together.

"Groups like this," he wrote, "immediately learn to respect each member as equals regardless of race, color, national origin, or status.

"The fear of the streets and street violence hastened our group to bond fast and tight. We bonded in one night. . . . Internal conflict did not exist within our group. And I can only attribute that to the nature of our group interest. Already, there was conflict swirling around us from the drug dealers and users. We never had time to focus upon anything but unity and togetherness."

Feeling at Home in Your Own Neighborhood

In the end, perhaps what is most important in keeping the GFEDDs and the Takoma Coalition involved in patrolling and other activities over the long haul is the way it makes them feel about the community they live in. In a racially diverse community people are not always able to see what they have in common until some external purpose that they share and some common activity offers them an opportunity to grow comfortable with one another.

For Roger Conner, it has made all the difference. "For a white person living in a predominantly black neighborhood, just having people to your face be welcoming and generous gives you the feeling that you're not an alien surrounded by people who dislike them," he says.

And for Jaime Velez, an activity like orange hatting is essential for creating a sense of community in an urban neighborhood. "I don't know about the suburbs, but in the cities, people are on the go. They're behind closed doors. But this is basic—who lives where, and so how is so-and-so? How is the family?

"Otherwise, what is neighborhood? Is it a nice front yard? There are many people who have been here for ages that are locked behind their doors, or they just drive to the front of their house and walk in. You never even know if they have legs. They always are in their car. And I don't want to know what people are doing, I'm not nosy, but I want to feel that this is my neighborhood. And this makes you feel like, I know people. I know who they are. They live in my neighborhood."

The Future

Will the Takoma Coalition ever stop patrolling? Will a day come when they no longer need to spend their evenings guarding their streets from crime and violence?

"Sometimes I find myself wondering where will it all go," says Patty Walker. "For how many years will it continue? I never would have thought we would be standing out there four years. . . . And I wonder how many more years I'm going to be out there. Yet I'm one of those who has the feeling that if we don't stay out there on the corner, they, the big they, are going to be standing on the corner."

"How would you feel if you stayed in this neighborhood and were standing out there till the end of your days?" I ask her.

"I'd just accept that that was what living in this neighborhood is all about," she said.

Thomas and Sarah Green are hopeful that the drug problem in America will run its course, and that they will not have to spend their old age standing under a street lamp on the corner of Georgia and Aspen. "I don't see myself, 80, 90 years old, having to go out on the corner," says Thomas.

"However," Sarah jumps in. "I do see our group staying together. Orange Hats may not be patrolling, but as long as our friends, the core group is here, we will always be doing something together."

Notes

This chapter originally appeared in 1994 as a "Case Study in Community Action," published by The Communitarian Network, Washington, D.C. It is reprinted here with permission.

1. For safety and privacy, Young's name, and all of the names of the Takoma Park residents quoted in this study, have been changed.

2. These data are drawn from the *Heritage Foundation Policy Review*, "D.C. Blues: The Rap Sheet on the Washington Police," Winter 1993.

4

Building Community Capacity to Prevent Violence through Coalitions and Partnerships

David M. Chavis

Over the past ten years, community coalitions have been increasingly used to address a variety of complex and entrenched social and health problems, especially in poor and underserved communities. Government and foundation prevention initiatives have embraced coalitions and partnerships as major components of their strategies to address tobacco use (e.g., National Cancer Institutes' PROCEED and COMMIT programs), alcoholism and other substance abuse (e.g., Center for Substance Abuse Prevention's Community Partnership Program and the Robert Wood Johnson Foundation's Fighting Back), maternal and child health (e.g., Health and Human Services' Healthy Mothers Healthy Babies), crime (community policing efforts), economic deprivation (e.g., Housing and Urban Development's Empowerment Zones and the Ford Foundation's Family and Neighborhood Project), school reform (e.g., Annie Casey Foundation), cancer and cardiovascular disease (e.g., Centers for Disease Control's PATCH program and the Henry J. Kaiser Family Foundation's and W. K. Kellogg Foundation's community health promotion programs) and the overall revitalization of communities (e.g., HUD's Building Communities Together program). Coalition initiatives not only cover a range of social and health problems, but also range in geographic scope (e.g., national, state, region, county, city, neighborhood, and school) and membership strategies (e.g., public agencies, public and private agencies, multiple sectors, spiritual institutions, business, government, and grass-roots leaders, etc.).

Definitions of Coalitions and Partnerships

Butterfoos et al. (1993) reported that early definitions of coalitions reflected "short term loosely structured intra- and inter-organizational alliances, and blurred distinctions between coalitions and other types of groups." Feighery and Rodgers (1992) offered a definition that probably reflects the most current use of the term: "an organization of individuals representing diverse organizations, factions or constituencies who agree to work together in order to achieve a common goal." Other authors have emphasized that contemporary community coalitions are also formal, multipurpose, and long-term alliances (Butterfoos et al. 1993; Chavis et al. 1993). The term *partnership* has lately been used more frequently in relation to domestic programs to reflect their multisectoral (e.g., spiritual, business, government, grassroots citizens, schools) makeup (Center for Substance Abuse Prevention 1994). The term partnership also implies the shared and long-term commitment of effective community coalitions; everybody brings something of value to the table.

Coalitions are uniquely characterized by the paradox of participant advocacy and commitment of resources to both the organization they represent and the coalitions themselves (Butterfoos et al. 1993; Mizrahi and Rosenthal 1993). This paradox is a source of conflict inherent in a community coalition that requires a great deal of attention (Mizrahi and Rosenthal 1993; Speer and Chavis 1994). Coalitions of groups that are composed of members from diverse sectors and with more resources are more likely to experience this conflict to a greater degree.

The Functions of Coalitions in Prevention Strategies

It should not surprise the student of social policy that, despite the enthusiasm for coalescing, there is a lack of clarity in most coalition initiatives as to why coalitions might help solve problems, and little evidence that they can accomplish the types of changes they are undertaking. Moreover, a viable strategic understanding of why we should invest so much in coalitions is still rare in most current national initiatives, apart from the sense that everyone needs to be involved in problem-solving and communities need to combine resources and reduce duplication. Coalitions are difficult enough to successfully maintain when diverse groups have a tangible immediate goal. When the goals of the coalition become more complex and distant, they can easily become tumultuous and/or inactive.

Community coalitions for prevention are capable of ten primary functions according to reviews of the literature (Butterfoos et al. 1993; Chavis et al. 1993). Coalitions can:

1. broaden the mission of member organizations and develop more comprehensive strategies;
2. develop wider public support for issues;
3. increase the influence of individual community institutions over community policies and practices;
4. minimize duplication of services;
5. develop more financial and human resources;
6. increase participation from diverse sectors and constituencies;
7. exploit new resources in a changing environment;
8. increase accountability;
9. improve capacity to plan and evaluate; and
10. strengthen local organizations and institutions to respond better to the needs and aspirations of their constituents.

There is little evidence in the literature that indicates that coalitions have a unique ability to develop new programs, such as (specific) services. The programs of member organizations in current community coalition efforts tend to be more comprehensive and more fully engage the community (Butterfoos et al. 1993). Several national initiatives have begun to expect that, and the results are unclear and not encouraging (Institute for Social Analysis 1993). That is not to say that coalitions funded to develop programs are incapable of actually developing programs and interventions. However, at this time it is questionable as to whether they are in most cases any more effective or efficient in developing new service programs than other types of organizations.

Coalitions can be very expensive, more in terms of time and energy than money. They can deplete the resources of their membership; this is especially true of the already overextended community-based organizations (Speer and Chavis 1994). Therefore, we must be cautious in regard to our application of this tool. Two recent collections of articles on

coalitions and community organizations document the vast efforts, conflicts, disappointments, and variety of initiatives that come under the
banner of building coalitions and other similar community organizations
(Goodman et al. 1993; Mizrahi and Morrison 1993). These two collections of articles by practitioners and researchers review the literature and
make their own contributions. They largely reflect what Butterfoos et al.
(1993) refer to as "wisdom literature" with regard to coalitions—impres-
sions, perceptions, and descriptions that are valid only within the context
of the study parameters and not generalizable. Rarely do these studies
show the larger outcomes of coalition efforts. Most often, their effects are
characterized as singular and immediate (e.g., starting a program, passing
legislation, getting an agency to respond to a community need). This may
be due to the fact that, until recently, coalitions have been viewed as
temporary relationships focused on immediate outcomes (Butterfoos et al.
1993). Only recently have larger, more systematic studies begun to
examine the popular strategy of coalition building, and what impact it
may have on complicated, entrenched problems and long-term outcomes
(Butterfoos et al. 1993).

Coalitions and the Prevention of Violence, Alcoholism, Drug Abuse, and Juvenile Delinquency

Coalitions show promise in the prevention of violence, alcoholism, drug
abuse, and juvenile delinquency because of the complexity and interdependence of these problems and the systemic and community basis of their
causes.

Several recent studies concluded that these problems stem from a
variety of factors, including fragmented communities and families, a sense
of hopelessness and powerlessness, and economic deprivation (American
Psychological Association Commission on Youth and Violence 1993;
Curtis and Currie 1990; Hawkins et al. 1992). According to the American
Psychological Association Commission on Youth and Violence (1993),
"social forces, such as prejudice, economic inequality, and attitudes
toward violence in mainstream culture interact with the influences of early
childhood to foster the expression of violence."

Community coalitions, properly designed and supported, could create
a multifaceted and comprehensive community development strategy. This
is necessary for member organizations to adequately develop their own

capacity to take on the challenge of violence reduction. The member communities can work alone or within an organization—that is within the mandate of the (sponsoring) institution, and within the needs or desires of their constituents.

Community Capacities for Prevention

Community capacity is defined in this article as the ability to effectively develop, mobilize, and use resources to manage change. Community coalitions can enhance the capacity of local leaders, organizations, and community institutions in (activating) individual communities to prevent violence and other social and health problems. One of the most important and achievable goals of a community coalition is to develop a learning community (Knowles 1970; Senge 1990). A learning community can be seen as a system where organizations and "people continually expand their capacities to create the results they truly desire, where new and expansive patterns of thinking are nurtured, where collective aspirations are set free, and where people are continually learning how to learn together" (Senge 1990). Capable communities are learning communities. The following capacities are proposed as necessary for communities to prevent social problems such as violence:

Resource acquisition and mobilization
- increased resources for prevention and community development
- recruitment and use of volunteers and other nonmonetary resources
- fund-raising strategies, structures, and resources
- learning/intellectual
- knowledge and skills
- enabling system (workshops, seminars, consultations, information and referral networks)

Political
- inter-institutional linkages and practices that promote prevention and community development
- setting goals, planning
- goal attainment

- processes and structures that foster responsiveness and account-ability
- leadership development and support

Psychosocial
- mobilization and management of social relations
- sense of community, caring
- development and maintenance of organizations, communities
- appropriate and effective help-seeking
- organizational structure and climate

How Coalitions Can Enable Community Capacity Building

An enabling system is a coordinated network of organizations, which nurture the development and maintenance of a grassroots community development process through the provision of resources, incentives, and education (Butterfoos et al. 1993; Speer and Chavis 1994). Coalitions can manage, sponsor, network, or broker the components of this system in order to build community capacity. The components or types of assistance that coalitions need to make available to individuals and institutions constitute a variety of types of assistance that function to build community capacity and include the following elements:

Training and Consultation

This involves team, staff, local trainer, and leadership training, as well as consultation on community, organizational, and programmatic issues and strategies.

Information and Referral

Coalitions can disseminate information on model programs, provide data on community conditions, research information and resources (e.g., funding, training, conferences, consultants, volunteers).

Networking and Coalition Development

Assistance can be provided in order to form networks and coalitions at local levels (e.g., neighborhood) or among institutions and people with common interests and needs (e.g., grassroots organizations, youth workers). Networks consist of organizations and individuals interested in common problems, issues, and strategies who meet to exchange information, common training, and technical assistance needs. Coalitions are made up of organizations and institutions working together through communication, coordination, and collaboration in order to solve community problems.

Communications

Coalitions can be most effective in their capacity building only if they foster communications among members, the public, and larger systems. Coalitions can promote communication through newsletters, television and radio programs (e.g., community access cable stations), conferences, and electronic bulletin boards.

Incentive Grants and Recognition

Coalitions can encourage innovation, experimentation, and diffusion of successful local programs by developing funds to incubate new strategies, and provide public recognition and awards to successful local collective efforts.

Public Information and Social Marketing

Coalitions can use the media (electronic and print) to promote public involvement and ownership of initiatives. They can also assist in the identification of public priorities, concerns, and resource usage. Coalitions can facilitate the fit between public needs, preferred methods of service delivery, and agency responses. Coalitions can even increase public access to resources by publishing printed or electronic resource directories.

Research and Evaluation

Coalitions can facilitate their communities' learning process through research and evaluation services. These are services generally too expensive and involved for any one agency to provide to the community alone. Coalitions can sponsor or conduct action research projects; evaluate systems, services, and products; facilitate the evaluation of local programs, and train local evaluators to work more effectively and appropriately with community leadership; provide feedback on research findings; and develop action principles to guide strategy development.

Examples of Community Coalition
Capacity Building in Two Cities

Two coalitions for drug abuse prevention in New Jersey were funded by the Center for Substance Abuse Prevention (CSAP) Community Partnership program for between $250,000 and $300,000 annually for three years. The two partnerships were in cities near to each other with populations of approximately 60,000 (Community A) and 120,000 (Community B) persons. These cities were slowly recovering from decline. The community partnerships were primarily assisted by an intermediary support organization, the Center for Social and Community Development's Urban Community Development Program (UCDP) at Rutgers University. The UCDP managed an enabling system for these and three other partnerships in the state (Butterfoos et al. 1993; Speer and Chavis 1994). The UCDP was under contract to the partnerships to provide evaluation and other support services (training, staff field supervision, consultation, organizational and resource development). The UCDP strategy was to use the coalition to build the cities' capacities to comprehensively develop their communities and strengthen their basic institutions based on the strategy described in Chavis et al. (1993). The partnerships also received training and technical assistance through CSAP-supported intermediaries. This assistance was coordinated through learning plans developed by UCDP for the partnership members and their organizations, neighborhood leaders, and partnership staff.

These two multilevel community partnerships, each with a comprehensive community development agenda that evolved over a twenty-two-month period beginning on November 1, 1991, demonstrated all the capacity-building functions of a coalition described previously. These brief descriptions illustrate the potential of coalitions when there is this level of support.

Community A Partnership

The Community A partnership included five working committees of citywide and neighborhood leaders focusing on problem areas such as crime, education, housing, and health. The partnership had four professional staff: a director and three community development specialists that reported to a lead agency. A citywide citizen organization was the lead agency. The staff of the partnership and the Urban Community Development Program (UCDP) developed three new leader-dominated neighborhood organizations to provide grassroots support and action for partnership initiatives.

Accomplishments

Partnership members worked with the local board of education and neighborhood leaders to bring the Cities in Schools (CIS) program to a school in one of the targeted neighborhoods. The neighborhood CIS program was placed under the auspices of one of the neighborhood coalitions developed by the partnership. Community A partnership's youth, education, and recreation committee served as the official CIS steering committee without having the board of education develop its own separate committee.

The partnership and neighborhood leaders, working with city officials and the State Department of Community Affairs, were successful in bringing Community Action Agency designation to the partnership's lead agency. This brought additional resources and tensions to the process. The staff formed a citywide youth organization. The partnership members worked with emerging youth leaders on an antidrug block party for youth.

A neighborhood coalition successfully advocated for the reform of the Basic Skills Instruction program in all of the city's schools. The Basic Skills program was the city's Chapter I program to provide an educational enrichment program for at-risk and disadvantaged youth. Most neighborhood leaders thought it was tracking. The neighborhood coalition members felt that the program targeted minority youth for marginal futures. Students generally remained in the program for almost all of their school career and, according to policy, could not receive a grade greater than a C.

This neighborhood coalition started a youth media production program in conjunction with the public schools. The Department of Recreation has supplied a $1,000 seed grant in support of this effort. Another neighborhood coalition cleaned up a park and its surrounding area that was plagued by drug dealing. Several schools and other community institutions participated in a tree planting event at the park.

The three neighborhood coalitions also worked collaboratively to negotiate with the police department and the mayor's office to implement community policing strategies.

Community B Partnership

The Community B partnership created six working committees and took on an even more comprehensive, multifaceted approach to building the capacity of local organizations to prevent drug and alcohol abuse. This partnership also had broad representation from citywide institutions and neighborhood leaders. The lead organization was a church-initiated, citywide citizen organization similar to the lead organization in Community A. There was a director and four community development specialists. Committees were established to implement neighborhood-based responses to the city's drug problem in conjunction with the eight neighborhood coalitions created by UCDP and partnership staff.

Accomplishments

Partnership members and UCDP and partnership staff worked with the city police department to implement a pilot community policing program in the one neighborhood.

This partnership initiated working with the Community A partnership and successfully held a hearing on banking practices cosponsored by the state's banking commission. At the hearing, minority residents of the two nearby cities gave testimony concerning deceptive practices by mortgage companies and realtors and their poor record of reinvesting in the community. The state's banking regulations for mortgage companies were changed following the hearing. The state banking commissioner acknowledged the influence of the hearing on the changes. The partnership was able to identify citizens who could convincingly testify, and who would not normally be accessible to regulatory agencies.

The partnership's economic development committee developed plans for a community credit union for residents, businesses, and institutions in the less wealthy sections of the city.

Partnership members worked with the neighborhood coalitions and local banks to hold a banking fair in a bankless neighborhood. Mortgage lending information was distributed as well as information on how to improve credit ratings.

The partnership sponsored, with the Neighborhood Coalition and other local institutions, a walking tour for the city's federal delegation to point out housing conditions in the coalition's neighborhood.

The youth and families committee completed a proposal to sponsor a Youth Build program, a federally funded, combined job-training program for young adults, and a housing program. It appears very likely that the proposal will be funded at the time of the writing of this paper.

One coalition of neighborhood leaders and institutions held a campaign against negative stereotyping on billboards in their area. The campaign has led to the removal of one billboard and the provision of free space for an advertisement promoting community involvement on the other.

The partnership health committee, neighborhood coalitions, the major hospitals, and social service providers in the city held health fairs in two neighborhoods. Over 1,000 people attended the two sessions, which provided information and referral as well as health screening services.

The youth and families committee and one neighborhood coalition held a Youth and Family Fair in which area residents were informed of existing programs in the city for families and youth.

The neighborhood coalitions worked together on citywide campaigns. They worked with the police department to implement several new strategies to combat the city's drug problem. Their Seven Point Program included a return to foot patrols in high crime areas, having the police work with other city departments to close drug-dealing sites, working with community groups to pressure landlords to keep their properties from being used for illegal drug sales, and counseling area youth on alternatives to simply hanging out on the streets.

Outcomes of the Capacity-Building Process

The outcomes of these accomplishments are not completely clear as yet. However, these two partnerships generated a number of organizations, and therefore allowed for more people and institutions to participate (Butterfoos et al. 1993; Chavis et al. 1993). The neighborhood coalitions allowed for greater grassroots ownership and participation in the initiatives (Chavis et al. 1993). The decentralization of planning and the implementation of strategies through committees and neighborhood coalitions was an effective structure for responding to a chaotic and rapidly changing environment (Butterfoos et al. 1993; Institute for Social Analysis 1993). After three years it was not possible to determine reduction in alcoholism or other substance abuse, especially due to the limitations of current measures of community drug and alcohol use and limited resources. A large majority of residents surveyed by telephone, however, did report noticing greater activity in their neighborhood by police, schools, hospitals, and neighborhood organizations. What you can see most clearly from the accomplishments of the first twenty-two months was that the leaders of organizations were getting smarter, better skilled, and more motivated to try new practices. These two partnerships demonstrated their capacity to create a better learning community.

A Policy to Build Community Capacity and Prevent Violence

In order to build the violence-prevention capacities of communities, their social and economic infrastructure must be strengthened and well integrated at the local level. There must be an investment in the social infrastructure through mediating institutions that connect with families, schools, churches, community organizations, and businesses. Government must build its capacity to use mediating institutions to invoke substantial change. Institutions at all levels will need to be engaged in a process that builds community capacity to develop healthy families and communities. Families and communities can receive the resources and opportunities they need for their development through a multilevel community partnership and coalition system. This system can help facilitate the current reformation of our mediating institutions. First, we must renovate the social and local economic infrastructure so that our institutions can do their jobs. Schools must be able to educate, hospitals must be able to promote health, businesses must be able to develop jobs, and spiritual and civic institutions must be able to strengthen the moral and spiritual fiber of our communities.

Note

This chapter originally appeared in the *Journal of Health Care for the Poor and Underserved,* Volume 6, 1995, pp. 234-44. It is reprinted here with permission.

References

American Psychological Association Commission on Youth and Violence. 1993. *Violence and Youth: Psychology's Response.* Vol. I. Washington, DC: American Psychological Association.

Butterfoos, F. D., R. M. Goodman, and A. Wandersman. 1993. "Community Coalitions for Prevention and Health Promotion." *Health Education Research* 8: 315-30.

Center for Substance Abuse Prevention. 1994. *The Community Prevention Coalitions Demonstration Grant Program.* Program announcement no. 94-02. Rockville, MD: U.S. Public Health Service.

Chavis, D. M., P. Speer, I. Resnick, and A. Zippay. 1993. "Building Community Capacity to Address Alcohol and Drug Abuse: Getting to the Heart of the Problem." In *Drugs and Community,* edited by B. C. Davis, A. J. Lungio and D. Rosenbaum, 251-84. Springfield, IL: Charles C. Thomas.

Curtis, L. A., and E. Currie. 1990. *Youth Investment and Community Construction: Street Lessons on Drug and Crime in the Nineties.* Washington, DC: Milton S. Eisenhower Foundation.

Feighery, E., and T. Rodgers. 1992. "Building and Maintaining Effective Coalitions." *How to Guides in Community Health Promotion,* Vol. 12. Palo Alto, CA: Stanford Health Promotion Resource Center.

Goodman, R. M., I. N. Burdine, E. Meehan, K. McLeroy, eds. 1993. "Community Coalitions for Health Promotion." *Health Education Research* 8: 305-453.

Hawkins, J. D., R. F. Catalano., and Associates. 1992. *Communities that Care: Action for Drug Abuse Prevention.* San Francisco: Jossey-Bass.

Institute for Social Analysis. 1993. *Evaluation of the Second Year of the Community Partnership Program.* Rockville, MD: Public Health Service/Center for Substance Abuse Prevention.

Knowles, M. S. 1970. *The Modern Practice of Adult Education.* New York: New York City Press.

Mizrahi, T., and J. D. Morrison, eds. 1993. *Community Organization and Social Administration: Advances, Trends. and Emerging Principles.* Binghamton, NY: Haworth Press.

Mizrahi, T. and B. B. Rosenthal. 1993. "Managing Dynamic Tensions in Social Change Coalitions." In *Community and Social Administration: Advances, Trends and Emerging Principles,* edited by T. Mizrahi and J. D. Morrison, 11-40. New York: Haworth Press.

Senge, P. M. 1990. *The Fifth Discipline: The Art and Practice of Learning Organizations.* New York: Doubleday.

Speer, P. W., and D. M. Chavis. 1994. "Community Coalitions and Rural Practice." In *Sowing Seeds in the Mountains: Community-Based Coali-*

tions for Cancer Prevention and Control, edited by R. A. Couto, N.K. Simpson, and G. Harris, 138-51. Bethesda, MD: National Institutes of Health, National Cancer Institute.

III. Race and Class

5

Toward a Theory of Race, Crime, and Urban Inequality

Robert J. Sampson and William Julius Wilson

Our purpose in this chapter is to address one of the central yet difficult issues facing criminology race and violent crime. The centrality of the issue is seen on several fronts: the leading cause of death among young black males is homicide (Fingerhut and Kleinman 1990, p. 3292), and the lifetime risk of being murdered is as high as 1 in 21 for black males, compared with only 1 in 131 for white males (U.S. Department of Justice 1985). Although rates of violence have been higher for blacks than whites at least since the 1950s (Jencks 1991), record increases in homicide since the mid-1980s in cities such as New York, Chicago, and Philadelphia also appear racially selective (Hinds 1990; James 1991; Recktenwald and Morrison 1990). For example, while white rates remained stable, the rate of death from firearms among young black males more than doubled from 1984 to 1988 alone (Fingerhut et al. 1991). These differentials help explain recent estimates that a resident of rural Bangladesh has a greater chance of surviving to age forty than does a black male in Harlem (McCord and Freeman 1990). Moreover, the so-called drug war and the resulting surge in prison populations in the past decade have taken their toll disproportionately on the minority community (Mauer 1990). Overall, the evidence is clear that African-Americans face dismal and worsening odds when it comes to crime in the streets and the risk of incarceration.

Despite these facts, the discussion of race and crime is mired in an unproductive mix of controversy and silence. At the same time that articles on age and gender abound, criminologists are loath to speak openly on race and crime for fear of being misunderstood or labeled racist. This situation is not unique, for until recently scholars of urban poverty also consciously avoided discussion of race and social disloca-tions in the inner city lest they be accused of blaming the victim (see Wilson 1987). And when the topic is broached, criminologists have reduced the race–crime debate to simplistic arguments about culture versus social structure. On the one side, structuralists argue for the primacy of "relative deprivation" to understand black crime (e.g., Blau and Blau 1982), even though the evidence on social class and crime is weak at best. On the other side, cultural theorists tend to focus on an indigenous culture of violence in black ghettos (e.g., Wolfgang and Ferracuti 1967), even though the evidence there is weak too.

Still others engage in subterfuge, denying race-related differentials in violence and focusing instead on police bias and the alleged invalidity of official crime statistics (e.g., Stark 1990). This in spite of evidence not only from death records but also from survey reports showing that blacks are disproportionately victimized by, and involved in, criminal violence (Hindelang 1976, 1978). Hence, much like the silence on race and inner-city social dislocations engendered by the vociferous attacks on the Moynihan Report in the 1960s, criminologists have, with few exceptions (e.g., Hawkins 1986; Hindelang 1978; Katz 1988), abdicated serious scholarly debate on race and crime.

In an attempt to break this stalemate we advance in this chapter a theoretical strategy that incorporates both structural and cultural argu-ments regarding race, crime, and inequality in American cities. In contrast to psychologically based relative deprivation theories and the subculture of violence, we view the race and crime linkage from contex-tual lenses that highlight the very different ecological contexts that blacks and whites reside in regardless of individual characteristics. The basic thesis is that macrosocial patterns of residential inequality give rise to the social isolation and ecological concentration of the truly disad-vantaged, which in turn leads to structural barriers and cultural adapta-tions that undermine social organization and hence the control of crime. This thesis is grounded in what is actually an old idea in criminology that has been overlooked in the race and crime debate—the importance of communities.

The Community Structure of Race and Crime

Unlike the dominant tradition in criminology that seeks to distinguish offenders from nonoffenders, the macrosocial or community level of explanation asks what it is about community structures and cultures that produces differential rates of crime (Bursik 1988; Byrne and Sampson 1986; Short 1985). As such, the goal of macrolevel research is not to explain individual involvement in criminal behavior but to isolate characteristics of communities, cities, or even societies that lead to high rates of criminality (Byrne and Sampson 1986; Short 1985). From this viewpoint the "ecological fallacy" inferring individual-level relations based on aggregate data is not at issue because the unit of explanation and analysis is the community.

The Chicago School research of Clifford Shaw and Henry McKay spearheaded the community-level approach of modern American studies of ecology and crime. In their classic work *Juvenile Delinquency and Urban Areas*, Shaw and McKay (1942) argued that three structural factors, low economic status, ethnic heterogeneity, and residential mobility, led to the disruption of local community social organization, which in turn accounted for variations in crime and delinquency rates (for more details see Kornhauser 1978).

Arguably the most significant aspect of Shaw and McKay's research, however, was their demonstration that high rates of delinquency persisted in certain areas over many years, regardless of population turnover. More than any other, this finding led them to reject individualistic explanations of delinquency and focus instead on the processes by which delinquent and criminal patterns of behavior were transmitted across generations in areas of social disorganization and weak social controls (1942, 1969, p. 320). This community-level orientation led them to an explicit contextual interpretation of correlations between race/ethnicity and delinquency rates. Their logic was set forth in a rejoinder to a critique in 1949 by Jonassen, who had argued that ethnicity had direct effects on delinquency. Shaw and McKay countered:

> The important fact about rates of delinquency for Negro boys is that they, too, vary by type of area. They are higher than the rates for white boys, but it cannot be said that they are higher than rates for white boys in comparable areas, since it is impossible to reproduce in white communities the circumstances under which Negro children live. Even if it were possible to parallel the low economic status and the inadequacy of institutions in the

white community, it would not be possible to reproduce the effects of segregation and the barriers to upward mobility. (1949, p. 614)

Shaw and McKay's insight almost a half century ago raises two
interesting questions still relevant today. First, to what extent do black
rates of crime vary by type of ecological area? Second, is it possible to
reproduce in white communities the structural circumstances in which
many blacks live? The first question is crucial, for it signals that blacks
are not a homogeneous group any more than whites are. Indeed, it is
racial stereotyping that assigns to blacks a distinct or homogeneous
character, allowing simplistic comparisons of black–white group differences in crime. As Shaw and McKay recognized, the key point is that
there is heterogeneity among blacks in crime rates that correspond to
community context. To the extent that the causes of black crime are not
unique, its rate should thus vary with specific ecological conditions in the
same way that the white crime rate does. As we shall now see, recent
evidence weighs in Shaw and McKay's favor.

Are the Causes of Black Crime Unique?

Disentangling the contextual basis for race and crime requires racial
disaggregation of both the crime rate and the explanatory variables of
theoretical interest. This approach was used in recent research that
examined racially disaggregated rates of homicide and robbery by
juveniles and adults in over 150 U.S. cities in 1980 (Sampson 1987).
Substantively, the theory explored the effects of black male joblessness
and economic deprivation on violent crime as mediated by black family
disruption. The results supported the main hypothesis and showed that
the scarcity of employed black males relative to black females was
directly related to the prevalence of families headed by women in black
communities (Wilson 1987). In turn, black family disruption was substantially related to rates of black murder and robbery, especially by
juveniles (see also Messner and Sampson 1991). These effects were
independent of income, region, density, city size, and welfare benefits.

The finding that family disruption had stronger effects on juvenile
violence than on adult violence, in conjunction with the inconsistent
findings of previous research on individual-level delinquency and broken
homes, supports the idea that the effects of family structure are related to
macrolevel patterns of social control and guardianship, especially for
youth and their peers (Sampson and Groves 1989). Moreover, the results
suggest why unemployment and economic deprivation have had weak or

inconsistent direct effects on violence rates in past research—joblessness and poverty appear to exert much of their influence indirectly through family disruption.

Despite a tremendous difference in mean levels of family disruption among black and white communities, the percentage of white families headed by a female also had a large positive effect on white juvenile and white adult violence. In fact, the predictors of white robbery were shown to be in large part identical in sign and magnitude to those for blacks. Therefore, the effect of black family disruption on black crime was independent of commonly cited alternative explanations (e.g., region, density, age composition) and could not be attributed to unique cultural factors within the black community given the similar effect of white family disruption on white crime.

To be clear, we are not dismissing the relevance of culture. As discussed more below, our argument is that if cultural influences exist, they vary systematically with structural features of the urban environment. How else can we make sense of the systematic variations *within* race for example, if a uniform subculture of violence explains black crime, are we to assume that this subculture is three times as potent in, say, New York as in Chicago (where black homicide differs by a factor of three)? In San Francisco as in Baltimore (3:1 ratio)? These distinct variations exist even at the state level. For example, rates of black homicide in California are triple those in Maryland (Wilbanks 1986). Must whites then be part of the black subculture of violence in California, given that white homicide rates are also more than triple the rates for whites in Maryland? We think not. The sources of violent crime appear to be remarkably invariant across race and rooted instead in the structural differences among communities, cities, and states in economic and family organization.

The Ecological Concentration of Race and Social Dislocations

Having demonstrated the similarity of black-white variations by ecological context, we turn to the second logical question. To what extent are blacks as a group differentially exposed to criminogenic structural conditions? More than forty years after Shaw and McKay's assessment of race and urban ecology, we still cannot say that blacks and whites share a similar environment especially with regard to concentrated urban poverty. Consider the following. Although approximately 70 percent of all poor non-Hispanic whites lived in nonpoverty areas in the ten largest U.S. central cities (as determined by the 1970 census) in 1980, only 16 percent of poor blacks did. Moreover, whereas less than 7 percent of poor whites lived in extreme poverty or ghetto areas, 38 percent of poor blacks lived in such areas (Wilson et al. 1988, p. 130). In the nation's largest city, New York, 70 percent of poor blacks live in poverty neighborhoods; by contrast, 70 percent of poor whites live in nonpoverty neighborhoods (Sullivan 1989, p. 230). Potentially even more important, the majority of poor blacks live in communities characterized by high rates of family disruption. Poor whites, even those from "broken homes," live in areas of relative family stability (Sampson 1987; Sullivan 1989).

The combination of urban poverty and family disruption concentrated by race is particularly severe. As an example, we examined race-specific census data on the 171 largest cities in the United States as of 1980. To get some idea of concentrated social dislocations by race, we selected cities where the proportion of blacks living in poverty was equal to or less than the proportion of whites, *and* where the proportion of black families with children headed by a single parent was equal to or less than that for white families. Although we knew that the average national rate of family disruption and poverty among blacks was two to four times higher than among whites, the number of distinct ecological contexts in which blacks achieve equality to whites is striking. In not one city over 100,000 in the United States do blacks live in ecological equality with whites when it comes to these basic features of economic and family organization. Accordingly, racial differences in poverty and family disruption are so strong that the "worst" urban contexts in which whites reside are considerably better than the average context of black communities (Sampson 1987, p. 354).

Taken as a whole, these patterns underscore what Wilson (1987) has labeled "concentration effects," that is, the effects of living in a neighborhood that is overwhelmingly impoverished. These concentration effects, reflected in a range of outcomes from degree of labor force attachment to social deviance, are created by the constraints and opportunities that the residents of inner-city neighborhoods face in terms of access to jobs and job networks, involvement in quality schools, availability of marriageable partners, and exposure to conventional role models.

The social transformation of the inner city in recent decades has resulted in an increased concentration of the most disadvantaged segments of the urban black population especially poor, female-headed families with children. Whereas one of every five poor blacks resided in ghetto or extreme poverty areas in 1970, by 1980 nearly two out of every five did so (Wilson et al. 1988, p. 131). This change has been fueled by several macrostructural forces. In particular, urban minorities have been vulnerable to structural economic changes related to the deindustrialization of central cities (e.g., the shift from goods-producing to service-producing industries; increasing polarization of the labor market into low-wage and high-wage sectors; and relocation of manufacturing out of the inner city). The exodus of middle- and upper-income black families from the inner city has also removed an important social buffer that could potentially deflect the full impact of prolonged joblessness and industrial transformation. This thesis is based on the assumption that the basic institutions of an area (churches, schools, stores, recreational facilities, etc.) are more likely to remain viable if the core of their support comes from more economically stable families in inner-city neighborhoods (Wilson 1987, p. 56). The social milieu of increasing stratification among blacks differs significantly from the environment that existed in inner cities in previous decades (see also Hagedorn 1988).

Black inner-city neighborhoods have also disproportionately suffered severe population and housing loss of the sort identified by Shaw and McKay (1942) as disrupting the social and institutional order. Skogan (1986, p. 206) has noted how urban renewal and forced migration contributed to the wholesale uprooting of many urban black communities, especially the extent to which freeway networks driven through the hearts of many cities in the 1950s destroyed viable, low-income communities. For example, in Atlanta one in six residents was dislocated by urban renewal; the great majority of those dislocated were poor blacks (Logan and Molotch 1987, p. 114). Nationwide, fully 20 percent of all central-city housing units occupied by blacks were lost in the period 1960–70 alone. As Logan and Molotch (1987, p. 114) observe, this displacement does not even include that brought about by more routine market forces (evictions, rent increases, commercial development).

Of course, no discussion of concentration effects is complete without recognizing the negative consequences of deliberate policy decisions to concentrate minorities and the poor in public housing. Opposition from organized community groups to the building of public housing in their neighborhoods, de facto federal policy to tolerate extensive segregation against blacks in urban housing markets, and the decision by local governments to neglect the rehabilitation of existing residential units (many of them single-family homes), have led to massive, segregated housing projects that have become ghettos for the minorities and disadvantaged (see also Sampson 1990). The cumulative result is that, even given the same objective socioeconomic status, blacks and whites face vastly different environments in which to live, work, and raise their children. As Bickford and Massey (1991, p. 1035) have argued, public housing is a federally funded, physically permanent institution for the isolation of black families by race and class and must therefore be considered an important structural constraint on the ecological area of residence.

In short, the foregoing discussion suggests that macrostructural factors both historic and contemporary have combined to concentrate urban black poverty and family disruption in the inner city. These factors include but are not limited to racial segregation, structural economic transformation and black male joblessness, class-linked out-migration from the inner city, and housing discrimination. It is important to emphasize that when segregation and concentrated poverty represent structural constraints embodied in public policy and historical patterns of racial subjugation, notions that individual differences (or self-selection) explain community-level effects on violence are considerably weakened (see Sampson and Lauritsen 1994).

Implications

The consequences of these differential ecological distributions by race raise the substantively plausible hypothesis that correlations of race and crime may be systematically confounded with important differences in community contexts. As Testa has argued with respect to escape from poverty:

> Simple comparisons between poor whites and poor blacks would be confounded with the fact that poor whites reside in areas which are ecologically and economically very different from poor blacks. Any observed relationships involving race would reflect, to some unknown degree, the relatively superior ecological niche many poor whites occupy with respect to jobs, marriage opportunities, and exposure to conventional role models. (quoted in Wilson 1987, pp. 58-60)

Regardless of a black's individual-level family or economic situation, the average community of residence thus differs dramatically from that of a similarly situated white (Sampson 1987). For example, regardless of whether a black juvenile is raised in an intact or single-parent family, or a rich or poor home, he or she will not likely grow up in a community context similar to that of whites with regard to family structure and income. Reductionist interpretations of race and social class camouflage this key point.

In fact, a community conceptualization exposes the "individualistic fallacy" the often-invoked assumption that individual-level causal relations necessarily generate individual-level correlations. Research conducted at the individual level rarely questions whether obtained results might be spurious and confounded with community-level processes. In the present case, it is commonplace to search for individual-level (e.g., constitutional) or group-level (e.g., social class) explanations for the link between race and violence. In our opinion these efforts have largely failed, and so we highlight contextual sources of the race–violence link among individuals. More specifically, we posit that the most important determinant of the relationship between race and crime is the differential distribution of blacks in communities characterized by (1) *structural social disorganization* and (2) *cultural social isolation*, both of which stem from the concentration of poverty, family disruption, and residential instability.

Before explicating the theoretical dimensions of social disorganization, we must also expose what may be termed the "materialist fallacy" that economic (or materialist) causes necessarily produce economic motivations. Owing largely to Merton's (1938) famous dictum about social structure and anomie, criminologists have assumed that if economic structural factors (e.g., poverty) are causally relevant it must be through the motivation to commit acquisitive crimes. Indeed, "strain" theory was so named to capture the hypothesized pressure on members of the lower classes to commit crime in their pursuit of the American dream. But as is well known, strain or materialist theories have not fared well empirically (Kornhauser 1978). The image of the offender stealing to survive flourishes only as a straw man, knocked down most recently by Jack Katz, who argues that materialist theory is nothing more than "twentieth-century sentimentality about crime" (1988, p. 314). Assuming, however, that those who posit the relevance of economic structure for crime rely on motivational pressure as an explanatory concept, is itself a fallacy. The theory of social disorganization *does* see relevance in the ecological concentration of poverty, but not for the materialist reasons Katz (1988) presupposes. Rather, the conceptualization we now explicate rests on the fundamental properties of structural and cultural organization.

The Structure of Social (Dis)organization

In their original formulation Shaw and McKay held that low economic status, ethnic heterogeneity, and residential mobility led to the disruption of community social organization, which in turn accounted for variations in crime and delinquency rates (1942, 1969). As recently extended by Kornhauser (1978), Bursik (1988), and Sampson and Groves (1989), the concept of social disorganization may be seen as the inability of a community structure to realize the common values of its residents and maintain effective social controls. The *structural* dimensions of community social disorganization refer to the prevalence and interdependence of social networks in a community both informal (e.g., the density of acquaintanceship; intergenerational kinship ties; level of anonymity) and formal (e.g., organizational participation; institutional stability) and in the span of collective supervision that the community directs toward local problems.

This social-disorganization approach is grounded in what Kasarda and Janowitz (1974, p. 329) call the "systemic" model, where the local community is viewed as a complex system of friendship and kinship networks, and formal and informal associational ties are rooted in family life and ongoing socialization processes (see also Sampson 1991). From this view social organization and social *dis*organization are seen as different ends of the same continuum of systemic networks of community social control. As Bursik (1988) notes, when formulated in this way, social disorganization is clearly separable not only from the processes that may lead to it (e.g., poverty, residential mobility), but also from the degree of criminal behavior that may be a result. This conceptualization also goes beyond the traditional account of community as a strictly geographical or spatial phenomenon by focusing on the social and organizational networks of local residents (see Leighton 1988).

Evidence favoring social-disorganization theory is available with respect both to its structural antecedents and to mediating processes. In a recent paper, Sampson and Lauritsen (1994) reviewed in depth the empirical literature on individual, situational, and community-level sources of interpersonal violence (i.e., assault, homicide, robbery, and rape). This assessment revealed that community-level research conducted in the past twenty years has largely supported the original Shaw and McKay model in terms of the exogenous correlates of poverty, residential mobility, and heterogeneity. What appears to be especially salient is the *interaction* of poverty and mobility. As anticipated by Shaw and

McKay (1942) and Kornhauser (1978), several studies indicate that the effect of poverty is most pronounced in neighborhoods of high residential instability (see Sampson and Lauritsen 1994).

In addition, recent research has established that crime rates are positively linked to community-level variations in urbanization (e.g., population and housing density), family disruption (e.g., percentage of single-parent households), opportunity structures for predatory crime (e.g., density of convenience stores), and rates of community change and population turnover (see also Bursik 1988; Byrne and Sampson 1986; Reiss 1986). As hypothesized by Sampson and Groves (1989), family disruption, urbanization, and the anonymity accompanying rapid population change all undercut the capacity of a community to exercise informal social control, especially of teenage peer groups in public spaces.

Land et al. (1990) have also shown the relevance of *resource deprivation, family dissolution,* and *urbanization* (density, population size) for explaining homicide rates across cities, metropolitan areas, and states from 1960 to 1980. In particular, their factor of resource deprivation/affluence included three income variables median income, the percentage of families below the poverty line, and the Gini index of income inequality in addition to the percentage of population that is black and the percentage of children not living with both parents. This coalescence of structural conditions with race supports the concept of concentration effects (Wilson 1987) and is consistent with Taylor and Covington's finding (1988) that increasing entrenchment of ghetto poverty was associated with large increases in violence. In these two studies the correlation among structural indices was not seen merely as a statistical nuisance (i.e., as multicollinearity), but as a predictable substantive outcome. Moreover, the Land et al. (1990) results support Wilson's argument that concentration effects grew more severe from 1970 to 1980 in large cities. Urban disadvantage thus appears to be increasing in ecological concentration.

It is much more difficult to study the intervening mechanisms of social disorganization directly, but at least two recent studies provide empirical support for the theory's structural dimensions. First, Taylor et al. (1984) examined variations in violent crime (e.g., mugging, assault, murder, rape) across sixty-three street blocks in Baltimore in 1978. Based on interviews with 687 household respondents, Taylor et al. (1984, p. 316) constructed block-level measures of the proportion of respondents who belonged to an organization to which coresidents also belonged, and the proportion of respondents who felt responsible for what happened in the area surrounding their homes. Both of these dimensions of informal social control were significantly and negatively related to community-level variations in crime, exclusive of other ecological factors (1984, p. 320). These results support the social-disorganization hypothesis that levels of organizational participation and informal social control especially of public activities by neighborhood youth inhibit community-level rates of violence.

Second, Sampson and Groves's analysis of the British Crime Survey in 1982 and 1984 showed that the prevalence of unsupervised teenage peer groups in a community had the largest effects on rates of robbery and violence by strangers. The density of local friendship networks measured by the proportion of residents with half or more of their friends living in the neighborhood also had a significant negative effect on robbery rates. Further, the level of organizational participation by residents had significant inverse effects on both robbery and stranger violence (Sampson and Groves 1989, p. 789). These results suggest that communities characterized by sparse friendship networks, unsupervised teenage peer groups, and low organizational participation foster increased crime rates (see also Anderson 1990).

Variations in these structural dimensions of community social disorganization also transmitted in large part the effects of community socioeconomic status, residential mobility, ethnic heterogeneity, and family disruption in a theoretically consistent manner. For example, mobility had significant inverse effects on friendship networks, family disruption was the largest predictor of unsupervised peer groups, and socioeconomic status had a significant positive effect on organizational participation in 1982. When combined with the results of research on gang delinquency, which point to the salience of informal and formal community structures in controlling the formation of gangs (Short and Strodtbeck 1965; Sullivan 1989; Thrasher 1963), the empirical data suggest that the structural elements of social disorganization have relevance for explaining macrolevel variations in crime.

Further Modifications

To be sure, social-disorganization theory *as traditionally conceptualized* is hampered by a restricted view of community that fails to account for the larger political and structural forces shaping communities. As suggested earlier, many community characteristics hypothesized to underlie crime rates, such as residential instability, concentration of poor, female-headed families with children, multiunit housing projects, and disrupted social networks, appear to stem directly from planned governmental policies at local, state, and federal levels. We thus depart from the natural market assumptions of the Chicago School ecologists by incorporating the political economy of place (Logan and Molotch 1987), along with macrostructural transformations and historical forces, into our conceptualization of community-level social organization.

Take, for example, municipal code enforcement and local governmental policies toward neighborhood deterioration. In *Making the Second Ghetto: Race and Housing in Chicago, 1940–1960*, Hirsch (1983) documents in great detail how lax enforcement of city housing codes played a major role in accelerating the deterioration of inner-city Chicago neighborhoods. More recently, Daley and Mieslin (1988) have argued that inadequate city policies on code enforcement and repair of city properties contributed to the systematic decline of New York City's housing stock, and consequently, entire neighborhoods. When considered with the practices of redlining and disinvestment by banks and "blockbusting" by real estate agents (Skogan 1986), local policies toward code enforcement that on the surface are far removed from crime have in all likelihood contributed to crime through neighborhood deterioration, forced migration, and instability.

Decisions to withdraw city municipal services for public health and fire safety, presumably made with little if any thought to crime and violence, also appear to have been salient in the social disintegration of poor communities. As Wallace and Wallace argue, based on an analysis of the "planned shrinkage" of New York City fire and health services in recent decades, "The consequences of withdrawing municipal services from poor neighborhoods, the resulting outbreaks of contagious urban decay and forced migration which shred essential social networks and cause social disintegration, have become a highly significant contributor to decline in public health among the poor" (1990, p. 427). The loss of social integration and networks from planned shrinkage of services may increase behavioral patterns of violence that may themselves become "convoluted with processes of urban decay likely to further disrupt social networks and cause further social disintegration" (1990, p. 427). This pattern of destabilizing feedback (see Skogan 1986) appears central to an understanding of the role of governmental policies in fostering the downward spiral of high crime areas. As Wacquant has recently argued, federal U.S. policy seems to favor "the institutional desertification of the urban core" (1991, p. 36).

Decisions by government to provide public housing paint a similar picture. Bursik (1989) has shown that the planned construction of new public housing projects in Chicago in the 1970s was associated with increased rates of population turnover, which in turn were related to increases in crime. More generally, we have already noted how the disruption of urban renewal contributed disproportionately to housing loss among poor blacks.

Boiled down to its essentials, then, our theoretical framework linking social-disorganization theory with research on urban poverty and political economy suggests that macrosocial forces (e.g., segregation, migration, housing discrimination, structural transformation of the economy) interact with local community-level factors (e.g., residential turnover, concentrated poverty, family disruption) to impede social organization. This is a distinctly sociological viewpoint, for it focuses attention on the proximate structural characteristics and mediating processes of community social organization that help explain crime, while also recognizing the larger historical, social, and political forces shaping local communities.

Social Isolation and Community Culture

Although social-disorganization theory is primarily structural in nature, it also focuses on how the ecological segregation of communities gives rise to what Kornhauser (1978, p. 75) terms *cultural* disorganization the attenuation of societal cultural values. Poverty, heterogeneity, anonymity, mutual distrust, institutional instability, and other structural features of urban communities are hypothesized to impede communication and obstruct the quest for common values, thereby fostering cultural diversity with respect to nondelinquent values. For example, an important component of Shaw and McKay's theory was that disorganized communities spawned delinquent gangs with their own subcultures and norms perpetuated through cultural transmission.

Despite their relative infrequency, ethnographic studies generally support the notion that structurally disorganized communities are conducive to the emergence of cultural value systems and attitudes that seem to legitimate, or at least provide a basis of tolerance for, crime and deviance. For example, Suttles's (1968) account of the social order of a Chicago neighborhood characterized by poverty and heterogeneity supports Thrasher's (1963) emphasis on age, sex, ethnicity, and territory as markers for the ordered segmentation of slum culture. Suttles found that single-sex, age-graded primary groups of the same ethnicity and territory emerged in response to threats of conflict and communitywide disorder and mistrust. Although the community subcultures Suttles discovered were provincial, tentative, and incomplete (Kornhauser 1978, p. 18), they nonetheless undermined societal values against delinquency and violence. Similarly, Anderson's (1978) ethnography of a bar in Chicago's south-side black ghetto shows how primary values coexisted alongside residual values associated with deviant subcultures (e.g., hoodlums), such as "toughness," "getting big money," "going for bad," and "having fun" (1978, pp. 129-30, 152-58). In Anderson's analysis, lower-class residents do not so much "stretch" mainstream values as "create their own particular standards of social conduct along variant lines open to them" (1978, p. 210). In this context the use of violence is not valued as a primary goal but is nonetheless expected and tolerated as a fact of life (1978, p. 134). Much like Rainwater (1970), Suttles (1968), and Horowitz (1987), Anderson suggests that in certain community contexts the wider cultural values are simply not relevant they become "unviable."

Whether community subcultures are authentic or merely "shadow cultures" (Liebow 1967) cannot be resolved here (see also Kornhauser 1978). But that seems less important than acknowledging that community contexts seem to shape what can be termed *cognitive landscapes* or ecologically structured norms (e.g., normative ecologies) regarding appropriate standards and expectations of conduct. That is, in structurally disorganized slum communities it appears that a system of values emerges in which crime, disorder, and drug use are less than fervently condemned and hence expected as part of everyday life. These ecologically structured social perceptions and tolerances in turn appear to influence the probability of criminal outcomes and harmful deviant behavior (e.g., drug use by pregnant women). In this regard Kornhauser's attack on subcultural theories misses the point. By attempting to assess whether subcultural values are authentic in some deep, almost quasi-religious sense (1978, pp. 1-20), she loses sight of the processes by which cognitive landscapes rooted in social ecology may influence everyday behavior. Indeed, the idea that dominant values become existentially irrelevant in certain community contexts is a powerful one, albeit one that has not had the research exploitation it deserves (cf. Katz 1988).

A renewed appreciation for the role of cultural adaptations is congruent with the notion of *social isolation* defined as the lack of contact or of sustained interaction with individuals and institutions that represent mainstream society (Wilson 1987, p. 60). According to this line of reasoning, the social isolation fostered by the ecological concentration of urban poverty deprives residents not only of resources and conventional role models, but also of cultural learning from mainstream social networks that facilitate social and economic advancement in modern industrial society (Wilson 1991). Social isolation is specifically distinguished from the culture of poverty by virtue of its focus on adaptations to constraints and opportunities rather than internalization of norms.

As Ulf Hannerz noted in his seminal work *Soulside*, it is thus possible to recognize the importance of macrostructural constraints that is, avoid the extreme notions of the culture of poverty or culture of violence, and yet see the "merits of a more subtle kind of cultural analysis" (1969, p. 182). One could hypothesize a difference, on the one hand, between a jobless family whose mobility is impeded by the macrostructural constraints in the economy and the larger society but nonetheless lives in an area with a relatively low rate of poverty, and on the other hand, a jobless family that lives in an inner-city ghetto neighborhood that is influenced not only by these same constraints but also by the behavior of other jobless families in the neighborhood (Hannerz 1969, p. 184; Wilson 1991). The latter influence is one of culture the extent to which individuals follow their inclinations as they have been developed by learning or influence from other members of the community (Hannerz 1969).

Ghetto-specific practices such as an overt emphasis on sexuality and macho values, idleness, and public drinking are often denounced by those who reside in inner-city ghetto neighborhoods. But because such practices occur much more frequently there than in middle-class society, largely because of social organizational forces, the transmission of these modes of behavior by precept, as in role modeling, is more easily facilitated (Hannerz 1969). For example, youngsters are more likely to see violence as a way of life in inner-city ghetto neighborhoods. They are more likely to witness violent acts, to be taught to be violent by exhortation, and to have role models who do not adequately control their own violent impulses or restrain their own anger. Accordingly, given the availability of and easy access to firearms, knives, and other weapons, adolescent experiments with macho behavior often have deadly consequences (Prothrow-Stith 1991).

The concept of social isolation captures this process by implying that contact between groups of different class and/or racial backgrounds either is lacking or has become increasingly intermittent, and that the nature of this contact enhances effects of living in a highly concentrated poverty area. Unlike the concept of the culture of violence, then, social isolation does not mean that ghetto-specific practices become internalized, take on a life of their own, and therefore continue to influence behavior no matter what the contextual environment. Rather, it suggests that reducing structural inequality would not only decrease the frequency of these practices; it would also make their transmission by precept less efficient. So in this sense we advocate a renewed appreciation for the ecology of culture, but not the monolithic and hence noncontextual culture implied by the subculture of poverty and violence.

Discussion

Rejecting both the "individualistic" and "materialist" fallacies, we have attempted to delineate a theoretical strategy that incorporates both structural and cultural arguments regarding race, crime, and urban inequality in American cities. Drawing on insights from social-disorganization theory and recent research on urban poverty, we believe this strategy provides new ways of thinking about race and crime. First and foremost, our perspective views the link between race and crime through contextual lenses that highlight the very different ecological contexts in which blacks and whites reside regardless of individual characteristics. Second, we emphasize that crime rates among blacks nonetheless vary by ecological characteristics, just as they do for whites. Taken together, these facts suggest a powerful role for community context in explaining race and crime.

Our community-level explanation also departs from conventional wisdom. Rather than attributing to acts of crime a purely economic motive springing from relative deprivation an individual-level psycho-logical concept we focus on the mediating dimensions of community social organization to understand variations in crime across areas. Moreover, we acknowledge and try to specify the macrosocial forces that contribute to the social organization of local communities. Implicit in this attempt is the incorporation of the political economy of place and the role of urban inequality in generating racial differences in community structure. As Wacquant observes, American urban poverty is "preeminently a *racial poverty* . . . rooted in the *ghetto* as a historically specific social form and mechanism of racial domination" (1991, p. 36, emphasis in original). This intersection of race, place, and poverty goes to the heart of our theoretical concerns with societal and community organization.

Furthermore, we incorporate culture into our theory in the form of social isolation and ecological landscapes that shape perceptions and cultural patterns of learning. This culture is not seen as inevitably tied to race, but more to the varying structural contexts produced by residential and macroeconomic change, concentrated poverty, family instability, and intervening patterns of social disorganization. Perhaps controversially, then, we differ from the recent wave of structuralist research on the culture of violence (for a review see Sampson and Lauritsen 1994). In an interesting methodological sleight of hand, scholars have dismissed the relevance of culture based on the analysis of census data that provide no measures of culture whatsoever (see especially Blau and Blau 1982). We believe structural criminologists have too quickly dismissed the role of values, norms, and learning as they interact with concentrated poverty and social isolation. In our view, macrosocial patterns of residential inequality give rise to the social isolation and concentration of the truly disadvantaged, engendering cultural adaptations that undermine social organization.

Finally, our conceptualization suggests that the roots of urban violence among today's 15- to 21-year-old cohort may stem from childhood socialization that took place in the late 1970s and early 1980s. Consider that this cohort was born between 1970 and 1976 and spent its childhood in the context of a rapidly changing urban environment unlike that of any previous point in U.S. history. As documented in detail by Wilson (1987), the concentration of urban poverty and other social dislocations began increasing sharply in about 1970 and continued unabated through the decade and into the 1980s. As but one example, the proportion of black families headed by women increased by over 50 percent from 1970 to 1984 alone (Wilson 1987, p. 26). Large increases were also seen in the ecological concentration of ghetto poverty, racial segregation, population turnover, and joblessness. These social dislocations were, by comparison, relatively stable in earlier decades. Therefore, the logic of our theoretical model suggests that the profound changes in the urban structure of minority communities in the 1970s may hold the key to understanding recent increases in violence.

Conclusion

By recasting traditional race and poverty arguments in a contextual framework that incorporates both structural and cultural concepts, we seek to generate empirical and theoretical ideas that may guide further research. The unique value of a community-level perspective is that it leads away from a simple "kinds of people" analysis to a focus on how social characteristics of collectivities foster violence. On the basis of our theoretical framework, we conclude that community-level factors such as the *ecological concentration of ghetto poverty, racial segregation, residential mobility* and population turnover, *family disruption,* and the dimensions of local *social organization* (e.g., density of friend-ship/acquaintanceship, social resources, intergenerational links, control of street-corner peer groups, organizational participation) are fruitful areas of future inquiry, especially as they are affected by macrolevel public policies regarding housing, municipal services, and employment. In other words, our framework suggests the need to take a renewed look at social policies that focus on prevention. We do not need more after-the-fact (reactive) approaches that ignore the structural context of crime and the social organization of inner cities.

Note

This chapter originally appeared in *Crime and Inequality,* edited by John Hagan and Ruth D. Peterson, Stanford University Press, Stanford, CA, 1995, pp. 37-54. It is reprinted with permission.

References

Anderson, E. 1978. *A Place on the Corner.* Chicago: University of Chicago Press.

———. 1990. *Streetwise: Race, Class and Change in an Urban Community.* Chicago: University of Chicago Press.

Bickford, A., and D. Massey. 1991. "Segregation in the Second Ghetto: Racial and Ethnic Segregation in American Public Housing, 1977." *Social Forces* 69: 1011–36.

Blau, J. R., and P. M. Blau. 1982. "The Cost of Inequality: Metropolitan Structure and Violent Crime." *American Sociological Review* 47: 114–29.

Bursik, R. J., Jr. 1988. "Social Disorganization and Theories of Crime and Delinquency: Problems and Prospects." *Criminology* 26: 519–52.

———. 1989. "Political Decision-Making and Ecological Models of Delin-quency: Conflict and Consensus." In *Theoretical Integration in the Study of Deviance and Crime,* edited by S. Messner, M. Krohn, and A. Liska. Al-bany: State University of New York Press.

Byrne, J., and R. J. Sampson. 1986. "Key Issues in the Social Ecology of Crime." In *The Social Ecology of Crime,* edited by J. Byrne and R. J. Samp-son, 1–22. New York: Springer-Verlag.

Daley, S., and R. Mieslin. 1988. "New York City, the Landlord: A Decade of Housing Decay." *New York Times*, February 8.

Fingerhut, L. A., and J. C. Kleinman. 1990. "International and Interstate Comparisons of Homicide Among Young Males." *Journal of the American Medical Association* 263: 3292–95.

Fingerhut, L., J. Kleinman, E. Godfrey, and H. Rosenberg. 1991."Firearms Mortality Among Children, Youth, and Young Adults 1–34 Years of Age, Trends and Current Status: United States, 1979–88." *Monthly Vital Statistics Report* 39: 1–16.

Hagedorn, J. 1988. *People and Folks: Gangs, Crime and the Underclass in a Rustbelt City*. Chicago: Lake View Press.

Hannerz, U. 1969. *Soulside: Inquiries into Ghetto Culture and Community*. New York: Columbia University Press.

Hawkins, D., ed. 1986. *Homicide Among Black Americans*. Lanham, MD: University Press of America.

Hindelang, M. J. 1976. *Criminal Victimization in Eight American Cities*. Cambridge, MA: Ballinger.

———. 1978. "Race and Involvement in Common Law Personal Crimes." *American Sociological Review 43*: 93–109.

Hinds, M. 1990. "Number of Killings Soars in Big Cities Across U.S." *New York Times*, July 18, p. 1.

Hirsch, A. 1983. *Making the Second Ghetto: Race and Housing in Chicago, 1940–1960*. Chicago: University of Chicago Press.

Horowitz, R. 1987. "Community Tolerance of Gang Violence." *Social Problems* 34: 437–50.

James, G. 1991. "New York Killings Set Record in 1990." *New York Times*, April 23, p. A14.

Jencks, C. 1991. "Is Violent Crime Increasing?" *The American Prospect* (Winter): 98–109.

Jonassen, C. 1949. "A Reevaluation and Critique of the Logic and Some Methods of Shaw and McKay." *American Sociological Review* 14: 608–14.

Kasarda, J., and M. Janowitz. 1974. "Community Attachment in Mass Society." *American Sociological Review* 39: 328–39.

Katz, J. 1988. *Seductions of Crime: The Sensual and Moral Attractions of Doing Evil*. New York: Basic.

Kornhauser, R. 1978. *Social Sources of Delinquency*. Chicago: University of Chicago Press.

Land, K., P. McCall, and L. Cohen. 1990. "Structural Covariates of Homicide Rates: Are There Any Invariances Across Time and Space?" *American Journal of Sociology* 95: 922–63.

Liebow, E. 1967. *Tally's Corner*. Boston: Little, Brown.

Leighton, B. 1988. "The Community Concept in Criminology: Toward a Social Network Approach." *Journal of Research in Crime and Delinquency* 25: 351–74.

Logan, J., and H. Molotch. 1987. *Urban Fortunes: The Political Economy of Place.* Berkeley: University of California Press.

Mauer, M. 1990. *Young Black Men and the Criminal Justice System: A Growing National Problem.* Washington, DC: The Sentencing Project.

McCord, M., and H. Freeman. 1990. "Excess Mortality in Harlem." *New England Journal of Medicine* 322: 173–75.

Merton, R. 1938. "Social Structure and Anomie." *American Sociological Review* 3: 672–82.

Messner, S., and R. J. Sampson. 1991. "The Sex Ratio, Family Disruption, and Rates of Violent Crime: The Paradox of Demographic Structure." *Social Forces* 69: 693–714.

Prothrow-Stith, D. 1991. *Deadly Consequences.* New York: HarperCollins.

Rainwater, L. 1970. *Behind Ghetto Walls: Black Families in a Federal Slum.* Chicago: Aldine.

Recktenwald, W., and B. Morrison. 1990. "Guns, Gangs, Drugs Make a Deadly Combination." *Chicago Tribune,* July 1, Section 2, p. 1.

Reiss, A. J., Jr. 1986. "Why Are Communities Important in Understanding Crime?" In *Communities and Crime,* edited by A. J. Reiss, Jr., and M. Tonry, 1–33. Chicago: University of Chicago Press.

Sampson, R. J. 1987. "Urban Black Violence: The Effect of Male Joblessness and Family Disruption." *American Journal of Sociology* 93: 348–82.

———. 1990. "The Impact of Housing Policies on Community Social Disorganization and Crime." *Bulletin of the New York Academy of Medicine* 66: 526–33.

———. 1991. "Linking the Micro and Macrolevel Dimensions of Community Social Organization." *Social Forces* 70: 43–64.

Sampson, R. J., and W. B. Groves. 1989. "Community Structure and Crime: Testing Social-Disorganization Theory." *American Journal of Sociology* 94: 774–802.

Sampson, R. J., and J. Lauritsen. 1994. "Violent Victimization and Offending: Individual, Situational, and Community-level Risk Factors." In *Understanding and Preventing Violence: Social Influences,* edited by A. J. Reiss, Jr., and J. Roth, Vol. 3, 1-114. Washington, DC: National Academy Press.

Shaw, C., and H. McKay. 1942. *Juvenile Delinquency and Urban Areas.* Chicago: University of Chicago Press.

———. 1969. Rev. ed. *Juvenile Delinquency and Urban Areas.* Chicago: University of Chicago Press.

Short, J. F., Jr. 1985. "The Level of Explanation Problem in Criminology." In *Theoretical Methods in Criminology,* edited by R. Meier, 51–74. Beverly Hills, CA: Sage.

Short, J. F., and F. L. Strodtbeck. 1965. *Group Process and Gang Delinquency.* Chicago: University of Chicago Press.

Skogan, W. G. 1986. "Fear of Crime and Neighborhood Change." In *Communities and Crime,* edited by A. J. Reiss, Jr., and M. Tonry, 203–29. Chicago: University of Chicago Press.

Stark, E. 1990. "The Myth of Black Violence." *New York Times*, July 18, p. A21.

Sullivan, M. 1989. *"Getting Paid": Youth Crime and Work in the Inner City.* Ithaca, NY: Cornell University Press.

Suttles, G. 1968. *The Social Order of the Slum.* Chicago: University of Chicago Press.

Taylor, R., and J. Covington. 1988. "Neighborhood Changes in Ecology and Violence." *Criminology* 26: 553–90.

Taylor, R., S. Gottfredson, and S. Brower. 1984. "Black Crime and Fear: Defensible Space, Local Social Ties, and Territorial Functioning." *Journal of Research in Crime and Delinquency* 21: 303–31.

Thrasher, F. 1963. *The Gang: A Study of 1,313 Gangs in Chicago.* Rev. ed. Chicago: University of Chicago Press.

U.S. Department of Justice. 1985. *The Risk of Violent Crime.* Washington, DC: U.S. Government Printing Office.

Wacquant, L. 1991. "The Specificity of Ghetto Poverty: A Comparative Analysis of Race, Class, and Urban Exclusion in Chicago's Black Belt and the Parisian Red Belt." Paper presented at the Chicago Urban Poverty and Family Life Conference, University of Chicago.

Wallace, R., and D. Wallace. 1990. "Origins of Public Health Collapse in New York City: The Dynamics of Planned Shrinkage, Contagious Urban Decay and Social Disintegration." *Bulletin of the New York Academy of Medicine* 66: 391–434.

Wilbanks, W. 1986. "Criminal Homicide Offenders in the U.S.: Black vs. White." In *Homicide Among Black Americans,* edited by D. Hawkins, 43–56. Lanham, MD: University Press of America.

Wilson, W. J. 1987. *The Truly Disadvantaged: The Inner City, the Underclass, and Public Policy.* Chicago: University of Chicago Press.

————. 1991. "Studying Inner-City Social Dislocations: The Challenge of Public Agenda Research." *American Sociological Review* 56: 1–14.

Wilson, W. J., R. Aponte, J. Kirschenman, and L. Wacquant. 1988. "The Ghetto Underclass and the Changing Structure of American Poverty." In *Quiet Riots: Race and Poverty in the United States,* edited by F. Harris and R. W. Wilkins, 123–54. New York: Pantheon.

Wolfgang, M., and F. Ferracuti. 1967. *The Subculture of Violence.* London: Tavistock.

6

Crime and the Racial Fears
of White Americans

Wesley G. Skogan

Fear of black crime covers the streets like a sheet of ice.
—Senator Bill Bradley[1]

It is widely assumed that expressions by many whites of concern about crime are rooted to a significant degree in their fear of black people. One popular news magazine states that many white people seem to be unduly troubled by black people, especially young black men; white people are often afraid of some danger that may exist solely in the imagination (Minerbrook 1992). Of course, fear is not necessarily a bad thing; it can be a rational response to the conditions of one's life and guide purposeful action. Fear reflects people's individual vulnerability to crime and its harmful consequences, risks in their neighborhood, and their personal victimization experiences and those reported by their families and friends. However, it may also be that white Americans translate their unease about race relations into beliefs about crime, and vice versa, a linkage of potentially great divisiveness. This chapter reviews research on the nexus between them. It examines linkages between fear and white attitudes toward blacks and the anxiety created by close residential proximity between the two groups.

Focusing on the fears of whites should not obscure the fact that black Americans are even more fearful. Research documents that they are

119

fearful mostly for the same reasons that whites are fearful, and their higher level of fear reflects the fact that those common causes afflict their communities more severely. This chapter focuses on white fear because it is one of the most compelling political constructs of our time. It is evoked as an explanation for white backlash against progressive social and economic policies, the declining prospects of the Democratic Party, and as a source of divisiveness that threatens the fabric of urban life. Concern about common crime—street mugging, sexual assault, and the like—is not the only outcropping of the racial fears of whites. Another is resistance to school busing (Taylor 1986). In both instances, white fear partly is deliberately constructed by those who are in a position to profit from its divisiveness. Most prominently, they are politicians, among whom "playing the race card" is a time-tested political ploy. In 1988, presidential candidate George Bush horrified audiences with his story of a man convicted of murder who raped a Maryland woman while he was on furlough from a Massachusetts prison. The president personally made no reference to Willie Horton's race, but someone was quick to come up with his picture. In that campaign, Horton was a wedge issue.

There is only a limited amount of useful research on the nexus of race and fear, for several reasons. For one, so many aspects of American life are racially encoded that it is difficult to tease out statistically the separate consequences of factors such as crime, school quality, neighborhood satisfaction, property values, neighborhood racial change, and the like. In a segregated society, many things covary strongly with race. For another, what Senator Bradley (1992) termed a "cloak of silence and denial" surrounds the general race-crime nexus in many circles. Prominent among them have been the federal agencies that pay for expensive research ventures involving large-sample surveys; they have been, in my experience, unwilling to fund investigations that touch too closely on controversial racial attitudes. Crime is also an issue area where the facts of the case as measured by arrests, reports by crime victims, and self reports of offending all point to higher rates of criminality among black Americans, confounding prejudiced attitudes with doses of realism that make it difficult to interpret the pulse of white opinion.

Some research closely skirts the two issues. For example, there is a great deal of research on the social and economic determinants of how much cities spend on policing. These studies, which are summarized in a book by Pamela Irving Jackson (1989, pp. 1-46), find that police strength is politically determined by a complicated set of socially patterned interests and that the local level of crime plays only a limited role in the process. More straightforward seems to be the role played by indicators of racial economic inequality, inner-city riots, and the relative size of the minority population. More is spent on policing in cities where white interests appear to be threatened.

The present chapter reviews direct studies of the problem. A few are ethnographic reports by researchers who immersed themselves in the lives of residents of urban neighborhoods and emerged to tell their stories. The other studies are based on interviews with large samples of survey respondents who were quizzed about crime, fear, and the character of their neighborhoods. Some of these surveys also questioned white respondents concerning their racial attitudes, and those studies present the most complete—and complex—view of the topic.

The Stinchcombe Model of Race and Fear

Perhaps the best-known statement of the problem was advanced by Arthur Stinchcombe and his associates (1980). Their explanation of fear of crime, which is illustrated in Figure 1, hinges on the racial composition of people's neighborhoods. They examined the problem using data from the General Social Survey (GSS), a yearly national survey. The GSS measures fear by asking if there is a place within a mile of their home where respondents are afraid to walk alone at night. Stinchcombe and his colleagues began by equating the distribution of black people with the distribution of crime. They cited what they dubbed "well-known statistics" to argue that "the most fear-producing crimes are all 'ghetto crimes'" and that "crimes that make people afraid are more concentrated among black people" (Stinchcombe et al. 1980, pp. 43, 47). For example, they showed that blacks were arrested for murder, robbery, and rape at a rate that is disproportionate to their numbers in the population and that blacks were more frequently victimized by violent crime. As part of the argument, they used the GSS to document that victimization of whites was disproportionately high when they lived closer to black people. Whites living in integrated neighborhoods were a little more than twice as likely as those living in segregated neighborhoods to be robbed and about 1.4 times as likely to be burglarized. They therefore felt justified in using reports by survey respondents of how close they live to concentrations of black people as a "measure of objective risk" of victimization by black people (Stinchcombe et al. 1980, p. 44). The latter construct is depicted in italics in Figure 1, for risk of victimization was not actually measured in the data that they used to test their explanation of fear.

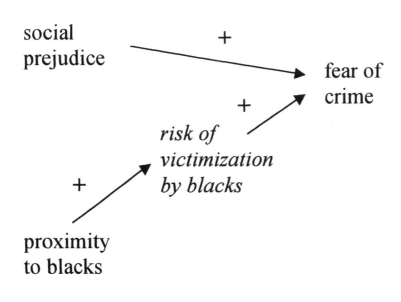

Figure 1. Stinchcombe Model of Fear

It is important to note that this part of Stinchcombe's model is intended to explain fear of crime among all Americans, not just whites. In the data, blacks were more fearful than whites, a finding that is consistent from study to study. However, Stinchcombe did not directly examine the question of whether blacks living in black neighborhoods were more fearful than those living in integrated surroundings, because the number of blacks doing so is painfully small in a national survey. Because of the numbers involved, when he examined the data for "everyone," he was in practice examining the views of whites. He found that the proportion of people who were fearful was substantially higher in integrated areas even when controlling for other factors. These included living in big cities (more fear), sex (women are more fearful), age (fear is higher among old people), household composition (living alone magnifies fear), and individual victimization (fear provoking). Gun ownership was at first glance reassuring, for people who owned guns were less fearful. However, self-reports of gun ownership were lower than usual among whites (and blacks) living in big cities and among whites living near blacks. When these and the other factors just enumerated were controlled for, the effect of gun ownership disappeared.

The other part of Stinchcombe's model, what he dubbed the "irrational" part, applies only to whites. As illustrated in Figure 1, he also examined the statistical relationship between fear and a three-question measure of whites' views of black people. It combined responses to questions about laws against interracial marriage, objecting to someone in the family bringing a black person home to dinner, and whether or not anyone in the family had actually brought a black person home to dinner. As it was weighted heavily toward intimate social activity, it is not clear that this was the best possible indicator for a study of attitudes related to street crime. However, those falling at the prejudiced end of the scale were more fearful even when the racial composition of their neighborhoods was controlled for.

It is important to note that the link between prejudice and fear was not due to higher levels of prejudice among whites in close contact with blacks; in fact, quite the opposite was the case. Figure 2 presents the results of my own reanalysis of data from more recent years of the GSS (1988, 1989, and 1990). It uses a different indicator of racial prejudice, an index combining responses to two measures of whites' views of black participation in society's most public institutions. The first measure assesses their views of the acceptability of white and black children's going to school together under the circumstance of varying racial composition of the school. The most prejudiced whites (only 4 percent of the total) objected to white children's going to school with even a few blacks, while the most liberal (40 percent) did not object to their going to school mostly with blacks. The second component of the prejudice measure is based on responses to a question about "white people's right to a racially segregated neighborhood." At the most liberal end, 50 percent of respondents disagreed strongly that whites had such a right, while the polar group (8 percent of all whites) agreed strongly that they did. In combination, 28 percent of whites took the most liberal stance on both questions, while 2 percent of whites took the most prejudiced stance (the questions are presented in an appendix to this chapter).

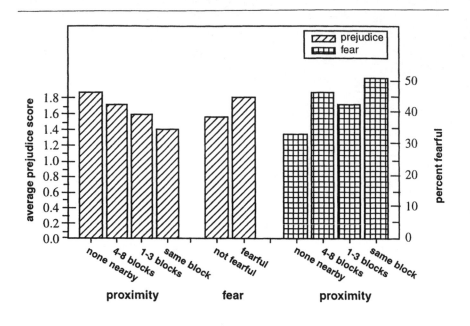

Source: National Opinion Research Center, General Social Survey, 1988-90.

Figure 2. Racial Prejudice and Fear Among Whites

As before, fear was measured by the presence of a location nearby where respondents were afraid to go alone after dark. Whites' proximity to blacks was measured by a question asking if blacks lived nearby and a follow-up question determining "how far away" measured in city blocks, using the response categories presented in Figure 2.

As Figure 2 illustrates, on a national basis, racial prejudice was in fact somewhat lower among whites who reported living in close proximity to blacks. As the left side of the figure indicates, average prejudice scores dropped with increasing proximity. This was true of both the school segregation and the residential segregation subcomponents of the measure. The causes for this might run both ways. Certainly, many whites are financially and socially able to distance themselves from blacks to an extent appropriate to their racial attitudes; many of the more prejudiced just move away. At the same time, people living together may (the evidence is mixed) learn to get along, especially if they share cultural values or are not competitors for the same jobs or houses (Adams et al. 1991, pp. 22-25; Anderson 1990, pp. 28-30; Merry 1980; Sigelman and Welch 1993). In either event, the decline in both measures of prejudice with increasing proximity is impressive in light of the fact that interracial proximity is not at all an abstract, far-away issue for whites who indicated that black people lived within eight blocks of their home.

On the other hand, Figure 2 indicates that whites who were fearful were also somewhat more prejudiced, so there may be a causal link between the two. Again, the relationship between the two could run in either direction. Stinchcombe argued that fear leads to prejudice, as whites rationally assessed official and media images of the extent of black crime and then generalized the results into beliefs about the appropriate place of blacks in society. The argument that fear of crime is a code word for racism takes the opposite view, that whites project their general attitudes toward black people onto resonant social issues such as crime. These data are not very suitable for deciding between the two views, but it is an important research question.

Figure 2 also documents that the whites' proximity to blacks was related to fear. Those who reported that no black people lived nearby were the least fearful, while those living closest to blacks were the most fearful. The gap between the two polar groups was 20 percentage points. Stinchcombe's rationality-of-fear argument was that it is simply riskier for whites to live near blacks, so proximity leads to fear.

The tenacity of the link between racial prejudice, proximity to blacks, and fear of crime is illustrated in Table 1. It presents the results of a logistic regression analysis examining the impact of those factors on fear while simultaneously controlling for a host of other well-established correlates of fear. The list of control factors is longer than Stinchcombe's tabular analysis allowed. It includes age, gender, education, whether respondents lived alone, whether they had children living at home, region of the country, city size, and whether respondents had been the victim of a burglary or robbery. It also includes a control for being old and female in combination. However, when all of these factors are controlled for, both the residential proximity of blacks and prejudice (measured by whites' views of the appropriate role of black people in society) remained independently linked to fear.

Table 1
Logistic Regression Analysis of
Fear Among Whites

	Coefficient	Sig.
proximity	**.2039**	**.0002**
prejudice	**.1409**	**.0012**
live in south	.5134	.0002
female	1 .8375	.0000
city size (log)	.2298	.0000
crime victim	.4991	.0416
elderly	.2508	.2159
have children	- .1150	.4656
age & sex	.0042	.4870
live alone	.0760	.6029
education	.0278	.6523
Constant	3 .4207	.0000

Note: Overall 72.6% correctly classed
Number of cases 1396

The Liska Model of Race and Fear

A second prominent statistical model of the determinants of fear of crime was advanced by Allen Liska and his associates (1982). It takes into account the objective risk of victimization, measured directly by citywide victim surveys, and the city-size factor that was so prominent in the results of the GSS. It does not include a direct measure of the racial attitudes of whites but takes into account several important features of their environment: the relative size of the black population in the city where they live, the extent of racial segregation in housing patterns there, and the likelihood that crimes against them will be interracial in character. Liska finds that residential segregation calms white fear, while interracial crime exacerbates it.

The factors comprising the Liska model are illustrated in Figure 3. Unlike Stinchcombe's, this model is cast at the city level rather than at the individual level. The data on crime and fear were drawn from official sources and large (10,000 respondent) surveys conducted by the Census Bureau in twenty-six large cities. The cities varied considerably in level of fear. In the surveys, respondents were asked how safe they felt out alone in their neighborhood at night. Only 27 percent of those interviewed in San Diego felt either unsafe or very unsafe; the comparable figure for residents of Newark, New Jersey, was 58 percent.

Liska's causal explanations for this large variation are illustrated in Figure 3. Unlike Stinchcombe, he measured crime rates directly, using official statistics from the Federal Bureau of Investigation. He found that the robbery rate was a strong predictor of fear among whites and that it was much more potent than city size. However, the interesting parts of the model lie in the middle of the diagram. Whites were more fearful in cities with larger black populations, independent of the crime rate. A measure of residential segregation was included that indicated how separately blacks and whites lived their lives in each city, and there was also a direct effect of this on white fear. Where blacks and whites lived separately, whites were less fearful.

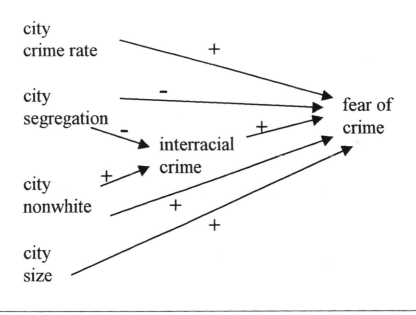

Figure 3. Liska Model of Race and Fear

Furthermore, the extent of interracial crime in each city had an added effect on white fear; in fact, its effect was the strongest of all the elements in the model. Interracial victimization was measured in the city surveys by asking victims to describe their attackers. For statistical purposes, Liska used the percentage of robberies against whites in each city that were perpetrated by nonwhites as a general indicator of the extent of interracial crime. He and his colleagues note that "robbery . . . is the epitome of dangerous street crime in which the offender is a stranger whose racial identity is generally known to the victim" (Liska et al. 1982, p. 764). As depicted in Figure 3, interracial crime was more common in cities with more nonwhites and in cities that were less segregated. In turn, the extent of interracial crime was the strongest determinant of white fear, followed by the robbery rate.

In Liska's model, it is both risk of victimization and who is doing the victimizing that matters to white city residents. He and his colleagues interpret their data as suggesting that "cultural dissimilarity between whites and nonwhites makes interracial crime appear particularly uncertain, violent, and dangerous to whites" (Liska et al. 1982, p. 767). Residential segregation was directly related to lower levels of white fear, perhaps by reducing the day-to-day visibility of blacks and the frequency with which whites came into contact with them. Segregation was also linked to lower levels of fear indirectly by dampening the rate of interracial crime. Statistically, the effects of segregation and the racial composition of the cities were felt most strongly via the extent of interracial crime.[2]

Other Research on Race and Fear

Beyond these studies, most research examining fear of crime and racial fears of white Americans puts the problem in simpler terms and does not include measures of whites' racial attitudes. Instead, these studies focus solely on the link between racial proximity and fear. For example, Gertrude Moeller conducted interviews with 764 residents of Illinois during the early 1980s (Moeller 1989). Based on questions in the survey, she classified respondents as living in neighborhoods that were virtually all black, of mixed composition, or virtually all white. Like other studies, hers found that blacks and whites lived in proximity primarily in big cities. She measured fear of crime using the same "is there a place where you would be afraid to walk alone" question used by the GSS. The survey found that blacks were generally more fearful than whites and that fear went up sharply with city size. When she statistically controlled for other correlates of fear, including age, gender, education, income, and size of place, she found that whites living in black or integrated neighborhoods were distinctly more fearful. Differences in fear associated with this condition were less than differences in fear due to gender or city size, but otherwise whites living in proximity to blacks were more fearful than anyone else, including the elderly.

Jeanette Covington and Ralph Taylor (1991) found roughly the same pattern in a survey of residents of Baltimore, Maryland. Their "subcultural diversity" approach to the issue postulated that "fear of crime . . . results from living in proximity to others whose cultural background is different from one's own. The manners and behaviors of persons belonging to these different groups [are] difficult to interpret and thus fear-inspiring" (Covington and Taylor 1991, p. 232). Their research controlled for an impressive list of factors that have been shown to be related to fear, including both personal factors (age, gender, education) and neighborhood factors (crime rate, various social disorders, racial composition). They measured fear by combining responses to questions asking how fearful respondents would feel being out alone in their neighborhood during the day and at night. Controlling for many other factors, they found that residents of mostly black neighborhoods were more fearful. Further, fear was higher than expected among people whose racial identity did not fit their context. They found that the more different people were from their neighbors in terms of the racial composition of their neighborhood, the more fearful they were. This effect was apparent for both blacks living in white areas and whites living in black areas, leading them to characterize it as the effect of "cultural diversity" rather than simply "white fear." This was an important conclusion and runs contrary to Stinchcombe's argument that proximity to whites makes all Americans feel safer. Black residents of white neighborhoods, sometimes facing threats or harassment and more often the targets of humiliation and contempt, would recognize the concept.

What about the benefits of living together? Sally Engle Merry (1980) studied the consequences of residential racial integration in a small multiracial housing project in San Francisco. She evaluated the proposition that integration leads to increased social contact between racial and ethnic groups, which in turn leads to increasing tolerance of one another among residents. I noted earlier that the evidence for this hypothesis is quite mixed, and Merry's contribution is a pessimistic one. She found that living together exacerbated tensions between the black, white, Hispanic, and Chinese residents of the project. Frictions between residents were all interpreted racially, and prejudice and hostility grew rather than diminished over time. Residents hung on because the housing was good and the price was right, but members of each ethnic group kept to themselves or found social ties outside the project. They did not trust other project residents enough to sustain anticrime efforts; in fact, they victimized each other with relative impunity because they remained strangers. No one could criticize or exercise control over children of another background. Chinese residents in particular lived in fear of black youths, who remained strangers even while living in their midst.

Conclusion

These studies suggest several conclusions. First, racial differences in fear usually are smaller than differences associated with gender or age, but often they are next on the list. Blacks are much more fearful of crime, and these studies document that there are good reasons for this. Blacks are more likely to be victimized and to live in neighborhoods where serious crime is more frequent. Some of this race-related difference is due to the concentration of black survey respondents in bigger cities, where everyone is more fearful. Another fraction of the racial difference in fear documented in surveys is due to neighborhood-level differences in social disorder, physical decay, and economic collapse. In a segregated society, race goes along with many other area-level factors that contribute to fear, and the more segregated conditions are in any particular research environment, the more closely they covary and the more difficult it is to untangle their effects.

Second, among whites, residential proximity to black people is related to fear of crime. The link between the two is both direct and further exacerbated by the tie between residential integration and the extent of interracial crime. These links persist even in studies controlling for alternative explanations for fear. It is important to note in this regard that the bulk of whites reporting that black people live nearby live in larger cities. Cities are places where levels of victimization, social disorganization, and aspects of physical decay that are linked to fear of crime are more common (Skogan 1990, pp. 21-50). In cities, whites also live closer to all of the other factors that cluster with race in our segregated society and that themselves have an impact on fear. The statistical controls described previously doubtless do not account for all of the effects of these city and neighborhood factors. Race brings with it so many tightly coupled social and economic factors that these studies probably overestimate how much white fear is due to racial proximity and how much it is due to proximity to other factors that scare all Americans but cannot be statistically untangled from race.

Third, the link between residential proximity and fear persists despite the fact that whites living close to blacks register lower levels of prejudice than do those who are more distant. Whites living in close proximity to blacks voice fewer objections to sharing their schools and neighborhoods with them. This may be because they have learned to get along, but it is more likely because, through choices about where they live, many whites have sorted themselves into residential patterns that reflect their attitudes. Research generally suggests that close contact between blacks and whites breeds favorable attitudes only under unlikely circumstances: when they are of roughly equal status yet not in competition with one another for jobs, housing, or power. The statistical analysis described earlier indicated that this measure of prejudice was indeed related to fear of crime, but its effect was independent of the proximity of whites to black people.

In this regard, it is important that white society is becoming more tolerant and egalitarian with regard to selected racial attitudes. A 1942 national poll found that 72 percent of Americans thought black people should eat in separate restaurants, a response that is virtually unheard of today. The percentage of whites tolerant of abstract or personal issues like inter-racial marriage or bringing people of color home to dinner has climbed to near universality. Very few whites object to mingling with blacks at the workplace. In addition, whites' opinions about blacks have become more variegated; their views on one dimension do not necessarily correspond with their views on another, and views on racial matters have become linked to larger political and ideological views on issues such as individual responsibility, the role of the government, and compensatory public policies generally. This leads Paul Sniderman and Thomas Piazza (1993) to conclude that racism per se is a minor force in contemporary American politics, especially when defined in Gordon Allport's classic terms as outright hostility and rejection based solely on categorical criteria. Instead, racial cleavages are driven by bundles of social and

economic issues that involve or have implications for race but are not—
among whites—dominated by it.[3]

However, whites continue to be particularly resistant to proposals that
involve school busing or close residential proximity to black people or
more generally to policies that promise to interfere with their ability to act
on their preferences via markets and, through them, to maintain their
dominant position (Page and Shapiro 1992, pp. 67-80). These issues were
raised by the school and neighborhood integration components of the
racial-attitude measure employed earlier and they—not who is coming to
dinner—lie near the problematic core of black-white relations at the end of
the twentieth century. And the image of black lawlessness remains perva-
sive. In one 1991 national survey, the statement that "blacks are aggressive or violent" was the most frequently endorsed negative stereotype on a
list of five, approved by 52 percent of whites (Sniderman and Piazza
1993, p.45).[4] As Andrew Hacker (1992, p. 188) put it,

> The dread whites feel of black crime goes beyond actual risks or probabili-
> ties. The visage of Willie Horton stirred fears in parts of the country where
> black faces are seldom seen. . . . The feeling is not simply that crime is out
> of control. Far more troubling is the realization that white citizens can be
> held in thrall by a race meant to be subservient.

The persistent links between fear, proximity, and whites' desire to retain
their dominance of their most intimate institutions are not likely to wane
anytime soon.

Appendix: Measuring Racial Prejudice

The GSS administered fear of crime, racial proximity, and racial prejudice
measures to half of a national sample for the years 1988, 1989, and 1990. 1396
respondents answered these and the list of demographic questions discussed in
the text. The racial prejudice measure was created by combining responses to
questions about school and neighborhood integration. The correlation between
the two subcomponent measures was .42.

Attitude toward school integration.

Score		Frequency
0	does not object to children going to school with mostly blacks	40%
1	objects to children going to school with mostly blacks, but does not object to children going to school with half blacks	38%
2	objects to children going to school with half blacks, but does not object to children going to school with a few blacks	18%
3	objects to children going to school with even a few blacks	4%

Attitude toward neighborhood integration.

Score		Frequency
0	disagree strongly that whites have a right to live in a segregated neighborhood	50%
1	disagree slightly that whites have a right to live in a segregated neighborhood	26%
2	agree slightly that whites have a right to live in a segregated neighborhood	15%
3	agree strongly that whites have a right to live in a segregated neighborhood	8%

Notes

This chapter originally appeared in the *Annals of the American Academy of Political and Social Science*, Volume 539, 1995, pp. 59-71. It is reprinted here with permission.

1. See Bradley (1992).

2. In otherwise unrelated research on the statistical correlates of police strength, Liska and his colleagues (1981) also find that the relative size of the black population is more strongly linked to city expenditures on policing in less segregated cities than it is in highly segregated cities.

3. See also Jackman (1994, pp. 33-43).

4. Interestingly, this view was also endorsed by 59 percent of black respondents; Sniderman and Piazza think this is because both views are "rooted in part in a common reality" and are also consistent with views of black violence represented by the mass media.

References

Adams, Carolyn, David Bartlet, David Elesh, Ira Goldstein, Nancy Kleniewski, and William Yancy. 1991. *Philadelphia: Neighborhoods, Division, and Conflict in a Postindustrial City*. Philadelphia: Temple University Press.

Anderson, Elijah. 1990. *Streetwise: Race, Class, and Change in an Urban Community*. Chicago: University of Chicago Press.

Bradley, Bill. 1992. *Congressional Record*, 26 March, p. S4242.

Covington, Jeanette, and Ralph B. Taylor. 1991."Fear of Crime in Urban Residential Neighborhoods." *Sociological Quarterly* 322: 231-49.

Hacker, Andrew. 1992. *Two Nations*. New York: Scribner.

Jackman, Mary R. 1994. *The Velvet Glove: Paternalism and Conflict in Gender, Class and Race Relations*. Los Angeles: University of California Press.

Jackson, Pamela Irving. 1989. *Minority Group Threat, Crime, and Policing*. New York: Praeger.

Liska, Allen E., Joseph J. Lawrence, and Michael Benson. 1981. "Perspectives on the Legal Order: The Capacity for Social Control." *American Journal of Sociology* 87: 413-26.

Liska, Allen E., Joseph J. Lawrence, and Andrew Sanchirico. 1982. "Fear of Crime as a Social Fact." *Social Forces* 603: 760-70.

Merry, Sally Engle. 1980. "Racial Integration in an Urban Neighborhood: The Social Organization of Strangers." *Human Organization* 391: 59-69.

Minerbrook, Scott. 1992. "Commentary: A Different Reality for Us." *U.S. News & World Report* (11 May): 36.

Moeller, Gertrude L. 1989. "Fear of Criminal Victimization: The Effect of Neighborhood Racial Composition." *Sociological Inquiry* 592: 209-21.

Page, Benjamin I., and Robert Y. Shapiro. 1992. *The Rational Public*. Chicago: University of Chicago Press.

Sigelman, Lee, and Susan Welch. 1993. "The Contact Hypothesis Revisited." *Social Forces* 713: 781-96.

Skogan, Wesley G. 1990. *Disorder and Decline: Crime and the Spiral of Decay in American Cities*. New York: Free Press.

Sniderman, Paul M., and Thomas Piazza. 1993. *The Scar of Race*. Cambridge, MA: Harvard University Press.

Stinchcombe, Arthur. 1980. *Crime and Punishment: Changing Attitudes in America*. San Francisco: Jossey-Bass.

Taylor, D. Garth. 1986. *Public Opinion and Collective Action: The Boston School Desegregation Conflict*. Chicago: University of Chicago Press.

IV. Community Policing

7

A Tale of Two Targets: Limitations of Community Anticrime Actions

Michael E. Buerger

The rhetoric of community policing ascribes to the community a great power to regulate itself, shake off its fear of crime by forming "partnerships" with the police, and re-establish community norms that will successfully resist the encroachments of the criminal element. Unfortunately, the early returns from the field suggest that its successes in this regard are modest, that community policing initiatives have so far failed to tap the great wellspring of "community" believed to lie waiting for the proper catalyst (e.g., Rosenbaum 1988, p. 375).

The literature suggests that the sine qua non of community organizing is an already-organized community; that of crime prevention, an area not subjected to crime. So, too, appears to be the case with community policing, which like its predecessors does best in the areas which need it least.

The ineffectiveness of community crime-prevention efforts has already been well documented (Rosenbaum 1986, 1988; Rosenbaum, Lewis, and Grant 1986). Community, neighborhood, and even block organizations are difficult to form and more difficult to maintain. Rarely does membership exceed a small fraction of the resident pool, and active members are even fewer. Both nominal and active memberships tend to be dominated by homeowners and by white residents in racially mixed areas; in some cases rival organizations arise and are dominated by competing ethnic groups that address different issues (Skogan 1988, p. 46). Community-based organizations (CBOs) that form around a single issue such as crime generally fail to thrive unless they can broaden their focus (Yates 1973). "Anticrime organizations are often most successful in communities that need them least . . . [and] least common where they appear to be most needed—in low-income, heterogeneous, deteriorated, renting, high-turnover, high-crime areas" (Skogan 1988, pp. 42, 45). Despite this lack of tangible results, Neighborhood Watch and community organizing continue to be promoted as the community-based answer to the crime problem. The reasons for this are threefold.

First, the promotional aspect of anticrime organizing is theory-poor, and prone to the same "means over end" syndrome for which Goldstein (1979, 1990) criticizes the police. Hypothesized outcomes are elevated to the status of achievable goals, when in fact they are not. Activities are promoted as though they are certain to achieve the goals, when frequently they do not. One of the prime directives of the community organizers' bible is the command to "celebrate your small successes" as a means of generating more participation in the process, but somewhere along the way, small successes (the *means* of recruiting additional participation) came to substitute for the bigger successes being sought after (the *ends* of reduced crime and increased social cohesion). The disparity between the two is not lost on the marginal participants, who may celebrate as a victory the closing of a crackhouse, but continue to see the drug trade continue unabated as the dealers shift tactics in response to pressure (Buerger 1992). The result is the dashing of unrealistic expectations on the part of participants, a loss of belief in the efficacy of the process, and ultimately the withdrawal of support.

Second, past efforts to develop community-based anticrime efforts have created a national infrastructure of organization, literature, and vocabulary. Persons or groups looking for solutions to new crime and disorder problems in their community (including police departments under pressure to "solve" those problems) encounter a well-developed network of promotional materials that promise a cheap, certain, and (at least on the surface) relatively easy solution. Not only are there national organizations promoting the technology, but there is a well-developed popular literature that promotes the early "small successes" of previous efforts.

Those success stories usually come from the earlier stages of the organizing effort, bereft of the tempering experience of longer observation. The long-term perspective is more dismal, and does not appear in the promotional materials for obvious reasons. Evaluations like those of Rosenbaum and Skogan, cited herein, are buried in academic journals unread by the general public. Because no institutional memory exists, the programs are adopted as a cure on the basis of their promotional advertising. Each new generation then relearns the lessons of the previous one as the "panacea phenomenon" (Finckenauer 1982) repeats itself, unrealistic expectations giving way first to discouragement, then abandonment, when the inadequate means fail to deliver the promised outcomes.

The final reason for the survival of these "permanently failing technologies" is that there are no alternatives, and the limited successes are sufficient to sustain the approach in the absence of competing strategies. There is little new under the sun, no new "silver bullets" of interpersonal technologies available to slay the great ogre of crime. To a large degree, both research and policy are driven by a need to assume that existing technologies *can* work, even if they have not done so in the past.

The record is not completely negative. Community anticrime organizations serve as a platform for encouraging target-hardening activities against a limited range of crimes (Rosenbaum 1988), and some of those endeavors have produced positive outcomes (Yin 1986; Rosenbaum 1988; for a slightly different perspective, see Lurigio and Rosenbaum 1986). Following Skogan's assessment that "fear is linked to despair rather than positive action" (Skogan 1988; citing Skogan and Maxfield 1981), community organizing at least represents an avenue for positive action. The benefits may redound primarily to those who choose to participate (Fisher 1993), but the actions at least preserve (for a time) a committed core of "local elites" around whom may be centered other, more robust programs should they become available. But in the final analysis, both target-hardening and participation produce *individual* benefits, not collective ones:

> Although neighborhood studies have underscored the importance of social interaction in developing informal social control, neighborhood crime prevention programs have been unable to set in motion the social interaction, territoriality, surveillance, and other behaviors that theoretically are expected at the block or neighborhood level. (Rosenbaum 1988, p. 375)

Since these areas are the ultimate goals of community organizing,[1] this failure of community-based organizing should promote a new look at the technology of community anticrime activity. Clinging to an insufficient technology does not further the search for better solutions. Indeed, using satisficing technologies as a crutch may even impede or censor efforts to develop a better alternatives.

Theory failure is exacerbated by three flaws in the academic communities' approaches to the situation. First, there has been a persistent confusion of two radically different concepts (social disorganization and political organizing) that share a common root word. Second, the search for the proper unit of analysis upon which to predicate database research has fostered a debilitating shrinkage of the concept of community, which creates an inadvertent hybrid of the "blaming the victim" syndrome (Ryan 1976). Third, academic contributions to the discussion of disorder and crime—the nominal targets of the community organizing—focus either on surface symptoms or on macrolevel processes. With only a few exceptions, academic researchers resolutely decline to look at contributing factors that are invisible to the large data sets, particularly the decision-making processes in the private sector.

Community organizing (in its myriad forms) is enjoying a resurgence under the community policing movement, which is promoting a technology with no proven efficacy. The traditional explanations of the failure of watch-style organization tend to be those of inadequate resources and implementation failure (the two are integrally linked). This article proposes that we ought to begin thinking in terms of theory failure, that a robust technology is being squandered because it is being asked to take on the wrong task, focusing its efforts on unresponsive targets.

Community Policing

The concept of community policing has been with us for more than a decade, though its actual implementation has been as fragmented as the American police establishment itself (Buerger 1993; Eck 1994). Some communities have always enjoyed the "partnership" aspect of community policing and have never experienced the alienation of police from the citizens they serve. Others have grabbed on to "community policing" only in a time of scandal and crisis, wielding its promises like a shield to ward off earned criticism. Regardless of how the departments come to community policing, though, they are limited to a fairly standard bag of police-initiated schemes.

Community policing as it is now practiced is an echo of the wedding aphorism, "Something old, something new; something borrowed, something blue." "Something blue" is a giveaway, of course: it puns on the blue uniform of the police to suggest that there is a unique way in which the police combine the other components in the turbulent environment of the streets. Though it is possible to articulate reasons why such an outcome may be expected, the proposition reprises the problem of elevating hypothesized outcomes to the level of attainable goals. Community policing to date has been too program-based and too limited in scope, both geographically and in terms of police participation, to declare this possibility a fact (Buerger 1993).

"Something borrowed" comes from the field of corporate management: the concepts of participatory management, quality of service, and customer orientation that are in at least the vocabulary of community policing. Though it may provide a new wrinkle to police services, it is primarily an internal development, a change in the mindset of the police, away from the detached, expert "just the facts, Ma'am" professionals whose services were so in demand that they could dictate the nature of service delivery to their desperate clients. The operational gains of this movement could be applied as profitably in traditional reactive deployment and crime attack schemes as in community policing.

The "something old" is the wide range of programs and practices that have been brought in under the community policing umbrella: community organizing activities and crime prevention technologies, foot patrols, school liaison programs, Police Activity Leagues (PAL), and a host of other community outreach programs. All of these components have honorable histories that predate the advent of community policing; indeed, critics of community policing often score the "old wine in new bottles" promotion of these existing programs as emblematic of something new (see, e.g., Bayley 1988; Eck 1994). Though the problem-solving approach is of more recent vintage, it too has become a tactical and strategic pillar of community policing. Foot patrols and their slightly more mobile counterparts on two wheels and four legs existed for tactical purposes well before the advent of community policing.

"Something new" is the police role as catalyst in mobilizing other public and private agencies on a common problem. Where this is really happening, it is one of the true innovations of police service to have appeared under the community policing label. However, this role merely adopts one of the goals of the old Alinsky-style organizations, to improve city services to the neighborhoods (Bailey 1974). What had been accomplished by community organizing is now given over to the police with the approval of the community organization.

Nowhere in this scheme is there an articulated substantive role for the community.[2] Little attention has been given to a definition of the community commensurate with the vast promise imbedded in the rhetoric of community policing. Even less has been spared for defining the role that can be reasonably expected of "the community," howsoever it should be defined. Though some departments and localities are engaged in honest efforts to make the promises a reality, community policing by and large remains a unilateral action on the part of the police. Community participation seems to be limited to four primary roles (singly or in combination), of which three are police-related.

Standard Community "Partnership" Roles

The lowest form of partnership is a traditional one, with the community acting as the "eyes and ears of the police." Members of the community provide information about crime, criminals, suspicious persons, and undesirable conditions in their neighborhoods. Traditionally, citizens have done this through 911 calls and other mobilizations and by assisting investigators with follow-up inquiries. In the newer models of problem- and community-oriented policing, this role may be discharged informally by interacting with a beat officer, as well as more formally in concert with other citizens, as members of a precinct advisory group or other formal organizations. In each case, the citizen contribution to the "partnership" is legitimization for police actions.

A second citizen role is that of cheerleader, frequently intervening on behalf of the police in the political arena. This tends to be a collective role: responding to surveys on citizen satisfaction with the police, and staging demonstrations in support of the police generally, or in support of particular actions. Though organizations and spokespersons usually lead such efforts, the role can be filled by individuals as well, through letters to the editor, calls and letters to holders of political office, and media person-on-the-street interviews.

The third role is also a publicly supportive one, but it backs up the "warm fuzzies" with monetary assistance. The most well-known example is the collective action of the taxpayers in Flint, Michigan, passing two successive tax measures to fund foot patrol (Trojanowicz 1983, 1986). More recently, such participation has tended to be more modest, programmatic supplements to the agency's budget. It comes largely though not exclusively from the business community: donating space for ministations, paying for equipment for bicycle patrols or special outreach programs, etc. This form of community support is not unique to the community policing phenomenon (particularly the corporate support, which has a long history), but it is better-orchestrated. It is a tangible, recognizable thing that the community can *do* as its part of the partnership.

Finally, there is the statement-making role of the community, which can be done in concert with police action or independently. In a variety of ways, the community makes a statement that it will not tolerate certain types of behaviors. Short-term statements consist of vigils and demonstrations, typified by the annual Take Back the Night rallies across the nation. Longer-term statement activity generally involves the posting of signs (Drug-Free School Zones declarations, or the Criminal Beware! messages directed at the furtive and black-clad cartoon figure of the old Neighborhood Watch signs[3]), although some activities like Court Watch also make statements to selected respectable targets. Ironically, it is those statements that are directed at the nominal servants or allies of the community which get the greatest response, and thereby hangs a tale.

Statement-Making Behavior

Statement-making attends almost all activities in which community-based organizations participate, particularly the inauguration of new efforts and the attainment of the "small victories" of organizing efforts. With every closed crackhouse, with every john sweep, with every new posting of a Drug-Free School Zone, someone announces, "We're making a statement to the criminal element that we won't tolerate this any more."

A statement, as employed by community activists, is confrontational. It is a line drawn in the sand—"you go no farther"—and implicit in the drawn line is an "or else," the threat of opposition and sanctions for continued misconduct. The collective statements of communities have two distinctly different targets, however: Respectable and Disreputable. The key to the effectiveness of statement-making as an anticrime tactic may lie more in target selection than in any inherent efficacy of the technique.

Respectable Targets

Respectable targets are far more amendable to community action than disreputable ones for two reasons. The community has a greater capacity to deliver the threatened sanctions to respectable targets because of structural factors, and respectable targets are less capable of levying retributive actions against communities (though they are not entirely incapable of it, at least in some portions of the political arena).

For a judge, the presence of community members in his or her courtroom implies their discontent with the judge's proclivities, particularly what the community perceives to be lenient sentencing. The "or else" is the microscope of media attention, with its implied threat of embarrassment (being exposed as a judicial deviant, unconcerned with the greater good of the community). In jurisdictions where judges are elected, or serve, as renewable term appointees, "embarrassment" translates into political opposition, either for the elected judge or their elected patron.

Statement-making has been the primary weapon of collective community action.[4] It is a weak technology, in that it can only operate in a milieu where the rules are known and agreed to by all participants, where moral suasion is recognized as a legitimate lever.

If the statement is sufficiently loud, or persistent, the target has two options: back down (the usual outcome), or resist. When resistance occurs, it is usually in the form of (singly or in combination) moral outrage, denial of the accusation, and the proffering of an alternate interpretation of the record. Resistance is most likely to be offered by a special subset of the "respectable targets" class, the marginally respectable proprietors of nuisance establishments.

Marginally Respectable Targets

Owners of sex-oriented bookstores, buildings that house saunas and massage parlors, dive bars, and slum apartment buildings (among other properties) constitute marginally respectable targets for community action. Their establishments are responsible for unsavory conditions in the community, but are nominally protected by law. Nevertheless (unlike the Disreputable Targets class), their claims to respectability force upon them a vulnerability to both community pressures and the formal regulatory agencies which the community can call upon.

Intermediate cases may or may not yield to community statement-makers, depending upon the strength and duration of the statement. A handful of picketers in front of an "adult" entertainment establishment may be dismissed as a fringe element. Patrons may brush by them easily (though they may do so with averted faces, and quit the establishment by another door). When the picket lines and media attention are shifted to the proprietor's suburban neighborhood, the focus becomes the owner's projected image of respectability.

Statements may be answered by other statements, however. Proprietors of such establishments court the media and regulatory bodies with alternative definitions, casting the issue in terms of First Amendment freedom of expression, portraying its clientele as "consumers" rather than "deviants," and so on. As most activists know, the proprietors of marginal establishments live elsewhere, and have considerable financial and political resources (either above-board or under-the-table, or both). In addition, long experience in riding out the periodic moral crusades that target their establishments has given them a thick skin against expressions of moral outrage. And in the normal state of politics (that is, absent a coherent or robust opposition), even a specious prima facie argument in defense of unsavory activities serves to justify inaction on the part of the formal regulatory bodies.

If the community action gains sufficient numbers, the political balance begins to shift. Massive, sustained protest carries with it implied threats of political action against the regulatory agents, who are more vulnerable to public pressure. That dynamic targets (by implication) the more respectable political actors who influence (by direction or protection) regulatory actions. As community activists understand, a sufficient quantum of community opposition will outweigh specious arguments in defense of unsavory threshold activities.

If the *character* of the protest changes, so too does the nature of the contest. When picket lines are supplemented by video cameras (and the implied if not overt threat of publication of names, or pictures, or license plates), the focus is shifted from the establishment onto the individual patrons, whose projected image of respectability is at odds with the deviant image they know their neighbors associate with the consumption of pornography. By directly affecting the patrons, the community may indirectly affect the establishment, which (the activists hope) either will go out of business or at least move to areas of lower guardianship in response to declining sales (see, e.g., Skogan's [1990] treatment of the distribution of such establishments).

Disreputable Targets

A direct "statement" to the criminal population is a far different matter. Whether attempting to move loiterers or drunks off one's property, or interposing one's self between a drug seller and a potential buyer, direct "statements" to the criminal or disorderly run the risk of eliciting equally direct, physically violent "statements" in response.

Many police departments actively discourage direct citizen intervention into illegal activities for exactly this reason.[5] As a result, community-based "statements" directed at disreputable targets tend to be merely symbolic, talismanic phrases uttered in hopes of warding off evil manifestations. But in many areas, despite various short-term successes, the talismans have little lasting effect: the magic wears off fairly quickly. For the statements to have an impact, someone has to be listening and disposed to respond. There is little evidence that the criminal element is disposed to respond (though they may shift locales temporarily as a convenience), and none that the retreatists are even listening.[6]

Those with a stake in conformity wish to preserve the good image that their neighbors hold of them, as that image is an important part of their own self-definition. Though they may resort to the predictable forms of resistance noted above, they will "get the message" when their counterarguments are rejected, and conform. Those who have rejected conformity, and those who feel they have been rejected by the mainstream, have different responses. Two groups are important to community policing, and to the establishment of a role for the community: those who retreat into passivity, and those who react with anger and violence.

Those who have retreated into drugs and alcoholism, who are ready-made victims for predators and pimps, nevertheless constitute a major part of the fear-producing ambience in the "Broken Windows" scenario. To their number may be added the large numbers of mentally ill persons who live on the street (though some of them fit the category of the violent more than that of the passive). Repeated arrest, even repeated victimization, is not enough to force the personal crisis that would lead them to seek help to change their lives, and it is unlikely that the moral exhortation of "statements" will do so, either. As an exasperated police officer once asked, "What can you do to people for whom jail is a higher standard of living?"

The second group is comprised of those who have chosen a more aggressive response to their disenfranchisement, and are equally impervious to moral suasion. Their self-justification process denies the legitimacy of the majority viewpoint, thereby exempting them from any debasement of their own image. As Weisburd (1989) has noted in a different context, social deviance becomes justified as resistance to what the subculture defines as deviance on the part of the majority.[7] In the ghetto streets, violence is justified because of the dog-eat-dog nature of their world; the more sophisticated among them will claim it is a lesson that they learned from their oppressors. To expect persons such as gang members (who are effectively insulated from both the outrage and the approval of mainstream society by an alternative social system) to respond to "statements" from a source they hold to be morally bankrupt and physically powerless is simply foolishness. Sherman's (1993) theory of defiance is instructive in this regard, and a caution against simplistic expectations for the realization of hypothesized outcomes of inadequate technologies.

For all the rhetoric about empowering the community, or the community "taking responsibility" for itself, when it comes down to cases the police establishment reverts back to a community role that simply enhances the police response to crime and disorder. Rather than "empower" the community to act in its own interest, this model calls upon them to help focus police crime-fighter activities. Subsidiary actions, including acting as witnesses in criminal trials, and even serving in a Court Watch capacity to try to influence sentencing patterns, also support the formal criminal justice system, and do not address the wider task of using the interventions as a springboard for building community cohesion. And it may be that is proper to do so.

In the neighborhoods most affected by crime and least attended by the formal institutions of government and society, regulating the behavior of other persons takes two forms: direct intervention (either individually or collectively) or indirect, usually by calling the police. The language of community policing that attempts to shift the burden of direct intervention back onto the shoulders of a community that is neither well defined nor necessarily competent may well be advocating more harm than good. At the very least, it may be setting citizens up for failure, mobilizing them by a resort to moral outrage and directing their energies at targets that are generally impervious to moral outrage.

Toward a Working Definition of Community

Before we can assign a meaningful role to the community in the supposed partnership, we should ask two related questions: What is the stake of the community in the endeavor? What tasks lie within the capacity of an organized community? From the perspective of a police program, the first question is probably best answered by Bursik and Grasmick (1993b, p. 15):

> The residents of neighborhoods share a common goal of living in an area relatively free from the threat of crime. . . . Therefore, social control represents *the effort of the community to regulate itself and the behavior of residents and visitors* to the neighborhood to achieve this specific goal. (emphasis added)

Accepting such a definition turns the second question into an inquiry of how the community can regulate the behavior of residents and visitors to the neighborhood. More specifically, the question is, "What can the community do—in what specific activities can it engage—that will bring about this desired end?" Our theories and hypotheses of community action begin to fail us when we consider these questions, because the necessary preconditions do not exist in the ragged neighborhoods. Arriving at a proper role for the community requires a reexamination of our definitions of "community" and a similar inquiry into the nature of social organization and disorganization.

Part of the difficulty in the search for a proper community role lies in the imprecise and multiple uses of the word "community." Webster's dictionaries give us several different meanings:

1. a social group of any size whose members reside in a specific locality, share government, and have a common cultural and historical heritage;
2. a social group sharing common characteristics or interests and perceived or perceiving itself as distinct in some respects from the larger society within which it exists (usually preceded by the): the business community, the community of scholars;

3. society at large; the public, or people in general;
4. common character; similarity; likeness, as community of spirit;
5. the people living in the same district, city, etc., under the same laws;
6. the district, city, etc. where they live.[8]

The use of community in the rhetoric of community policing is imprecise, usually referring to society at large (Definition 3) or the people living in a given bounded district (Definition 5) as if they were organically linked by common concerns inherent in Definitions 1 and 2. Though that may be true at a metaphysical level, it has little practical impact under conditions where only Definition 5 holds any truth; it makes even less sense under conditions in which Definition 6 is imposed as if the district lines corresponded to a distinct subcommunity like Definition 2. As many commentators have noted before, the community that is society at large is in fact comprised of multiple communities of limited liability.

In order to break out of the cyclical and serial failures of community organizing, we need to reevaluate two assumptions of the criminal justice research field. First, we need to broaden our understanding of community beyond the narrow, geographically-based subdivisions that inform database research. Second, we need to understand community participation and individual expectations not in the terms dictated by the prepackaged vocabulary of the crime prevention industry, but in terms meaningful to the people we are attempting to recruit, the disenfranchised persons we are trying to persuade to change their behavior.

The Constricted Community

The search for the proper unit of analysis for research using social indicator databases has warped our notion of community. The overwhelming dominance of the Chicago School, with its impressive laboratory of "natural areas," has indelibly linked the concept of community with that of neighborhood, a place of distinct and discrete boundaries. Community is now spoken of only in terms of geographical areas (blocks, neighborhoods, census tracts) that are pitted against each other for resources, without reference to a more egalitarian sense of the larger community.

As a consequence, the notion of a community of "limited liability" put forward by Janowitz (1967) and Suttles (1972), "characterized by the partial and differential involvement of their residents" (Bursik 1988, p. 536) is often described as a negative facet of modern urban neighbor-hoods. The other side of that coin, however unspoken or unrecognized it has been, is that of membership in a larger, more expansive community that recognizes the legitimacy of the person based upon what they contribute to the lateral community, regardless of where they live. In the lateral communities that cut across territorial lines, the Murray Kempton definition of neighborhood, "A neighborhood is where, when you go out of it, you get beat up" (Bursik and Grasmick 1993b, p. 5), is utterly unthinkable.

Outside the sociological debate, when we speak of communities where peoples' lives are totally defined by the geographic territory in which they live (outside of which they "get beat up"), we often use another term: ghetto. If we shift the terms of the debate and speak of ghettos—which are the products of ghettoization, a process *enforced upon* the residents by persons living elsewhere—we find ourselves dealing not with impartial (and seemingly implacable) social forces, but with a series of deliberate decisions made by human beings.

Block-busting in real estate (Bailey 1974; Bursik 1986, citing Holt and Pacyga 1979; Skogan 1986, 1990); a visible abandonment of investment in both the real estate and the human capital of an area,[9] of which disinvestment (Skogan 1986) and redlining in the mortgage, insurance, and other industries are symptoms (Allen 1992; Associated Press 1991a; Baden and Ison 1992; Brenner and Spayd 1993a, 1993b, 1993c; Grady and Nickerson 1992; Reuters 1993; St. Anthony and Woods 1993); the prevalence of gun stores and liquor-selling establish-ments (Sanchez 1994); the targeting of "special markets" for special cigarettes and enhanced alcohol products; demolition and new civic works and highway construction (Skogan 1986), and other similar practices are all activities foisted upon the least organized areas by more powerful groups. The overt demagoguery cited by Skogan (1986, 1990) is supplemented by a climate of racially charged resentment and exclusion (Skogan 1988, p. 57, citing Taub, Taylor, and Dunham 1984) and a host of subtle, cumulative statements that foster for some a feeling of despair (Associated Press 1991b; Cohn and Vobejda 1993; Ison 1992; Levinson 1992; National Urban League 1993; Nazario 1993; Peterson 1991; Raspberry 1993; Rommel 1991; Thompson 1993; von Sternberg 1992)[10] and give rise to quasi-theories such as the antiblack racial conspiracy that was recently in vogue. Bursik and Grasmick (1993b, p. 53), describing the work of Taylor and Covington (1988), summarize this as "the increasing social isolation of the urban underclass leads to a heightened sense of relative deprivation, which in turn should increase the likelihood of violent crimes."

In the radical[11] view, it is those deliberate decisions, and those human beings who make them, which are the appropriate targets for community action. However, the Alinsky model is promulgated upon influencing political controls, and as the late Speaker of the House Tip O'Neill was fond of saying, "All politics is local." In some cases, local political decisions are insufficient to sway corporate interests. As a general rule, the farther from the community the decision-making process is conducted, the less likely that statement-making (or even boycotts) will be effective. National and multinational corporations are effectively insulated from embarrassment, and the isolation of corporate headquarters from the influences of local governments (except perhaps in their headquarters cities) undercuts the effectiveness of community statements and reduces them to entreaties.

"Organized" versus "Organizing"

In certain areas, particularly the most crime-infested inner city neighborhoods, the question of regulation of behavior actually turns on the still-unanswered question of the Implant Hypothesis (Rosenbaum 1987): whether or not a group of dedicated individuals can implant a set of social values that will make a ragged neighborhood viable again. Though initial efforts to implant social cohesion produced negative results, the catalyst role of the police—both in terms of their hypothesized ability to mobilize citizen participation and their demonstrated ability to mobilize other agencies—may conceivably tip the balance in a positive direction.

But the "socially organized" communities that the Implant Hypothesis seeks to replicate did not arise from organizing efforts. Social organization existed as a result of other factors relating to the establishment of what came to be recognized as "a community." McGahey (1986, p. 232) notes that prior research efforts "concentrate on the informal social controls provided by stable neighborhoods [and] illuminate how stable neighborhoods control or manage street crime but have not said much about how neighborhoods decay or lose control." The contributions of disorder and fear of crime to that decay have been mapped (see, e.g., Skogan 1990 on disorder, and Lewis and Salem 1986 on fear of crime), but it seems more appropriate to view them as part of the "feedback loops" than as prime movers.

A persistent confusion of two radically different concepts that share a common root word masks the essential nature of the problem. Skogan (1988, p. 40, emphasis added) has articulated the working hypothesis of the community approach as follows:

> The community approach *assumes* that contemporary crime problems reflect the decline of the traditional structure of urban neighborhoods [which] are disorganized because the informal control they once exerted has largely disappeared. If disorganization is the root of the crime problem, organization is the solution.

The shift in language is of critical importance here: disorganized (a condition) is employed in its sociological sense, and organizing (an activity) in a political one. Political organizing has clearly identified, reputable targets; those targets are amenable to the statement-making pressures of CBOs because they are structurally vulnerable to the pressures that such statements can create. The social conditions that constitute "social disorganization" are neither clear nor especially amenable to statement-making. They are amorphous, frequently vested in decision-making processes and bodies that are far removed from the effective reach of CBOs.

Social (sociological) disorganization has been operationally defined in a variety of ways for database research on the ecological correlates of crime: socioeconomic status of residents, percentage minority and/or percentage youth, and family and household stability (Taylor and Covington 1988); family structure, official sanctions, and local incarceration risk (Sampson 1986); the ability of a community to supervise and control teenage peer groups, local friendship networks, and local participation in formal and voluntary organizations (Sampson and Groves 1989); socioeconomic status, economic deprivation, and regulatory capacity (Bursik and Grasmick 1993a), among others. Esbensen and Huizinga (1990) discovered different types of social disorganization, and different types of drug use, in Denver neighborhoods similarly identified as "high-crime" areas. Their findings that "community descriptors are not distributed uniformly among socially disorganized areas" suggested that "subtypes or segments of communities may exist that help predict the behavior of their residents" and "it is important for future research endeavors to evaluate carefully not only the conceptualization of social disorganization but also the operationalization of this theoretical construct" (1990, p. 706).

None of these macrolevel indicators are directly amenable to the intervention tactics of CBOs. They are precisely and merely what social scientists label them: social *indicators*, not the social processes themselves. The sociological bias[12] of the large data set research gives us a macrolevel description of the *results* of neighborhood and community decline, but neither illuminate the causes of that decline nor provide any practical insight into where and how to intervene to change the described dynamics.[13] Though such knowledge is valuable, it has limited utility for policy decisions because it is incomplete, and retrospective.

The basic framework of the Alinsky organizations—using block clubs as a means of organizing the community politically, to put pressure on either the sources of the illicit practices or on government regulatory agencies to intercede against those sources—is the same that is employed by modern-day block clubs and CBOs. The modern twist, however, is that CBOs are now exhorted to apply collective pressures against the disreputable elements in the communities. Except for community patrols—which are simultaneously a turf-claiming and a surveillance activity, and which usually culminate in the mobilization and informing of the police about illicit or unsavory persons and episodes—the techniques of applying such pressure are not defined.

The Alinsky-style organizations were known for their confrontational tactics, which were designed to exact the penalty of public embarrassment against chosen reputable targets: nominal guardians in the political machine who defaulted on their obligations to the community residents, and marginally respectable individuals in the private sector. The modern heirs of the Alinsky organizing efforts have eschewed confrontation for a more cooperative stance: though confrontation remains a possibility, the limited availability of effective coercive tactics (Buerger 1994) relegate that to a last resort. A greater emphasis is placed on regulatory processes in an attempt to define third-party responsibilities and secure participation in social control activities (Buerger and Green 1994).

Visible Symptoms, Invisible Causes

Perhaps the most serious failure of community-based crime-prevention efforts is its equation of symptoms with causes. The symptoms—whether they be the UCR crime rate, or observations and measurements of social and physical "disorder"—are the result of other processes to which scholars only infrequently allude, and which are well beyond the control of local residents. It is no accident that the list of citations that follows the discussion of redlining and general social disenfranchisement comes primarily from the news media: they report the results of efforts to develop specific social *process* information that is invisible to the social *indicator* databases. Such information comes largely through investigative reporting and/or investigation by guardian agencies, a process which has an implied advocacy position that is anathema to the canons and conceits of academic research. However, that information is more focused than social indicator research, and more vital than sociological descriptions of trends to the policy decisions that attempt to change (or compensate for) the toxic social by-products of the processes.[14]

To be effective, protest, statement-making, or any other activities mounted by community organizations must be directed at targets that have a direct link to the condition being created. By wrongly identifying effects as causes, the current structure of community anticrime efforts leaves the needy communities in the lurch. It asks the community's least capable residents to band together, and Canute-like to wade out into the tide of human misery and command it to stop.

To change that dynamic, policy decisions must incorporate information that is generally not available through the large social-indicator data sets. To produce lasting outcomes, the program efforts must address the milieu and problems as defined in the view of the target population, not as defined elsewhere.

As Rosenbaum (1988, pp. 363-64) points out, this is an area where anticrime programs such as those promulgated by community policing initiatives have substantial opportunity to miss the mark:

> Another major lesson from these experimental programs is that organizing and sustaining community interest in activities directed at reducing opportunity and creating informal social control are considerably more difficult in low-income, heterogeneous areas that are most in need of crime prevention assistance. . . . Asking residents to "join together" and "watch

out for suspicious persons" is asking a great deal in neighborhoods characterized by high levels of fear and distrust, a disproportionate number of "strangers," and a host of other problems. In fact, local voluntary organizations in these areas often express a preference for the "social problems" approach to community crime prevention rather than opportunity reduction (Bennett and Lavrakas 1988; Podolefski 1983), recognizing that crime is not caused by "strangers" from outside the neighborhood but by local problems that affect local residents, such as drug abuse, unemployment, and poor housing.

Looking at the task from this perspective poses a much different tactical situation. While academics massage large databases in an effort to conclude scientifically whether unemployment and poor housing do or do not have causal properties vis-à-vis crime, the people have a very good, usable understanding of how those conditions affect their environment and their lives.

Formal education levels may well be low in the target areas, but that does not mean that the residents are bereft of intelligence or savvy. They understand (at the intuitive level if not the verbal one) the dissonance between the stranger-oriented rhetoric of the watch-style programs and the facts of their immediate environment. They "vote with their feet" by withholding additional participation when organizers propose solutions that do not speak to their personal conditions and capacities. Asking them to believe that the crime and disorder problems that assail them on a daily basis will be ameliorated by the simple act of coming to a meeting once or twice a month is, at best, naive.

Even if participation could be guaranteed, there is still the problem of human capital. Effective organization is most severely needed in the geographic areas that have served as the "home of last resort" for those with the fewest personal and financial resources. Asking them to shoulder the burden of undoing the social effects of corporate and political practices is both unfair and unrealistic.

Conclusion

The anticrime activities of community-based organizations attack symptoms as though they were causes. They are attempting to apply a limited technology—that of organizing on a block, neighborhood, or communitywide basis, which has been lifted out of its original context—

against a target that has neither a structural means of responding to such pressures nor any incentive to do so. Adversarial tactics that depend upon either confrontation and moral persuasion are ineffective against criminal or corporate targets that are impervious to both.

In the worst areas, organizers must grapple with the Herculean task of mobilizing the most discouraged, least capable members of society, and set them to the task of changing or redirecting the decisions made by the elite, using only the tool of public appeals and expressions of moral outrage. Municipal and private bureaucracies are organized to respond to pressure.[15] The essence of politics is to summon sufficient pressure to be the group *responded to* rather than the one ignored. Community organizing can be successful in this regard if the target of the community's symbolic statements has a stake in being responsive.

The criminal elements are not so organized. Their raison d'être serves a small corporate interest, and those who deal in drugs are in a position to exert control over their market. The demand-driven field of supplying human vices is like a hydra, regenerating itself after every defeat, and occasionally corrupting its opponents. It is not reasonable to expect it to yield to "statements" alone when it has so effectively thwarted aggressive suppression efforts by law enforcement. Rather than fostering a belief that somehow the community must shoulder the burdens of controlling the dangerous elements through informal means, we should properly leave that type of confrontational work to the police: informal social control works to maintain the boundaries of those at the threshold, but is powerless against those who have already defined themselves as outside the law. We need to recognize that in the short term, the community will be represented only by a small cadre of local elites, who need realistic goals and tactics.

New Roles, New Solutions

Skogan (1988) notes four main ways in which community organizations can affect crime: (1) capture problem-solving resources; (2) confront external enemies; (3) push crime prevention; and (4) activate informal internal control. Skogan and Rosenbaum have both demonstrated the poor record of accomplishment in the third category; I have suggested indirectly that the "friendly takeover" of the Alinsky-style organizations by the former targets (the agents of local government) will most likely vitiate their capacity to do the second.

The track record in the first category is better. Organized community groups have had success mobilizing city agencies on particular problems, be they derelict buildings, abandoned cars, street prostitution, or crack houses. But the catch-22 of community organizing is that limited victories over small problems are not enough to create—for the disenfranchised or for the corporate interests—a stake in a geographical area where none of the attributes of a more capable and stable community are present.

It is the fourth area that is the most important and in which the accomplishments of community organizing have been most meager. It is there, however, that the greatest gains can be made. But the capacity for internal control must be rebuilt, and that cannot be accomplished with monthly, weekly, or even daily exhortational meetings that do little more than say, "Do more of what's already failed." The crucial task facing community organizations, with or without the support of community policing, is to rebuild the human capital of the besieged areas.

Focus should be brought to bear on the conditions in the same order that they occurred: if the broken windows theory is correct, it was community decline that signaled the availability of the area to the dissolute and the criminally minded. People—including and perhaps especially the powerful, nonresident elite—had already given up on the community. Merely sweeping the vulgar from the streets will not correct that basic problem, and sooner or later the tide of undesirables will flow back again.

One possible avenue is to divert community-based efforts into long-term interactions with public and private agencies that have the power to rebuild the infrastructure vital to community. Since community coalitions have a much stronger track record in mobilizing agencies with a mandate to be responsive, those agencies should be their targets rather than the criminal or disruptive elements living in, coming to, or passing through the neighborhoods.[16]

A second avenue is a long-term proposal that would require outreach to those persons who have physically, symbolically, or mentally abandoned the inner core. The upscale and safe suburban communities are fond of establishing "sister city" relationships in other parts of the globe, but what are truly needed are "sister neighborhoods" in other parts of the same city or metropolitan area. The "sister neighborhoods" concept would operate like an expanded version of a mentoring program, bringing human capital into the areas devoid of them, working individually or in groups on literacy skills, social skills, job skills and placement . . . whatever is needed to end "the increasing social isolation" of the constricted communities. This is a huge and delicate undertaking. It requires a strong police role to establish safety parameters for the volunteers. It requires careful planning and monitoring because the trust relationship can be easily killed by any whiff of patronizing attitudes. And it will involve providing those who volunteer the skills to deal with difficult people, in part so that they do not get "conned" or victimized by their partners, but more importantly so that the volunteers can see beyond the facade of social aspect to deal with the real issues, and accomplish real change.

In a sense, organizing and maintaining a "sister neighborhoods" effort is even more complex and difficult than dealing with the criminal element. It asks too much of those who have too little. The proper role of community organizers—who will be the community in the initial stages—is to identify and recruit capable broker organizations outside the geographic community. Those broker organizations—certainly church groups and already active organizations like Habitat for Humanity—are in a better position to recruit volunteers from the outer neighborhoods, and perhaps to take on the job or orientation and training. Other targets for the neighborhood activists will continue to be the police, city agencies, and potential funding sources, but those resources alone will not be sufficient as long as the community remains an island.

Ultimately, effective crime control lies in the successful reintegration of the inner-city islands of neglect into the larger community. That task must not be based on confrontational tactics of exclusion. Though it is a more difficult road, it can be accomplished only through strategies of inclusion. Those who have the resources must extend to those bereft of them the necessary first steps (and second, and third, as is necessary) of rebuilding the network of mutual trust and obligation *across* geographic boundary lines, undoing the handiwork of generations of class and racial exclusion. A stake only in a constricted community, identified by lines on a map and otherwise abandoned, is no incentive to the disenfranchised to invest their own meager human capital in obeying a set of shared rules that favor the fortunate. The only meaningful incentive is a stake in the larger community that represents, in tangible ways, the promise of the American dream.

Notes

This chapter originally appeared in *Crime & Delinquency,* Volume 40, 1994, pp. 411-36. It is reprinted with permission. The research was supported by the National Institute of Justice through a Visiting Fellowship, Grant #92-IJ-CX-0011. The opinions expressed herein are those of the author alone, and do not represent or purport to represent those of the National Institute of Justice or the U.S. Department of Justice.

1. It is tempting to suggest that in some areas, the organizations most successful at promoting these activities are the gangs, and that they operate on the same basic principle as the racially motivated bands of toughs in "defended communities" (e.g., Bursik and Grasmick 1993b, p. 3, citing Heitgerd and Bursik 1987, and p. 56, citing Suttles 1972 and Hirsch 1983; Skogan 1990, p. 25), but the argument is specious. Whatever case might be made for the gangs' ability to establish territoriality, promote surveillance, challenge strangers, and promulgate member adherence to common rules, gang behavior is a perverse mirror, a distortion of true community. Unlike the youths arrested for "turf defense" crimes in the defended neighborhoods, gangs constitute an aberration of community, not its representatives.

2. Indeed, the "police-as-broker" role of community policing has in some cases annexed the community role in the name of "partnership." The police act as agents for the community instead of the community acting on its own behalf, which had been a goal and the technique of the Alinsky-style organizations.

3. The "Stranger" implied by the neighborhood watch signs, and indeed by much of the rhetoric of the block- and neighborhood-watch movements (i.e., "be aware of people who don't belong in your neighborhood") are essentially a manifestation of middle-class fears (see, e.g., Skogan 1988, pp. 45, 49-51). The concept of "criminal invasion" that is implied by the signs, and more explicit in Wilson and Kelling's (1982) "Broken Windows" hypothesis, is only possible in neighborhoods where there is little crime, and where delinquency is familiar and explainable, if not tolerated, as "hijinks." The "neighborhoods at the tipping point" (which Wilson and Kelling identify as the natural focus for police disorder control strategies) are as far a cry from these neighborhoods as they are from the devastated inner-city neighborhoods where community anticrime organizing is least successful. Although the problems they address are vastly different, the available technologies are applied indiscriminately in each type of neighborhood. This chapter recognizes the difference, and concentrates on the inner-city rather than on suburban, "defended," or tipping-point neighborhoods . . . though the arguments here presented may apply as well to the latter. This distinction constitutes a variation of the "two targets" theme that is worth exploring at a later time.

4. Economic boycott is also an available weapon, but to be effective, boycotts require a much greater degree of community participation that most

CBOs have been able to marshal. Boycotts are also risky, insofar as flight and abandonment of an area by the target of the boycott is a possible outcome. Shrewd target selection and available alternatives are vital to using boycott as a tool; like other forms of coercion, it is often most effective as a backdrop to negotiated settlements of grievances, an implied threat rather than an imposed sanction.

5. Though they will publicly praise those who are visibly successful, so as not to lose the public's esteem or their own credibility.

6. The difference between "making a statement" to persons who maintain a stake in conformity, and making a statement to those who have none, is like night and day. As someone once observed in a different context, Gandhi's tactics on nonviolent resistance worked against the British, who ultimately tired of the brutality required to maintain the *raj* because that conduct was in conflict with their own view of themselves as a civilized people: but it is much less likely that he would have prevailed against German Nazis or Stalinist Cossacks, who reveled in brutality. In another vein, Boston Globe columnist Mike Barnicle once noted that traditional Mafia intimidation tactics worked against peaceable shopkeepers who merely wished to be left alone, and who had a static capital investment—their stores—that was easy to target; it had no impact on mobile, angry young men armed with Uzis and willing to meet violence with violence.

7. Weisburd's work deals with Jewish settler violence on the West Bank, an eerie foreshadowing of Baruch Goldstein's killings of Islamic worshipers in a Hebron mosque on February 25, 1994. The two portraits of Goldstein that emerged in the media in the wake of the massacre—one a hero of biblical proportions, the other a fanatical murderer—vividly illustrate the turn by which each side labels the other "deviant."

8. Definitions 1 and 2 are from *Webster's Encyclopedic Unabridged Dictionary of the English Language,* Portland House (a division of Dilythium Press, Ltd.), New York, 1989, page 298. Definitions 3-6 are from *Webster's New Universal Unabridged Dictionary,* Deluxe Second Edition, based on *Webster's New Twentieth Century Dictionary,* Second Edition, New York, Doset and Baber, a division of Simon and Schuster, 1979.

9. Suttles's discussion of expressed attitudes in Chicago (1990, pp. 45-48), for instance, is instructive.

10. The list is entirely stochastic, compiled by a quick rifling of convenient files of newspaper clippings. It could easily be expanded, probably to a length exceeding that of this chapter.

11. As used by Saul Alinsky (and other 1960s types, in differing contexts), this self-bestowed label is a badge of honor; it was only the members of the establishments that Alinsky-style organizations targeted for confrontation (and, puckishly, the Establishment) who used "radical" as a pejorative.

12. "Bias" in the neutral sense rather than the pejorative sense of distorted judgment. In this case, as in a tendency to select for one particular outcome: a preference for *knowledge about* the phenomena under study, rather than knowledge that would inform a change process.

13. Indeed, academe's promotion of its own products tends to be limited to simple statements of possibilities—such as Taylor and Covington's (1988, p. 583) "If such dynamics hold also at the community or neighborhood level . . . such findings *can be used to shape intervention or self-help strategies*" [emphasis added]—but leaving any and all policy design to persons who have little or no idea of how to apply such findings for that purpose. The academics' refusal to apply their theories is a point of complaint with practitioners, frequently and pointedly voiced to field researchers.

14. This is the case even in the most benign situations, setting aside suspicions (and in some cases direct evidence) that the "zones of transition" identified by Park and Burgess, and Shaw and McKay, are not deliberately created and maintained by large corporate interests as a future investment. The evidence here is mixed: Skogan (1988) notes that,

> An important but often overlooked role is also played by big institutional actors with an investment to protect. Hospitals, universities, banks, utilities, churches and other institutions with large and difficult-to-uproot stakes in deteriorating communities can often be found behind the scenes, supplying money and staff to support local organizing efforts. (p. 43, citing Taub, et al. 1977 and Taub, Taylor and Dunham 1984)

Against that positive role, however, are the profits that those same institutions may reap from maintaining the status quo, as for instance when urban universities move to annex adjacent depressed neighborhoods for expansion of the schools' physical plants.

15. Though it is simultaneously true that such organizations seek to minimize such pressures, and will ignore them until they reach a certain threshold level.

16. Though community-based organizations should continue to mobilize police services for those matters—if for no other reason than that safety is integral to their ability to attract long-term investment—their efforts may be more fruitful if they focus on an infrastructure for community building. Though crime and disorder must be resisted simultaneously, so as not to poison the well, it is time to stop thinking in terms of crime as the only barrier to community well-being.

References

Allen, J. Linn. 1992. "Mortgage Bias Riles Fannie Mae." *Chicago Tribune*, August 31.

Associated Press. 1991a. "Housing Bias Found in Half of Bids You Rent, Buy; Market Unfriendly to Blacks, Hispanics Alike." *Minneapolis Star Tribune*, August 31.

————.1991b. "Study Finds Significant Earnings Gaps for Blacks, Whites." *Minneapolis Star Tribune*, September 20.

Baden, Patricia Lopez, and Chris Ison. 1992. "Investigation of Paragon Cable Launched in Wake of Allegations." *Minneapolis Star Tribune*, May 14.

Bailey, Robert Jr. 1974. *Radicals in Urban Politics: The Alinsky Approach.* Chicago: University of Chicago Press.

Bayley, David H. 1988. "Community Policing: A Report from the Devil's Advocate." In *Community Policing: Rhetoric or Reality*, edited by J. R. Greene and S. D. Mastrofski, 225-38. New York: Praeger.

Bennett, Susan F., and P. J. Lavrakas. 1988. *Evaluation of the Planning and Implementation of the Neighborhood Program.* Final process report to the Eisenhower Foundation. Evanston, IL: Northwestern University, Center for Urban Affairs and Policy Research.

Brenner, Joel Glenn, and Liz Spayd. 1993a. "A Pattern of Bias in Mortgage Loans: Statistics Show Blacks at a Disadvantage." Separate But Unequal, three-part series, part 1. *Washington Post*, June 6.

————.1993b. "Area Blacks Have Worst Bank Access." Separate But Unequal, three-part series, part 2. *Washington Post*, June 7.

————.1993c. "Bankers Describe Roots of Bias: Cultural Prejudice and Traditional Home Loan Rules Hurt Blacks." Separate But Unequal, three-part series, part 3. *Washington Post*, June 8.

Buerger, Michael E. 1992. "Defensive Strategies of the Street-Level Drug Trade." *Journal of Crime & Justice* 152: 31-51.

————. 1993. "The Challenge of Reinventing Police and Community." In *Police Innovation and Control of the Police: Problems of Law, Order, and Community*, edited by D. Weisburd and C. Uchida, 103-24. New York: Springer-Verlag.

————. 1994. "The Problems of Problem-Solving: Resistance, Interdependencies, and Conflicting Interests." *American Journal of Police* 133: 1-36.

Buerger, Michael E., and Lorraine A. Green. 1994. "Deviant Persons, Deviant Places, and Third-Party Policing." Paper presented to the annual meeting of the Academy of Criminal Justice Sciences. Chicago.

Bursik, Robert J., Jr. 1986. "Ecological Stability and the Dynamics of Delinquency." In *Communities and Crime, Crime and Justice: A Review of Research* Vol. 8, edited by A. J. Reiss, Jr. and M. Tonry, 35-66. Chicago: University of Chicago Press.

————. 1988. "Social Disorganization and Theories of Crime and Delinquency: Problems and Prospects." *Criminology* 264: 519-51.

Bursik, Robert J., Jr., and Harold G. Grasmick. 1993a. "Economic Deprivation and Neighborhood Crime Rates, 1960-1980." *Law and Society Review* 272: 263-83.

————. 1993b. *Neighborhoods and Crime: The Dimensions of Effective Community Control*. New York: Lexington.

Bursik, Robert J., Jr., Harold G. Grasmick, and Mitchell B. Chamlin. 1990. "The Effect of Longitudinal Arrest Patterns on the Development of Robbery Trends at the Neighborhood Level." *Criminology* 283: 431-50.

Cohn, D'Vera, and Barbara Vobejda. 1993. "Few Blacks Reach Top in Private Sector, Census Finds." *Washington Post*, January 18.

Eck, John. 1994. Plenary session address to the annual meeting of the Academy of Criminal Justice Sciences. Chicago.

Esbensen, Finn-Aage, and David Huizinga. 1990. "Community Structure and Drug Use: From A Social Disorganization Perspective." Research note. *Justice Quarterly* 74: 691-709.

Finckenauer, James O. 1982. *Scared Straight! and the Panacea Phenomenon*. Englewood Cliffs, NJ: Prentice-Hall.

Fisher, Bonnie. 1993. "What Works: Block Watch Meetings or Crime Prevention Seminars?" *Journal of Crime and Justice* 161: 1-27.

Goldstein, Herman. 1979. "Improving Policing: A Problem-Oriented Approach." *Crime and Delinquency* 25: 236-58.

————. 1990. *Problem-Oriented Policing*. Philadelphia: Temple University Press.

Grady, William, and Matthew Nickerson. 1992. "Insurer Redlining Banned: U.S. Appeals Court Extends Protection of Fair Housing Law." *Chicago Tribune*, September 22.

Heitgerd, Janet L., and Robert J. Bursik, Jr. 1987. "Extra-Community Dynamics and the Ecology of Delinquency." *American Journal of Sociology* 92: 775-87.

Hirsch, A. R. 1983. *Making the Second Ghetto: Race and Housing in Chicago 1940-1960*. New York: Cambridge University Press.

Ison, Chris. 1992. "Paragon is Accused of Shunning Poor Areas." *Minneapolis Star Tribune*, May 13.

Janowitz, Morris. 1967. *The Community Press in an Urban Setting*. 2nd edition. Chicago: University of Chicago Press.

Levinson, Arlene. 1992. "Racism is Becoming a Real Drag: It Undercuts Economic Growth while Adding Cost to Society." Associated Press byline. *Sunday Post-Crescent*, Appleton-Neenah-Menasha, WI. July 2.

Lewis, Daniel A., and Greta Salem. 1986. *Fear of Crime: Incivility and the Production of a Social Problem*. New Brunswick, NJ: Transaction.

Lurigio, Arthur J., and Dennis P. Rosenbaum. 1986. "Evaluation Research in Community Crime Prevention: A Critical Look at the Field." In *Community Crime Prevention: Does It Work?* edited by D. Rosenbaum, 19-44. Beverly Hills, CA: Sage.

McGahey, Richard M. 1986. "Economic Conditions, Neighborhood Organization, and Urban Crime." In *Communities and Crime, Crime and Justice: A Review of Research* Vol. 8, edited by A. J. Reiss, Jr. and M. Tonry, 231-70. Chicago: University of Chicago Press.

National Urban League. 1993. *The State of Black America.* Washington, DC: National Urban League.

Nazario, Sonia. 1993. "Odds Grim For Black Men In California: Study Shows Group's Prospects Eroding." *Washington Post,* December 12.

Peterson, David. 1991. "Unequal Justice for Young Blacks?" *Minneapolis Star Tribune,* August 20.

Podolefsky, A. M. 1983. *Case Studies in Community Crime Prevention.* Springfield, IL: Thomas.

Raspberry, William. 1993. "Lots Of Reasons, One Bad Result." *Washington Post,* August 15.

Reuters. 1993. "Black Applicants for Mortgages Rejected More." *Minneapolis Star Tribune,* November 5, p. 19A.

Rommel, Rick. 1991. "Decline Seen in Blacks Who Own Homes; 80's Reversed Earlier Trends." *Milwaukee Sentinel,* September 2.

Rosenbaum, Dennis P. 1986. "The Problem of Crime Control." In *Community Crime Prevention: Does It Work?* edited by D. Rosenbaum, 11-18. Beverly Hills, CA: Sage.

———. 1987. "The Theory and Research Behind Neighborhood Watch: Is It a Sound Fear and Crime Reduction Strategy?" *Crime and Delinquency* 33: 103-34.

———. 1988. "Community Crime Prevention: A Review and Synthesis of the Literature." *Justice Quarterly* 53: 323-95.

Rosenbaum, Dennis P., Dan A. Lewis, and Jane A. Grant. 1986. "Neighborhood-Based Crime Prevention: Assessing the Efficacy of Community Organizing in Chicago." In *Community Crime Prevention: Does It Work?* edited by D. Rosenbaum, 109-33. Beverly Hills, CA: Sage.

Ryan, William. 1976. *Blaming The Victim.* Rev. ed. New York: Vintage.

Sampson, Robert J. 1986. "Crime in Cities: The Effects of Formal and Informal Social Control." In *Communities and Crime, Crime and Justice: A Review of Research.* Vol. 8, edited by A. J. Reiss, Jr. and M. Tonry, 101-62. Chicago: University of Chicago Press.

Sampson, Robert J., and W. Byron Groves. 1989. "Community Structure and Crime: Testing Social-Disorganization Theory." *American Journal of Sociology* 944: 774-802.

Sanchez, Rene. 1994. "In Parts of D.C., Alcohol is Everywhere: Some Say Density of Liquor Stores Threatens Their Neighborhoods." *The Washington Post*, March 20, pp. A1, A6-A7.

Sherman, Lawrence W. 1993. "Defiance, Deterrence, Irrelevance: A Theory of the Criminal Sanction." *Journal of Research in Crime and Delinquency* 304: 445-73.

Skogan, Wesley G. 1986. "Fear of Crime and Neighborhood Change." In *Communities and Crime, Crime and Justice: A Review of Research*. Vol. 8, edited by A. J. Reiss, Jr. and M. Tonry, 203-29. Chicago: University of Chicago Press.

———. 1988. "Community Organizations and Crime." In *Crime and Justice: A Review of Research*. Vol. 10, edited by M. Tonry and N. Morris, 39-78. Chicago: University of Chicago Press.

———. 1990. *Disorder and Decline: Crime and the Spiral of Decay in American Neighborhoods*. New York: Free Press.

Skogan, Wesley G., and Michael G. Maxfield. 1981. *Coping with Crime: Individual and Neighborhood Reactions*. Beverly Hills, CA: Sage.

St. Anthony, Neal, and Willard Woods. 1993. "Minority Mortgages: Where the Money Goes." Three-part series. *Minneapolis Star Tribune*, November 6-8.

Suttles, Gerald D. 1972. *The Social Construction of Communities*. Chicago: University of Chicago Press.

———. 1990. *The Man-Made City: The Land-Use Confidence Game in Chicago*. Chicago: University of Chicago Press.

Taub, Richard P., George P. Surgeon, Sara Lindbolm, Phyllis B. Otti, and Amy Bridges. 1977. "Urban Voluntary Associations, Locally Based and Externally Induced." *American Journal of Sociology* 83: 425-42.

Taub, Richard P., D. Garth Taylor, and Jan Dunham. 1984. *Patterns of Neighborhood Change: Race and Crime in Urban America*. Chicago: University of Chicago Press.

Taylor, Ralph B., and Jeanette Covington. 1988. "Neighborhood Changes in Ecology and Violence." *Criminology* 264: 553-89.

Thompson, Tracy. 1993. "Study Finds Subtle Discrimination in Area Job Interviews." *Washington Post*, January 15.

Trojanowicz, Robert C. 1983. *An Evaluation of the Neighborhood Foot Patrol Program in Flint, Michigan*. East Lansing, MI: Michigan State University, National Neighborhood Foot Patrol Center.

———. 1986. "Evaluating a Neighborhood Foot Patrol Pro-gram: The Flint, Michigan, Project." In *Community Crime Prevention: Does It Work?*, edited by D. Rosenbaum, 157-78. Beverly Hills, CA: Sage.

von Sternberg, Barbara. 1992. "Minorities' Prospects Plunge in Minnesota." *Minneapolis Star Tribune*, December 10.

Weisburd, David. 1989. *Jewish Settler Violence: Deviance and Social Reaction*. University Park, PA: Pennsylvania State University Press.

Wilson, James Q., and George L. Kelling 1982. "Broken Windows." *The Atlantic Monthly* (March): 29-38.

Yates, Douglas. 1973. *Neighborhood Democracy: The Politics and Impacts of Decentralization.* Lexington, MA: Lexington (Heath).

Yin, Robert K. 1986. "Community Crime Prevention: A Synthesis of Eleven Evaluations." In *Community Crime Prevention: Does It Work?,* edited by D. Rosenbaum, 294-308. Beverly Hills, CA: Sage.

8

"Angels in Marble": Problems in Stimulating Community Involvement in Community Policing

Randolph M. Grinc

Community policing is the new orthodoxy of American policing. It has become a flourishing alternative to what many police administrators view as the failure of professional policing to deal effectively with crime and quality-of-life issues, and jurisdictions throughout the country have instituted efforts designed to focus on a wide variety of crime and other quality-of-life problems that occur in specific neighborhood settings (Goldstein 1990; Kelling and Moore 1988a; McElroy, Cosgrove, and Sadd 1993; Moore and Kelling 1983; Police Foundation 1981; Skolnick and Bayley 1986; Sparrow, Moore, and Kennedy 1990; Trojanowicz 1983; Trojanowicz and Bucqueroux 1990). In fact, in cities with populations of 50,000 or more, 50 percent of the police officials responding to a recent survey by the FBI and the National Center for Community Policing said that they had implemented community policing, and another 20 percent anticipated doing so within the next year (Trojanowicz 1993). Community policing has been heartily endorsed by the Clinton administration as a key element in its efforts to fight crime and revitalize cities. The administration has set aside $150 million in its fiscal year 1993 supplemental budget to begin hiring 100,000 community police officers across the nation (U.S. Department of Justice 1994).

In 1990 the Bureau of Justice Assistance (BJA) awarded grants to eight jurisdictions to implement Innovative Neighborhood-Oriented Policing (INOP) programs. The purpose of INOP was to provide police departments with funds to implement community policing initiatives that would target drug demand reduction. In June 1991, the Vera Institute of Justice was awarded an eighteen-month grant from the National Institute of Justice (NIJ) to conduct an evaluation of the INOP projects.

The Purpose and Settings of the BJA-Funded INOP Programs

When BJA awarded grants (ranging from $100,000 to $200,000 for the first year) to eight urban and suburban police departments in 1990 under the INOP program, its major objective was to encourage community policing drug demand reduction initiatives at the neighborhood level. The eight jurisdictions that received INOP grants—Hayward, California; Houston, Texas; Louisville, Kentucky; New York, New York; Norfolk, Virginia; Portland, Oregon; Prince George's County, Maryland; and Tempe, Arizona—developed diverse community policing initiatives. They did, however, share some common features—some form of heavy street enforcement activity; a focus on drug demand reduction in targeted communities; and an attempt to create an array of "partnerships" with community groups and various public and private agencies.

Yet the differences among the projects were far more striking than their similarities. The projects varied in the size of the locality in which they were implemented—ranging from a population of under 200,000 in Hayward and Tempe to over 7,000,000 in New York City. They also differed in terms of the size of the police departments that designed their projects—from fewer than 200 police officers in Hayward, to nearly 30,000 in New York City. The projects also differed substantially in their experience with the community policing approach. In most sites (Tempe, Portland, Prince George's County, Louisville, Norfolk, and Hayward), INOP represented the departments' first effort at implementing a community policing initiative. Houston and New York, by contrast, have relatively long histories in the implementation of community policing dating back to the early 1980s. The way in which the eight sites used their INOP funds varied as well. For example, in Houston and Norfolk, the primary emphasis was on heavy street-level enforcement activities. One site

(Portland) placed greater emphasis on the delivery of community-based social services, such as drug prevention education and treatment. Several of the sites (Portland, Prince George's County, Tempe) used funds to open satellite offices. Hayward and New York used their funds to purchase motor homes that were intended to provide a place for community organizations to hold meetings and obtain information about available social services.[1]

The Research Design

The INOP research began in June 1991, well after the start of most of the INOP projects, and the data collection ended in August 1992, while most of the projects were still in operation. As a result of the timing of the research (determined by NIJ), it was not possible to design a typical evaluation involving collection of both quantitative and qualitative data in a "pre-post" design. Also, the projects were very dissimilar in design and were at varying stages of implementation, and statistical data were not available in many of the sites. The research thus relied almost entirely on qualitative data. During three sets of weeklong visits to each site, research staff collected observational data and conducted intensive interviews with police personnel, community leaders, residents, and members of other public and private agencies involved in the INOP projects. Interviews were conducted with individual members of these groups and homogeneous focus groups (i.e., focus groups did not mix police and community respondents in a single group). There were 522 people interviewed across the eight sites. Respondents were asked questions about the INOP projects and community policing in general; their perceptions of the project's effectiveness; their perceptions of the community's role in community policing; and their expectations for the future of community policing. All interviews were tape recorded with the permission of respondents and were transcribed. Transcribed interviews were entered onto personal computers using a free-form text database manager that made the data accessible for coding and analysis. Data were interpreted qualitatively using systematic, computer-assisted analysis.[2]

The results of the first site visits revealed that the eight programs were so highly differentiated that it would be impossible, given time and fiscal constraints, to compare them directly. There were, however, cross-site patterns linking the eight sites; these commonalities were the problems surrounding the implementation of community policing. Early analysis of the data showed that each site had experienced the same problems of implementation regardless of whether the jurisdiction was a city with extensive experience with community policing (e.g., Houston, New York), or one in which INOP represented a pilot community policing demonstration project (e.g., Portland, Tempe). For example, all the INOP sites experienced problems in getting their police officers to accept the new roles, behaviors, and expectations required by the community policing approach. All the sites except one had failed to establish adequate problem-solving links between the police department and other city agencies. Finally, all the INOP projects experienced extreme difficulty in getting community residents involved in community policing.

The Community Question

Although there is little agreement among theorists and practitioners on the precise definition of community policing (Bayley 1988; Mastrofski 1988; Murphy and Muir 1985), there is one central tenet that they share—that the police and the community must work together to define and develop solutions to crime and quality-of-life problems. Proponents of community policing, however, have often been criticized for failing to define adequately what is meant by community (Manning 1988; Murphy 1988). Often, community is taken to mean residents who historically have been excluded from mainstream society—poor, minority residents of inner-city neighborhoods (Eck and Rosenbaum 1994).

Although there has been virtually no research conducted on the community role in community policing, community theories indicate that social order is primarily the outcome of informal social processes rather than the result of formal social control mechanisms such as police activity. It is thus important to stimulate citizen participation in crime prevention and problem-solving activities (Bursik and Grasmick 1993; Byrne and Sampson 1986; Rosenbaum 1988). In addition, without community involvement many problems would escape the attention of the police, and solutions to those problems might be more difficult to develop (Eck and Spelman 1987). It has been suggested that involving community residents in problem-solving will make them feel that the police are being responsive to their concerns, which will, in turn, make them feel safer and improve police-community relations. With the active participation of community residents in the crime prevention process, real crime can be expected to decline as well (Eck and Rosenbaum 1994). Thus, increasing the level and quality of interaction between police officers, individual community residents, and existing community organizations is central to all forms of community policing. Although there may be some controversy over the precise role of the community in community policing, few theorists or practitioners would deny that the active participation of community residents is of central importance to its success. It is therefore surprising that police departments have paid so little attention to the education and inclusion of community residents in their transitions to community policing. Indeed, in most cases community policing is an isolated police department phenomenon including neither community residents nor other city agencies (Sadd and Grinc 1994b).

In a radical departure from the era of "professionalism" in policing, in which the police claimed a monopoly on the responsibility for crime control, under community policing the police argue that they can do little about crime, social disorder, or the myriad other quality-of-life problems that affect communities without the active assistance of community residents (Kelling and Moore 1988b). Indeed, in describing community policing as the new professionalism, Skolnick and Bayley (1986) write, "the new professionalism implies that the police serve, learn from, and are accountable to the community. Behind the new professionalism is a governing notion: that the police and the public are co-producers of crime prevention" (pp. 212-13). Thus what the police can accomplish in reducing criminal activity, social disorder, and fear, is heavily dependent on the partnerships that they form with community residents. The police provide guidance and assistance, but they are unable to create a safer environment without the involvement of residents (Goldstein 1990; Trojanowicz and Bucqueroux 1990).

Community policing's emphasis on the new role of the community as partner and co-producer of neighborhood safety is a key element distinguishing it from traditional or professional policing in which communities were given little, if any, formal role in policing their own neighborhoods. Indeed, professional or bureaucratic policing emphasized and encouraged the police officer's detachment from the community (Greene and Taylor 1988). In light of the failure of professional-era policing, police administrators and theorists of community policing, like the English statesman Disraeli, look out on the community as a vast, inchoate mass, and see in it an "angel in marble." Ordinary community residents represent a vast, untapped resource in the fight against crime, disorder, and fear. How to unleash the potential for effective organization lying dormant in communities will prove itself to be the greatest challenge facing community policing. As one police administrator in Norfolk, for example, observed,

> Our biggest problem is community partnerships. . . . [We institute community policing] in mostly low-income areas where they have a high incidence of crime. . . . We have to teach those civic leaders and those residents . . . how to become empowered, how to seek out resources that are available . . . the [law enforcement] stages of PACE (Norfolk's community policing) are easy . . . the community partnership stage is the most difficult, time consuming, and resource draining.

Norfolk's problem in stimulating community involvement and building partnerships was not unique; all eight INOP sites experienced extreme difficulty in establishing a solid community infrastructure on which to build their community policing programs.

Levels of Knowledge about INOP Project Structure and Goals

To determine how involved community residents were in the community policing process, residents were asked what they knew about the INOP projects and community policing in general. In all eight INOP sites, community residents' knowledge of community policing's existence, goals, and tactics varied greatly. Interviews showed that the level of understanding that residents had about INOP or community policing in general was closely linked to their status in the community. Thus community leaders with close and frequent interaction with the police had a higher level of knowledge about INOP or community policing than did ordinary residents who did not belong to any organized community group. Even the most enlightened community leaders in all eight sites, however, had only a limited understanding of INOP project goals and tactics.

The first and highest level of knowledge about INOP and community policing was found among local community leaders. Neighborhood Alert leaders in Hayward, Blocks Organizing Neighborhood Defenses (BOND) board members in Houston (both block watch groups), or residents' council members in Portland's target area, for example, knew a great deal more about project goals, strategies, and tactics than did their membership, and a great deal more than the average citizen not associated with a community group. A well-informed residents' council member in Portland, for example, said,

> I think the police are trying to do community policing through the residents. You police your own neighborhood and [the police] are here to assist us. [The police] will teach us how to do this. The goal of the project is to make this a drug-free and a crime-free zone.

However, even among community leaders, few knew many details about the INOP projects or community policing in general. For example, all the INOP projects were designed to include an interagency component that would secure the cooperation and participation of other city and private agencies in the INOP effort. Few community leaders in any of the sites knew of other agencies involved in their projects.

A second level of knowledge was found among "ordinary" residents (i.e., those not members of any formal community organizations), members of community groups, and employees of city agencies other than the police. These people knew that there was a program operating in specific neighborhoods (or, more frequently, that there was an increased police presence in their area), but few of them knew that the programs were related to community policing. A community leader in Norfolk, for example, thought that information about PACE had been "disseminated pretty well" in PACE target areas, but that the average person in the target areas, although aware of an increased police presence, probably knew little about the project:

> I think the average person, if you said "PACE," they'd say, "Yeah, that's some kind of program that the police department has to get the community involved." But when you start getting more specific than that in your questions, I don't think that they [know].

Similarly, in Houston, a member of a community association said,

> Well, . . . people might have seen what was happening when more policemen had come through and got the [drug dealers] off of the street. But [I don't think] that they knew why that was happening. . . . My aunt likes to sit on her front porch—a lot of the older people like to sit on the front porch—so she told me, "Yes, I noticed it (i.e., more police activity)." . . . But when I was listening to her this morning, asking her about the name of it and everything, she didn't [know]—just wasn't knowledgeable.

The lowest level of knowledge was found among respondents (usually ordinary community residents with no community group affiliation) who had no idea that any police program was operating in their neighborhoods. In all eight sites, these people were most likely to be senior citizens (who, because of high fear levels, present an especially difficult challenge for officers engaged in community outreach). According to most community leaders and individual residents in all of the INOP sites, their respective police departments did not adequately inform or educate residents affected by the projects about the goals and objectives of the projects or the role of the community resident. Indeed, when asked if they thought that the larger community was aware of the INOP project or community policing in general, most community leaders said that they did not think either was known to the average resident. For example, a Norfolk beat officer responsible for patrolling several public housing projects found that ordinary residents on his beat were unaware of PACE per se:

> People in the community know the PACE officers and they still don't know about [the substance of PACE. We've got to get past the [community] leaders [in making information available]. . . . We're not telling people, educating people (i.e., "ordinary residents").

This problem manifested itself in all eight INOP sites to one degree or another. Even in Portland's Iris Court Community Policing Demonstration project, a project directly affecting only 159 residents (many of these only children), project staff admitted that community outreach was their major problem.

The lack of knowledge about the INOP projects (or community policing in general) also extended to other city agencies. As a rule, employees of other city and private agencies that were supposed to be involved in the INOP projects often knew very little. Police officials in nearly every city scheduled appointments for Vera research staff to interview city officials whose departments were "actively involved" in the INOP projects. In fact, many such officials admitted that they had never heard of the projects or community policing. They did, however, routinely cooperate with the police. During an interview with a large group of INOP project officers in Tempe, for example, one officer angrily asserted that other city agency officials and workers did not understand the Beat 16 INOP project or the principles of community policing underlying it. Later, a second officer complained that most officers within the police department did not understand the project or the community policing approach. It is difficult to imagine how workers in other city agencies (or community residents) should be expected to understand the tenets of community policing and their roles in the process if, as these officers agreed, most members of the police department do not understand them.

Sources of Knowledge about
INOP and Community Policing

Although community leaders often knew a great deal about the structure and goals of INOP projects, ordinary residents in public housing neighborhoods that were often the targets of the INOP projects would often define community policing or specific INOP projects only in terms of the picnics and block parties that were so often used as vehicles for community outreach. They generally knew little or nothing of the substance of community policing or the INOP projects.

Whereas community leaders often heard about the INOP projects directly from officers involved in the projects (in community meetings), the primary sources of knowledge for many of the poorest of area residents were social functions such as parties, barbecues, and neighborhood "fairs" of one sort or another. Such events may serve the positive social function of bringing residents together (with the hope that this will help create solidarity among residents), but constitute outreach in only the broadest sense of the term.

The problem with social events such as block parties is that they do virtually nothing to inform or educate residents about community policing and their role in it. A member of a residents' council in Portland, for example, described the annual block party/job fair as a great success in which "everybody" from Iris Court (the Portland project site) would turn out. Even people (estimated at over 300) from outside Iris Court would attend the event. However, as a form of outreach and a vehicle for stimulating interest and active involvement in community policing, such events produced poor results:

> Whenever we have a free event, the whole complex will show up. When something requires work or when we need to raise money for the [residents'] council, nobody shows up. . . . They [police] have these projects going on so people will become involved. . . . When you throw a block party or any kind of party, they show up. But when we knock on doors [to encourage residents to attend a meeting] they say, "Okay, I'm coming."

But when we start working, they are not there. But let the food come up and everybody's up here, not only [from Iris Court], but from outside [the neighborhood] too! . . . There's more people who show up for the parties than who get involved in organizing. There's really just a handful of us that always show up to organize things and there's a large group that comes for the fun part. That hasn't changed much over the last year—the same people who plan and do the work stays the same.

When asked if the projects had any effect on the level of community organization, many residents across the eight INOP sites answered that the projects had increased the level of community organization and involvement in community policing. However, many residents tended to associate large turnouts for barbecues and picnics as manifestations of community organization, solidarity, and involvement in their INOP projects. Larger turnouts for community meetings, or significant increases in the number of people volunteering for community-based crime prevention efforts that were part of all eight INOP projects, would be better indicators of increased solidarity and community organization. When questioned further, residents made it clear that community organization and involvement in the projects had not changed significantly since the projects began. In nearly every instance, residents reported that only a small core group of residents were involved in the INOP projects.

Putting the "Community" into Community Policing: Issues in Stimulating Community Involvement

The assumption is often made by both practitioners and theorists of community policing that, once educated about the benefits of community policing, community residents will embrace and actively participate in the community policing process. It is often an explicit or implicit assumption that, in those communities where organization does not exist, community policing should take an active role in organizing them (Goldstein 1990; McElroy et al. 1993). The experience of the INOP projects, however, suggests that such assumptions largely ignore or grossly underestimate the level of hostility that has existed between the police and members of poor and minority communities who have often borne the brunt of police abuses. In light of this historical relationship between the police and minority communities that are most often the targets for new community policing initiatives such as the INOP projects, practitioners and theorists alike would be better off asking, Why should community members be willing to involve themselves in community policing? Among police officers involved in the INOP projects, this issue did not completely escape the attention that it deserves. One officer in New York said,

> You know, one of the untested assumptions about community policing . . . is that the community wants to be involved in this project, in this grand idea (i.e., community policing). The police department is [officially] behind it, moving full speed ahead . . . but there is one untested assumption . . . that the community wants to be in partnership [with the police], that they want to be involved.

Data collected from the eight INOP sites strongly suggest that community residents generally have no interest in becoming involved in community policing efforts. The reasons for the lack of community participation in the INOP projects may seem all too familiar to experienced police administrators, beat officers, and community leaders, but some may have received little thought. Although police officials and project officers may have attempted to address some of the barriers to community participation (especially fear), others are ignored completely in community outreach efforts, in part because police officials have no idea about how to address them. However, because these eight, very different, INOP efforts all encountered the same problems in stimulating community involvement, they provide police administrators and community groups interested in instituting community policing in their own cities with valuable information regarding the obstacles they will have to confront in generating community involvement.

Fear of Retaliation from Drug Dealers

Across all eight sites, the explanation most frequently offered for the lack of community involvement in the INOP projects (and community policing in general) was residents' fear of retaliation from drug dealers. One Neighborhood Alert leader in Hayward, for example, said,

> People on this block will not get more involved because they are afraid. It's difficult for us to even advertise that we're with the Neighborhood Watch or to pass out flyers, because when they (i.e., drug dealers) see us on the street passing out flyers, they automatically harass us, we're automatically labeled . . . as snitches. . . . People are afraid of that, and they don't want to

get involved in anything that's going to upset the street anymore than it already is, and they are just afraid of retaliation. . . . The fear is so strong that it's going to take the street being patrolled [by police officers] 24 hours a day before the people are actually going to feel better.

Residents in several cities also expressed fear of reprisals from drug dealers because when they would call 911 to make a complaint, responding police officers would come to the resident's door to question them. In Norfolk, for example, a resident explained that:

I find that most community people are fearful [of reprisals]. A lot of the fear comes from . . . when you call [the police] up on the telephone, your home telephone number pops up [on the dispatcher's computer screen]. Then the officers come to your house, and people would say that you're with the police and they label you [a snitch]. And, you know, with all the drugs and things around here, you hate to be labeled as calling the police. So we in the community, when we meet with the [PACE] officers, we say that we did not want this to happen.

Similarly, in Louisville, several residents complained that:

You call the police, okay? And then what the police would do, instead of them going and checking out what you said, they would come to your home and knock on your door. . . . People are going to see them come there! . . . So people wouldn't call [the police].

All theories guiding community policing make perceptions of fear a central concern. Implicitly or explicitly, most community policing proponents incorporate the theory of "broken windows" (Wilson and Kelling 1982) into their own programs. According to Wilson and Kelling, the police need to emphasize their order-maintenance function (i.e., attending to disorderly behaviors such as people "hanging out" and public drunkenness). Such behavior, if neglected by police, leads to increased incivilities, lessened informal social control, and increased fear among community residents. Left unattended, such conditions increase levels of community decay and make neighborhoods susceptible to intrusion by outside criminal elements. This, in turn, generates even higher levels of fear. Community policing is expected to lead residents to feel safer because beat officers will concentrate on the incivilities and disorders that inspire fear in residents.[3]

It may be, however, that fear is so deeply ingrained among residents in lower-income communities (where virtually all community policing programs are targeted) that it may not be possible for community policing alone (through foot-patrol, community organizing, and other tactics) to reduce fear to the degree that will allow residents to feel safe enough to "police themselves" and "take back their streets." It may be, therefore, that community policing finds itself confronted by a major contradiction. It appears that for community policing to attain its goal of fear reduction, it must first make the streets safe from the perspective of community residents. For this to happen, the level of real crime must drop, according to respondents. However, most theory on community policing seems to assert that, without the active participation of the community, the police cannot reduce the incidence of crime and disorder and thus reduce fear. An officer in Prince George's County argued that, before residents will get involved, they must be less fearful. This will come about as a result of increased enforcement efforts:

> Our initial step was first to show them that we are doing something . . . a lot of these people are scared and they are not going to go out there just because you tell them to go—"Hey, lets start a march against drugs or a neighborhood crime watch!" . . . We have to go into their neighborhoods and show them that we actually do care . . . make lock ups!

This, of course, is precisely what policing in the professional era attempted to do. Its perceived failure to make urban streets safer through aggressive enforcement gave rise to community policing. The designers of many of the INOP projects (Houston, Tempe, Portland, and Hayward) began or preceded their projects with intensive traditional law enforcement efforts. To reduce fear in Houston, for example, two districts engaged in "zero tolerance," whereby all crime and disorder become the target of enforcement. In Portland, the police bureau prefaced its INOP project (consisting almost entirely of social service delivery) with an intensive enforcement effort to evict drug-using or -trafficking tenants in the Iris Court public housing target site. The Portland police, in association with the Housing Authority of Portland, also implemented a "trespass" enforcement effort, whereby nonresidents guilty of engaging in criminal behavior or causing other problems (the incivilities discussed by Kelling and Moore 1988b) would be excluded from the site. In Tempe, the INOP project included "Sweep 16," in which all major drug dealers in the target area were arrested.

Such efforts, however, may well serve to produce unintended and negative effects. Residents almost unanimously applauded police efforts to increase the level of enforcement in their neighborhoods (for almost all residents, the more police presence in their neighborhoods, the better). During such crackdowns, residents reported feeling somewhat safer. However, many of these heavy enforcement efforts are short-lived and therefore do not have the desired effect of reducing residents' fears in the long run. When this is the case, they may actually create an additional crisis of legitimacy for the police as residents begin to define community policing as just another program in which services are "here today, gone tomorrow."

The Historically Poor Relationship between the Police and the Community

Common wisdom among police officers holds that, "95 percent of the community is good and law-abiding. These are the people with whom we must work." However, one of the untested assumptions of community policing is that residents want closer contact with the police, and further, want the responsibility for reducing the incidence of crime in their neighborhoods (Greene and Taylor 1988; Manning 1984). The assumption is that people who do not routinely violate the law, the vast majority of all neighborhood residents who are "good," will eventually come to work cooperatively with the police. These are the people who are the logical target audience for the community policing approach. Data collected in interviews with residents, however, cast doubt on these assumptions.

Some research (Block 1971) has found that among minority residents, those who are afraid of the police are often the same residents who are afraid of criminal activity. According to a large number of community residents, a major reason why residents do not involve themselves with community policing projects or are hostile to any police initiative, is the historically poor relationship between the police and the residents of poor, minority communities. This observation was often made by residents who fall into the police category of "good." Such relationships, most common in those areas of the city usually chosen as the target sites for community policing demonstration projects, will not be easily changed. One resident in Louisville, for example, explained,

> There has been such a negative view of the police. People don't trust them. . . . And most of those who are policing us do not live in our area so, therefore, they don't understand what we're going through. . . . So, there's a lot of misunderstanding—no communication at all. . . . That's the

kind of attitude [distrust of the police] that the community has. . . . Attitudes are learned, . . . So for 20 years they're taught that the police are no good. . . . You know, it's a lot of hard work to get somebody to change their perspective of something like the police department all of a sudden when you've been taught all your life to think a certain way about them.

A community leader in Hayward reported that she had experienced great difficulty in communicating to her neighbors what community policing was all about because of the extreme level of distrust that residents feel toward the police: "In the beginning, they [residents] wouldn't even listen to me. They're (i.e., the police) bad, period! Not that the police even know about this because it's all behind the scenes." Similarly, a residents' council member in Portland argued that even though the police had made outreach efforts at the Iris Court INOP site, few people used the contact office because of their fear and distrust of the police:

> The only people that are willing [to go into the contact office] are the ones that basically be in there all the time (i.e., the core group of resident organizers). The rest of them . . . are scared of it 'cause it's the police. The only time they want to be bothered is if their boyfriend is beating them up, or they've been threatened or something like that. That's the only time they want to be bothered with the police, but other than that they brush them off.

At the very least, these findings call into question the assumption that even good people desire a closer relationship with the police and are willing to assume a greater responsibility for social order in their own neighborhoods through the community policing process. As Manning (1988) has observed, so long as the police exercise violence in the name of the state, they will be despised by many in poor communities and will always represent the potential for violence to all (even those the police define as good) community residents.

Apathy

During the course of interviews with police administrators and police officers assigned to the INOP projects, it became apparent that many police officers had become increasingly hostile toward community residents who, because of apathy or lack of interest in "bettering their own lives," refused to get involved in community policing efforts. Such a perspective fails to appreciate the depth of distrust and fear of the police among residents in areas where community policing projects are usually initiated. Such areas are typically poor, disorganized areas of the city where residents have for generations borne the brunt of police abuses. The apparent unwillingness of residents to involve themselves with the police may thus be less a product of apathy than of fear and suspicion grounded in their largely negative experiences with the police in the past.

However, police officers across sites sometimes reported increased hostility toward community residents who, because of their perceived apathy, refused to involve themselves in the INOP projects. Police officers, many of whom were extremely enthusiastic at the beginning of the INOP projects, often found themselves demoralized because of the lack of community enthusiasm and involvement. One officer in Norfolk, for example, said,

> There's maybe three or four people in each community involved and the rest are apathetic. They are either hopeless or they have no hope. They don't think it can work and aren't doing anything to make it work—maybe because they don't feel safe yet . . . or they feel it's just another scam. And then, some are just bad people. . . . I say the community is like a bunch of baby birds, "Gimme, gimme, gimme, gimme!" And they . . . oughta start getting out there and getting their own stuff. Until they do that, this program won't work. The officers will just have disdain for them.

As an illustration of that disdain, officers involved in the Tempe project recalled a community cleanup effort in which almost no community residents participated:

> R1: Well, see, I don't think the community has bought into this yet.

> R2: Yeah, but what we've been doing [regarding community cleanups] is getting people from ASU (Arizona State University) who do their fraternity or sorority volunteer work. You know, some of these people (i.e., community residents) are just downright lazy and they won't do anything for themselves.

> R3: Exactly. I've been to all the cleanups but one. You've got a handful of people doing it all. Most of them won't do it. And see, they (residents) know our city [sanitation] crew [will clean up]. . . . Everybody just throws trash by the side of the road because they know it's going to get cleaned up by the city free of charge. . . . I mean, they don't even want to take it to a dumpster.

R4: That can be a little discouraging because you'll have some people who bring all these people in from other agencies to help the community, but the community don't want to help themselves. To give you an example . . . I was cleaning some fields and all of these guys are out and it's 112 degrees. We're sweating to death on a Saturday and we look up, and there's a couple of the homeowners sneering at us, sitting there drinking beers and watching us. And I start thinking, "Wait a minute. What's wrong with this picture?" I'm in this neighborhood on my Saturday, cleaning this guy's yard, and he's sitting there drinking a Budweiser!

R5: I look around and there's a couple of ASU fraternity guys and me pulling weeds, [one police officer] had brought his brand new lawn mower the day before and had it [broken], and there isn't a single person from the community participating. I'm going, "Wait a minute! I don't mind doing this, but where's the neighborhood? I got weeds at my own house I could be working on if they're no more interested than this!" I have some real concerns about perpetuating, sort of, our welfare society where all we do is give, give, give, because I really believe that that has led to a lot of the apathy that we're experiencing today.

Indeed, among police officers not involved in the INOP projects, the feeling that the INOP projects constituted welfare was a common idea. Portland's Iris Court project, for example, was almost entirely devoted to the delivery of social services to 159 residents of one housing complex. The project emphasized education and health services delivery as a means to reduce the demand for drugs. Several officers here, however, asserted that such welfare services made residents more dependent on others:

This sounds funny, but we started off giving everybody stuff, giving out badges to the kids. Give them this or that. You can't drive down the street now without giving them a sticker. . . . It seems we are sending the wrong message by doing all these goody give-aways—there was candy, free parties, free chicken. . . . It's true you got to have a party once in a while, but it was getting out of hand here! Everything is kind of like a handout— "Come along with our program and look at all the goodies you'll get!"

The lack of involvement on the part of poorer residents in the INOP sites, however, may be less a product of apathy or laziness, than a demystification of community policing's perspective on community involvement. From a resident's perspective, there are a large number of rational reasons why it is difficult to inspire the community to trust and help the police.

The Fleeting Nature of "Projects" to Help Poor Communities

Another reason for a lack of community involvement was the feeling among residents that projects (not only police projects, but others as well) come and go all the time in poor communities. Why, they reason, should community policing be any different? There is a healthy skepticism in poor communities that projects designed to help them are going to be anything but short-lived. Residents of neighborhoods targeted by the INOP projects have empirical experience with projects that emerge to help them in one way or another, but which disappear when funding for them runs out. One volunteer in the New York INOP project, for example, claimed that outreach efforts had largely failed because:

> What normally happens in the community is that something (i.e., a project) comes in and you just start to get the feel of it, and then it's pulled out. You know, it's pulled out because it wasn't doing what anyone thought it should be doing. . . . But what normally happens in the East Harlem community is that programs come in and you start to warm up to them, and you start to develop a relationship to them, but they get pulled out. So that creates skepticism in the community, because you don't know if you want to participate or not because you don't know how long it's going to be there.

Because of the fleeting nature of projects in poor communities, the credibility of any city- or government-sponsored project to help the community is suspect among residents. In Louisville, a police administrator observed,

> The folks over [in public housing] are used to talking police programs, they have for years and they haven't given the police department a lot of credibility. They know that when there's federal bucks out there, that we'll throw some program in there and then, when the money runs out, the program dies. So when the COP program started getting publicity, I don't think anyone over there [in the target site] really cared.

In addition, many respondents felt that the police were pulling out of their communities too soon after delivering a high level of services. In Portland, for example, several residents' council members argued that at the inception of the INOP project, they had two officers who walked through the housing project every day. Other officers regularly drove through the complex. By the time of the final Vera site visit, however, residents complained that the level of police service had declined dramatically. Many residents, they said, felt that the police had withdrawn too soon. The level of personal contact with residents had also declined.

R1: When I see the police now, they drive in and out.

R2: I see the same things. They go [into the contact office] and make their reports. I don't see them doing nothing here. They go inside and then you don't see them no more. . . . I've gone in [the contact office] to make a report and they've told me, "Tell the manager." It was about a dope-dealing car. A car that was selling drugs right on the sidewalk. I took the license plate number. I took it to them and they said, "Take it to the manager. Take it to the Housing Authority." . . . You call the police now and they don't show up.

R3: I'm here every day and I don't see a [police] car come in.

R1: That's what it is [another project]. When I was moving in here, I was told that there are always police around here, there was a community policing office right here; you'll always see a cop at night. I never see cops here at night, not once!

R2: I think it's a lot of patrol officers that don't take the time. They'd just as soon sit on Union Avenue, one [patrol] car facing one way, one facing the other, and they have their meeting right there, whereas at one time they met here. . . . It's just, like, at one time you'd see two or three cars [come through at night] and now you hardly see them at all.

If they remain unchanged, such perceptions will contribute to a crisis of legitimacy for community policing. These perceptions were most apparent in projects that relied on strong enforcement efforts. In theory, such crackdowns (i.e., sweeps in Norfolk, trespass enforcement in Portland, zero tolerance in Houston) are designed to reduce the level of fear in a community to the point where residents can actively organize and "reclaim their streets." In practice, the duration of such crackdowns is generally far too short for fear to be reduced significantly. When a high level of enforcement is provided and then withdrawn suddenly, the general response of residents is anger. In such instances, the police lose credibility and the project loses legitimacy in the eyes of residents.[4] A representative of a city agency in Norfolk, for example, explained,

Well, when we first started, when I first started working with PACE, I was just like a resident, really foolish. I thought [the police] were going to come in and clean up. And, yeah, they did for a moment . . . they were just so fantastic, it was just unbelievable! . . . They were able to reduce [drug activities] for a short period of time. Well, what happens after this? The police can't stay here forever, and it became apparent to me that the next step would be to help the communities to keep that kind of [drug] activity out. Now, it's up to the community to just say to the dealers, "You will not come back!" And I don't mean it for you to stand out there with guns, but that you start coming out, you start being visible. You start bringing city resources and services back into the community, and that's what I thought PACE would eventually do. I think that they left too soon. . . . And after you get past the police, the community is not quite sure what happens next. I know what is supposed to happen, but I don't know how you make it happen. I think that [the police] left at a key point . . . they should have had a backup unit in there working with the tenant groups, so when the police did pull out, you start having [the community] willing to take charge of something. They followed it up with a community service day, it was like a celebration. Everybody bought into that and then the resources left . . . [the community] didn't really see anyone in there working to pull them together to make sure that they were able to continue the work after the police left.

Although intensive enforcement efforts such as those seen in many of the INOP projects may make clear and immediate impacts on the levels of crime and fear in any community, their long-term impacts are highly suspect. There is no evidence to suggest that such crackdowns can (either alone or in concert with other agencies) inspire the level of community organization and participation that is necessary to maintain those effects. Without a solid infrastructure of community support and organization, it is unlikely that such enforcement measures will have any enduring value.

Residents Do Not Understand
Their Role in Community Policing

If, as community leaders reported, most residents are unfamiliar with the INOP projects specifically, or community policing generally, it is difficult to see how residents could be inspired to organize around and participate in these efforts. All the INOP sites were hampered by a lack of fundamental resources and experience in their attempts to generate community organization and involvement. Although these departments recognized the immediate need to train their officers in community policing strategy and tactics, none had taken steps to provide adequate information to members of the community. As Goldstein (1990) has observed, "conveying sound, accurate information is currently one of the least used, but potentially most effective, means the police have for responding to a wide range of problems" (pp. 114-18). Although meeting with community groups has been the preferred method for conveying information to the public, Goldstein notes, little attention has been given to the type of information that is presented or the most effective way to present it.

One type of information needed by community groups is training on the fundamental principles of community policing. Another is the role of the community. Any potential for the success of community policing will be limited if major commitments to community education and training are not forthcoming. Thus far, police departments have de facto viewed community policing as an isolated police department phenomenon. When police departments make the decision to adopt community policing principles and tactics, they take the logical step of training and educating their officers in this new approach. The education of organized community groups and individual residents is an afterthought. Often, departments rely solely on beat officers who have been trained to impart information to the community, but the INOP experience shows that this approach is inadequate. One community leader in Hayward, for example, believed that few people in the city had any knowledge of community policing and argued that, even as a well-informed community activist, she was unsure of what the police meant by "partnership" and what the community's role was in community policing:

> Well, I just think that the average person doesn't have a clue what it (i.e., community policing) means, all they know is that if you call the police, somebody pays attention. . . . But the one question that never gets answered to my satisfaction by the police department is—they want this "partnership," right? But I still can't figure out exactly what we are supposed to do in the partnership. I don't think that question has been thought through.

Although most of the INOP projects attempted to involve residents in some manner (e.g., volunteers in Tempe and New York; helping residents form councils in Portland; allowing residents to take part in interagency problem-solving sessions in Norfolk), even community leaders are generally uncertain about the fundamental role of community residents in community policing. Most respondents, for example, when asked what the police meant when they asked residents for help under community polic-

ing, answered that the police wanted residents to be their "eyes and ears."
As some residents in Houston said,

> R1: We're supposed to be their eyes and ears. . . . That's the way that I un-
> derstand it. . . . That's the way that we can help them. If we see something
> going on, we must call them.

> R2: It seems that they are asking for our help more often. Not to be more or
> less doing their work, but they figure that we can help them by letting them
> know what is going on.

Most police officers involved in the INOP projects generally defined
help in the same way as residents. An officer in New York, for example,
said,

> The only way that we can get to know who the players are in drug activity
> or criminal activity is by getting members of the community to either
> phone in that information or write in that information. Then that informa-
> tion is disseminated to the agency or group of police officers who will deal
> with that particular instance. . . . Without the community giving us the in-
> formation, we just wind up answering 911 emergencies.

Some officers, mostly administrators more knowledgeable about the
theory of problem-oriented community policing, added that residents need
to actively participate in problem identification and problem-solving and
become better organized. However, it is difficult to see how community
policing could be successful in creating community organization where it
has not existed in the past, especially because most officers interviewed
believed that the police department is not the appropriate agency to help
communities organize.

When residents were asked how the police request for help under
community policing differed from the help police had requested under
traditional policing, most respondents were hard-pressed to answer. Those
who did generally thought that under community policing the police were
nicer and more genuine in their request and also seemed more willing to
help residents and community groups. Those community leaders who had
a better understanding of community policing thought that help went
beyond being the police department's eyes and ears. A community resident
in Prince George's County, for example, said that help meant

> [providing] information, involvement [in community policing projects],
> attending meetings, helping to clean up the streets, educating the police as
> to the problems [in the community], and cooperating with the police.

At least three of the INOP sites (Tempe, Prince George's County, and Hayward) had instituted "citizens academies" that can provide at least one avenue for education of the public in community policing. Too often, however, such academies focus on introducing the public to the police role and thus emphasize "ride alongs" designed to encourage a better appreciation of the police role. However, if these academies do not properly instruct residents in the community role in community policing, they will not advance the effort to institutionalize community policing.

It must be remembered that community residents have been conditioned for more than one-and-a-half centuries to view the police officer as crime fighter. During the era of professional policing, the police actively discouraged community participation in order maintenance and problem-solving. The lack of participation and enthusiasm in the INOP projects and community policing in general is thus not so much a manifestation of apathy or laziness as it is a historical product of the era of professionalism and the conflict and distance it created between the police and the public.

Heterogeneous Populations in Many
Target Sites Make Outreach Efforts Difficult

Several of the INOP projects targeted areas where the resident population was extremely heterogeneous and formal community organizations were nonexistent. Such heterogeneity makes it difficult for the police to respond to divergent community demands and provide equitable services to competing groups (Gottlieb 1993). The Hayward police, for example, must deal with a number of ethnic groups that do not welcome police intervention in neighborhood problems. In addition, in several of the sites (Hayward, Houston, and Tempe), many residents speak no English and no police officers speak the language of the area residents. In Houston, for example, one resident reported that she had stopped attending area BOND (a citywide block watch organization) meetings because they were conducted only in English. She also reported that Spanish-speaking friends on her block would ask her what had transpired at the BOND meetings, but she could not tell them.[5]

In several of the sites (particularly, Tempe, Houston, and Hayward), many residents also told researchers that there were a considerable number of undocumented residents living in INOP target areas. Because they feared the police, there was no chance of them becoming involved in any police initiative.[6] A community leader in Hayward, for example, explained why her efforts to increase the membership in her branch of Neighborhood Alert had met with failure:

> No, we (i.e., residents of the neighborhood) haven't contributed to [community policing] at all. . . . I would speak about my street. Not involved at all. . . . It's [ethnically] mixed—Afghans, Iraqi, Guatemalans, American Blacks, Nicaraguans. It's very hard to organize because the Afghans are very suspicious of the police . . . they will not get involved. The Iraqis will help you, but they don't want to be seen getting involved [with the police]. It is perhaps that in some cases, they are not citizens yet; they have green cards, but they do not want to get in trouble. . . . It's hard in our area . . . people are too [ethnically] mixed, the racial conflicts, and so on. . . . For instance, there are lots of Black people that live there. So, I would confront them and say, "Would you like to help us?" They say, "Yes, I'm against crime, but I cannot go against my own people." Afghans, for instance, they tell us, "No, we don't trust the police; police is paid off!"

Indeed, in a survey of available research, Greenberg and Rohe (1986) show that there is an absence of shared norms regarding the definition of social order in heterogeneous, lower-income neighborhoods. Thus, establishing community consensus on problems and their solutions will be no easy task in neighborhoods characterized by heterogeneous populations.

Areas Targeted by INOP
Projects are Highly Disorganized

Community policing theories hold that the community must become an active partner with the police before crime and other quality-of-life problems can be effectively addressed. One problem for community policing is that the poorer areas of cities that are generally the testing grounds for community policing projects are highly disorganized. These are the areas of cities characterized by poverty, unemployment, poor educational systems, and high crime rates. In such areas, it is often difficult to find well-organized community groups attempting to address quality-of-life issues.

The question facing the police is, Who will organize the residents of troubled areas so that they can work in partnership with the police? Because the police have the mandate to fight crime, they have also been encouraged to take the lead in developing community partnerships with community organizations and other city agencies (Lavrakas 1985; Rosenbaum, Hernandez, and Daughtry 1991). Also, because the police are asking for the public to assist them in the transition to community policing, it would appear, as Goldstein (1990) has suggested, that the initial responsibility for generating community organization where it does not exist must fall to the police. It is, however, unclear why the police should be successful in stimulating organization where none has existed in the past. This is an especially difficult problem given the extreme distrust with which people in poor, minority communities view the police.[7]

Such an effort at community organization, however, may be undertaken by the police along with other appropriate city agencies. In Portland, for example, where the Iris Court project serves people living in public housing, the police have asked the Housing Authority of Portland to assist the residents in forming a residents' council.

Most residents in the eight INOP target sites reported that the level of community organization in their neighborhoods was only average or low and that this had been the case for some time. Most attributed the lack of active community groups to fear, and as one resident put it, "People here are just trying to survive day-to-day. That's what life here is all about."

Intragroup Conflict among Community Leaders and Residents

According to residents and police officers, a common barrier to organizing residents in the INOP sites was conflict among community leaders and residents about issues to be addressed and delegation of tasks. In several of the sites, personality conflicts among residents and community leaders was cited as a major reason why more residents refused to become involved with a block watch, residents' council, or other civic association connected with the INOP effort.

It is often forgotten in rhetorical references to the community in the community policing literature that the community is often an assemblage of competing groups. That people live in the same ecological space and possess the same racial and class backgrounds is by no means an indication that they define values and problems in the same way. Even where the population targeted by an INOP project was highly homogeneous (in Portland and Norfolk, for example), there were ongoing conflicts among residents regarding the direction they should take with regard to community problems.

In Portland, for example, several key respondents reported that a core group of residents, by insisting on controlling each project, kept other Iris Court residents from getting more actively involved in the project:

> Well, some people don't want to get involved because of a certain individual that they cannot get along with that's real bossy. That [issue] has been addressed several times . . . [but] they keep letting that person go on. . . . I don't think that's a good idea. A lot more people would get involved if that certain individual would step down.

In an effort to encourage broader participation among residents at Iris Court, the Housing Authority of Portland instituted training for the residents council that offers instruction on resolving intragroup conflict. Because many residents have never been part of a formal group decision-making process like the council, the training offers basic instruction on things such as running a meeting and communicating effectively. This form of education or training would appear to be essential for residents in many, if not most, areas targeted by community policing projects.

What Does the Community Want?

One of the things that distinguishes community policing from professional-era policing is its recognition that policing must be guided by the values and perceptions of community residents. A major task that lies ahead of police departments engaged in a transition to community policing will be how to determine the values of the many groups that make up any given community. Some of the INOP sites used surveys (e.g., Portland and Hayward) of residents in an effort to determine their perceptions of quality-of-life problems. As many critics of community policing have argued, however, determining the will or values of any given community will not be accomplished easily (Mastrofski 1988; Weatheritt 1988). This is particularly true of neighborhoods characterized by highly heterogeneous populations.

For the purposes of the present research, respondents were asked how they would improve the INOP project, and more generally, how they would improve community policing in their city. If the respondent had never heard of their INOP project or community policing, they were asked for their recommendations on how they would improve the quality of policing in their city. Across the eight sites, a number of patterned responses appeared.

Most residents, for example, said that they did not know their beat officer or, if they did, complained that he or she was rarely assigned to them for a sufficient period of time. Many residents who were aware that community policing was operating in their cities argued that the police department should assign a regular beat officer to their community for at least several years, if possible. It would take this long, respondents argued, for the officer to get to know his or her beat and its people well enough to have a lasting impact on crime and other quality-of-life problems. Often, they argued, they had been promised a regular beat officer only to see that officer reassigned without explanation within a year of assignment to the area. The Portland INOP project, for example, had established a Neighborhood Response Team consisting of two officers who spent a great deal of time at the inception of the project walking through the Iris Court public housing complex. During this time they were, by most reports, successful in establishing rapport with a large number of residents. However, according to residents, the presence of these officers in the area declined dramatically over time, and other patrol officers were seen only occasionally in the Iris Court police contact office—they did not walk through the complex.[8] As one community leader said,

> Officers regularly change here. Now, [two officers assigned as Neighborhood Response Team] have stayed here pretty regularly since the [community policing] contact office started, but they are also involved in some other community policing sites . . . so we don't see as much of them . . . but the regular beat officers, yes, they do change quite regularly. And that is a problem . . . the first two officers [assigned to the housing complex] actually sat down and listened to us as . . . intelligent human beings . . . we gave them information . . . it gets more difficult as time goes by to have to reestablish that trust relationship over and over with [new beat of officers] on various shifts. . . . It has been brought up as an issue. Sometimes . . . they have to reassign people because of the budget and because of the trouble spots in the community and that's what I hear a lot—other trouble spots . . . they need to reassign these officers. Now, most [beat officers] come right in, especially at night, most of them are just coming in to have lunch. They might write their reports, but one of the things that I was really hoping is that the officers would be walking and talking among our residents. I think that's one of the biggest differences between Iris Court

community policing office and what's going on out at Columbia Villa—those Multnomah County Sheriffs, whatever shift they work, they're out walking among the residents and getting to know the kids . . . that hasn't happened here. We've voiced that as an issue, and the police response has been too much area, too little time, and we seem to have taken care of 90 percent of the drug- and gang-related problems here ourselves, so "Gee, nice job. And our officers will get their lunch, do their report, and get out!"

Many residents in the eight sites argued that they had been promised that they would have a regular beat officer who would be responsible for their community for an extended period of time. Officers, however, would often be reassigned for a number of reasons, or had beats so large and covering several communities that residents had no idea who their beat officers were. Such actions on the part of police departments (especially when the explicit promise of regular beat officers has been made) may severely undermine public trust and confidence at a time when the police most need to encourage it. It must be distinctly understood that, for most community residents, the beat officer is the most visible and accessible symbol of community policing. A large number of residents defined a program on the basis of their relationship with one or two beat officers who, in effect, came to embody community policing. Indeed, it was common across sites to hear residents distinguish between INOP project officers who they defined as the good officers (or "our officers") who made an effort to interact with area residents and solicit their help, and everyone else in the police department. When these trusted officers are withdrawn with little explanation, any newly assigned officers must necessarily spend a great deal of time developing working relationships with community residents. The interview data show that community residents take the problem of revolving beat officers most seriously. If police departments are uncertain of their ability to provide communities with steady beat officers, they must make clear to community leaders and residents the reasons for this at the outset. The failure to do this may result in a further weakening of an already tenuous legitimacy accorded community policing by community residents.

Although many residents were happy to see more patrol officers in their areas at the inception of the INOP projects, they were less pleased when those officers disappeared after a number of months. Residents in most of the sites often complained that during the late night and early morning hours, when high visibility beat officers would be most welcomed by residents, there would be few, if any, officers seen on patrol.

Residents thus argued for increased high visibility patrol at those times when problems most often occurred.

Interviews also showed that community residents expect police officers to be "crime-fighters" above all else. Because they lack sufficient information about what community policing is, residents sometimes expressed concern that a community policing approach would make policing "soft" on crime and criminals. This, they agreed, was unacceptable. One community leader in Hayward, for example, although claiming to be a staunch supporter of community policing, argued that the police department's abandonment of its TNT (a buy-and-bust enforcement tactic) was a mistake and attributed its demise to the new community policing approach:

R: Another thing was . . . TNT. Okay, that was a wonderful outfit, I'm telling you! I saw them in action! I think that they are necessary in an area like our area.

I: Why did TNT stop operating?

R: Because the new COPPS (Hayward's community policing program) program came and they (i.e., the police) got more gentle and so on. TNT— it's rough! . . . They just jump out of nowhere and all those hoodlums are taken away! . . . If they didn't get them for drugs, 9 times out of 10 there was stolen property or whatever.

I: If this was so effective, why was it disbanded?

R: Because the COPPS program came in. Because TNT was aggressive on the street. The COPPS program, we understand, is supposed to assume that not everybody is a criminal, which is true, but the criminals don't need nice cops!

The importance that community residents place on crime fighting is found in their responses to the question, How will we know if community policing has been successful? In virtually every instance, residents defined the success of community policing in terms of crime and fear reduction. However, a great many residents also pointed to other, and equally important criteria, as a measure of success. One frequently mentioned measure of the success of community policing was better relationships between community residents and police officers. One resident in Portland, for example, said,

The police will have a better image for one thing. . . . The hostility towards the police. I would love to see that come down. . . . basically, I would love to see a community policing where people can go and talk to the police without being in fear [of the police].

Better relationships between police and community residents often rested on the idea that long-term beat officers would be assigned to communities. Beat officers, many residents thought, would be in the best position to improve relations with the community. As we have already seen, it was common for residents to define community policing in terms of the beat officer—certainly the most visible manifestation of the community policing approach. Indeed, the beat officer represents the community policing ideals of personalized service through face-to-face interaction between police officers and community residents and the police department's enduring commitment to the community through permanently assigned beat officers (Trojanowicz and Bucqueroux 1990). However, many residents were dismayed that they did not really know their beat officers, or if they did, these officers were often transferred after a relatively short time. Thus the primary means for reestablishing good police-community relationships—the beat officer—was often negated. As several community leaders in Hayward argued,

R1: You know, we're supposed to have the same beat officers [over time]. I don't feel that yet. . . . I don't know who to call! . . . I haven't a clue, and I'm fairly tuned in!

R2: I think that what community policing is about is the opportunity for local policemen to acquire a beat that they feel comfortable with—to get an opportunity to feel comfortable with the residents of that particular community—so that they can pretty much get a feel for the neighborhood, the areas that are the potential problems and some of the people that are the problems. And they interact with some of the people that are helping to prevent it and, therefore, put a lid on things. . . . And also, I think, when an officer is responsible for a particular area, he's more prone to go into that area and look it over and check it out. So you get a feeling that you have a presence there . . . he's like, your personal guy. You know, you feel like you have more confidence that way.

R3: What he just said, that's what the program was all about, was to assign an officer in your area for 18 months. But they keep switching them around lately.

R2: And you can't get acquainted!

Another Hayward community leader argued that the level of community organization and communication will be an important indicator of community policing's efficacy:

> [Another measure of success] will be the networking or communications within the community. The last 10 years, people have spent behind closed doors not wanting to get involved. . . . I think [community policing] is going to bring people back closer together again like we were 10 years ago.

Many community leaders, however, argued that community policing could not be a success without more effective outreach and education efforts on the part of the police department and city government. Without effective outreach, city residents will not understand their role in the community policing process. As one community resident in Norfolk observed,

> [The police] came in with some kind of community services day and that was a one-shot introduction [to PACE]. If you are talking about understanding all about what PACE is about, that is certainly not adequate enough to make that happen . . . but I'm really concerned that many residents are still in question [about the meaning of PACE and community policing] because [the community service day] gave them the impression that the police are going to come in to save the day, and in fact, everything but that has happened. But that impression is still out there, so it costs us.

Conclusion and Policy Implications

Because the public is convinced that traditional policing has failed to reduce crime and disorder, community policing has become an increasingly popular police reform movement. Whether it will succeed where professional era policing failed will in theory depend on the active involvement of community residents in the community policing process. The current research suggests that the apparent popularity of community policing among residents is not sufficient to promise their active involvement in the process. Although very different in design and implementation, all the INOP projects experienced extreme difficulty in stimulating community resident participation. Even in Houston and New York, both of which have a decade of experience with community policing, generating community involvement proved to be the most difficult implementation problem for the INOP projects. Community leaders across the INOP sites believed that most residents did not know about the projects or community policing in general, and interviews with residents suggested that this was generally the case. In the absence of effective outreach mechanisms that go beyond small-core groups of community leaders and residents, it is difficult to imagine that average community residents will ever understand community policing or their role in it.

The data strongly suggest, however, that the task of involving residents is likely to be quite difficult because community residents may not want to involve themselves in community policing. The reasons for this include high levels of fear, skepticism that community policing will be anything but another short-lived police program, the heterogeneous populations and disorganization that often characterize communities, intragroup conflict among community leaders and residents, and the poor relationship between the police and residents in poor, minority communities that historically have borne the brunt of police abuses. The relationship between the police and members of communities that are most often the targets of community policing initiatives has been characterized by conflict and distrust for over 150 years—a formidable obstacle to the successful implementation of community policing. Indeed, because even "good" residents in these communities are skeptical of police motives, police officers may sometimes become more alienated from the public if they interpret the lack of community involvement as apathy and laziness. Such a perspective fails to appreciate the depth of distrust and fear of the police among residents in minority communities.

If they are to realize even the less ambitious objectives of community policing (e.g., improved police-community relations), police and government administrators have little choice but to develop more effective means of community education, outreach, and organizing. This objective should be pursued in concert with those public and private agencies best equipped for the task. If a commitment to community education and organization is not forthcoming from local governments, it is difficult to imagine that community policing will realize whatever potential it may possess. Unquestionably, the education and training of community residents and leaders will require a Herculean effort. The transformation of police department structure and subculture, and the process of educating police officers about community policing, will by contrast be a relatively simple task.

Notes

This chapter originally appeared in *Crime & Delinquency*, Volume 40, 1994, pp. 437-68. It is reprinted with permission. The information presented in this chapter was collected under a grant awarded to the Vera Institute of Justice by the National Institute of Justice (award #91-DD-CX-0012). Points of view in this document are those of the author and do not necessarily represent the official position of the U.S. Department of Justice.

1. Space limitations prohibit a detailed description of the eight INOP projects. A description and analysis of the structure and implementation of the INOP projects can be found in Sadd and Grinc (1994a).

2. Much of the data presented in this article in the form of quotations are found in Sadd and Grinc (1994b).

3. Greene and Taylor (1988), in an examination of the broken windows theory, find little or no evidence in existing research to support the theory. The association between incivility and fear of crime seems to be confined to neighborhoods that are neither exceptionally poor and disorganized nor those that are particularly well-to-do.

4. The Vera Institute's research on the NYPD's Tactical Narcotics Teams (TNT) showed that heavy short-term, street-level drug enforcement did not affect significantly the level of fear in three Brooklyn communities. In addition, the level of community organization and community participation did not change. Residents interviewed for the study generally argued that the short duration of TNT (three months in any one target precinct) made little, if any, difference in the level of street-level drug dealing. Residents claimed that as soon as the crackdown ended, drug dealing almost always resumed at its former level (Sviridoff et al. 1992).

5. In an attempt to reach the large Spanish-speaking population in their INOP target site, the Houston Police Department has recently started publishing its BOND newsletter in English and Spanish.

6. Vera's research on the NYPD's TNTs revealed that one reason for the lack of community involvement in the TNT effort was the large number of undocumented people living in a TNT target precinct. Because of their legal status, such individuals avoided any contact with the police. In addition, some ethnic groups living in areas targeted by TNT came from nations where the police were feared for their brutality. Because of their experiences with the police in their own country, Haitians, for example, steadfastly refused to involve themselves with the police (Sviridoff et al. 1992).

7. In their research on New York's community policing program, McElroy et al. (1993) found that beat officers were most successful in working with members of the community in those areas where there were existing community groups. In neighborhoods characterized by a lack of formal community

organizations, beat officers were generally unsuccessful in stimulating community involvement.

8. Officers in charge of this project argued that a heavy police presence at Iris Court was no longer necessary because crime and civil disorder had declined dramatically. Many residents disagreed.

References

Bayley, David H. 1988. "Community Policing: A Report From the Devil's Advocate." In *Community Policing: Rhetoric or Reality,* edited by J. R. Greene and S. D. Mastrofski, 225-37. New York: Praeger.

Block, R. 1971. "Fear of Crime and Fear of the Police." *Social Problems* 19: 91-100.

Bursik Robert J., and Harold G. Grasmick. 1993. *Neighborhoods and Crime: The Dimensions of Effective Community Control.* New York: Lexington.

Byrne, J. M., and R. S. Sampson, eds. 1986. *The Social Ecology of Crime.* New York: Springer.

Eck, John E., and Dennis P. Rosenbaum. 1994. "The New Police Order: Effectiveness, Equity, and Efficiency in Community Policing." In *The Challenge of Community Policing: Testing the Promises,* edited by D. P. Rosenbaum, 3-23. Thousand Oaks, CA: Sage.

Eck John E., and W. Spelman. 1987. *Problem-Solving: Problem-Oriented Policing in Newport News.* Washington, DC: Police Executive Research Forum.

Goldstein, Herman. 1990. *Problem-Oriented Policing.* New York: McGraw-Hill.

Gottlieb, M. 1993. "Crown Heights Study Finds Dinkins and the Police at Fault in Letting Unrest Escalate." *The New York Times,* July 21, p. 1.

Greenberg, S. W., and W. M. Rohe. 1986. "Informal Social Control and Crime Prevention in Modern Urban Neighborhoods." In *Urban Neighborhoods: Research and Policy,* edited by Ralph B. Taylor, 79-118. New York: Praeger.

Greene, Jack R., and Ralph B. Taylor. 1988. "Community-Based Policing and Foot Patrol: Issues of Theory and Evaluation." In *Community Policing: Rhetoric or Reality,* edited by J. R. Greene and S. D. Mastrofski, 195-223. New York: Praeger.

Kelling, George L., and Mark H. Moore. 1988a. "The Evolving Strategy of Policing." *Perspectives on Policing,* No. 4. Washington, DC: National Institute of Justice and Harvard University.

———. 1988b. "From Political Reform to Community: The Evolving Strategy of Police." In *Community Policing: Rhetoric or Reality,* edited by J. R. Greene and S. D. Mastrofski, 3-25. New York: Praeger.

Lavrakas, Paul J. 1985. "Citizen Self-Help and Neighborhood Crime Prevention Policy." In *American Violence and Public Policy,* edited by L. A. Curtis, 87-115. New Haven, CT: Yale University Press.

Manning, Peter K. 1984. "Community Policing." *American Journal of Police* 3: 205-27.

———. 1988. "Community Policing as a Drama of Control." In *Community Policing: Rhetoric or Reality,* edited by J. R. Greene and S. D. Mastrofski, 27-45. New York: Praeger.

Mastrofski, Stephen D. 1988. "Community Policing as Reform: A Cautionary Tale." In *Community Policing: Rhetoric or Reality,* edited by J. R. Greene and S. D. Mastrofski, 47-72. New York: Praeger.

McElroy, Jerome, Colleen Cosgrove, and Susan Sadd. 1993. *Community Policing: The CPOP in New York.* Newbury Park, CA: Sage.

Moore, Mark H., and George L. Kelling. 1983. "To Serve and Protect: Learning From Police History." *The Public Interest* 7 (Winter).

Murphy, Christopher. 1988. "Community Problems, Problem Communities, and Community Policing in Toronto." *Journal of Research in Crime and Delinquency* 25: 392-410.

Murphy, C., and G. Muir. 1985. *Community-Based Policing: A Review of the Critical Issues.* Ottawa: Solicitor General of Canada.

Police Foundation. 1981. *The Newark Foot Patrol Experiment.* Washington, DC: Police Foundation.

Rosenbaum, Dennis P. 1988. "Community Crime Prevention: A Review and Synthesis of the Literature." *Justice Quarterly* 5: 323-95.

Rosenbaum, D. P., E. Hernandez, and S. Daughtry, Jr. 1991. "Crime Prevention, Fear Reduction, and the Community." In *Local Government Police Management,* edited by W. A. Geller, 96-130. Washington, DC: International City Management Association.

Sadd, Susan, and Randolph M. Grinc. 1994a. *Innovative Neighborhood-Oriented Policing: Descriptions of Programs in Eight Cities.* New York: Vera Institute of Justice.

———. 1994b. *Issues in Community Policing: Problems in the Implementation of Eight Innovative Neighborhood-Oriented Policing Projects.* Washington, DC: National Institute of Justice.

Skolnick, Jerome H., and David H. Bayley. 1986. *The New Blue Line: Police Innovations in Six American Cities.* New York: Free Press.

Sparrow, Malcolm K., Mark H. Moore, and David M. Kennedy. 1990. *Beyond 911: A New Era for Policing.* New York: Basic Books.

Sviridoff, Michele, Susan Sadd, Richard Curtis, and Randolph Grinc. 1992. *The Community Effects of Street-Level Narcotics Enforcement: A Study of* the New York City Police Department's Tactical Narcotics Teams. New York: Vera Institute of Justice.

Trojanowicz, Robert C. 1983. *An Evaluation of the Neighborhood Foot Patrol Program in Flint, Michigan.* East Lansing: Michigan State University.

―――. 1993. *Community Policing Survey of Jurisdictions Over 50,000 People.* East Lansing: Michigan State University.

Trojanowicz, Robert C., and Bonnie Bucqueroux. 1990. *Community Policing: A Contemporary Perspective.* Cincinnati, OH: Anderson.

U.S. Department of Justice. 1994. "Second Round of Police Hiring Grants Announced." *Weed and Seed In-Sites* 2(2), (February): 1.

Weatheritt, Mollie. 1988. "Community Policing: Rhetoric or Reality?" In *Community Policing: Rhetoric or Reality,* edited by J. R. Greene and S. D. Mastrofski, 153-75. New York: Praeger.

Wilson, James Q., and George L. Kelling. 1982. "Broken Windows." *Atlantic Monthly* (March): 29-38.

9

Civil Liberties and Aggressive Enforcement: Balancing the Rights of Individuals and Society in the Drug War

Dennis P. Rosenbaum

Since the mid-1980s, the United States has been engaged in a "war" against illegal drugs. The rhetoric of war has underscored the severity of the drug problem from the perspective of the news media, government officials, and the general public. To a large extent, inner-city neighborhoods across the country feel besieged by the drug problem and by the violent consequences of engaging in this war. Open-air drug markets, drive-by shootings, and other forms of unmitigated violence are now commonplace on the streets of poor, inner-city communities. With few exceptions, the level of violent crime has risen dramatically over the past five years in large U.S. cities where the major drug battles have been fought. Police statistics indicate that the rate of reported violent crime rose 22 percent from 1986 to 1990, with the number of homicides increasing almost 14 percent (Federal Bureau of Investigation 1991).

This chapter addresses a number of related questions about the drug war: What types of aggressive street-level enforcement programs have been promoted by police and communities that might jeopardize the individual liberties protected by the U.S. Constitution? What role has the community played in supporting these antidrug crackdowns, and what factors distinguish residents who support strong enforcement from those who oppose such actions? Addressing these questions helps us to assess the costs and benefits of the street-level war against drug dealers and users.

The Role of the Community

Although this war has a significant international component, which includes U.S. efforts to eradicate crops in other countries, incapacitate drug "kingpins," and interdict drugs at the U.S. boarder, the primary thrust of the war effort has been on the homefront—in the streets and dwelling units of America's cities. On the domestic front, the impetus for government action came from the grass roots. Witnessing the growth of local drug markets and drug-related violence, many community residents decided they were fed up and needed to take action. Over the past five years, community organizations and community leaders have played a major role in mobilizing civic-minded residents who were fearful and angry about drug dealers/users living and working in their neighborhoods. An impressive array of community-based antidrug strategies have been developed and implemented in many cities. As one example, the Bureau of Justice Assistance funded a ten-site Community Responses to Drug Abuse National Demonstration Program (CRDA). Our evaluation of the CRDA program, funded by the National Institute of Justice, found that local groups worked hard to stimulate citizen participation in a number of areas, including community awareness activities (e.g., rallies and marches, community meetings), enforcement activities (e.g., reporting drug "hot spots," closing drug houses, working for stiffer penalties), treatment services (e.g., referrals and networking with treatment agencies), and prevention (e.g., drug education in schools, youth and parent programs). However, equal attention was not paid to each of these areas. The bulk of their community-based efforts was directed at enhancing enforcement activities and encouraging citizens to work with police to remove drug dealers and users from the area (see Rosenbaum et al. 1992).

The primary objective behind a wide range of community antidrug programs is to identify, arrest, prosecute, and incapacitate local drug dealers and drug users. On the positive side, this means that local community organizations and law enforcement agencies have developed (in many cases, for the first time) a cooperative, mutually supportive relationship rather than a relationship based on conflict and blame. On the negative side, this means that community groups are not spending as much time on prevention and community-building, but rather are pursuing the criminal justice system as the primary solution to their neighborhood drug problems. In the language of the Justice Department's Weed and Seed program, there has been intensive efforts to "weed out" drug activity, but much less effort to "seed" the neighborhood with prevention and treatment programs.

Essentially, citizens have called upon the police to work with them to identify and arrest drug offenders. Neighborhood watches and patrols generate anonymous tips from citizens about drug "hot spots," which give police the information (and rationale) necessary to conduct drug raids, close drug houses, and perform area sweeps. The creation of drug-free school zones, driven by community action, stiffens the penalty for drug violations near schools and requires police enforcement in order to have maximum impact. Citizens have also called upon prosecutors and judges to work with them to insure that drug offenders are properly punished and not sent back out the "revolving door" of the criminal justice system. To insure this result, court monitoring by volunteers has become a common practice among community organizations. Community groups have also supported legislative action in many areas (in addition to drug-free school zones) for the specific purpose of increasing the penalties associated with drug activity. Community groups have pushed for laws and ordinances pertaining to nuisance abatement, asset forfeiture, unfair business practices, drug paraphernalia retailing, beepers at school, and other areas. Because community support for these antidrug laws inevitably places considerable pressure on the police to act, the enforcement function and the dangers inherent in this function, deserve special attention.

Drug Enforcement

During the 1980s, the government at all levels dramatically increased its effort to penalize those involved in the illegal drug business, whether they be users or sellers. Under the Antidrug Abuse Act of 1986, Congress strengthened enforcement programs by adding thousands of law enforcement officers and creating mandatory sentences for drug traffickers. In 1989, President Bush created the Office of National Drug Control Policy, which produced a comprehensive, multibillion dollar plan for attacking the nation's drug problem. The plan gave particular emphasis to reducing drug trafficking through increased use of criminal justice sanctions.

The federal government has tried many different strategies for reducing the supply of drugs in the United States, including eliminating crops from the country of origin, interdiction at the border, high-level enforcement directed at drug kingpins, and street-level enforcement to stop local dealers (Moore 1988). The limited effectiveness of crop eradication, interdiction, and high-level enforcement strategies is now apparent to the astute observer. Foreign governments are not always fully cooperative, locations to grow crops are virtually unlimited, U.S. boarders are too large to patrol effectively, and eliminating drug kingpins does not insure than their organizations will crumble. To make matters worse, the U.S. government has been criticized for giving too much attention to reducing the *supply* of drugs and not enough attention to reducing *demand*.

These factors, along with increased community pressure for action against local drug markets and gang violence, has generated a renewed interest in street-level enforcement directed at local dealers, gang members, and drug users. Indeed, this has become a major focal point of the drug war. Local residents and community leaders are working closely with police on the front lines to "take back the streets and buildings" from drug offenders. The strategies and tactics they have employed to achieve this end have become the source of considerable debate among legal scholars, news reporters, and politicians. There is little question that police powers have been expanded in recent years by the courts as a weapon for fighting the drug war. The real question is whether these additional powers, or the way they are applied, have effectively undermined the civil liberties guaranteed under the Constitution's Bill of Rights. That is, have we sought to increase *collective* safety at the price of *individual* liberty or privacy?

Is Drug Enforcement a Threat to Civil Liberties?
Some Debated Tactics

The Siege Mentality

In his 1989 Inaugural address, President Bush referred to the drug problem as a "scourge" that must be eliminated, and he committed substantial criminal justice resources to combat the problem. At the conclusion of the Gulf War, the president called upon Americans to assemble another coalition, this time, to rejuvenate the ongoing "war" against drug dealers and other criminals here at home (Bush 1991). Describing our nation's efforts to reduce drug abuse and crime in terms of "war" is an attempt to underscore the severity of the problem and mobilize public support for swift action. However, there are dangers hidden in this approach to public policy. Defining the problem as a national crisis may increase the risk that individual liberties will become another "casualty of war." In reviewing the history of wars and the Bill of Rights, Finkelman (1990, p. 2) notes that "Most of our wars have led to some deprivations of individual rights and liberties." We only need to look at the internment of 120,000 Japanese-Americans during World War II for a clear-cut example of how concerns about "national security" can override civil liberties.

In the late 1980s, the drug problem in the United States was defined by the media, politicians, and the general public as a major national crisis, and illegal drugs were seen as a threat to the basic fabric of our society. In 1988 and 1989, national surveys found that drugs were viewed as the most important problem facing the nation. Commenting on the "siege" mentality that pervaded the country at this time, Treaster (1990, p. 5) observed, "the crisis is so severe that intangible liberties may hardly seem to compare with daily horrors: drug deals and shoot-outs on street corners, entire inner-city buildings under the control of drug gangs." Indeed, legal scholars and civil libertarians have argued that the crisis/siege/war mentality, which has served to justify the courts' gradual expansion of police powers, has subtly eroded the constitutional protections against invasions of privacy and other threats to individual freedoms. A closer look at some of the key drug enforcement strategies employed by law enforcement agencies (and supported by the public) will shed additional light on the veracity of these claims.

Area Crackdowns

To eliminate hot spots of drug activity on street corners or specific geographic areas, police have increasingly turned to multifaceted crackdowns. These enforcement activities include: surveillance of known dealing locations, undercover drug buys, undercover drug sales, stopping and questioning suspected buyers and sellers, the use of anonymous tips from drug "hot lines," arrests for possession, arrests for various misdemeanors (e.g., disorderly conduct, loitering), aggressive traffic and parking enforcement, and the seizure of vehicles (see Kleiman et al. 1988).

Collectively, these street-level crackdowns may lead to the incapacitation of a few serious dealers, but they are generally intended to reduce the opportunity for retail drug dealing in that particular area by making it difficult for persons to buy or sell drugs. The basic idea is to "hassle" persons suspected of drug activity (Moore 1988).

As part of these efforts, police have increasingly relied on stop-and-frisk tactics. For many years, the courts have allowed the police to stop, frisk, and detain someone simply on the basis of "suspicion" (*Terry v. Ohio* 1968). However, the suspicion was connected with the potential for violence and/or the presence of weapons. Now, the suspicion is that the suspect is carrying illegal drugs from one location to another, which does not present the same immediate danger in most circumstances. Typically, the police will have time to apply for a search warrant once the presumed drugs have arrived at their destination (cf. Finkelman 1990). In any event, the "suspicion" often depends on the officer's profile of a drug courier, which may result in the stopping and hassling of many innocent citizens.

Perhaps the most difficult aspect of police crackdowns is knowing where to draw the line between breaking up local street markets and hassling innocent citizens. Clearly, that line has been crossed on occasion, as in the case of Philadelphia's "Operation Cold Turkey," where officers made nearly twice as many arrests for disorderly conduct as they did for narcotics, and the program was stopped after four days because of public complaints and a lawsuit (Kleiman 1988). Often, arrests for narcotics are *not* the primary outcome of police crackdowns. The potential for abuse of police authority in drug enforcement is described by Kleiman (1988, p. 14): "Street enforcement may involve the stopping and questioning of many citizens without any basis for arrest. The difficulty of making narcotics cases that will stand up in court has even driven some narcotics officers to manufacture evidence and to perjure themselves." Yet, for every complaint about crackdowns, police executives and city officials tend to report that the larger problem is community pressure to continue the operation, even when observation indicates that the drug market has been dispersed or eliminated.

If street-level crackdowns were effective at eliminating drug markets, this might take some of the sting out of complaints about civil liberties. However, the evidence is quite mixed and very limited (see Hayeslip 1989; Kleiman et al. 1988; Sherman 1990). Clearly, law enforcement has been able to increase substantially the number of narcotics arrests, and in some cities, effectively disperse drug markets and other criminal activity for short periods. (Even here, the evaluations are very weak and inconclusive.) Still, there is no evidence in larger cities that the targeted drug activity has not been displaced to other locations or that the reduction in activity can be sustained for more than a few months. Sherman (1990) cites six crackdowns where a "residual" deterrent effect was observed, but most of these involved minor offenses. Hence, the general public and policymakers have placed their confidence in programs where the potential costs to individual liberties may be significant and the benefits to the public remains uncertain.

Stops on Highways, at Airports, and Other Locations

As an important component of the drug war, highway patrols have set up roadblocks and profiles to identify persons transporting drugs. The most notorious example comes from Volusia County, Florida, where Sheriff Robert Vogel, Jr. and his officers regularly stop and search cars that fit their profile of a drug courier. The sheriff's office also uses a sign that reads "Narcotics Inspection Ahead," and officers then stop any vehicle that slows or makes a U-turn. If the officers find a large amount of cash, but no drugs, the cash is confiscated and the driver is released (Mydans 1989). The pervasiveness of these practices is unknown, but in Volusia County, the victims are starting to fight back and several lawsuits have been filed.

In addition to highway traffic, law enforcement agents also stop airport travelers who fit their profile of a drug courier. Lawsuits from such stops have generated important legal decisions that extend the *Terry* stop-and-frisk ruling and justify the use of such profiles to stop individuals.

The development of drug courier profiles is now a widely used law enforcement strategy to fight the drug war. The Supreme Court has approved the use of profiles to briefly detain airport travelers and the use of dogs to help locate drugs hidden in luggage. To justify these investigative stops without probable cause, the courts have created the concept of "reasonable suspicion," which allows officers to conclude that criminal activity "may be afoot." What constitutes reasonable suspicion is not clear, but the use of profiles is meant to help clarify matters. According to William Lenck, profiles "represent the collective wisdom of law enforcement personnel, whose experience tells them that individuals who commit certain kinds of offenses tend to look, act, and react in particular ways" (cited in Police Executive Research Forum 1990).

The use of drug courier profiles seems to create a significant legal problem because local profile factors often do not uniquely identify drug couriers and are not based on scientific research. The profile used by Sheriff Vogel, for example, often includes characteristics such as: driving a large car with out-of-state tags, driving at the speed limit to avoid suspicion, driving on a known drug corridor (e.g., Interstate 95), and other descriptors that will produce a large number of "false positive" stops. Such general hunches are not sufficient to justify a warrantless search or seizure under the Constitution and will inconvenience many innocent travelers.

Stops by DEA agents at the bus station in Buffalo, New York, illustrate this point. Agents reported stopping and searching approximately eighty passengers per month who fit their drug courier profile, but this activity resulted in only three to four arrests on average (Finkelman 1990). Even when law enforcement officers have "reasonable suspicion" (and not just a nonspecific hunch) that the person is carrying drugs, the stop-and-frisk tactic can be overused.

One of the major problems with the use of profiles is that minorities are too easily singled out as fitting the profile of a drug courier. Although few agencies will openly admit to this practice, the disproportionate number of minority arrests for drug offenses certainly raises questions about the fairness of the enforcement process throughout the country.

Housing Sweeps, Raids, and Evictions

Police surveillance and raids of individual dwelling units have long been an important component of the drug war. Most experts now recognize that such activity has little impact on the overall drug problem in a community, either because arrests often do not lead to extended incapacitation or because the arrestees are quickly replaced by other drug offenders in the marketplace. In the present context, the concern is that raids can sometimes victimize innocent residents or be conducted without sufficient evidence. Newsweek reported the consequences of police enforcing the law with the wrong address:

> The Stokes were home watching television early one evening when a heavily armed D.C. SWAT team came crashing through their door. George Stokes was ordered to the floor at gunpoint, somehow sustaining a gash on his head in the process. His wife, understandably terrified, fell down the

cellar stairs as she tried to run away from the band of black-uniformed intruders. (Morganthau 1990, p. 18)

Unfortunately for the D.C. police, a local camera crew was there and captured the entire event on television.

Another controversial enforcement tactic has been the use of sweeps in multifamily units, especially public housing. In many U.S. cities, residents of high-rise public housing have lived in extreme fear as they confront frequent gang violence and drug marketing. They have turned to the housing authorities and police for help and their requests for assistance have been granted. To make it easier to evict drug dealers, the Department of Housing and Urban Development (HUD) has changed its regulations requiring a pre-eviction hearing, and local management has followed up with aggressive sweep programs. Beginning in 1988, the Chicago Housing Authority initiated Operation Clean Sweep, which involves sealing off a particular housing project (sometimes sealed for forty-eight hours), conducting door-to-door inspections, and requiring residents to show identification of residency. Evictions swiftly follow for persons in possession of drugs or living in the building without a lease.

Using asset forfeiture laws, public housing tenants have been swiftly evicted *prior to* any hearing or legal decision regarding the justifiability of such actions. In some cities, innocent tenants have been evicted because another member of their household was suspected of a drug violation. In Berkeley, California, Alexandria, Virginia, and other places, tenants have found themselves evicted and federal rent subsidies stopped when evidence of drug dealing was found in their home, *regardless* of whether they were involved in any way (Mydans 1989).

HUD has spotlighted Chicago's Operation Clean Sweep as a national model for other housing authorities to replicate. A successful lawsuit by the ACLU has forced the Chicago Housing Authority to modify its program to provide additional protection of individual rights and due process. (See Juffer 1990, for a critique of the program.) In Los Angeles, police paid $3 million to settle a suit by residents of public housing regarding the use of warrantless searches.

The public housing sweeps have an important component that should not be overlooked. Apparently, the majority of residents are strongly supportive of the sweeps and want them to continue. Vince Lane, the widely respected executive director of the Chicago Housing Authority, reports that he cannot keep up with the number of tenant requests for sweeps, and he is convinced that the program is restoring the rights and freedoms of good tenants who want to live in a safe, drug-free environment. Laurence H. Tribe, a constitutional expert at Harvard Law, offers a slightly different perspective: "Whole communities in public housing, because they see themselves as victims of drug violence, willingly invite the police to cut procedural corners to conduct what amounts to kangaroo courts aimed at expelling suspected drug dealers" (Treaster 1990).

Use of Anonymous Tips

Anonymous informants have been used effectively to identify drug dealers since the early 1970s, and recently, they have worked closely with police investigators to report drug activity through programs such as Crime Stoppers or local drug hot lines (see Rosenbaum, Lurigio, and Lavrakas 1987). Thousands of anonymous hot lines are currently being used in the drug war, both by police agencies and by private employers. While the provision of anonymity allows informants to report illegal drug activity without fear of retaliation, it has also opened the door to potential abuses of this privilege and to false reporting of information about neighbors, acquaintances, lovers, competitors, and others without sanction. Nevertheless, the courts have generally upheld the use of anonymous tips as providing "reasonable suspicion" (in the totality of the circumstances) and, therefore, as a justification for investigatory stops, consent searches, or other police contacts. Again, citizens have shown a strong willingness to participate as informants in these programs without reservation.

Asset Forfeiture

To date, the most powerful weapon employed in the drug war has been the seizure of personal assets. In general, the public and community organizations have endorsed asset forfeiture programs, expressing only one reservation—that they have not been able to share in the proceeds.[1]

Asset forfeiture is defined as "the divestiture without compensation of property used in a manner contrary to the laws of the sovereign" (*U.S. v. Rhodesian Stone Statutes*, C.D. Cal. 1978). The 1984 Comprehensive Forfeiture Act allows the government to seize all property derived from illegal drug sales or property used "in any manner or part" to violate federal drug laws. The primary intent of the law was to prevent drug profits from being sheltered and reinvested in future illegal activity, but forfeiture laws have also become a major source of revenue for law enforcement. During the 1990 fiscal year, the Drug Enforcement Administration alone made 18,293 domestic seizures of nondrug property, worth more than $1 billion (Timrots, Byrne, and Finn 1991).

One of the major concerns regarding asset seizure programs is that the fundamental presumption of innocence in our justice system is often ignored. As Finkelman (1990, p. 51) notes, "the law allows the sequestration of private property solely on the basis of suspicion or indictment." Hence, tenants have been evicted; subsidies stopped; bank accounts frozen; and cars, houses, boats, and other property seized *prior to* any trial. Being accused (not convicted) is sufficient for a citizen to lose virtually all of his/her assets. Furthermore, forfeiture laws typically allow law enforcement officers to seize a person's property even if he/she is unaware than the property was used to house or transport drugs.

The CBS news program "Street Stories" (July 9, 1992) described the case of the Swickla family, whose home was seized by federal prosecutor Leslie Ohta. The prosecutor admitted that the house was never searched for marijuana and the sole piece of evidence was the testimony of a former drug dealer, who apparently was told that his sentence would be reduced if he turned in another drug offender. The Swickla family has paid over $30,000 in legal fees to defend themselves against these charges. CBS referred to this story as the "90s version of McCarthyism."

Even citizens who take actions against drug users can find themselves the victims of this powerful law enforcement weapon. When Gussy May Grant's husband passed away, grandchild and other friends moved in with her and brought along a lifestyle of illegal drug use. Fed up but unable to persuade them to leave, this sixty-nine-year-old woman called the police to have them removed. When she refused to press drug charges, the police seized her house (Gross 1992).

Asset seizure seems to shift the burden of proof from the state to the defendant, who must prove that he/she is innocent and/or that the seized property was not used for drug activity. Moreover, regardless of one's innocence or guilt, the defendant would have difficulty obtaining the necessary resources for a legal defense. Because the law generally allows for the seizure of drug-generated assets that are transferred to third parties, it effectively prevents suspected drug dealers from hiring qualified defense attorneys, since attorneys' fees can be seized by the prosecution. Providing the government with this degree of control over defense attorneys also raises questions about whether defendants' right to a counsel (Sixth Amendment) has been jeopardized.

For big drug dealers, with substantial assets, these concerns about civil liberties may seem trivial and the public's sympathy may be limited. But for the "little guy" at the other end of the economic scale, the situation is quite different. While asset forfeiture laws were intended for the "big fish" involved in organized crime, the fact remains that the vast majority of seizures involve smaller items seized from the "small fish" (McAnany 1991). In fact, persons living in poverty are often the target of these enforcement initiatives. In Lawrence, Massachusetts, for example, the police have confiscated Medicaid and food stamp identification cards for individuals arrested (but not convicted) for drug violations.

Privatizing Public Areas with Barricades

Fearful that crime and drugs are out of control, some communities have taken the extreme measure of erecting street barriers on public streets to exclude the criminally minded from entering the area. In a dozen Miami neighborhoods, citizens have blocked off public streets with orange barrels and some have established checkpoints with private guards (Schmalz 1988). The guards serve as gatekeepers to the area—they stop cars, question the drivers, record license plates of suspicious vehicles, and control the gate. Obviously, the guards are legally required to let all cars pass through, but the stop is intended to deter some vehicles. The dangers of abuse are always present in this type of arrangement, and there is legitimate concern that minorities will be stopped more frequently.

Similarly, in 1990, the Los Angeles Police Department began "Operation Cul-de-Sac" in several neighborhoods by installing concrete barricades and signs which read "Open to Residents Only" (Baker, Rogers, and Annin 1990). One difference between the Miami and L.A. programs is that in L.A., the police are conducting drug and gang crackdowns within the barricaded areas. Before implementing the program in the first neighborhood, L.A. police conducted a survey of 563 residents and found that 558 supported their plans to intervene. As one resident told *Newsweek*, "I will readily accept anything that will make a difference." The police have plans to implement the program throughout Los Angeles.

Gang Membership and Anti-Loitering Enforcement

Now that gangs are being blamed for much of the urban violence and drug marketing, a law enforcement crackdown on gang membership is gaining momentum. Among the more extreme actions are laws which outlaw gang membership or gang association. The ordinance in Seminole County, Florida, makes it a crime to be a gang member. Similarly, a wide range of antiloitering laws have been created or "dusted off" in recent years. In Washington, D.C., an antiloitering ordinance gives police the power to close off certain streets, order everyone out, and arrest persons who gather in a group of two or more. In Chicago, a 1992 antiloitering law gives police the authority to disperse any group of two or more individuals when one of them is a known gang member (Davis 1992). Enforcing this ordinance will require police to develop accurate lists of known gang members. Most of these antiloitering ordinances appear to be in conflict with the First Amendment right to free association, and, therefore, a challenge to their constitutionality can be expected. In Los Angeles, the ACLU blocked the city's attempt to require residents of a particular neighborhood (troubled by gangs) to carry proof of residency in that area, similar to South Africa's "pass laws" (Morganthau 1990).

Whether or not the constitutional protections guaranteed in the Bill of Rights are being squeezed by the above-mentioned enforcement programs could be the subject of legitimate debate, but these are not the most extreme proposals or enforcement programs. Some examples include: a proposal by the Delaware State Senate to institute public whippings for drug dealers (Mydans 1989); a request by Aldermen Edward Smith in Chicago to bring in the national guard to help fight crime and drugs in his community (Geller 1990); the deportation of immigrants arrested for gang activity in forty-one Chicago suburbs (Houston 1992); and a random drug testing program required of all sixth, seventh, and eight graders at St. Sabina's Roman Catholic Church in Chicago.

The Problem of Race

The civil liberties of most Americans are not immediately threatened by the enforcement programs described above. The most aggressive initiatives are typically carried out in low-income neighborhoods comprised largely of African-Americans, Hispanics, or other minorities. As a result, our nation's jails and prisons are presently overcrowded with minorities.

In urban areas across the country, African-Americans and Hispanics are disproportionately subject to arrest on drug charges. In Washington, D.C., a study by the Rand Corporation found that 99 percent of the adults charged with drug distribution between 1985 and 1987 were African-Americans (Reuter, MacCoun, and Murphy 1990). In Texas, Tackett (1990) reports that most of the defendants in drug cases are poor Hispanics who had dropped out of high school. In New Jersey, the aggressiveness of the highway patrol is apparent in one study conducted by the Public Defender's office: Although African-Americans comprised less than 5 percent of all travelers on the New Jersey Turnpike with out-of-state plates, they comprised more than three-quarters of those arrested on drug and weapons charges, and only 40 percent of the arrests state-wide (see Sullivan 1990).

As a result of these arrest patterns, our jails, prisons, and probation systems are being filled with minorities. The Washington, D.C. Sentencing Project reported that roughly one-in-four African-American males in the 20-29 age range is under the control of the corrections system.

The differential rate of contact with the criminal justice system can be directly linked to the drug war on the streets. The Uniform Crime Reports offer a clear picture of the pattern of arrest by race for the nation as a whole (FBI 1991): In 1990, 43 percent of the persons 18 and older who were arrested and charged with drug abuse violations were African-American (56% were white). For drug arrestees under 18, the majority were African-American (51% vs. 48% white), yet African-Americans accounted for only 28 percent of *all* teen arrests. Thus, the drug crackdown seems to be especially harsh on minority teens.

More evidence of a crackdown on minority youths comes from national data on youth detention facilities (Snyder 1990): Between 1985 and 1987, the number of minority youths (African-American and Hispanic) held in public detention facilities increased by more than 30 percent, while the number of white youths detained increased by only 1 percent.

If minorities are using substantially more drugs than whites, perhaps the above arrest and detention statistics would not be so surprising. But the racial distribution of illegal drug use in America is inconsistent with this pattern of arrests. Specifically, the *vast majority* of individuals who use illegal drugs are white—not African-American or Hispanic. A look at data on the most widely used illegal substances provides the documentation: The 1990 National Household Survey on Drug Abuse shows that 34 percent of whites aged 12 and older have used marijuana in their lifetime, compared with less than 32 percent of African-Americans and 30 percent of the Hispanic population (National Institute on Drug Abuse 1991). Stated differently, the 65.5 million marijuana users include 53.5 million whites, 7.3 million African-Americans, and 4.7 million Hispanics. Similarly, whites are more likely than minorities to have used the drug at the center of the drug war—cocaine (11.7% of whites vs. 10.0% of African-Americans vs. 11.5% of Hispanics).

Going to the heart of the problem, new search and seizure laws, police crackdowns, and other aggressive enforcement plans have given police additional discretionary powers, allowing them to develop profiles and make stops on the basis of "suspicion" and/or prior experience as a police officer. This approach to the drug war is likely to encourage prejudicial responses that are unfavorable to disadvantaged and minority communities, whereby skin color is too often associated with drug activity. Clearly, stop-and-frisk tactics in Los Angeles and Boston have already aroused complaints about police harassment of minorities (Morganthau 1990). Unfortunately, at a time when community policing practices are being praised and widely implemented, the current rules of the drug war can heighten the tension between the police and minority communities, even though community residents have, themselves, demanded these crackdowns.

Public Opinion: Who Supports Aggressive Enforcement?

Aggressive enforcement programs to stop illegal drug traffic have received mixed support. Some news reporters, civil libertarians, academics, and community leaders have express concern and even condemnation of these new programs, arguing that civil liberties are being eroded. However, a different viewpoint is offered by many local residents, who often express support for these aggressive antidrug activities.

Americans appear willing to sacrifice some liberties to enhance public safety and reduce crime and drug abuse. A 1989 national survey by Gallup found that, when given a choice, most Americans (79%) are more worried about "some criminals being let off too easily" than they are about the "constitutional rights of some people accused of committing a crime" (16%). However, when asked about specific situations, the public is not willing to endorse all intrusive police actions. The same national poll found that most Americans (again 79%) are opposed to allowing the police to search a home without a warrant.

A Study of Citizens' Beliefs

To shed some light on the nature and extent of public support for individual liberties in the context of aggressive antidrug programs, the author conducted a study of community perceptions and attitudes. Survey data were collected in six low-income neighborhoods in the Bronx, Chicago, Cleveland, Hartford, Oakland, and Waterloo, Iowa, as part of an evaluation of the Community Responses to Drug Abuse (CRDA) demonstration. These inner-city, predominantly minority neighborhoods were targeted for antidrug programs by local community organizations because the areas were judged to have significant crime and drug abuse problems. Random samples of residents in each neighborhood were drawn using reverse directories. In the fall of 1989, telephone interviews were completed with 1,168 respondents.

Because these data were collected from persons living in neighborhoods with relatively severe drug problems, the question remained whether similar beliefs about individual liberties would be held by a broader sample of citizens. To examine this question, one survey question about civil liberties and enforcement was included on the annual Chicago Area Survey Project conducted by the Northwestern University Survey Laboratory. Using the random digit dialing technique, this telephone survey captured a random sample of residents (including unlisted phone numbers) in the Chicago metropolitan area. The coverage was very broad, including urban and suburban residents of Cook, DuPage, and Lake County. In contrast to the neighborhood samples, which were predominantly minority residents from working and lower class families, this metropolitan sample of 1,026 residents was considerably more representative of the nation as a whole.

Extent of Belief in Individual Rights

The six-city neighborhood-level survey included three questions pertaining to the respondent's belief in individual rights (or conversely, the respondent's support for strong police enforcement powers). As shown in

Table 1
Citizens' Beliefs about Individual Rights (vs Police Enforcement Powers)*

Statement	*Response Options (%)*			
	Agree Strongly	Agree Somewhat	Disagree Somewhat	Disagree Strongly
A. The government should have the right to seize the property of suspected drug dealers, even before they have gone to trial.	47.1	17.4	16.5	19.0
B. The government should have the right to evict suspected drug dealers from their homes, even if they haven't been convicted in court.	31.2	16.6	22.6	29.6
C. The police should have the right to round up suspected drug users, even if they don't have specific evidence against them.				
Inner-city Neighborhoods	37.4	20.0	18.7	24.0
Chicago Metropolitan Area	12.3	35.1	38.8	13.7

*N=1168 for inner-city neighborhoods; N=1026 for Chicago Metropolitan Area.

Table 1, two items (a and b) focused on suspected drug *dealers* and whether the government should be allowed to seize their property or evict them prior to trial. A third item (c) focused on drug *users* and whether the police should be allowed to round them up "even if they don't have specific evidence against them." This item was included on both the neighborhood surveys and the Chicago metropolitan area survey.

The results shown in Table 1 indicate that a *majority* of residents living in neighborhoods with high drug activity were in favor of aggressive police actions to seize the property of suspected drug dealers prior to trial (64.5%) and to "round up" suspected drug users without specific evidence against them (57.4%). Furthermore, nearly half (47.8%) of the local residents were in favor of evicting suspected drug dealers prior to trial.

In these inner-city neighborhoods, the frustration with open drug markets and violent crime may have driven many local residents to reduce their support for civil liberties in exchange for a possible reduction in these visible problems by means of enforcement. The question is whether this same pattern of results would be found in a metropolitan area sample in which most respondents do *not* live in high-drug areas. As shown in Table 1, support for aggressive enforcement against suspected drug users is not as strong in the random sample of Chicago area residents (47.4%) as it is in high-drug neighborhoods (57.4%). Apparently, when respondents live outside "the war zone" and do not see the drug markets and criminal violence on a daily basis, they can afford to express more support for civil liberties.

Who Believes in Individual Rights?

Within the inner-city neighborhoods, responses to the three questions showed considerable variation of opinion. When faced with the same set of neighborhood conditions, the question becomes—Who in the community is inclined to support aggressive enforcement programs to stop drug activity and who is inclined to oppose such actions because of concern about encroachment upon individual liberties?

To address this question, the three survey items were combined to form a single index of Belief in Individual Rights.[2] Several variables were identified as potential predictors of residents' tendency to support either individual rights or aggressive enforcement.

The general notion which guided the first hypothesis can be stated as follows: When community residents perceive a threat to their safety, property, or their neighborhood as a result of the drug problem, they will be motivated to endorse whatever action is deemed necessary to eliminate this threat. In the context of a challenge to civil liberties, the first hypothesis can be stated as follows: The greater the perceived threat, the more inclined residents will be to relinquish constitutionally guaranteed liberties in favor of drug enforcement. Threat was measured in several ways: fear of victimization (two separate items: personal and property crime), prior victimization experience (two separate items: personal and property crime), and perceptions of the severity of the drug/crime problem.[3]

A second hypothesis focuses on the perceived efficacy of actions by individual citizens versus police enforcement programs. Theoretically, the drug threat can be eliminated by the actions of individual citizens or by working with the police to forcibly remove the drug offender. The second hypothesis can be stated as follows: When residents lack confidence in their own ability to improve the neighborhood, they will be more inclined to support aggressive police action at the cost of civil liberties. Furthermore, residents will be more likely to support antidrug enforcement programs (and sacrifice liberties) when they believe that such enforcement programs are effective in removing the drug problem.[4]

Finally, a third hypothesis focused on several demographic correlates of the Belief-in-Individual-Rights index. Assuming that minorities and women would perceive the drug problem as a greater threat to their community (as documented in the fear of crime literature), they were expected to be more supportive of police crackdowns than their counterparts. Also, civil liberties should receive less support from residents with less income and education. This prediction is based on the idea that such individuals may have less awareness of their constitutional rights and probably had greater exposure to aggressive police behavior, which may desensitize them to such actions.

Survey Results

Logistic regression was used to test the above-stated hypotheses and generate the best model for predicting Belief in Individual Rights.

Table 2 shows the regression results from the neighborhood-level surveys. The data were not supportive of the first hypothesis. Residents' attitudes about individual liberties were not influenced by their fear of victimization, victimization history, or perceptions of the severity of the crime/drug problem. Some confirmation of the hypothesis could be found in data showing that parents who were worried about their children's safety were less supportive of individual liberties (i.e., suspects rights) than parents who were not afraid for their children (not shown in Table 2). Furthermore, the fact that respondents in the Chicago metropolitan survey, with a broader sample (including nonurban residents from less threatening environments), were less enthusiastic about aggressive enforcement than the inner-city samples (see Table 1) might be construed as indirect support for the threat hypothesis.

The second hypothesis could only be tested with the neighborhood-level data, but the results provided consistent support for this prediction. Residents' endorsement of individual rights was weakened (and their support for strong police action was strengthened) when they: (a) lacked confidence in their own ability to improve the neighborhood, and (b) be-

Table 2
Logistic Regression Results for Factors Predicting
Belief in Individual Rights

Predictor Variables	Wald Statistic	(Standard Error)
African-American	0 .08	(.19)
Hispanic	3 .80*	(.30)
Gender	0 .28	(.17)
Age	6 .77**	(.07)
Income	0 .09	(.09)
Education	24 .15***	(.11)
Occupancy Status	0 .02	(.19)
Fear of Personal Crime	0 .63	(.09)
Fear of Property Crime	2 .19	(.08)
Victim of Personal Crime	1 .19	(.24)
Victim of Property Crime	0 .16	(.23)
Perceived Individual Efficacy	3 .11 ms	(.09)
Perceived Program Effectiveness	17 .54***	(.24)
Perceived Severity of Problem	0 .89	(.17)

N = 703
ms = marginally significant, p < .10
* p < .05
** p < .01
*** p < .001

lieved more strongly in the effectiveness of antidrug enforcement programs. The latter was the stronger predictor of belief in individual rights.[5]

Finally, demographic variables were among the strongest predictors of belief in individual liberties. In the inner-city samples, persons with less education and Hispanics were significantly less supportive of individual liberties and more supportive of aggressive enforcement than their counterparts. Being African-American or from a low-income household, however, did not have an independent effect upon one's belief in individual rights after controlling for the effects of other variables.

Overall, the pattern of results produced from the Chicago metropolitan survey was similar to the neighborhood samples. As shown in Table 3, a good set of demographic predictors emerged from this logistic regression analysis. The strongest predictors of belief in individual rights were race

Table 3
Logistic Regression Results for Factors Predicting Belief in Individual Rights: Chicago Metropolitan Area Random Sample

Predictor Variables	Wald Statistic	(Standard Error)
African-American	10 .67***	(.19)
Hispanic	9 .24**	(.32)
Gender	6 .48**	(.15)
Age	2 .75	(.08)
Income	14 .80***	(.07)
Education	4 .71**	(.07)
Occupancy Status	4 .63*	(.18)

N = 834
* p < .05
** p < .01
*** p < .001

and income: African-Americans, Hispanics, and persons of lower income were the most willing to discard individual protections in favor of aggressive police enforcement. In addition, support for individual rights was weaker among females, renters, and persons with less education. Age was not a significant predictor of belief in individual liberties.[6]

While confirming the general pattern of findings at the neighborhood level, the metropolitan survey results also show that African-Americans (as well as Hispanics) were less supportive of individual liberties than whites. Furthermore, this survey underscored the importance of income, which may be a surrogate measure of exposure to disorder, crime, and drug markets. Again, persons of low income were significantly less tolerant of drug users and less respectful of their rights than persons of higher income, perhaps because of their greater exposure to the violent and disorderly aspects of the drug market. In the inner-city samples, the effects of race and income may have been weakened by the lack of variance.

The demographic findings from the metropolitan survey are illustrated in Table 4. The differences are sizable and dramatic. To summarize, supporters of strong police intervention against drug users tend to be persons of less income and less education, as well as females, renters, and minorities. In addition, the neighborhood inner-city surveys showed that

Table 4
Belief in Individual Rights as a Function of Personal Characteristics:
Chicago Metropolitan Area Random Sample

Personal Characteristics	Belief in Individual Rights *(% Who Agree that Police Should "Round Up" Suspected Drug Users Even without Sufficient Evidence)*
Race	
Hispanic	73.7
African-American	59.5
White	42.5
Education	
Some High School or less	74.6
High School Graduate	51.0
Some College	44.6
College Graduate or more	39.9
Income	
$20,000 or less	61.4
$20,001-$40,000	52.0
$40,001 or more	35.7
Gender	
Female	53.4
Male	43.0

N=1,026

persons who were willing to exchange individual liberties for strong police powers were more likely to believe in the effectiveness of enforcement programs for stopping drugs, and lack confidence that individual citizens can make a difference by themselves. Taken as a whole, the findings are consistent with the general argument that the most disadvantaged residents and those who feel a lack of power to correct the drug problem by themselves will call upon the police to "do whatever it takes" to remove the local drug problem.

Conclusions

This chapter has addressed what is believed to be a critical issue in the "drug war," namely, balancing society's need to maintain a safe and secure community with every individual's need to be protected against unreasonable searches, seizures, and other intrusions by government. Several arguments have been developed, either explicitly or implicitly: (1) that the rhetoric of the "drug war" (and the crisis mentality engendered by this terminology) has provided the justification for additional police powers that would be unnecessary during "peace time"; (2) that many community-based antidrug initiatives have worked to strengthen aggressive enforcement programs rather than focus on preventing crime and rebuilding communities; (3) that some street-level enforcement programs, *as currently practiced*, stand as a threat to civil liberties; (4) that this threat is more real and substantial in inner-city minority communities where race and crime are often confused; (5) that most citizens support the "war on drugs" and are willing to sacrifice some liberties to achieve a police crackdown on drug dealers and users; and (6) that public support for aggressive enforcement is the strongest among persons most likely to be the target of that enforcement, namely African-Americans, Hispanics, low income residents, renters, and persons of limited education.

Many writers and commentators have recognized the potential dangers to individual freedom that are presented by the war on drugs, but few have recognized the central role of the community in supporting these actions. If nothing else, this chapter highlights the importance of community support for law enforcement policies, and in doing so, points to the complex (and seemingly contradictory) nature of inner-city community attitudes about policing. Residents of neighborhoods with visible drug markets have repeatedly called for police crackdowns on their own neighbors and their calls have been heard. Yet prior surveys have documented that minorities are strongly opposed to police use of excessive force—more so than whites. For several years, these competing forces have caused this author to speculate about when a backlash would emerge (Rosenbaum 1990). As it turns out, the anger exploded in 1992 when the acquittal of Los Angeles police officers for the severe beating of Rodney King opened the door to a new round of urban riots. While police brutality is universally condemned (because of its relatively indisputable and visible nature), the loss of privacy, personal property, and other infringements upon individual liberties are subtle and protracted police actions whose fairness and adverse consequences are not readily apparent to the observer. As a result, the public does not always see the price tag of aggressive stops and searches, until it is too late.

While it is certainly not "too late" to protect the constitutionally guaranteed freedoms that have made this country a very desirable place to live, the present trend is sufficiently troublesome that policy analysts would be remiss not to conduct a careful cost-benefit analysis of the drug war at the street level. On the benefit side, the public has endorsed these enforcement programs because *they believe that such actions are the most effective way to reduce the drug problem.* Unfortunately, the evaluation literature on this subject is very limited and has given insufficient attention to critical issues such as the possible displacement of drug markets, the frequency of illegal searches or seizures (and the number of "false positives"), and most importantly, the long-term effects of these programs on drugs and crime.

The potential costs of aggressive street-level enforcement are noteworthy. In addition to possible violations of civil liberties, serious consideration must be given to (1) the intensification of violent crime that can result from tightening or displacing drug markets; (2) the adverse effects on the overall administration of justice that accrue from overloading our courts with drug cases at the expense of other criminal and civil matters (Labaton 1989), and (3) the potential damage to police-community relations that can result from these confrontations.

Although the vast majority of illegal drugs are consumed by whites and not by minorities, the visibility of inner-city drug markets and the pleas for outside intervention have led to a concentration of police crackdowns in minority neighborhoods. The urban riots of 1992 have caused our nation to become more introspective in the search for causes (e.g., see *Newsweek*, May 18, 1992; *U.S. News and World Report*, May 11, 1992). Not only is there a "new" recognition that the problems of the ghetto are a reflection of rising poverty and urban neglect, there is a growing awareness of the extent to which these communities have been victimized by police actions and prejudicially characterized by outsiders as places where only criminals reside. The sense of injustice that runs through the urban ghetto seems to be at an all-time high. As the anger continues to fester, we must carefully examine our policing strategies to make sure that the most popular antidrug initiatives ultimately serve to strengthen (rather than weaken) the target communities.

In the midst of all this critical "outside" analysis, the community's perspective must not be lost. Academics, news reporters, and civil libertarians can easily stand back and criticize the police, the government, and the community for promoting aggressive programs at the expense of individual liberties. But often these critics enjoy liberties that are denied on a daily basis to honest, decent citizens who live in high-crime, high-drug neighborhoods. Drive-by shootings, open-air drug markets, gangs hanging out, street hassles, and other daily threats to safety can generate extreme levels of fear of crime, self-imposed behavioral restrictions, and other measures to protect oneself and loved ones. The civil rights of drug dealers and users seem unimportant in an environment where law-abiding citizens no longer feel free to leave their home for groceries or to sit out on their front porches during hot summer days. Residents have become so fed up that they have asked the police to "do whatever it takes" to correct these conditions.

Understanding and sympathizing with these angers and frustrations does not imply that one approves any particular solution to this problem. While the government has viewed these crackdowns as a means to redress the perceived imbalance between individual and community rights, in a free society, every possible effort must be made to protect individual liberties, despite the level of threat that is perceived. As Morgan (1991) reminds us, "Without a doubt, law enforcement's primary responsibilities are to uphold the law *and* to protect civil liberties." To insure that this happens, police officers must be extremely well trained, knowing what rights citizens are entitled to, knowing how to respect citizens' privacy and human dignity, and knowing that the abuse of police powers is morally and legally intolerable. Similarly, the time has come for citizens to be thoroughly educated about their own rights, as reflected in the Bill of Rights, so that abuses of authority can be detected and reported. *Good* law enforcement and civil liberties should never be incompatible!

In the final analysis, the real question is this—Are these street-level enforcement programs the best investment of scarce resources, and have we thoroughly explored alternative strategies for reducing the drug problem? Certainly, crackdowns and other intrusive initiatives play an important function in dispersing visible drug problems, at least in the short run. If these enforcement programs continue to expand, however, it is this author's opinion that they will conflict with a multitude of community policing strategies designed to develop a trusting relationship between the police and the community they serve (cf. Rosenbaum,

Hernandez, and Daughtry 1991). While enforcement activities may solve immediate problems, a permanent reduction in crime and disorder problems will require the establishment of informal social controls or mechanisms for neighborhood self-regulation (Rosenbaum 1988; Skogan 1990), as well as a broad-based willingness to address the "root causes" or social problems underlying criminality (Rosenbaum 1991). Self-regulating communities are places where local residents trust each other, trust the police, and feel sufficiently efficacious to work with government and other service agencies to solve or at least contain a wide range of social problems. Anonymous tip lines, surveillance cameras, door-to-door consent searches, buy-and-busts, and other antidrug programs, when not used judiciously, are incompatible with the development of trust, cooperation, and community efficacy.

Finally, to conclude that the police regularly abuse their authority would be misleading. Oftentimes, they are simply doing their job as mandated by the general public and as legalized by the courts. The record clearly indicates that, over the past decade, the courts have expanded police powers in the area of search and seizure to combat what the public saw as a national crisis in the late 1980s. Although the drug problem is no longer front page news, the additional police authority remains intact and will be used as needed for other criminal investigations. In 1989, 64 percent of the American public felt that drugs were "the most important problem facing the country," but three years later (1992), only 2 percent of the public still held this to be true (CBS/*New York Times* polls, cited in Treaster 1992). Despite this change in public sentiment, the machinery and policies of the drug war is in place and working harder than ever.

This situation underscores the importance of citizen participation in the planning, implementation, and evaluation of all antidrug or anticrime programs that may affect their lives. Ultimately, government must continue to operate by "the consent of the governed." The public should be fully knowledgeable of the many alternatives to enforcement and be given opportunities to participate in decisions about how best to improve public safety. Furthermore, with education and empowerment, community residents are better equipped to communicate their desire to protect one of our nation's greatest assets—the promise to safeguard individual liberties from excessive government intervention.

For better or worse, the final responsibility for police *and* community actions rests with those being served by such actions. Consequently, it is incumbent upon the citizenry to continuously monitor and evaluate anticrime and antidrug initiatives, making every effort to determine whether these programs and policies are sensible, measured, and appropriate to the problem at hand. Justice Thurgood Marshall, in his 1989 dissent from the court's decision to support random drug testing of railway workers, summarized the problem this way:

> Precisely because the need for action against the drug scourge is manifest, the need for vigilance against unconstitutional excess is great. History teaches that grave threats to liberty often come in times of urgency, when constitutional rights seem too extravagant to endure. (Mydans 1989)

Notes

This chapter originally appeared in *Drugs and the Community: Involving Community Residents in Combating the Sale of Illegal Drugs,* edited by Robert C. Davis, Arthur J. Lurigio, and Dennis P. Rosenbaum, 1993, pp. 55-82, Springfield, IL, Charles C. Thomas. It is reprinted here with permission. Research findings reported in this chapter were supported under award #89-IJ-CX-0026 from the National Institute of Justice. Points of view expressed in this chapter are those of the author and do not necessarily represent the official position of the U.S. Department of Justice.

1. At present, most of the revenues from seizures are returned to law enforcement agencies to strengthen their drug enforcement programs.

2. Reliability analysis indicates that these items "hang together" reasonably well, with an alpha coefficient of .78.

3. A five-item Problem Severity index was formed after factor analysis confirmed unidimensionality and reliability analysis produced an alpha coefficient of .84.

4. Program effectiveness was measured using a nine-item unidimensional index, with an alpha of .78. Each item asked respondents to rate the effectiveness of specific antidrug strategies on a four-point scale ("very effective" to "not very effective"). Most of the items dealt with joint police-citizen enforcement programs (e.g., drug hot lines, patrols/watches, stiffer penalties around schools). Perceived individual efficacy was measured by a single item that asked respondents "Overall, how much of an effect can a citizen, like yourself, have on reducing problems in your neighborhood?" (4-point scale ranging from "Big effect" to "No effect").

5. The effect of individual efficacy was only marginally significant, $p < .07$.

6. A closer look at the age distribution revealed that persons under 60

share similar beliefs about the need to protect individual rights, while those over 60 would rather see suspected drug users arrested.

References

Baker, J. N., P. Rogers, and P. Annin. 1990. "The 'Walled Cities' of L.A." *Newsweek*, May 14, pp. 24-25.

Bush, G. H. W. 1991. "President's Anti-crime Address" before law enforcement executives in Washington DC, National Public Radio, March 5.

CBS News. 1992. "Street Stories," with Ed Bradley, July 9.

Davis, R. 1992. "Loitering Law Clears Hurdle Despite Fears." *Chicago Tribune*, May 19, sec. 2, p. 1.

Federal Bureau of Investigation. 1991. *Crime in the United States.* 1990 Washington, DC: U.S. Government Printing Office.

Finkelman, P. 1990. "The Second Casualty of War: Civil Liberties and the War on Drugs." Paper presented at the annual meeting of the American Society of Criminology, Baltimore, November.

Gallup, G. Jr. 1989. *The Gallup Report*, Report No. 285. Princeton, NJ: The Gallup Poll, June.

Geller, W. A. 1990. "A Crime-Ridden Ward's Cry for Help." *Chicago Tribune*, May 16, sec. 1, p. 20.

Gross, G. 1992. "The Osgood File, CBS News" WBBM Radio, Chicago, July 26.

Hayeslip, D. W., Jr. 1989. "Local-Level Drug Enforcement: New strategies." *NIJ Reports*, No. 213, March/April.

Houston, J. 1992. "Deportation Gaining as Gang-Fighting Tool: Critics Raise Civil Rights Questions." *Chicago Tribune*, July 6, sec. 1, p.1.

Juffer, J. 1990. "Clean Sweep's Dirty Secret." *Chicago Reader* 20, no. 1 (October 5).

Kleiman, M. A. R. 1988. "Crackdowns: The Effects of Intensive Enforcement on Retail Heroin Dealing." In *Street-level drug enforcement: Examining the Issues*, edited by M. A. R. Kleiman. Washington, DC: National Institute of Justice.

Kleiman, M. A. R., A. Barnett, A. V. Bouza, and K. M. Burke. 1988. *Street-level Drug Enforcement: Examining the Issues.* Washington, DC: National Institute of Justice.

Labaton, S. 1989. "New Tactics in The War On Drugs Tilt Scales of Justice Off Balance." *New York Times*, December 29, sec. 1, p. 1.

Lane, V. 1991. "At Issue." Interviewed on Chicago's WBBM 78am radio April 21.

McAnany, P. 1991. "Asset Forfeiture as Policy." A paper delivered at the 1991 International Conference on Law and Society, Amsterdam, Netherlands, June.

Moore, M. 1988. "Drug Trafficking." *Crime File Study Guide*, Washington, DC: National Institute of Justice.

Morgan, R. 1991. "Knock and Talk: Consent Searches and Civil Liberties." *FBI Law Enforcement Bulletin* (November): 6-10.

Morganthau, T. 1990. "Uncivil Liberties: Debating Whether Drug-War Tactics Are Eroding Constitutional Rights." *Newsweek*, April 23, pp. 18-20.

Mydans, S. 1989. "Powerful Arms of Drug War Arousing Concern About Rights." *New York Times*, October 16, sec. 1, p. 1.

National Institute on Drug Abuse. 1991. *National Household Survey on Drug Abuse: Population Estimates 1990.* Washington, DC: U.S. Government Printing Office.

Police Executive Research Forum. 1990. "Use of Drug Courier Profiles." *Asset Forfeiture Bulletin* (May):1.

Reuter, P. 1988. "Can the Borders be Sealed?" *The Public Interest* 2: 51-152.

Reuter, P., R. MacCoun, and P. Murphy. 1990. *Money from Crime: A Study of the Economics of Drug Dealing in Washington DC.* Santa Monica, CA: Rand Corporation.

Rosenbaum, D. P. 1988. "Community Crime Prevention: A Review and Synthesis of the Literature." *Justice Quarterly* 5: 323-95.

———. 1990. "Community Empowerment and the War on Drugs: Balancing the Rights of Individuals and Society on the Battlefield." Presentation before the Faculty of the School of Public and Environmental Affairs, Indiana University at Indianapolis, April 25.

———. 1991 "The Pursuit of 'Justice' in the United States: A Policy Lesson in the War on Crime and Drugs?" *Canadian Police College Journal* 15: 239-55.

Rosenbaum, D. P., S. F. Bennett, B. D. Lindsay, D. L. Wilkinson, B. Davis, C. Taranowski, and P. J. Lavrakas. 1992. *The Community Responses to Drug Abuse National Demonstration Program Final Process Evaluation Report*, Prepared for the National Institute of Justice. Chicago, IL: Center for Research in Law and Justice, University of Illinois at Chicago.

Rosenbaum, D. P., E. Hernandez, and S. Daughtry, Jr. 1991. "Crime Prevention, Fear Reduction, and the Community." In *Local Government Police Management*, Golden Anniversary Edition, edited by W. A. Geller. Washington DC: International City Management Association.

Rosenbaum, D. P., and A. J. Lurigio. 1985. "Crime Stoppers: Paying the Price." *Psychology Today* (June): 56-61.

Rosenbaum, D. P., A. J. Lurigio, and P. J. Lavrakas. 1987. *Crime Stoppers: A National Evaluation of Program Operations and Effects.* Executive

Summary. Washington DC: U.S. Government Printing Office.

Schmalz, J. 1988. "Fearful and Angry Floridans Erect Street Barriers to Crime." *New York Times*, December 6, sec. 1, p. 1.

Sherman, L. W. 1990. "Police Crackdowns: Initial and Residual Deterrence," In *Crime and Justice*, Vol. 12, edited by M. Tonry and N. Morris. Chicago: University of Chicago Press.

Skogan, W. G. 1990. *Disorder and Decline: Crime and the Spiral of Decay in American Cities*. New York: Free Press.

Snyder, H. H. 1990. "Growth in Minority Detentions Attributed to Drug Law Violators." *Juvenile Justice Bulletin* (Update on Statistics). Reprinted from March, Office of Juvenile Justice and Delinquency Prevention.

Sullivan, J. F. 1990. "New Jersey Police are Accused of Minority Arrest Campaigns." *New York Times*, February 19, sec. B, p. 3.

Tackett, M. 1990. "Drug War Chokes Federal Courts." *Chicago Tribune*, October 14, sec. 1, p. 1.

Terry v. *Ohio*. 1968. 392 U.S. 1.

Timrots, A., C. Byrne, and C. Finn. 1991. "Fact Sheet: Drug Data Summary." Washington DC: Drugs and Crime Data Center and Clearinghouse, Bureau of Justice Statistics, November.

Treaster, J. B. 1990. "Is the Fight on Drugs Eroding Civil Rights?" *New York Times*, May 6, sec. 4, p. 5.

———. 1992. "Some Think the 'War on Drugs' is Being Waged on Wrong Front." *New York Times*, July 28, sec. 1, p. 1.

10

Disorder and the Court

George L. Kelling and Catherine M. Coles

In the current debate over what to do about crime in America, national political leaders focus on the "grand" crime issues—capital punishment, gun control, the length of prison sentences, and the number of police on the streets. But on the local level, the terms of debate are much different. There, the issues may seem relatively trivial: panhandling, lying down in public spaces, public drinking and drug use, prostitution, unsolicited window washing, public urination and defecation, loitering, and graffiti. Yet the skirmishes being fought over these issues in areas such as Boston's Dorchester, San Francisco's Tenderloin area, Milwaukee's Near West Side, Seattle's Wallingford area, and New York City's Columbia Heights may well determine whether or not these areas continue to decay.

What is going on? Why do local debates appear to center on problems so different from those focused upon in current national crime legislation? Isn't "serious" crime the real problem? Is it true, as Helen Hershkoff (1993, p. 1), of the American Civil Liberties Union argues, that: "In an effort to deal with the enormous increase in poverty and homelessness in cities across the country during the past decade, numerous municipalities are enforcing, with renewed vigor, long-dormant ordinances prohibiting the destitute from asking members of the public for money"? Are we resurrecting Victorian ideas of the "dangerous classes" and returning to the bad old days of arresting people for the "offenses" of poverty and homelessness?

No, we think not. The local issues are far more complex than such formulations would suggest. On the one hand, academics and civil libertarians properly worry about issues such as freedom of speech and due process. On the other, residents in many urban neighborhoods see controlling disorder as a last-ditch effort to restore safety and civility to streets, parks, and other public spaces. Crime statistics may rise or fall; citizens' daily "in your face" street experiences tell them that things are out of control and worsening.

The Law

Things have not always been as they are now. For most of American history, in nearly every state and in many municipalities, there were laws against begging, indigence, and traveling about the country without visible means of support.

Following the Depression and World War II, criticism of vagrancy and loitering laws became increasingly common. In 1972, in *Papachristou v. City of Jacksonville*, the Supreme Court struck down an anti-vagrancy statute. Then, in 1983, in *Kolender v. Lawson*, the Supreme Court struck down a California statute which required that loiterers produce identification and account for their presence on the request of a police officer.

Following the Supreme Court's decisions in *Papachristou* and *Kolander*, other courts overturned many vagrancy and loitering laws under the due process clause of the Fourteenth Amendment. States and municipalities got the message, and as a result police ceased to enforce, and district attorneys to prosecute under, those anti-begging and panhandling laws that remained on the books.

Other localities took a different path and passed more specific, behavior-directed statutes and ordinances. Both a 1965 Supreme Court decision, *Shuttlesworth v. City of Birmingham,* and a series of New York cases beginning in the late 1960s set forth the rule that while legislation prohibiting loitering alone was unconstitutional, legislation prohibiting "loitering for the purpose of" committing some specific unlawful act, such as prostitution, was acceptable.

In recent challenges to loitering laws, however, the courts have been presented not only with Fourteenth Amendment due process and equal protection arguments, but with assertions that such laws infringe upon the First Amendment right to free speech. In some cases the courts have found

First Amendment concerns sufficiently compelling to overturn even "loitering for the purpose of" laws, signaling a further shift in legal thinking. Legislators have responded by developing laws against very specific behaviors—lying down, asking a person for money more than once, not allowing people to move freely on sidewalks, etc. But even this strategy may not succeed if the courts continue to hold that the First Amendment rights of street people outweigh the countervailing interests of a community. It is this most recent judicial shift that is the concern of this chapter.

In a word, we believe that many of these decisions have gone too far, interfering with a community's ability to maintain order on its streets, in its parks, and in other public places. Furthermore, we believe that the resulting disorder has had serious social consequences—increasing fear and crime, and driving out law-abiding citizens.

But we believe that the root problem here is a social, and not just a legal, one. That is, in reaching their decisions, the courts have relied on current, popular assumptions about disorderly behavior—the assumptions accepted and promoted by the media, policymakers, and advocates. But, as a growing body of evidence indicates, the assumptions are incorrect. Refuting them must be the first step if we are to change the direction of recent court decisions.

The Problem

During the late 1980s and early 1990s, one of the authors of this chapter worked with New York City's Transit Authority Police Department to study the problems posed by the relatively small group of persons who used the subway to panhandle, "hang out," urinate and defecate, sleep, and consume drugs and alcohol. Passengers were increasingly fearful of this behavior, and surveys revealed that this was contributing to a decline in subway ridership: 97 percent of passengers reported taking some form of defensive action before entering the subway, 75 percent refrained from wearing expensive clothing or jewelry, 69 percent avoided "certain people," 68 percent avoided particular platform locations, and 61 percent avoided specific train cars.

Many social advocates and a good portion of the media argued that the problem in the subways was "homelessness," created by a lack of adequate housing and employment. These social advocates and the media were suspicious of relying on the police to address the problem, since the police, in their view, just wanted to "throw the bums out," regardless of the consequences. The advocates believed that those who did not want to allow the homeless to use the subway for shelter were the "well-to-do," who were disregarding the needs and interests of the poor. These assumptions were shared by much of the staff of the Metropolitan Transportation Authority (MTA) and the New York City Transit Authority. Repeated attempts were made to refer this population to agencies, give them food, transport them to shelters (provided by the Volunteers of America with MTA funding), and to bring social workers into the subway. These efforts, however, were for naught. As the number of people attempting to use the subway as a surrogate shelter continued to increase, pressure mounted on the subway's Transit Police Department (TPD) to do something.

The author's analysis—which consisted of observations, public surveys, and a literature review—suggested that popular conceptions were off the mark. Those who used the subway for shelter were a particularly troubled distillate of drug and alcohol abusers, the mentally ill, and criminals. MTA estimates indicated that at least 40 percent of the subway homeless were mentally ill. Substantial portions of the remainder were chronic alcohol and drug abusers. Some were genuinely homeless, but not because they were temporarily out of work or because there was a shortage of homes, as portrayed in the media. To the contrary, many were extraordinarily disturbed and in need of medical and social services. Many others lived off their criminal activities, which included preying on passengers.

The problem in the subway, then, was not homelessness per se; the problem was rule-violating behavior by an extraordinarily troubled group, mostly male, and in large part minority. This finding has been replicated in broader contexts: in New York City, 80 percent of the males in armory shelters abuse drugs or alcohol. In *A Nation in Denial: The Truth about Homelessness*, Alice S. Baum and Donald W. Burnes (1993, p. 75), both of whom worked with the homeless in social service roles, found that the popular portrayal of the "homeless problem" was way off the mark:

> (N)ewspapers, magazines, books, and television programs reported stories of homeless two-parent rust-belt families temporarily down on their luck or of homeless individuals who had recently been laid off from permanent employment. These stories led policymakers, politicians, and advocates to frame the issue as one of people not having homes and therefore being

"homeless." None of these descriptions bore any resemblance to the people we knew. Nor were they consistent with the emerging research, which documented that up to 85 percent of all homeless adults suffer from chronic alcoholism, drug addictions, mental illness, or some combination of the three, often complicated by serious mental problems.

In sum, the terms of the local debate have largely been framed by advocates of a particular, and scarcely disguised, political agenda—an agenda concerned with social injustice, society's inequitable distribution of wealth, and the general victimization of helpless street people. We have no quarrel with this political agenda per se, or attempts to implement it, even through the courts. Moreover, we believe that the concerns raised by homeless advocates are very much worthy of debate. Nevertheless, an alternative perspective exists and is supported by a substantial factual base. To the extent that courts ignore this perspective, and the facts that support it, and adhere to the usual ideas about the homeless, they are either inadvertently or wantonly supporting a political agenda and obfuscating the complex psychological, social, and economic problems that have led to our current urban crisis.

The Consequences

There are serious consequences of misunderstanding our troublesome street population: first, the very real emotional and social disabilities of this population are not recognized, let alone adequately addressed. Second, the enormous social consequences of this group's behavior—that is, the effects on other people—are not recognized. In the remainder of this article, we focus on the second of these consequences.

In many recent decisions, courts have tended either not to understand the enormous social consequences of fear and disorder, or to ignore them. Indeed, many have trivialized the problem, as did Judge Robert W. Sweet in *Loper v. New York City Police Dept.* (1992, p. 3):

A peaceful beggar poses no threat to society. The beggar has arguably only committed the offense of being needy. The message one or one hundred beggars sends society can be disturbing. If some portion of society is offended, the answer is not in criminalizing these people, debtor's prisons being long gone, but addressing the root cause of their existence. . . . Professor Kelling's approach would simply remove the messenger of bad news.

Judge Sweet suggests that society is offended by the notion of neediness. Perhaps, partially. But more importantly, individual citizens, of all social classes, are threatened by the behavior of, and the implicit and explicit threats made by, serious substance abusers, emotionally disturbed persons, some "peaceful beggars," and criminals. Not just panhandling, but prostitution, public urination and defecation, drunkenness, and obstreperousness all send a chilling message to citizens. This message is: things are out of control. For most citizens, disorder is the crime problem.

Disorder and Fear

Social science research confirms the link between disorder and fear. This link was demonstrated as early as 1967, when Albert Biderman and his associates found the connection in a survey of citizens in Washington D.C. Likewise Nathan Glazer (1979), suggested that ubiquitous graffiti on subway cars signaled riders that public officials did not have control. And if public officials could not control relatively minor problems such as graffiti, they certainly could not control serious problems such as robbery and assault. Graffiti and robbery were of one ilk to citizens.

The link between disorder and fear was brought to mainstream attention when James Q. Wilson and George L. Kelling (1982), published "Broken Windows" in the *Atlantic Monthly*. The article identified various violations of community norms that, while often codified as illegal, at times were not: public drinking, panhandling, prostitution, loud music, and graffiti.

The article discussed the link between disorder and community fear. Also, it argued that just as an unrepaired broken window sends a message that no one cares and invites more damage, so unattended disorderly behavior also acts as a signal that no one cares, with the result of more disorderly behavior and serious crime. Finally "Broken Windows" argued that disorder left unattended leads to a breakdown of community controls, and ultimately undermines the fabric of urban life and social intercourse. But much of this article's thesis was new and untested. Unlike the link between disorder and fear, which had been explored in previous research, the relationship between disorder and crime, and between disorder and further urban decay, had not.

Disorder and Serious Crime

In his book, *Disorder and Decline,* Wesley Skogan (1990), confirmed the correlation between disorder and serious crime. Using survey and observational data collected in forty residential neighborhoods in six U.S. cities, Skogan found that: (1) broad consensus existed among members of all racial and ethnic groups as to what constituted disorderly behavior; (2) disorder was a precursor to serious crime; and (3) disorder was also a precursor to further urban decay. By "precursor" to crime and urban decay, Skogan meant that disorder was found in the study to be one of several variables sequentially linked to crime and urban decay. There were other explanatory factors—such as poverty and family instability—but disorder was the single most powerful precursor of both serious crime and urban decay.

Skogan's findings clearly suggest that controlling disorderly behavior is important both because it will reduce fear (which will make people more comfortable in city streets, parks, and public transportation systems) and because it will discourage violent crime and help prevent urban decay. Contemporary experience confirms these findings. Focus groups in New Haven, Connecticut, surveys in the Fenway area of Boston, and interviews with suburbanites near San Francisco and with merchants in Brooklyn all show the same result: disorder creates fear. In response to this fear, citizens have abandoned parks and public spaces, refrained from using public transportation, turned from neighborhood shopping areas to malls, hired private security, locked themselves behind doors and barred their windows, purchased dogs and guns, and in some cases deserted cities entirely.

In other words, these findings show that it is crucially important for order to be maintained. When it is not, the social consequences can be severe.

Police Discretion

Most contemporary challenges to laws that restrict panhandling and other disorderly behavior allege that such laws allow the police to harass, intimidate, and arrest persons whose only crime is being poor, and that the laws thereby silence panhandlers and the message they send to society about poverty. In Florida and in New York, state courts have voiced the suspicion that laws against disorderly behavior lead to police intimidation of citizens on the streets in poor areas. Certainly police have supplied their critics with much ammunition. Historically, they have often treated African-Americans, among other groups, very poorly. Even recently, renegade police in New York, Detroit, and Los Angeles have captured headlines with their outrageous behavior.

Indeed, the issue at the heart of both policy and legal disputes about the maintenance of order is police discretion: how much police actually have, how much they should have, and how to control it. "Police discretion" is broader than just the individual officer's decision to arrest a person or not. It also includes the allocation of officers to neighborhoods; the establishment of police priorities; the setting of policies for the handling of civil disturbances and use of force, especially lethal force; the adoption of police tactics such as sweeps and undercover decoy units; and the use of other tactics, such as foot patrols—to mention just a few examples. For instance, the decision of the Transit Police Department to enforce rules and regulations aggressively in New York's subways was a discretionary one.

Attempts to influence or control police discretion have taken many forms. University of Wisconsin police expert Herman Goldstein (1993, p. 17), notes several:

> Legislatures have enacted statutes that curtail, clarify, guide, or mandate police actions (e.g., regarding stopping and questioning, strip searches, use of force). City councils have used their budgetary and legislative powers to set police priorities (e.g., marijuana enforcement, the decision to prosecute drug cases under federal law) and to control investigations (e.g., surveillance of political groups). The citizenry, through initiatives and referenda, have sought to provide more specific guidance to their police on the issues of local concern (e.g., marijuana enforcement, use of force). Prosecutors have been more assertive in making policy decisions affecting police practices regarding matters that are substantially of concern to them.

Furthermore, the police themselves have attempted to limit discretion by developing guidelines for officers to follow when making important policing decisions.

As we have also seen, courts have attempted to shape police conduct both directly and indirectly. Directly, courts have limited discretion through decisions such as *Miranda v. Arizona* (which requires that a suspect undergoing police interrogation be informed of his rights to an attorney and to remain silent), and *Mapp v. Ohio* (which established the exclusionary rule), both of which restrict criminal investigations, and by endorsing the development of guidelines that police must follow—for instance, guidelines about when police can use deadly force or conduct involuntary searches. Indirectly, courts have limited police discretion by encouraging legislatures to write laws that will pass constitutional muster.

We wish to emphasize that we have no quarrel with attempts to limit police discretion in the ways described above. Carefully crafted, specific laws that give the police "chunks" of authority to deal with a narrow range of problems are worthwhile, benefiting both the police and those they serve. Indeed, we believe that the more specific the law, the better. And, it is important to note, the police would largely concur with us on this.

An example is found in the NYCTA's old "obstructing" rule: it became clear to the task force that "obstructing" was a vague concept which police, and members of our task force, had difficulty defining. The rule left too much discretion to officers, which invited both formal legal challenges and street disputes. Upon closer analysis, we became aware that we were concerned ultimately not with obstructing, but with lying down, a specific behavior that is simpler to discern. (Though "lying down" still had to be defined—for instance, there is a difference between slouching on a bench and lying on it. And is a person leaning against a wall with his or her legs flat out on the ground lying down or not?) So, we returned to the Metropolitan Transit Authority's Board of Directors and requested that the rules be changed to forbid lying down rather than obstructing, which the Board did.

Police as Good Guys

Police misbehavior, and how to avoid it, have been major issues in the United States since the mid-nineteenth century. Retired Brandeis professor

Egon Bittner (1990, p. 356) drolly described portrayals of early American police: "Of all the institutions of city government in late-nineteenth-century America, none was as unanimously denounced as the urban police. According to every available account, they were, in every aspect of their existence, an unmixed, unmitigated, and unpardonable scandal." Virtually everyone had it in for nineteenth-century police. Progressives wanted to overturn machine politics, to which the police were closely linked. Social work was emerging as a profession, and its practitioners wanted police out of their business. Native urban residents—largely the English and Dutch—castigated the police for their reluctance to enforce vice laws in immigrant neighborhoods. Journalists and muckrakers revealed police scandal after police scandal. And early twentieth-century police thinkers—August Vollmer, Bruce Smith, Leonard Fuld, and others who were allied with the Progressives—portrayed the police in unflattering terms. No one defended the police.

When we read police history more carefully, however, a somewhat more complex picture emerges. What about the immigrants—the Irish, Italians, and Jews who moved into cities? Were they the targets of police abuse? Certainly police arrested some of them (although arrests during the nineteenth century were far less common than today), and we have no doubt that some police abused ethnic minorities.

But it was not as simple as that. Police provided urban residents and newcomers with an array of social services. Police stations were built with extra space, so that migrants who moved to cities would have a place to sleep for several nights until they found work and shelter. Historian Eric Monkkonen (1981) estimates that between 10 and 20 percent of America's population in the late nineteenth century came from families in which at least one member occasionally used police lodging facilities. Were the facilities commodious? No, as a matter of fact they were quite primitive. But in comparison to other social institutions of the time—poorhouses, for example—they probably weren't any worse. The original food and soup lines were also developed by police. Was the food plenteous and wholesome by today's standards? No, probably not. Nonetheless, nineteenth-century police were, as they are in many inner cities today, important dispensers of social services.

Moreover, during the nineteenth century, police were taught to get beggars into contact with agencies that might be able to help them. For example, the Rules and Regulations of the Boston Police Department (1863), ordered:

When any person begs in the street or goes from door to door soliciting alms, it shall be the duty of the officer to inquire the name and abode of such persons, and note the same for record, and to direct such person, if in distress, to the overseer of the poor of the ward where such person resides, or to any charitable association to his knowledge affording relief in similar cases.

Similarly, the Rules and Regulations of the Joliet (IL) Police Department (1891), specified:

The members of the department, are particularly enjoined to remove all beggars found begging in the streets. If on inquiry, they are found to be proper subjects for relief from the Town Supervisor, they are to be taken to the Town Supervisor, for relief and permanent aid; and if proven to be imposters or vagrants, to take them before the police justices to be dealt with according to law.

The provision of social services was not limited to adults and homeless immigrants: one of the major responsibilities of urban police was finding and returning lost children to their parents, or, if the parents could not be found, referring the children for other social services. So important were police in providing services that Monkkonen (1981), has concluded:

That police did not remain service oriented may have been a missed opportunity to help order American cities; that separate private agencies competed with the police in supplying social services may well have destroyed a potentially useful means of helping ordinary people resist the disorganizing effects of industrialized urban places.

Hardly police as "an unmixed, unmitigated, and unpardonable scandal"!

In fact, police were often considered too sympathetic to urban newcomers. They were reluctant, for example, to enforce vice laws in immigrant neighborhoods. (This is not terribly surprising, since many police were from these neighborhoods.) Industrialists considered urban police so unreliable in policing strikes (the police often sympathized with their working brethren) that, in some states such as Massachusetts and Pennsylvania, state police were created almost exclusively for the purpose of responding to labor unrest.

The Police Retreat, Partially

To extricate themselves from the battles between ward politicians and Progressives—who had very different visions of the business of police—early twentieth-century police reformers moved to narrow police functioning to areas about which there was little dispute: felonies such as murder, rape, robbery, assault, and burglary. While the enforcement of laws against Sunday selling ("blue laws"), drunkenness, prostitution, vagrancy, loitering, and other "vices" often pitted groups against each other and put the police in between, serious felonies were universally and unambiguously condemned. Everyone agreed that murder, for instance, was a serious problem. And so police became criminal "law enforcers," "crime fighters," and "the front end of the criminal justice system," whose job it was to arrest offenders. Furthermore, so as not to intrude too much into community life, police also became reactive, waiting to be called on the telephone, and frequently waiting until a serious crime had occurred before taking action.

So thoroughly was this strategy indoctrinated into the police culture that, even today, police are reluctant to get involved in order maintenance. When, for example, Loper challenged New York's anti-panhandling law in 1991, few police even knew that such a law existed, let alone cared whether or not it was challenged. In the subway, line officers were indignant and even appalled about getting into the business of order maintenance. Their job was to fight crime; dealing with the "homeless" was somebody else's job.

Nonetheless, the vast majority of police work in poor areas does not involve responding to incidents of "serious" crime; rather, it involves mediating conflicts and solving problems that confront the poor and needy. Police in major cities deal with literally thousands of complex and ambiguous cases each day, and handle most of them to the satisfaction of virtually everyone. Arrests are rare. In sum, every shred of research conducted over the past several decades demonstrates that police deal with an enormous range of problems, criminal and noncriminal, and that virtually every incident with which they deal is incredibly complex.

Take panhandling. What appears passive in one setting may seem aggressive in another: one person standing on a sidewalk at mid-day in a business area with a cup in his hand, quietly asking for quarters, is not particularly threatening; the same person, with exactly the same demeanor, standing at 9 P.M. in front of a brownstone when an elderly person returns and must unlock the door, is ominous. Similarly, four panhandlers standing in front of a restaurant, even if they are not behaving aggressively, may be more threatening than one panhandler in the same place. And just two passive panhandlers, framing each side of a subway entrance after the rush hour, can be menacing.

The condition of the panhandler is also significant. It is one thing to be approached by someone who appears sober and sane; it is quite another matter to be approached by someone who rants and raves, swears at those who pass by, suddenly lunges at other persons, but who, when panhandling, suddenly constrains his behavior. Similarly, an ostensibly courteous—shall we say obsequious—panhandler staggering from an overdose of drugs or alcohol is threatening because he is unpredictable, despite being relatively passive in the act of begging.

Finally, the circumstances of the person being approached are also relevant. A pregnant woman accompanied by a small child is far more vulnerable than is a robust male student. Similarly, a citizen who is moving feels far less vulnerable than one who is standing still.

So, given the complexity of police work, how should we go about providing police with the authority to deal with problems such as panhandling? First, be as specific as possible. Police will welcome specificity. They want neither legal challenges nor street hassles.

Second, although specificity is desirable, we must also recognize that there are limits to the extent to which laws can be made specific. Every street-wise person understands that dedicated hustlers play games. One can't lie down on the street? Then sit down and quibble about what constitutes lying down. One can't panhandle within so many feet of Grand Central Terminal (as one judge proposed)? Fine, then stay just outside of that perimeter. Or, develop new scams. Hold doors open for "fees." Get cabs for tourists. "Assist" people who are buying tokens for subways. "Direct" cars in public garages. The point is, it is impossible for legislators to frame laws that cover every contingency. Unrealistically specific laws will only lead to an endless "dance" between police and street people. As police move, hustlers adjust; as new laws are developed, police move again, and so on ad infinitum. Passing unrealistically narrow laws will only exhaust police in endless street quibbles.

Third, police must develop clear, formal guidelines for the use of discretion. These guidelines should be developed openly and in collaboration with citizens, prosecutors, and legal counsel. The New York City Transit Police Department worked very hard on this. The result? Although both ejections from the subway and arrests for rule-violating behavior and misdemeanors doubled in 1990, citizen complaints did not rise. Few police departments, however, have considered, let alone developed, guidelines of this sort.

Fourth, we must give up the false belief that police are eager to harass persons, especially minorities and the poor, if given the chance. Given the scope of police work, events of abuse and brutality are extraordinarily rare. Citizens of all ethnic and racial backgrounds recognize disorder and want something done about it. Skogan's research has documented the existence of a broad consensus, which cuts across race and class lines, on what constitutes disorderly behavior. Moreover, while elites and the media may see abuse as the primary policing problem in minority communities, residents point to police under-enforcement and passivity in the face of outrageous street behavior.

Fifth, we must be realistic about how much laws can accomplish. Giving police the ability to arrest persons who act in a disorderly manner will not eliminate the problem. No one really believes that Tampa's "loitering for the purpose of" prostitution law, for example, is going to eradicate prostitution. Indeed, more Draconian laws than Tampa's have failed in the past.

Finally, the sensational and simplistic views that have dominated thinking about the police must be recognized by the courts for what they are. Research that challenges these views has been piling up and ought to be taken seriously.

New York, a Success Story

In late October of 1989, in response to high levels of fear about a worsening crime problem, New York's Metropolitan Transportation Authority began to enforce its rules against panhandling, obstructing passengers, lying down, and other disorderly activities. In November, the Legal Action Center for the Homeless, along with two panhandlers, sued subway officials to overturn the ban on panhandling. Federal District Judge Leonard B. Sand ruled in January of 1990 that begging is deserving of First Amendment protection, and forbade the Authority from enforcing its rule. A month later, the Second Circuit Court of Appeals granted temporary relief from Judge Sand's order, permitting enforcement of the subway regulations; finally, in May of 1990, the Appeals Court reversed Judge Sand's decision, stating:

> The governmental interests in the prohibition of begging in the subway are more fully elucidated when the harms to be avoided are juxtaposed with the good to be sustained. The subway is not the domain of the privileged and powerful. Rather, it is the primary means of transportation of literally millions of people of modest means, including hard-working men and women, students and elderly pensioners who live in and around New York City and who are dependent on the subway for the conduct of their affairs. They are the bulk of the subway's patronage, and the City has an obvious interest in providing them with a reasonably safe, propitious and benign means of public transportation. In determining the validity of the ban, we must be attentive lest a rigid, mechanistic application of some legal doctrine gainsays the common good. In our estimation, the regulation at interest here is justified by legitimate, indeed compelling, governmental interests. We think that the district court's analysis reflects an exacerbated deference to the alleged individual rights of beggars and panhandlers to the great detriment of the common good. (*Young v. NYCTA* 1990, p. 158)

With the anti-panhandling rules allowed to stand, serious crime, especially robbery and assault, began a steep decline that has persisted through the present. Between 1990 and the end of the first quarter of 1994, robberies were cut by more than 52 percent and all felonies by 46 percent—stunning reductions that greatly exceed those in New York City and other urban centers.

This, then, is a success story. But there have been few attempts to replicate it elsewhere. And even if there were more, it is unlikely that many courts would agree with the Second Circuit Court of Appeals. Of course, restricting behavior on subways is different from restricting behavior on streets. Indeed, the Second Circuit Court's decision was based partially on the difference between city streets—the "quintessential public forum"—and subway stations, platforms, and cars.

But are subway spaces and the "classic public fora"—streets and parks—really all that different? Clearly in a city like New York, subways matter: they are part of a crucial transportation network, with vast commercial and social importance. But streets and parks matter too. They are more than mere sites for free speech or expression; they also have important social and commercial functions. Duke University professor Stanley Fish (1993, p. 91) recognizes this when he discusses the balancing of individual rights and governmental interests that courts undertake when they approach restrictions on speech:

> (T)he value of the "free speech" interest, which is a real interest, will vary with the underlying purpose for which some social space has been organized. It is only in the most peculiar and eccentric of social spaces, like a Hyde Park Corner, where the production of speech has no purpose other than itself that absolute toleration will make sense, and it is one of the oddities of "official" First Amendment rhetoric that such peculiar spaces are put forward as the norm. That is, First Amendment rhetoric presupposes the ordinary situation as one in which expression is wholly unconstrained and then imagines situations of constraint as special. But the truth is exactly the reverse: the special and almost-never-to-be-encountered situation is one in which you can say what you like with impunity. The ordinary situation is one in which what you can say is limited by the decorums you are required to internalize before entering. Regulation of free speech is a defining feature of everyday life, not because the landscape is polluted by censors, but because the very condition of purposeful activity (as opposed to activity that is random and inconsequential) is that some actions (both physical and verbal) be excluded so that some others can go forward. . . . When speech does matter, when it is produced in the service of some truth or preferred agenda, the sign of its mattering is the fact that only some forms of it will be welcome.

Though the Second Circuit Court of Appeals found that begging was neither speech nor expressive conduct deserving of First Amendment protection, other courts have declined to follow its lead. Indeed, most courts have approached legislation restricting begging and panhandling by attempting to determine in an abstract sense whether begging is speech (or symbolic conduct) deserving of First Amendment protection, without giving the weight that the Second Circuit Court did to public or societal interests. Most courts have found that begging or panhandling constitutes speech by virtue of the fact that beggars may communicate that "government benefits are inadequate" or "there are large numbers of poor and homeless in our country today." Other courts have held that even if the precise words do not carry a protected message, expressive acts do, so that as the Loper court suggested, the very presence of beggars conveys a message that society and government have abandoned them.

The logic here is troublesome. Most often, a beggar says something like the proverbial, "Brother can you spare a dime?" and someone else hears it and decides whether and/or how to respond. Calling a request, or often a demand, for money *speech*, however, does not end the matter. No absolute right to speech has ever existed. For the citizen to be told by courts that a street person is making a constitutionally protected statement about social injustice flies in the face of common sense and street experience, when most likely the panhandler is seriously disturbed, under the influence of drugs and alcohol, or seriously ill, but eager to make enough cash hits so that he or she can get more alcohol or drugs. So common is this scenario that Ken Smith, executive director of the New England Shelter for Homeless Veterans in Boston, has publicly requested that citizens not give panhandlers money. Why? Smith claims that the money is used to buy more drugs, which makes rehabilitation more difficult and makes panhandlers unsuitable for any sort of housing, including shelters.

If one begins not with the traditional question "Is begging speech?" (or protected action), but rather with an attempt to balance "the harms to be avoided with the good to be sustained"—to paraphrase the Second Circuit Court's decision—one may come to very different conclusions, not only concerning the interests of the public, but also the interests of the beggar.

Ultimately, these issues will be brought to the Supreme Court for settlement. The closest that the Court has come thus far to facing the question of whether begging is deserving of First Amendment protection is in *International Society for Krishna Consciousness v. Lee* (1992), where it dealt with the solicitation of funds (to be paid on the spot) by representatives of an organized religion, and found this to be protected speech. At the same time, the Court found that such speech could be restricted in New York City airport terminals, because they are not "public fora." We do not know whether this opinion will be extended by the Court in the future to include panhandling by individuals.

Even if the Supreme Court should find that begging is protected speech, however, it may well find that such protection is not absolute. If so, panhandling could still be prohibited if there were a compelling governmental interest in doing so. In previous decisions the Court has acknowledged that the cumulative effects of individual acts may be considered in weighing the potential harmful effects of speech or expressive conduct. And a few courts have addressed the rights of individuals to be left alone, or the rights of communities to safe streets.

Nevertheless, most courts have not fully, knowledgeably, or adequately assessed the public and governmental interests in regulating begging and other forms of disorderly behavior. Many courts continue to hold to the philosophical principles that historically underlie First

Amendment jurisprudence. While such an approach surely has value, the courts have all too frequently ignored empirical data, and even common sense. The stakes are high. For most citizens, the crime problem in cities *is* disorder.

Note

This chapter originally appeared in the *Public Interest*, No. 116, Summer 1994, pp. 57-74. It is reprinted with permission.

References

Baum, Alice S., and Donald W. Burnes. 1993. *A Nation in Denial: The Truth about Homelessness.* Boulder, CO: Westview Press.

Bittner, Egon. 1990. *Aspects of Police Work.* Boston: Northeastern University Press.

Boston Police Department. 1863. *Rules and Regulations.* Boston: Boston Police Department.

Fish, Stanley. 1993. *There's No Such Thing as Free Speech: and it's a Good Thing Too.* Oxford: Oxford University Press.

Glazer, Nathan. 1979. "On Subway Graffiti in New York." *Public Interest* 54 (Winter): 3-11.

Goldstein, Herman. 1993. "Confronting the Complexity of the Police Function." In *Discretion in Criminal Justice: The Tension Between Individualization and Uniformity*, edited by Lloyd Ohlin and Frank J. Remington. Albany: State University of New York Press.

Hershkoff, Helen. 1993. "Aggressive Panhandling Laws: Do These Statutes Violate the Constitution? Yes: Silencing the Homeless." *American Bar Association Journal* 79: 40.

Joliet Police Department. 1891. *Rules and Regulations.* Joliet, IL: Joliet Police Department.

Loper v. New York City Police Dept. 802 F. Supp. 1029 (S.D.N.Y. 1992), *aff'd*, 999 F. 2d 699 (2d Cir 1993).

Monkkonen, Eric. 1981. *Police in Urban America: 1860-1920.* New York: Cambridge University Press.

Skogan, Wesley. 1990. *Disorder and Decline: Crime and the Spiral of Decay in American Neighborhoods.* Berkeley: University of California Press.

Wilson, James Q., and George L. Kelling. 1982. "Broken Windows: The Police and Neighborhood Safety." *The Atlantic Monthly* (March): 29-38.

Young v. New York City Transit Authority. 903 F.2d 146 (1990).

V. Community Prosecution
and Sanctioning

11

Community Prosecution:
Portland's Experience

Barbara Boland

Community prosecution is, above all else, a local political response to the grass-roots public safety demands of neighborhoods—as expressed in highly concrete terms by citizens who live in them. Residents have immediate, specific crime problems they want addressed that the incident-based 911 driven system of justice is ill suited to handle. They are frustrated that no one listens, that nothing happens. Common problems involve quality of life and disorder issues. But in high-crime neighborhoods low-level disorders are now inextricably intertwined with the violent behaviors associated with the drug trade and gangs. In these neighborhoods the problem of public order is very serious. The nature of the crime problems and the local responses that are emerging to address them, differ radically from conventional notions about crime and crime fighting. Prosecutorial initiatives, for the most part, are arising outside the operational status quo of traditional organizational arrangements.

What is emerging in the Portland District Attorney's Office, and in other prosecutor offices around the country, is a redefinition of the elected prosecutor's institutional role in promoting order and controlling crime. Underlying this redefinition is a significant change in the institutional relationship of the prosecutor's office to citizens and police. Briefly, change is the creation of direct communication links and working relationships between individuals in the prosecutor's office and citizens and police

253

in neighborhoods, who collectively work together to devise strategies to prevent, suppress, solve or whatever is required (within the constraints of the law) to abate the problems that citizens identify as a threat to public safety and order in neighborhoods. Citizen participants in these activities (are not limited to but) most often represent neighborhood groups and citizen associations working on specific crime problems. Likewise, police officers are often (but are not limited to) community policing officers. These new arrangements are generating a multitude of rapidly emerging and constantly changing problem-oriented activities aimed at neighborhood crime.

This response to crime is to a significant degree a direct result of the crisis in public order that hit inner-city neighborhoods in the wake of the crack epidemic of the mid-1980s. The residents of high-crime city neighborhoods have since the 1970s been telling police and police researchers that low-level crimes of public order matter. When overlaid with the explosion in street level drug dealing that came with crack, the problem of public order, in the words of one Portland community activist, "became unbearable." The seriousness of the public order problem is drawing the prosecutor into the law enforcement task of street order maintenance, traditionally performed by the police.[1]

Over the last decade, prosecutors across the country got introduced to citizen demands for public order (both the serious and the seemingly trivial) and to the limitations of conventional crime control strategies for dealing with it via their response to drug crime. Neither drugs nor disorder are readily ameliorated by conventional incident-based enforcement strategies. Unlike the street robberies and burglaries that characterized the crime waves of the 1960s and 1970s, drug and disorder crimes involve patterned continuing behavior rather than discrete isolated incidents; victims are not typically individuals but neighborhoods or other geographic locations like business districts; and, with the exception of drug and gang related violence, seriousness more often derives from the collective nature of the activity rather than the seriousness of specific instances of it. Robberies and burglaries depend on stealth for success. A successful drug operation requires open control of public space. Convicting drug dealers removes individual perpetrators but the collective enterprise continues. That residents observe these activities on a daily basis, can identify suspects by face and street name, but calls to police result in no more than temporary interruptions heightens their frustration. The capacity of existing institutional arrangements to deal with this kind of behavior is, in short, limited.

In what follows I document the story of how the district attorney in Portland has responded to the public order issues Portland citizens want addressed: the genesis of the initiative, the nature of the activities, and the evolution of the experiment in its first five years. I then make a preliminary attempt to identify emerging elements of this new approach to law enforcement, but caution that "what this is" is still evolving. Portland's experiment with community prosecution focuses predominantly on quality of life and low-level disorders. Other offices are devising remarkably similar organizational responses to deal with serious violent crime. The New York County District Attorney's Office has community prosecution initiatives to deal with both quality of life and violent crime. In Washington, D.C. the U.S. Attorney's Office began community prosecution in the violent crime unit.

The Portland Community Prosecution Project: The Early Idea

In November of 1990, Michael Schrunk, district attorney for Multnomah County, Oregon (Portland), assigned Wayne Pearson, one of his most experienced senior deputies, to work for one year on a neighborhood-based pilot prosecution project in Portland's inner-city Lloyd District. The idea for the project came out of work with a group of District business people, concerned about crime and its consequences for the economic life of the area.

The Lloyd District, a roughly 100 square block area, is situated in the center of Portland just across the Willamette River from the city's vibrant downtown. Economic development efforts, implemented throughout the 1980s, were by the end of the decade well on their way to transforming this previously declining industrial-residential area into a major commercial business district. Developments included the Oregon Convention Center, a state financed office tower, and a new federal building. The MAX light rail system, built largely with federal dollars, by the mid-1980s conveniently connected the district to downtown and to east and west Portland. The public construction projects spurred a variety of privately financed investments including: renovation of the aging Lloyd Center shopping center into an upscale interior mall, new hotels and restaurants, and plans for a new multi-million dollar high tech sports arena for the Portland Blazers (the city's professional basketball team). In 1989, just as the Convention Center was about to open for business, government and civic leaders became legitimately worried that criminal activity in the District would negate the economic benefits these invest-ments were expected to bring into the city. Local citizens perceived the Lloyd District to be less safe than other area business districts. This perception, validated by official crime data, was compounded by the eruption of gang and drug problems in Portland's North/Northeast neigh-borhoods just north of the Lloyd District when the crack epidemic visibly arrived in Portland in 1988.

Lloyd area business leaders attacked the problem in accordance with long-standing local civic traditions. They formed an association, appointed a forty-member public safety committee, studied the issue, and came up with a carefully drafted public safety action plan. The committee included Schrunk, staff from his office, high-ranking members of the Portland Police Bureau (PPB), representatives of District businesses, adjacent residential neighbors, and public agency staff providing services to the district. The committee's draft plan succinctly stated the members con-cern:

> When the new Oregon Convention Center opens in September, 1990, the District will be the major gateway for hundreds of thousands of visitors to Portland each year. Most will not be familiar with Portland. . . . A major goal of the convention center and the private development efforts is to en-courage visitors to return again to the district, to Portland, and to Oregon. Creating a favorable impression on visitors, *including making them feel safe from criminal activity*, (emphasis added) is essential to meeting this goal. (Holladay [Lloyd] District Public Safety Action Plan 1990, p. 1)

The plan then outlined crime and the perception of crime in the district and listed specific strategies to address the problem. The strategies included private actions, such as upgraded lighting and better coordination of private security resources. But a clear message to local officials was: the committee thought intensified public law enforcement was crucial. The committee wanted more police officers, a common request of citizens concerned about crime, but they also wanted something unusual—a special prosecutor assigned to the Lloyd District. The committee wanted a special prosecutor to address their concern about the lack of consequences in the downtown courts for criminal activity that affected district busi-nesses. When the group failed to obtain federal funding through the governor's office for the special prosecutor project, they raised the money themselves. In essence the group made the offer to Schrunk to "buy their own prosecutor." The local weekly tabloid labeled the project "Hired Gun" (Redden 1990).

Despite widespread support for the District's overall anticrime plan, the idea of private businesses paying a special prosecutor's salary presented valid ethical issues. Critics, interviewed for the "Hired Gun" article, viewed the idea as a way for special classes of citizens (i.e., those with money) to get special services not available to others. Schrunk, though mindful of these concerns, decided that a one-year pilot project served the public interest. Safety in the Lloyd District was important to the general economic development of Portland. He accepted the private funding plan on the condition that, if the project were a success, eventual funding would be from public sources and all areas of the county would be served.

At the same time, the district attorney was alert to the fact that another coalition of business owners, community activists, and average citizens representing drug and gang plagued neighborhoods in North and Northeast Portland were similarly organizing and drafting anticrime action plans to address problems in Portland's North/Northeast neighborhoods. This area of the city includes some of Portland's highest crime and drug-infested neighborhoods. The Northeast Rescue Plan Action Committee's "Call to Action" plan did not include a request for a special prosecutor, but it clearly called for a vigorous law enforcement response from the local police, the FBI, the DEA, and a request to the Governor to deploy the National Guard to Northeast Portland neighborhoods (Northeast Rescue Plan Action Committee 1990).

In early 1992, about a year after Schrunk sent Pearson to work in the Lloyd District he dispatched, with funds from his own office budget, a second neighborhood DA, Mike Kuykendall, to work with citizens in North/Northeast. From that point on the project, so to speak, sold itself. When activist citizens groups (and the police) in other areas of the city and county began to hear about the work Pearson and Kuykendall were doing in the Lloyd District and North/Northeast, they stepped forward with their own requests. They "wanted one too."

The Association for Portland Progress, a downtown business association, funded a pilot Neighborhood DA (NDA) for downtown beginning in January of 1993. A fourth NDA was sent to work in the city of Gresham in the east end of the county in November 1993; initial funding came through the city of Gresham. The fifth NDA funded by the county went to work in southeast Portland in August of 1994. A sixth NDA went to work for Tri-Met, the regional transit authority, in mid-1995. A seventh went to work in a new police precinct in east Portland in late 1996.

The Neighborhood DA idea is obviously popular with Portland's activist citizens, and Schrunk has come very close to achieving his goal of complete county coverage and public funding, a major concern in the early days of the initiative. All attorneys' salaries are now paid out of public funds. Private funding continues only in the form of donated office space and clerical help in some locations. And with the exception of the "Hired Gun" article which appeared just after Pearson started work in the Lloyd District, there has been virtually no public criticism.

The Neighborhood DA project has struck a chord. This is something citizens want.

What Citizens Want

Citizens concerned about crime invariably state their demand "to do something" about it in traditional law enforcement terms. The drafters of the Northeast Rescue Plan unequivocally wanted more police to support their communities' fight against drugs and gangs. They even specified exactly what they wanted the increased troops to do. They wanted them to be visible; to control the streets, parks, and schools; to knock on the doors of drug houses to let the inhabitants know they knew what they were doing; and to employ major police sweeps to enforce the juvenile curfew. The "call to action" to the rest of the justice system was "to get coordinated to fast track the gangsters" (Northeast Rescue Plan Action Committee 1990, p. 3).

Lloyd District committee members, sought a somewhat less vigorous response, nonetheless they too stated their request in traditional law enforcement terms. They wanted more visible police presence in cars, on bikes, on foot, on horses; and the one-year special prosecutor project was supposed to focus on recidivist offenders (Fehrenkamp 1990).

Pearson, prior to being assigned to the District, thought that a problem-oriented approach would likely be more effective than traditional individual-oriented prosecution. Yet he too thought about ultimate project outcomes in traditional arrest and convict terms. In his assigned section of the Lloyd District public safety action plan, he envisioned something along the lines of an "enhanced case processing" approach.

Perpetrators become anonymous in the criminal justice system. . . . Through marshaling the support of the community, particularly at the time of trial and sentencing, the judges involved in these cases would be more aware of the effect of these crimes not only on the individual victim, but also on the businesses and neighborhood. ([Lloyd] District Public Safety Action Plan 1990, pp. A2-6)

In retrospect, Pearson observes that he went into the field with traditional notions about crime and prosecution. (Serious crime is the top priority.) Convicting the guilty so judges can impose appropriate punishment is the important task. When he got into the street, however, he quickly found that *what most bothered people on a daily basis was something different.* People who worked and lived in the Lloyd District, like everyone else wanted robbers and burglars caught and punished and rapid police response to emergencies, but they also wanted something else. They wanted something done about prostitution, public drinking, drug use, vandalism, street fights, littering, garbage, and car prowls. None of these behaviors fit traditional notions about serious crime, or, with the exception of car prowls (thefts from autos), are even counted in official measures of crime. Nor did complaints typically focus on specific criminal incidents, though Lloyd citizens did have specific ideas about the source of the district's problems—illegal camping in nearby Sullivan's Gulch.

Sullivan's Gulch, a wide natural gulch that forms the southern border of the District, houses the intersection of two major railroad lines that historically has been the point at which transients hop on and off north-south and east-west trains. Since the area is somewhat removed from residential neighborhoods, small numbers of transients who stay to camp are not a serious problem. By the late 1980s, however, the transient population had exploded. The number setting up more or less permanent residence and regularly venturing into neighboring areas, especially in the evening to buy liquor, drink, litter, fight, steal, etc., had become a threatening public nuisance. The problem coincided with the private and civic efforts to revitalize the District.

Disorder and Serious Crime

The immediate crime problem that concerned citizens in the Lloyd District is the classic problem of disorder that police researchers, beginning almost two decades ago, discovered is intimately linked to fear of crime and serious crime. Police research, most prominently the work of George Kelling and Wesley Skogan, on the links among crime, fear, and disorder, validates Lloyd's citizen's concern about seemingly minor criminal behavior. In brief, this research supports the commonsense citizen view that disorderly behavior breeds serious crime (Wilson and Kelling 1982).

The first scholarly observation that disorder is an important citizen concern came out of the Police Foundation's Newark, New Jersey, foot patrol experiment conducted in the mid-1970s to measure the effect on crime of assigning police officers to foot patrol beats. The conventional wisdom within the policing profession at the time was that foot patrol was an ineffective anticrime strategy. It had virtually been eliminated in most cities in the 1960s, thus the finding that foot patrol had no measurable impact on crime was not surprising to police researchers or progressive-minded police executives. But Kelling, who headed the evaluation team, and his fellow researchers reported another quite surprising result (Police Foundation 1981).

Even though serious crime had not been measurably reduced in neighborhoods with foot patrol beats, residents reported feeling safer. They said they thought crime had gone down and reported acting as if it had. They told researchers they went out more at night, had begun to leave their doors unlocked, and generally were taking fewer safety precautions. Shortly after the experimental results were published, Kelling wrote with James Q. Wilson the now widely referenced "Broken Windows" article in the *Atlantic Monthly,* interpreting the Newark results in light of Kelling's field observations, while walking with officers in foot patrol neighborhoods. What Kelling had observed, but the evaluation had failed to measure, was an "elevation of the level of public order." Specifically, Kelling observed foot patrol officers, in collaboration with people in neighborhoods, establish commonly understood and agreed upon rules of acceptable and disreputable public behavior. People who broke the rules were mostly asked to stop, move on, or go home. Arrests were required but only on occasion.

From this observation Wilson and Kelling drew two inferences. First, they argued that people's sense of crime in big city neighborhoods derives as much "from a sense that the street is disorderly, a source of distasteful, worrisome encounters" as from fear of serious crime. They supported this argument with data collected in the Newark evaluation and similar findings reported by other existing research studies. Second, they put forth the hypothesis that disorderly behavior left unchecked (like broken windows left unrepaired) is a sign that no one cares, inviting further damage, disorder, and serious crime. They inferred the process by which this occurs.

> The unchecked panhandler is, in effect, the first broken window. Muggers and robbers, whether opportunistic or professional, believe they reduce their chances of being caught or even identified if they operate on streets where potential victims are already intimidated by prevailing conditions. If the neighborhood cannot keep a bothersome panhandler from annoying passersby, the thief may reason, it is even less likely to call the police to identify a potential mugger or to interfere if the mugging actually takes place. (Wilson and Kelling 1982, p. 34)

Wilson and Kelling put forth the link between disorder and serious crime as a hypothesis worthy of empirical test. They had no data, at that point, to empirically test this part of their argument. Wesley Skogan (1990), in his book, *Disorder and Decline: Crime and the Spiral of Decay in American Neighborhoods*, published in 1990, is the first scholar to devise a serious empirical test of Kelling and Wilson's hypothesis.

Using data sets collected in several earlier studies, Skogan analyzed the crime, fear, and disorder nexus in forty inner-city neighborhoods of six cities: Atlanta, Chicago, Houston, Philadelphia, Newark, and San Francisco. The study data included surveys of citizens in all neighborhoods and field observations of neighborhood conditions in ten of the forty. Skogan replicated the link between disorder and fear found in prior studies. He also documented the fact that a broad consensus existed among diverse demographic groups as to what behavioral and physical conditions constitute disorder. (The most commonly cited disorders included public drunkenness and drug use, loitering gangs of youth, prostitution, vandalism, abandoned buildings, and garbage.) Up to that point academic work typically characterized disorderly behaviors as largely matters of opinion about appropriate public conduct that varied among ethnic groups and by social class. Most important, Skogan's work established an empirical link between disorder and serious crime.

While it is a common observation that high-crime and disorderly conditions are found in the same neighborhoods, it was not clear the extent to which disorder and serious crime are causally linked. Both could be independently caused by other neighborhood factors such as poverty, instability, and ethnic composition. Skogan's work established an independent causal link between disorder and serious crime. His statistical findings supported Wilson and Kelling's argument that disorder left unchecked leads to serious crime—lending credence to the view that direct action against disorder could have substantial payoffs in preventing crime.

Pearson, in other words, discovered in his first couple of months in the Lloyd District the problem police reformers and researchers had been working on for almost twenty years. The most common crime problems citizens in neighborhoods want addressed are low-level crimes of disorder, not just the serious index crimes that constitute official police and FBI measures of crime. In a more recent article Kelling discusses the distinction between serious crime and community crime problems. While the focus of criminal justice institutions has been on the former, they have, he believes, failed to address the latter. In particular, Kelling argues that using only official crime rates as a measure of performance fails to pick up important community concerns. "Lawlessness consists not just in the relatively rare "index" crimes counted by the FBI, but can also refer to an atmosphere of disorder in which it seems like these and less serious crimes and harassments might occur at any time" (Kelling 1992, p. 22).

Having come to this conclusion first hand Pearson, had to figure out what to do. "Once you see this," he comments, "the question is what do you do. Citizens can articulate the problem but they don't really know or understand that the traditional criminal justice system with its preeminent focus on serious criminal cases and procedural justice can't do much about it." That, he decided, is what he would have to do.

What the Neighborhood DAs Do

Before spending time in the street the Portland Neighborhood DAs pictured the job in traditional case-processing terms: they would bring into the courtroom the concerns of residents and businesses about particular cases and categories of crimes that impacted quality of life in neighborhoods. The Neighborhood DAs do advocate for the community on particular cases in court when that is an appropriate response (they do not themselves prosecute cases). But most of what they do is so radically different from traditional prosecution, that very early Schrunk changed the name from Neighborhood Prosecutor to Neighborhood District Attorney.

In generic terms what Neighborhood DAs do is work with citizens and the police to help them figure out how to control the negative street behavior and low-level disorder crime that threaten public safety in neighborhoods. They are, in the first instance, an access point for citizen concerns that do not fit into the traditional incident-based 911-driven system of justice. Part of the job is to provide answers, feedback, and explanations—especially explanations on why police, under the law, cannot do what citizens think they ought to be able to do to "deal with" offensive street conditions. Their core activity, however, is *coming up with alternative solutions.*

The Neighborhood DAs figure out what police and citizens "can do" about low-level crime and disorder that destroy legitimate neighborhood life. This includes searching all of the law, not just the criminal law, for legal solutions (development of civil remedies, for example); figuring out how to reconfigure existing resources (getting people to work together in new ways) so alternative strategies can proceed; and considerable behind-the-scene negotiation to bring diverse parties to agree on solutions and action plans. In this process the Neighborhood DA is a facilitator, legal counselor, negotiator, problem-solver, and community advocate. What they do not do is litigate. If that is needed the case is handed off to the downtown office.

Like community policing officers, Neighborhood DAs' work is by nature problem-, rather than incident-, oriented. Each neighborhood DA, while they advise police officers on many small projects, tends to work on six to ten major projects during the course of a year, and some projects continue indefinitely. In a sense the Neighborhood DAs' problem case file never closes. Once a problem is brought under control, they continue to monitor the situation themselves or through a network of citizens and neighborhood police officers in the impacted area. Part of the job is to "stay on it." If the problem returns or emerges in a new form (car prowls moving from the street into closed parking lots, for example) they adjust the strategy. Now that the entire county is covered, the unit as a whole has the capacity to look for and respond to displacement of crime from target locations to surrounding areas. Virtually all projects involve both police and citizen participants. Other city agencies are brought in on an as-needed basis.

The alternative character of what the Neighborhood DAs do and how they do it is illustrated by the strategy Pearson devised to attack the problem street conditions in the Lloyd District. Based on what citizens had identified as the underlying cause of the problem, illegal camping in Sullivan's Gulch, Pearson reasoned that increased police visibility and arrests of problem people were not likely to be effective in the long run. Traditional police tactics for dealing with negative street conditions typically involve an increase in targeted patrol, a crack down on the negative behavior, and then retreat. All too often when the additional police resources pull out, the problem reappears. Police agencies must respond to many competing demands on their resources. A strategy based on a permanent commitment of new resources is not realistic. On the other hand, intermittent arrests for the nuisance-makers are nothing but an occasional inconvenience.

Pearson instead focused his attention on figuring out how to clear up the transient camping situation in Sullivan's Gulch. If the citizen observation was correct, getting the campers to disperse would solve most of the problem. He devised a long-term plan that began with a police sweep and a major city clean up. For years the city had spent $40,000 to $60,000 each spring to clean up the garbage left by the Gulch campers. He then facilitated a collaborative team effort between citizens and police whereby the north slope of Sullivan's Gulch, which borders the Lloyd District, was prominently posted with neon-colored "no camping signs." The reverse side of the signs listed shelter locations where the truly homeless could find temporary housing. Citizen volunteers, in this case drawn from area businesses, were enlisted to do visual patrols of the Gulch by driving through at regular intervals during the day. When campsites were observed the citizen patrol faxed notification, detailing the exact camp location, to Pearson who passed the information on to the regular district patrol officer. The officer then went to the location and simply asked the camper(s) to leave. Arrests were rarely required, but the campers were *always* inconvenienced.

Eventually, with no prompting from Pearson, citizens themselves started asking the campers to leave (and clean up after themselves), eliminating further the demand on police resources. Pearson simultaneously facilitated the intervention of other city agencies to clean out the brush that created the cover campers depended upon to escape detection. He also got the city department of transportation to build inexpensive steel bar barriers under the highway viaducts to close off the cave-like shelters campers used to shield themselves from view.

There is no question that the illegal camping problem in Sullivan's Gulch has been eliminated. Grass now grows on the former site of "cardboard condominiums." Street conditions also improved in the Lloyd District. The next phase of Pearson's plan—to get liquor store owners to restrict voluntarily the sale of certain types of malt liquor and fortified wines, favored by campers—never had to be implemented. No one can say exactly where the campers went (the joking response is Seattle). While street people, in general, have not been cleared out of Portland, no similar aggregation of problem transients has reappeared in other parts of the city or nearby urban areas.

The Contrast with Traditional Prosecution

Pearson's approach to the Sullivan Gulch situation sounds so reasonable it's easy for courthouse outsiders to miss the innovation. That is how different this is from conventional prosecution. Without really consciously thinking about it, Pearson and the Neighborhood DA unit, which he now heads, are step by step redefining the district attorney's function to include the task of order maintenance, historically performed by the police. This is not to say that prosecutors in Portland, or elsewhere, are supplanting the police role in dealing with public order. They are rather augmenting it by providing the police with an expanded set of legal tools to respond to citizen problems for which the traditional criminal justice response is having no impact. In Pearson's words, this starts by getting attorneys' focus off the singular task of "hammering the defendant" in court and onto the problem of how to stop crime and abate disorderly situations. The critical first step is getting office attorneys to connect with citizens' view of what goes on in the street. When attorneys come to know what citizens know and see what the police see, they begin to understand the situational "handle the problem" perspective of citizens and police. They also come to understand that the court task of "holding individual defendants to account for committing specific criminal acts" is but one of a variety of legal tactics required to ameliorate neighborhood crime and disorder.

In the courthouse downtown an assistant prosecutor's work is governed, not by the neighborhood conditions that give rise to crime, but by the rules that govern all participants in adversary proceedings—formal rules of evidence, statutory definitions of crimes and punishments, and local court norms about the seriousness of crimes most worthy of judicial attention. In the routine business of prosecution this means sorting through the daily stream of arrests brought to the court by the police and making a judgment, case by case, from the facts the police deliver as to whether a particular individual can be proven to be legally culpable for having committed a specific criminal act, according to the procedural constraints imposed by the law. The all-important issue for the downtown system of justice is not generally whether a crime has occurred or even whether the person arrested is the culprit (these matters are in the routine case typically not in dispute), but whether the facts available meet the procedural standards of justice to demonstrate legal guilt in court.

In this process, it is the prosecutor's unique role to initiate the criminal proceedings designed to hold the guilty to account. In exercising this authority the public expects the office of the district attorney to act vigorously against law breakers, but simultaneously not to abuse the power of the office by accusing individuals of committing crime when the facts do not warrant. Deciding on which matters to proceed thus hinges critically on an assessment of whether a case can be proven at trial and on a staff of competent trial attorneys who can then in fact accomplish that task. Contrary to a great deal of misinformation (both popular and academic) regarding the insignificant role of trials in the court disposition process, in a well-managed court system trials set the standard and drive the system. In the American system of adversary justice there are powerful incentives against *routinely* moving forward cases that cannot withstand a trial standard of proof. Routinely taking forward cases that cannot be convicted at trial is likely, in addition to irritating judges, to provoke vigorous challenge by defense counsel (not to mention an embarrassing string of losses for the prosecutor). The most vexing administrative problem in moving criminal cases to disposition is not getting defendants to plead guilty (as is commonly stated), but getting them to come to terms with the fact that they must *either* plead guilty or go to trial. Defendants don't want to do either, they prefer dismissals. Skilled prosecutors know the quickest way to get a defendant to plead guilty is through credible threat of imminent trial.

Over the last twenty-five years or so, the trend in prosecution management has been to concentrate in the hands of key senior attorneys the highly discretionary decision about what matters are appropriate to take forward for serious prosecution. The organization's front line operatives (i.e., trial attorneys), not surprisingly, view their professional success in terms of how well they do in court on cases sent forward for adjudication. They are intensely focused on the task of obtaining convictions on the individual cases assigned to them and on acquiring the trial skills necessary to back up the organizational judgment that a given defendant is legally guilty. They are not remiss in thinking that what they do is fundamental to crime control—academic thinking, public opinion, and common sense support this view. But it also means the average trial attorney doesn't really think much (or have time to think much) about "crime" per se. He or she fails to consider how it happens in the street, the situational conditions that give rise to specific incidents of crime, or how to stop it— other than holding the guilty to account after the fact with the highest priority accorded to serious crimes. Thinking about what to do about small crimes and public order is not routinely viewed as part of the job.

The DA and Public Order

Both the legal tools and the organizational arrangements required for dealing with neighborhood problems of public order are markedly different from that which support the case-by-case, procedural justice of the court. The highly formalized rule-oriented work of the court seeks to strip away circumstances irrelevant to the task of affixing legal blame for a specific act to an individual, and to the extent possible routinize the work of dispensing equal justice to persons similarly charged. Dealing with public order requires taking all circumstances of the situation into account. This does not mean dispensing with individualistic procedural justice, but thinking through other ways, within the rule of law, to promote order and prevent crime. It means figuring out not just what to do about neighborhood drug dealers but also the landlords who unwittingly, negligently or corruptly rent to them; not just arresting the prostitutes but also dealing with the motel proprietors who facilitate and profit from their trade; not just catching shoplifters but also pursuing the convenience store fence who converts their contraband to cash for drugs. It also means figuring out how to use all areas of the law (not only the criminal law) to deal with situations attorneys "never see in the courthouse downtown."

As the work of the Portland Neighborhood DAs evolves, it is clear that the capability to adapt is critical. To be effective this new approach to neighborhood crime and order problems requires a highly flexible organizational arrangement that allows Neighborhood DAs to shape responses and legal tactics to meet the different needs of different neighborhoods and situations. What bothers the residents of one neighborhood may be irrelevant to the next. Conditions in given neighborhoods change over time. Street behaviors themselves are dynamic and constantly changing. Rigid operational prescriptions on how to proceed are not helpful.

Pearson's work in Sullivan's Gulch, for example, was essentially to coordinate a collaborative effort by citizens and police to send a clear, consistent, and constitutionally defensible message that illegal camping prohibited by local ordinance would not be tolerated in the Lloyd District. A clear consensus existed among area residents and business people that these minor infractions should not be tolerated because they were the underlying cause of a bigger problem. The downtown Neighborhood DA, in contrast, has devoted most of her energy to negotiating a sophisticated law enforcement response to open-air drug dealing (dominated by Mexican illegal aliens) in Old Town, an emerging entertainment district adjacent to downtown. To pull this off has required the resolution of numerous conflicting views of the problem among the diverse interests and varied agencies that converge in the downtown area including business owners, advocates for the Hispanic community, the Immigration and Naturalization Service, the U.S. Attorney's Office, the Portland Police Bureau, and the local courts and jails. In the view of one downtown business representative, just getting these diverse parties to the table so problem-solving could proceed was a major accomplishment. He had tried and failed. He attributes success to the negotiation skills of the downtown Neighborhood DA and the political prestige of the district attorney's office. The Downtown Neighborhood DA also did a tremendous amount of behind-the-scenes legal footwork to facilitate a mix of traditional and nontraditional law enforcement responses to the problem including: undercover missions by the FBI, indictments by the U.S. Attorney, conventional street enforcement by the Portland Police Bureau, and implementation of a Drug-Free Zone Ordinance that gives legal authority to police officers to arrest trespassing drug dealers who were previously arrested in the area on drug charges. The North/Northeast Neighborhood DA, on the other hand, has spent a great deal of time and effort helping citizen groups and police officers deal with the problem properties that arise from drug and gang activity in residential neighborhoods. A routine part of the North/Northeast Neighborhood DA's work is coming up with legal tactics to give official authority to police and citizen initiatives aimed at denying use of public and private space to persons using it to engage in illegal activities.

The common root giving rise to these varied approaches to neighborhood crime and disorder problems is an organizational arrangement that gets office attorneys directly linked to people who see daily what is going on in the street, frees them from the day-to-day demands of handling cases in court, and instead assigns them to work on the crime and disorder problems of specific geographic locations as articulated by the people who live and work in them. The problems of Portland's North/Northeast residential neighborhoods are common to drug-plagued neighborhoods in many other cities. Interactions among police, citizens, and the Neighborhood DAs that are occurring there illustrate how connecting the district attorney's office to police and citizens in neighborhoods gives rise to "a different response."

Getting Connected to Neighborhoods

In April 1992 (roughly one year after Pearson set up shop in the Lloyd District) Mike Kuykendall, equipped with a cellular phone and a truck for an office, set out to work with citizen groups in North/Northeast Portland. The area covers roughly one-quarter to one-third of the city's land area and includes approximately one-third of Portland's half million residents. By the time Kuykendall arrived, grassroots citizen groups and community policing officers were already actively working to combat neighborhood drug, gang, and liveability (Portland's term for disorder) issues.[2] His first task was to provide these groups with regular contact to the district attorney's office. At a minimum, Schrunk thought "people wanted access, say-so, and feedback." Of the twenty-two North/Northeast neighborhoods, about half were experiencing significant difficulties.

Problem neighborhoods fell into two groups. Complaints in the less seriously impacted centered on classic disorderly behaviors: public drunkenness, drug use, prostitution, trash, abandoned autos, illegal dumping, and so on. One of Kuykendall's first successes, in North Portland's Kenton neighborhood, was to help citizens curb chronic public drunkenness in the local business district. Armed with police data identifying eight problem-alcoholics as the source of several hundred "detox holds" in a twelve-month period, he, with citizen support, persuaded local liquor stores not to sell to the eight problem-drinkers. In higher crime neighborhoods closer to the inner-city core, disorderly behaviors intermix with drug and gang activity. Problem properties, drug and gang houses associated with the crack-cocaine trade, were the predominant problem. Most involved rental properties used either as locations for drug sales (drug houses) or as places where gang members hang out (gang houses). Both generate similar negative street behaviors—disruptive levels of noise and traffic, fights, indecent exposure, public drug and alcohol use, aberrant loitering, harassment of passersby, intimidation and shootings. Problem behaviors sometimes got threatening. One activist citizen who lead the attack on crack houses on his block, twice had his car bombed. At one point a prominent community organizer was demanding that the city station a police officer in front of every crack house. This behavior was not something citizens can stand up to alone. They needed law enforcement help.

Kuykendall established himself as available. In short order, he had "clients" seeking what he had to offer. Activist citizens and police agree that what he had that they *most* needed was legal expertise. Sometimes this meant up-front legal advice on tactics they wanted to try. For example, could landlords legally and constitutionally use police bureau criminal records to screen potential tenants to keep out convicted drug dealers? (Yes, as long as the same procedure applied to all applicants.) Sometimes legal expertise meant the mere presence of an assistant district attorney, for example, with police at problem property "knock and talk" sessions to give official authority to citizens complaints. Knock and talk is a community policing tool first used to connect officers to neighborhood problems and residents. In Portland (and elsewhere) police have found this to be a surprisingly effective tactic for deterring drug dealing from residential properties. It lets resident dealers know complaints are being taken seriously. Kuykendall reserved one day a week for what he called "roll day." He and a community policing officer working from a priority list, "rolled" through the precinct visiting problem properties that police were having difficulty resolving on their own.

Providing ad hoc backup to the police is an important part of what the Neighborhood DAs do, but early on Pearson and Kuykendall saw that their most valuable legal contribution was coming up with alternative legal options. A central function of the Neighborhood DA mission is to develop new legal tools citizens and police can use when existing tactics hit a brick wall. Such situations typically require not only new ideas and legal research but also coordinated action by varied agents—citizens, police, downtown justice, and other city agencies. "The best ideas come from citizens and police," Kuykendall comments. Support on the legal end, nonetheless, is critical to community efforts. "It has to be done right so the legal system will take it," if necessary, and even if the final solution turns out to be informally negotiated, having in place the legal back up ensures integrity. Informal solutions, in other words, are not based on bluff.

A good example of how this process works is the development of a particularly novel tool, the "citizen driven search warrant," that Kuykendall and Pearson devised to deal with low-level drug dealing at owner-occupied houses. Dealing by home owners is less common than dealing by tenants, but often more difficult to root out if dealers resist informal neighborhood efforts to get them to stop. Pearson and Kuykendall had been working on ideas to deal with such situations when a particularly stubborn problem property showed up on an otherwise quiet block in North Portland. Kuykendall's work report tells the story.[3]

On . . . a telephonic search warrant was successfully executed at 11 Ninth Street in the St. Dennis neighborhood. This location was an Operation Target property, and the warrant was served by Target officers and members of North Precinct's Neighborhood Response Team.[4] The property [had not previously responded] to the typical Target strategies—it was owner-occupied, making eviction through landlord-tenant law and the City's Nuisance Ordinances not possible. The residence met city code requirements and was not subject to Bureau of Buildings enforcement procedures. Taxes were current and not subject to scrutiny. The residents were not amenable to the Neighborhood Mediation program and had disregarded their warning letter from the Drugs and Vice Division (DVD).

With all this in mind, the decision was made to look at the more traditional option of obtaining a search warrant. DVD [was] unsuccessful in obtaining undercover buys, making this location a candidate for the telephonic search warrant we have researched in the past months, [provided] a citizen-neighbor informant could be located. Officer Lisa Branch canvassed the neighborhood and was able to locate a neighbor who had filed complaints with DVD for the past two years and who was willing to do anything to rid her neighborhood of this problem. After de-briefing the neighbor and providing her with copies of the Drug Observation Log Sheet that we prepared, the neighbor was instructed to watch the suspect location and record suspicious activities with as much particularity as possible. The resulting log contained observations of weeks of pedestrian and vehicular traffic at the location, most of which lasted for no more than three to four minutes. During that period, Officer Branch also performed random surveillance and was able to verify the accuracy of the informant's observations. After checking with the License Bureau and determining that there was no business license issued for that address, and gleaning corroborative information from police reports regarding the suspect location and its present occupants, it was determined that probable cause existed for a search warrant.

The affidavit was prepared and I met with Judge Abrecht to discuss the telephonic procedure. . . . Officer Branch then did additional surveillance at the suspect location, maintaining telephone contact with the neighbor informant. When the informant called to report the presence of a probable purchaser at the location who had entered and exited in a four-minute period, Officer Branch called Judge Abrecht from her surveillance point and read the affidavit and its fresh information. Judge Abrecht then authorized the search. North Precinct was contacted and the search warrant team arrived within 15 minutes. The search produced over 100 "bindles" of marijuana packaged for sale. The residents, Edward and Anne McCoy, both have been indicted for DCS I/PCS I[5] and the case has been assigned to Deputy DA Weintraub. As the North Precinct officers were leaving the scene with the suspects, about 20 neighbors and their children began clapping and cheering the officers' efforts, which was something I personally have never seen in the past. (Kuykendall, File Work Report)

As is often the case, this was not the end of the story. The McCoys were convicted and given probation with fairly stringent "civil behavior" conditions. The judge imposed a 10 P.M. curfew, required a log of visitors, specified no contact with neighbors and no alcohol or drug use on the property. The neighbors kept watch. The McCoys moved. Their son drove his car onto the citizen-informants lawn in retribution. Young McCoy subsequently was charged with stalking and received a thirty-day jail sentence and $750 fine. Kuykendall fronted for the neighborhood on the case downtown. Another incident would ratchet up to a Class C felony. Kuykendall briefed the regular district patrol officer about the situation, who agreed to perform low-level maintenance surveillance. The McCoys' property was ultimately sold, although they still reside in the St. Dennis neighborhood. As of this writing (several years after the incident) they remain in strict compliance with their terms of probation. Standard Operating Procedures (SOPs) were written for both the police and the court for future citizen-driven warrants. The tool is now regularly used in North/Northeast and other parts of Portland and Multnomah County.

Like the McCoys' marijuana operation, the neighborhood crime and disorder problems the Neighborhood DAs typically deal with require multifaceted action. In these situations, the Neighborhood DA capitalizes on community initiatives—empowering citizens and police to develop and implement public safety strategies. The attorneys figure out what they can do legally and then bring around other agencies and the criminal justice system (on an as-needed basis) to facilitate coordinated action. The strongest strategies incorporate multiple tactics. Street behavior is dynamic, and it is difficult to predict in advance how the problem-makers are going to respond. Success requires trying everything within reason, monitoring what happens, dropping what doesn't work, and adjusting tactics as events unfold. A network of actors—police, citizens, city government, downtown justice— is needed for effective action.

The Essence of Emerging Reform

The idea and practice of community prosecution are still evolving, nonetheless the experience of the Neighborhood DAs in Portland suggests several key themes regarding what this reform is, what it is not, and what it needs to take root. First, as I trust the foregoing examples have made clear, community prosecution is *not a program*—guided by clear-cut procedural rules, prescribed in advance interventions, uniformly applied across neighborhoods and similar situations, administered in a stable administrative environment. Nor is it a mere collection of tactics and strategies that once proved successful that are then routinized (although it can generate this, for example, setting up SOPs for successful legal tactics). Rather in the course of their problem-solving activities, the Neighborhood DAs have built a highly flexible new organizational arrangement that is not wedded to specific solutions or responses but to the task of getting one—to getting people to a doable action plan that brings down the level of street disorder in situations in which individualized guilt won't do—either because the adjudication of guilt is irrelevant, a mere inconvenience, or not enough. To get started this new arrangement for dealing with street disorder requires stout-hearted executives willing to delegate a lot of authority to line operatives, who work in the field out of his or her sight but in public view, and giving them space to figure out for themselves how to fashion responses to the crime and order problems in particular neighborhoods. Although the underlying demand is coming from citizens, the DA's office can't do this without the police. A serious effort necessitates a closer day-to-day working relationship with precinct officers than is now common practice. Loss of independent judgment is a risk. This is unfamiliar territory. Quick results are not certain.

Second, although the legal tactics the Neighborhood DAs devise more often than not involve alternatives to the conventional prosecutorial focus on litigation, their work is solidly grounded in fundamental traditions of the legal profession. They are applying what Mary Ann Glendon, Learned Hand Professor of Law at Harvard University, describes as the traditional order promoting skills of lawyers to an area of crime control—order maintenance—that has caused the police no end of grief for over a century.[6] In her book, *A Nation Under Lawyers*, in which she takes the legal profession, in general, to task for its exaltation over the last thirty years of "litigation, money making, and efforts to achieve social transformation through law" at the expense of what she argues are the more common order-affirming, peacemaking skills of the profession—she elegantly articulates the unique qualities lawyers bring to this task. Others share many of these qualities. She argues it is the following ensemble that is unique: the ability to narrow conflicts to precise issues in controversy; to grasp what is essential to individual parties to find common ground; to think through hypothetical cases in devising solutions so that trouble is avoided down the road; to understand others' perspective with detachment and respect; to minimize arbitrariness through reasoned argument; and above all the ability to apply the law. The one quality lawyers alone bring to peacekeeping is intimate mastery of the legal apparatus—"its history, its maintenance and proper functioning, awareness of its range of uses and understanding of its limitations," and its constitutional framework. In problem-solving, what lawyers bring to the table is "a vast fund of inherited experience . . . a record of the trials and errors of others in a huge range of variants on recurring human problems. Faced with a new variant a lawyer typically invents little, but adds adapts and rearranges much" (Glendon 1994, pp. 102-7).

This set of skills comes naturally to the Neighborhood DAs. They easily shift roles as the situation requires from problem-solver, to mediator, to consensus-builder, to legal strategist. Their innovative use of the law is mostly a reworking of long-established legal principles: the community's right to civilly sanction a public nuisance, to regulate commerce; the documentation of new fact patterns that justify a police search. An astute precinct captain understood the value of legal insight. "At first," he said, "I thought having the Neighborhood DAs around was just nice. But over time I realized how integral their work is to police efforts. When we work on problems citizens want addressed we inevitably run into thorny legal issues we can't handle by ourselves." It is the Neighborhood DAs who can provide the precise wording of ordinances to comply with constitutional restrictions, who write the briefs when challenges do arise, and who can draft legal documents that precisely define the negative behavior that is the problem. The attorneys who get involved in this work invariably find it rewarding, but like the DA they too must be sturdy individuals who can deflect the skepticism of their peers, who view their work of lesser value than trying cases. Eventually this starts to change but for a long time a Neighborhood DA is alone out on a limb.

Third, community prosecution is a reform effort from the bottom up. After nearly three decades in which public discourse about what to do about crime has been dominated by scholars, commentators, national commissions, and other distant experts, citizens are reclaiming their right to define the crime issue in terms of the specific concrete situations that affect their daily lives, and finally they are succeeding city by city, neighborhood by neighborhood, in forcing a response that only their locally elected representatives can deliver. Experts have much to offer—but it is their forte to abstract, to frame issues in dichotomous terms, to suggest either/or solutions that easily shift attention from the concrete facts of particular situations to ideologically intractable positions. In the community justice movement the seeds of reclaiming a voice in defining the crime issue for local institutions, where focus is on the concrete and consensus and balance are possible, is perhaps its most spectacular innovation. Community justice is the politics of the doable. Lacking elegant theory, it compensates by delivering in the real world.

Notes

This work was supported by Grant No. 94-IJ-CX-0004 awarded by the National Institute of Justice, Office of Justice Programs, U.S. Department of Justice. Points of view in this document are those of the author and do not necessarily represent the official position or policies of the U.S. Department of Justice. An earlier version of the chapter was prepared for the Workshop on the Prosecution in the Community at the Kennedy School of Government,

Harvard University, March 1996. A summary version appeared in the *National Institute of Justice Journal*, August 1996, Washington, D.C.

1. Scholarly studies of the police order maintenance function typically define order maintenance as the enforcement of low-level disorderly or disputatious public behaviors, such as "vagrancy," "disorderly conduct," "disturbing the peace," for which the law provides the police little statutory guidance in terms of behavioral definition, in contrast to serious criminal acts, like murder, which are precisely defined in state statutes. Disorderly behaviors are sometimes characterized as a largely uncodified set of behavioral norms about appropriate public conduct (see Skogan 1990, p. 5). The public order problem I refer to here includes these kinds of low-level disorderly behaviors but, in addition, the serious violent behaviors associated with the drug trade and street gangs.

2. North/Northeast has twenty-two Neighborhood Associations, part of a comprehensive network of over ninety associations formally associated with Portland's Office of Neighborhood Associations. In addition to citizen volunteers the Office of Neighborhood Associations provides paid crime prevention specialists to assist citizen anticrime efforts. The Police Bureau, as part of community policing reform, has assigned a Neighborhood Liaison Officer (NLO) to each Neighborhood Association; two to three officers in each of the city's four precincts to Neighborhood Response Teams (NRT) to work full time on crime and liveability problems; and has reduced the call loads of other designated district officers to free up time for crime problem-solving.

3. Names and locations have been changed and dates deleted.

4. Project Target is a community policing program targeting problem properties, staffed by designated district patrol officers. Neighborhood Response Teams are precinct-based community policing units devoted full time to problem-solving activities.

5. Delivery of a Controlled Substance Schedule I/Possession of a Controlled Substance Schedule I, a Class B Felony.

6. Police problems in dealing with the order maintenance function and their retreat from performing it are documented in Moore and Kelling (1983), Skogan (1990, Chapter 5), and Wilson (1968, 1969).

References

Fehrenkamp, Lee. 1990. "Memorandum on Neighborhood Prosecution Project." Metropolitan Exposition-Recreation Commission. Portland, Oregon.

Glendon, Mary Ann. 1994. *A Nation Under Lawyers*. New York: Farrar, Straus, and Giroux.

Holladay District Public Safety Committee. 1990. "The [Lloyd] Holladay District Public Safety Action Plan." Portland, Oregon.

Kelling, George. 1992. "Measuring What Matters." *The City Journal* (Spring): 21-33.

Kuykendall, Michael. "File Work Report." Multnomah County District Attorney's Office. Portland, Oregon.

Moore, Mark H., and George Kelling. 1983. "To Serve and Protect: Learning from Police History." *The Public Interest* 70: 49-65.

Northeast Rescue Plan Action Committee. 1990. "A Call to Action." Portland, Oregon.

Police Foundation. 1981. *The Newark Foot Patrol Experiment.* Washington, DC: The Police Foundation

Redden, Jim. 1990. "Hired Gun: Neighborhood Crime Got You Down? Buy Yourself a Prosecutor." *Willamette Week* (December 13-19), Portland, Oregon.

Skogan, Wesley G. 1990. *Disorder and Decline: Crime and Spiral of Decay in American Neighborhoods.* Los Angeles: University of California Press.

Wilson, James Q. 1968. *Varieties of Police Behavior.* Cambridge: Harvard University Press.

———. 1969. "What Makes a Better Policeman." *The Atlantic Monthly* (March): 129-35.

Wilson, James Q., and George Kelling. 1982. "Broken Windows." *The Atlantic Monthly* (March): 29-38.

12

Conditions of Successful Reintegration Ceremonies: Dealing with Juvenile Offenders

John Braithwaite and Stephen Mugford

The specter of failure haunts modern criminology and penology. Deep down many feel what some say openly—that "nothing works." That despite decades of study and debate, we are no nearer deterrence than we ever were and/or that more "humane" forms of treatment are mere masquerades concealing a descent into Kafkaesque bureaucracy where offenders suffer a slow and silent suffocation of the soul. Worse still, we fear that even when something does work, it is seen to do so only in the eyes of certain professionals, while "outside" the system ordinary citizens are left without a role or voice in the criminal justice process.

This chapter takes a different view. Rejecting the pessimism that pervades discussions about crime and punishment, it offers an optimistic view of at least one area—the punishment of juvenile offenders. It argues that it is possible to develop practices that "work" both in the sense of reducing recidivism and reintegrating offenders into a wider web of community ties and support and, at the same time, in giving victims a "voice" in a fashion that is both satisfying and also socially productive. Further, it links a theory (reintegrative shaming) and a practice (the reintegration ceremony) which explain how to understand and how to implement this success.

While there are elements that are quite distinctive about both the theory and practice of reintegrative shaming, there is also a great deal in common with the theory and practice of "making amends" (Wright 1982); restorative justice (Cragg 1992; Galaway and Hudson 1990; Zehr 1990);

reconciliation (Dignan 1992; Marshall 1985; Umbreit 1985); peacemaking (Pepinsky and Quinney 1991); redress (de Haan 1990); and feminist abolitionism (Meima 1990). We differ from abolitionists, however, in believing that it is right to shame certain kinds of conduct as criminal in certain contexts.

The rest of the chapter has two sections. The second section outlines some fieldwork which we have undertaken to examine such ceremonies, makes a relatively brief series of arguments which connect the theory of reintegrative shaming to the seminal paper by Garfinkel on degradation ceremonies, and outlines how the latter must be transformed to cover reintegration ceremonies. The major point of this section is a specification of the conditions for successful reintegration ceremonies. The third and longer section follows through the logic of such ceremonies, illustrating each point with material derived from the fieldwork and offering comments about policy and implementation.

Background to the Argument:
Reintegrative Shaming in Theory and Practice

The theory of reintegrative shaming (Braithwaite 1989, 1993) has been offered as a way of achieving two major aims. First, to recast criminological findings in a more coherent and productive fashion. Second, to offer a practical basis for a principled reform of criminal justice practices. Central to the endeavor is an understanding of the relationship between crime and social control which argues for the shaming of criminal *acts* and the subsequent reintegration of deviant *actors* once suitable redress and apology have been made. It is argued that societies that have low rates of common crime (such as Japan) rely more upon this type of social control, working hard at reforming the deviant through reconstructing his or her social ties. Conversely, high-crime societies (such as the United States) rely upon stigmatization, thus doing little to prevent cycles of re-offending.

This theory has clear practical implications and people involved in various reform programs have drawn on it in various ways—sometimes as an inspiration for reform blueprints (see e.g., Howard and Purches 1992; Mugford and Mugford 1991, 1992; O'Connell and Moore 1992), often as a way to articulate what they are trying to achieve and give it a sharper focus. Some, such as the New Zealand Maoris, have comprehended and applied the principles of the theory for hundreds of years (Hazlehurst

1985). Where we have heard of or been involved in programs, we have sought to carry out some limited fieldwork, which would help us to understand both what is practically possible and how we might refine our ideas.

This chapter utilizes such ongoing fieldwork, specifically observations of community conferences for twenty-three juvenile offenders in Auckland, New Zealand, and Wagga Wagga, Australia. In New Zealand, these conferences are called family group conferences. While there are differences between the approaches adopted in the two cities, both involve diverting young offenders from court and keeping them out of exclusionary juvenile institutions. Both programs subscribe to the philosophy of reintegrative shaming as outlined above. Shame and shaming is commonly used in both programs to describe what is going on; reintegration is commonly used in Wagga, while healing is more commonly used in Auckland for this aspect of the process. The approach in both cities involves assembling in a room the offender and supporters of the offender (usually the nuclear family, often aunts, uncles, grandparents, sometimes neighbors, counselors, even a teacher or football coach) along with the victim of the crime (and supporters of the victim, usually from their nuclear family) under the supervision of a coordinator—a police sergeant in Wagga, a youth justice coordinator from the Department of Social Welfare in Auckland. Auckland conferences usually only have single offenders, but can have multiple victims in the room. Wagga conferences often bring together multiple offenders who were involved jointly in the same offences with multiple victims. In the conferences we observed, the number of people in the room ranged from five to thirty. More systematic data from New Zealand puts the average attendance at nine (Maxwell and Morris 1993, p. 74). At both sites, the offender(s) plays an important role in describing the nature of the offence(s). The psychological, social and economic consequences of the offence—for victims, offenders, and others—are elicited in discussions guided by the coordinator. Disapproval, often emotional disapproval, is usually communicated by victims, and often by victim supporters and family members of the offender. At the same time, the professional who co-ordinates the conference strives to bring out support for and forgiveness toward the offender from participants in the conference.

A striking common feature of both locations is that the formal properties of the cautioning conference have come to take on a ceremonial or ritual character, based partly upon "common sense," itself expanded and tempered by experiences of what does and does not seem to work well.

With varying degrees of accomplishment, coordinators have developed procedures designed to ensure that the potential for shaming and reintegration of offenders is realized in practice. In so doing, they have effectively invented the reintegration ceremony, even if that is not what they would always call it. In this ceremony, identities are in a social crucible. The vision that an offender holds of himself as a "tough guy" or that victims have of him as a "mindless hooligan" are challenged, altered, and re-created (for example, as a "good lad who has strayed into bad ways").

Viewing these events as a reintegration ceremony recalls the seminal contribution of Harold Garfinkel (1956) on "Conditions of Successful Degradation Ceremonies." Perhaps the same kind of social structures and sociopsychological processes he analyses in that paper are at work here, but in different combination and directed to different ends? Posing the problem that way has been a productive way for us to organize our views of reintegration ceremonies and so we choose to use the Garfinkel approach as a way of outlining this rather different set of events.

By degradation ceremonies, Garfinkel meant communicative work that names an actor as an "outsider," that transforms an individual's total identity into an identity "lower in the group's scheme of social types" (1956, p. 420). Most criminal trials are good examples of status degradation ceremonies and this view of them became a central idea in the sociology of deviance, especially among labeling theorists (see Becker 1963; Schur 1973). For Erikson (1962, p. 311), for example, this communicative work constitutes "a sharp rite of transition at once moving him out of his normal position in society and transferring him into a distinctive deviant role." Moreover, Erikson continues, an ". . . important feature of these ceremonies in our culture is that they are almost irreversible" (1962, p. 311).

Such a view, however, is simplistic, exaggerated and overly deterministic (Braithwaite 1989). Most people who go into mental hospitals come out of them; many alcoholics give up drinking; most marijuana users stop being users at some point in their lives, usually permanently; most kids labeled as delinquents never go to jail as adults. Labeling theorists did useful empirical work, but their work was myopic, exclusively focused on "front-end" processes that certify deviance. Above all, they envisaged individuals as having "total identities." We suggest that by employing instead the notion of multiple identities one can recast the interest in transformation ceremonies, asking questions as much about ceremonies to decertify deviance as to certify it. While degradation ceremonies are about the sequence disapproval-degradation-exclusion, reintegration ceremonies are about the sequence disapproval-non-degradation-inclusion. In a reintegration ceremony, disapproval of a bad act is communicated while sustaining the identity of the actor as good. Shame is transmitted within a continuum of respect for the wrongdoer. Repair work is directed at ensuring that a deviant identity (one of the actor's multiple identities) does not become a master status trait that overwhelms other identities. Communicative work is directed at sustaining identities like daughter, student, promising footballer in preference to creating "master" identities like delinquent.

Considerable analytic and policy implications follow this refocusing from degradation to reintegration. Indeed, we suggest that the implication is a redesign of everything about contemporary criminal justice systems and everything about the labeling theory critique of those institutions. To achieve this, however, it is necessary to show where one must transcend earlier accounts. As a first step, we juxtapose in Table 1 Garfinkel's conditions of successful degradation ceremonies with our own conditions of successful ceremonies of reintegration. These latter were condensed from our observations and cast in a form that allows comparison and contrast. Eight of the conditions we specify for reintegration ceremonies involve presenting a deliberate twist on Garfinkel's conditions. The other six are based on observations and discussions and, we feel, address some of the theoretical neglects of the ethnomethodological tradition.

Reintegration Ceremonies in Practice

In this section, we outline each of the fourteen conditions identified in Table 1. For each one, we provide a detailed discussion, drawing on our field work observations.

1. *The event, but not the perpetrator, is removed from the realm of its everyday character and is defined as irresponsible, wrong, a crime.*

Courtroom ceremonies tend to degradation rather than reintegration—that is, they remove both event *and* perpetrator from the everyday domain in just the way suggested by Garfinkel. This is because the production-line technocracy and discourse of legalism makes it easy for the offender to sustain psychological barriers against shame for acts that the court defines as wrongful. It is hard for a person who we do not know or respect, who speaks a strange legal language, who forces us into a relationship of

Table 1

Conditions of Successful Degradation Ceremonies	Conditions of Successful Reintegration Ceremonies
1. Both event and perpetrator must be removed from the realm of their everyday character and be made to stand as "out of the ordinary."	1. The event, *but not the perpetrator*, is removed from the realm of its everyday character and is defined as irresponsible, wrong, a crime.
2. Both event and perpetrator must be placed within a scheme of preferences that shows the following properties: (a) The preferences must not be for event A over event B, but for event of *type* A over event of *type* B. The same typing must be accomplished for the perpetrator. Event and perpetrator must be defined as instances of a uniformity and must be treated as a uniformity throughout the work of the denunciation. (b) The witnesses must appreciate the characteristics of the typed person and event by referring the type to a dialectical counterpart. Ideally, the witnesses should not be able to contemplate the features of the denounced person without reference to the counter-conception, as the profanity of an occurrence or a desire or a character trait, for example, is clarified by the references it bears to its opposite, the sacred.	2. Event and perpetrator must be uncoupled rather than defined as instances of a profane uniformity. The self of the perpetrator is sustained as sacred rather than profane. This is accomplished by comprehending: (a) how essentially good people have a pluralistic self that accounts for their occasional lapse into profane acts; and (b) that the profane act of a perpetrator occurs in a social context for which many actors may bear some shared responsibility. Collective as well as individual shame must be brought into the open and confronted.
3. The denouncer must so identify himself to the witnesses that during the denunciation they regard him not as a private but as a publicly known person.	3. Coordinators must identify themselves with all private parties—perpetrators, their families, victims, witnesses—as well as being identified with the public interest in upholding the law.
4. The denouncer must make the dignity of the supra-personal values of the tribe salient and accessible to view, and his denunciation must be delivered in their name.	4. Denunciation must be both by and in the name of victims and in the name of supra-personal values enshrined in the law.
5. The denouncer must arrange to be invested with the right to speak in the name of these ultimate values. The success of the denunciation will be undermined if, for his authority to denounce, the denouncer invokes the personal interests that he may have acquired by virtue of the wrong done to him or someone else.	5. Nonauthoritative actors (victims, offenders, offenders' families) must be empowered with process control. The power of actors normally authorized to issue denunciations on behalf of the public interest (e.g., judges) must be decentered.

Table 1   (Continued)

6. The denouncer must get himself so defined by the witnesses that they locate him as a supporter of these values.	6. The perpetrator must be so defined by all the participants (particularly by the perpetrator himself) that he is located as a supporter of both the supra-personal values enshrined in the law and the private interests of victims.
7. Not only must the denouncer fix his distance from the person being denounced, but the witnesses must be made to experience their distance from him also.	7. Distance between each participant and the other participants must be closed; empathy among all participants must be enhanced; opportunities must be provided for perpetrators and victims to show (unexpected) generosity toward each other.
8. Finally, the denounced person must be ritually separated from a place in the legitimate order, i.e., he must be defined as standing at a place opposed to it. He must be placed "outside," he must be made "strange."	8. The separation of the denounced person must be terminated by rituals of inclusion that place him, even physically, inside rather than outside.
	9. The separation of the victim, any fear or shame experienced by victims, must be terminated by rituals of reintegration.
	10. Means must be supplied to intervene against power imbalances that inhibit either shaming or reintegration, or both.
	11. Ceremony design must be flexible and culturally plural, so that participants exercise their process control constrained by only very broad procedural requirements.
	12. Reintegration agreements must be followed through to ensure that they are enacted.
	13. When a single reintegration ceremony fails, ceremony after ceremony must be scheduled, never giving up, until success is achieved.
	14. The ceremony must be justified by a politically resonant discourse.

feigned respect by making us stand when she walks into the room, to touch our soul. Thus event and perpetrator remain united. One casts out both or neither. So the denunciation of the judge may degrade the offender but the process is so incomprehensible, such a blur, that all the judge usually accomplishes is some authoritative outcasting.

In contrast to formal courtrooms, community conferences in New Zealand and Wagga are held in less formal spaces. Conference coordinators purposively assemble actors with the best chance of persuading the offender of the irresponsibility of a criminal act. Close kin are prime candidates for commanding the respect that enables such persuasion, but with homeless or abused children the challenge is to discover whom the child does respect.[1] Perhaps there is an uncle who he feels sticks up for him, a football coach he admires, a grandmother he adores. The uncle, the football coach, and the grandmother must then be urged to attend. Normally, they are flattered to be told that they have been nominated as one of the few human beings this young person still respects. So they come. They come when the appeal to them is "to support and help the young person to take responsibility for what they have done." Thus the setting and the ceremonial character seek to "hold" the offender while allowing separation from the offence.

Victims play a crucial role in this, for they are in a unique position to communicate the irresponsibility of the *act*. Much delinquency is casual and thoughtless (O'Connor and Sweetapple 1988, pp. 117-18). The offenders who thought all they had done was to take fifty dollars from the house of a faceless person find that person is a vulnerable elderly woman who did without something significant because of the loss of the money. They learn that as a result of the break-in she now feels insecure in her own home, as does her next door neighbor. Both have invested in new security locks and are afraid to go out in the street alone because they have come to view the neighborhood as a dangerous place. Collateral damage from victimization is normal rather than exceptional and coordinators become expert at drawing it out of victims and victim supporters. Techniques of neutralization (Sykes and Matza 1957) that may originally have been employed, such as " . . . I am unemployed and poor while the householder is employed and rich" are seriously challenged when confronted by the elderly victim. Sometimes this shocks the offender. Other times it does not. Many of the worst offenders have developed a capacity to cut themselves off from the shame for exploiting other human beings. They deploy a variety of barriers against feeling responsibility. But what does not affect the offender directly may affect those who have come to support her. The shaft of shame fired by the victim in the direction of the offender might go right over the offender's head, yet it might pierce like a spear through the heart of the offender's mother, sitting behind him. It is very common for offenders' mothers to start to sob when victims describe their suffering or loss. So while display of the victim's suffering may fail to hit its intended mark, the anguish of the offender's mother during the ceremony may succeed in bringing home to the offender the need to confront rather than deny an act of irresponsibility.

Indeed, in our observations mothers often seize the ceremony of the occasion to make eloquent and moving speeches that they have long wanted to make to their child:

> I imagine life as a family living in a valley and the children gradually start to venture out from the family house in the valley. Eventually they have to climb up the mountain to get out of the valley. That mountain is adolescence. At the top of the mountain is a job. When they have that they can walk gently down the other side of the mountain into life. But there's another way they can go. They can decide not to climb the path up the mountain but to wander in the easier paths out into the valley. But those paths, while they are easier, lead to greater and greater darkness. I'm concerned that my little boy took one of those paths and I'm losing him into the darkness.

Coordinators work at bringing out collateral damage. Parents are asked: "How did this episode affect the family?" Offenders are asked: "How did mum and dad feel about it?" Typically, the offender will admit that their kin were "pretty upset." In Wagga, the coordinator then routinely asks why, and in a large proportion of cases young people will say something to the effect that the parents care about them or love them. This is the main chance the reintegrative coordinator is looking for. Once this is uttered, the coordinator returns to this again and again as a theme of what is being learnt from the conference. In the wrap-up, he will reaffirm that "Jim has learned that his mum and dad care a lot, that his Uncle Bob wants to help. . . ." This is not to deny that this strategy of reintegration can be mismanaged:

> Coordinator: "James, why are your parents upset?"
> James: [Silence]
> Coordinator: "Do you think it's because they care about you?"
> James: "Don't know."

Another way this path to reintegration can be derailed is when the parents indulge in outcasting attacks on their child. Coordinators sometimes manage this problem by intervening to divert stigmatization before it gets into full swing:

> Mother: "He used to be a good boy until then."
> Coordinator interrupts: "And he still is a good boy. No one here thinks we're dealing with a bad kid. He's a good kid who made a mistake and I hope he knows now that that's what we all think of him."

Even when serious stigmatic attacks are launched, the communal character of the encounter creates the possibility of reintegrative amelioration. The worst stigmatic attack we observed arose when the mother of a fourteen-year-old girl arrived at the conference. She told the coordinator that she was unhappy to be here. Then when she saw her daughter, who preceded her to the conference, she said: "I'll kill you, you little bitch." A few minutes into the conference, the mother jumped up from her seat, shouting: "This is a load of rubbish." Then pointing angrily at her shaking daughter, she said: "She should be punished." Then she stormed out. These events might have created a degradation sub-ceremony of great magnitude. Instead, the other participants in the room were transformed by it and developed a quite different direction. Victim supporters who had arrived at the conference very angry with the offender were now sorry for her and wanted to help. They learnt she was a street kid and their anger turned against a mother who could abandon her daughter like this. This dramatic example highlights two common processes seen in the conferences—the alteration of perspectives and the generation of social support. We believe these processes occur for two reasons:

(1) The more serious the delinquency of the young offender, the more likely it is to come out that she has had to endure some rather terrible life circumstances. Rather than rely on stereotypes they see the offender as a whole person (a point we return to later); and

(2) Participants at the conference have been invited on the basis of their capacity to be supportive to either the offender or the victim. Being supportive people placed in a social context where supportive behavior is expected and socially approved, they often react to stigmatic attacks with gestures of reintegration.

Even as they use stigmatic terms, ordinary citizens understand the concept of communicating contempt for the deed simultaneously with respect for the young person. An adult member of the Maori community caused tears to trickle down the cheeks of a huge, tough fifteen-year-old with the following speech:

> Stealing cars. You've got no brains, boy. . . . But I've got respect for you. I've got a soft spot for you. I've been to see you play football. I went because I care about you. You're a brilliant footballer, boy. That shows you have the ability to knuckle down and apply yourself to something more sensible than stealing cars. . . . We're not giving up on you.

2. *Event and perpetrator must be uncoupled rather than defined as instances of a profane uniformity. The self of the perpetrator is sustained as sacred rather than profane. This is accomplished by comprehending: (a) how essentially good people have a pluralistic self that accounts for their occasional lapse into profane acts; and (b) that the profane act of a perpetrator occurs in a social context for which many actors may bear some shared responsibility. Collective as well as individual shame must be brought out into the open and confronted.*

In speaking of degradation ceremonies, Garfinkel (1956, p. 422) says: "Any sense of accident, coincidence, indeterminism, chance or momentary occurrence must not merely be minimized. Ideally, such measures should be inconceivable; at least they should be made false." There must be no escape, no loophole. Rather, degradation insists upon fitting an identity of total deviant with a single, coherent set of motives into a black and white scheme of things. In contrast, a condition of successful reintegration ceremonies is that they leave open multiple interpretations of responsibility while refusing to allow the offender to deny personal responsibility entirely. In degradation ceremonies, the suppression of a range of motives and the insistence upon one account of responsibility allows the criminal to maintain (at least in her own eyes) an identity for herself as "criminal as victim," to dwell on the irresponsibility of others or of circumstances. When the crime is constructed as the bad act of a good person, uncoupling event and perpetrator, a well-rounded discussion of the multiple accountabilities for the crime does not threaten the ceremony as an exercise in community disapproval. The strategy is to focus on problem rather than person, and on the group finding solutions to the problem. The family, particularly in the New Zealand model, is held accountable for coming up with a plan of action, which is then ratified by the whole group. The collective shame and collective responsibility of the family need not detract from individual responsibility for the crime nor from community responsibilities, such as to provide rewarding employment and schooling for young people. Yet the collective assumption of responsibility moves the ceremony beyond a permanent preoccupation with the responsibility of the individual that might stall at the point of stigmatization and the adoption of a delinquent identity. The practical task of designing a plan of action is a way of putting the shame behind the offender, of moving from a shaming phase to a reintegration phase. Agreement on the action plan can be an even more ceremonial decertification of the deviance of the offender through institutionalizing a signing ceremony where offender, family, and police put their signatures side by side on the agreement. In signing such an agreement, the responsible, reintegrated self of the offender distances itself from the shamed behavior. The sacredness of the self is sustained through its own attack upon and transcendence of the profane act. Similarly, the collectivity of the family acknowledges its shame and takes collective responsibility for problem-solving in a way that transcends its collective shame.

3. *Coordinators must identify themselves with all private parties—perpetrators, their families, victims, witnesses—as well as being identified with the public interest in upholding the law.*

Garfinkel's third condition of successful degradation ceremonies is that the denouncer must claim more than a private role but must communicate degradation in the name of an [imaginary, unified, and static] public. This condition is explicitly incorporated into Western criminal law, wherein the police and the judge in a criminal trial are legally defined as fiduciaries of public rather than private interests. In community conferences, this totaling fiction is put aside. Coordinators have responsibilities to, and identify with, a plurality of interests. Reintegration and consensus on an agreement are quite unlikely unless the coordinator identifies with and respects all the interests in the room. Outside interests will put the agreement at risk unless the coordinator also speaks up on behalf of any public interest beyond the set of private interests assembled for the conference. This sounds demanding, perhaps even impossible. How can so many interests be juggled and a workable outcome reached? Our answer is simple—in practice consensus is reached more than 90 percent of the time at both research sites and in most of these cases the consensus is implemented (Maxwell and Morris 1993, p. 121).[2]

4. Denunciation must be both by and in the name of victims and in the name of supra-personal values enshrined in the law.

For Garfinkel, degradation ceremonies are enacted in the name of the supra-personal values of the tribe. We have seen that successful reintegration requires confronting the private hurts and losses from the crime as well. A key condition for the success of reintegration ceremonies is to get the victim to turn up. Where victims are institutions (like schools), this means getting victim representatives to turn up (e.g., the principal, elected student representatives). Blagg (1985) has discussed the greater problems of making reparation meaningful with impersonal victims. Victim or victim representative attendance has been nearly universally achieved in Wagga, but in New Zealand the success rate has been under 50 percent (Maxwell and Morris 1993, p. 75), though there is reason to suspect that the latter disappointing statistic has been improving in more recent times in New Zealand.[3] Some will be surprised at the near-universal success in Wagga and the recent higher success in New Zealand in getting victims along to conferences. But when the coordinator issues a combined appeal to private interest, public virtue (playing your part in getting this young person back on track) and citizen empowerment, the appeal is rather persuasive. In the words of Senior Sergeant Terry O'Connell—the key actor in adopting and developing the program at Wagga—the key is to "make the victim feel important and they will come." And important they are: in New Zealand victims can effectively veto any agreement reached at the conference, but only if they actually attend and listen to the arguments. Even in conventional dyadic victim-offender reconciliation programs in a noncommunitarian society such as the United States, victim interest in participation is quite high (Galaway 1985, p. 626; Galaway and Hudson 1975, p. 359; Galaway, Henzel, Ramsey, and Wanyama 1980; Novack, Galaway, and Hudson 1980; Weitekamp 1989, p. 82). Some of this may be sheer curiosity to meet the person who "did it."

When the victim and victim supporters turn up, of course, there remains the possibility that private hurts and losses will not be fully communicated to the offender. Sometimes the victim says that they suffered no real loss. For example, at one conference we attended, the victim said that the car stolen for a joy ride was found as soon as he noticed it to be missing and he could detect no damage. Here the coordinator must reiterate the public interest in being able to assume that one can park a car somewhere without constant worry that it might be stolen. Pointing out that "...it was a lucky thing for you and Mr. X [the victim] on this occasion" reinforces responsibility in the absence of specific private harm. Furthermore, in stressing the public as well as the private view of a crime, if the absence of private harm means that there is no direct compensation to be paid or worked for, conferences will usually agree to some community service work for the offender. Often there will be both private compensation and community work, signifying both the private and the public harm. The gesture of restoration to both community and victim, even if it is modest in comparison to the enormity of the crime, enables the offender to seize back pride and reassume a law-respecting, other-respecting, and self-respecting identity.

5. *Nonauthoritative actors (victims, offenders, and offenders' families) must be empowered with process control. The power of actors normally authorized to issue denunciations on behalf of the public interest (e.g,. judges) must be decentered.*

Degradation ceremonies for Garfinkel are about privileging authoritative actors with the right to denounce the profane on behalf of the tribe. Judges, for example, silence the denunciations of victims or pleas for mercy from relatives. Their role in the courtroom is simply as evidentiary fodder for the legal digestive system. They must stick to the facts and suppress their opinions. Consequently, they often emerge from the experience deeply dissatisfied with their day in court. For victims and their supporters, this often means they scream ineffectively for more blood. But it makes no difference when the system responds to such people by giving them more and more blood, because the blood lust is not the source of the problem; it is an unfocused cry from disempowered citizens who have been denied a voice.

Reintegration ceremonies have a [dimly recognized] political value because, when well managed, they deliver victim satisfaction that the courts can never deliver. In Wagga, a standard question to the victims is: "What do you want out of this meeting here today?" The responses are in sharp contrast to the cries for "more punishment" heard on the steps of more conventional courts. Offered empowerment in the way we have suggested, victims commonly say that they do not want the offender punished; they do not want vengeance; they want the young offender to learn from his mistake and get his life back in order. Very often they say they want compensation for their loss. Even here, however, it is surprising how often victims waive just claims for compensation out of consideration for the need for an indigent teenager to be unencumbered in making a fresh start.

Clifford Shearing attended two of the Wagga conferences with us. Struck by the readiness of victims not to insist on compensation claims but to press instead for signs of remorse and a willingness to reform, Shearing said, ". . . they all wanted to win the battle for his [the offender's] soul[4] rather than his money."

How can we make sense of outcomes that are so at odds with preconceptions of vengeful victims? In fact, even in traditional stigmatic punishment systems, victims are not as vengeful as popular preconceptions suggest (Heinz and Kerstetter 1981; Shapland, Willmore, and Duff 1985; Kigin and Novack 1980; Wietekamp 1989, pp. 83-84; Youth Justice Coalition 1990, pp. 52-54). Citizens seem extremely punitive and supportive of degradation ceremonies when asked their views in public opinion surveys. Distance, a stereotyped offender, and a simplification of evil conduce to public support for degradation ceremonies. But the closer people get to the complexities of particular cases, the less punitive they get (Ashworth 1986, p. 118; Doob and Roberts 1983; Doob and Roberts 1988). As we noted earlier, the reality of the meeting between victim, offender, and others tends to undermine stereotyping. Instead, immediacy, a particular known offender, and a complex grasp of all the situational pressures at work conduce to public support for reintegration.

Some reconciliations at family group conferences are quite remarkable. The most extraordinary case we know of involved a young man guilty of aggravated assault with a firearm on a woman who ran a lotto shop. The offender locked the woman at gunpoint in the back of her shop while he robbed her of over $1000. When the time for the conference came, she was mad, after blood. Yet after considerable discussion, part of the plan of action, fully agreed to by the victim, involved the victim housing the offender while he did some community work for her family! This is not an isolated case, although it involves the most dramatic shift of which we became aware. Occasionally, victims make job offers to unemployed offenders at conferences.

Unresolved fury and victim dissatisfaction is, of course, the stuff of unsuccessful reintegration ceremonies. An important recent New Zealand evaluation shows that failure as a result of such dissatisfaction remains (Maxwell and Morris 1993, p. 119). In fact over a third of victims who attended conferences said they felt worse after the conference, a result of insufficient attention to victim reintegration (see point 9 below).

It is not only victims who can benefit from the empowerment that arises from having cases dealt with in this nontraditional setting. Offenders and offenders' families are also very much empowered when community conferences work well. Maxwell and Morris (1993, p. 110) found that New Zealand conferences work better at empowering parents than offenders.[5] This is probably true in Wagga as well, though the Wagga approach rejects the Auckland tendency to give the arresting police officer the first opportunity to explain the incident of concern. Instead, the young person, rather than police or parents, are always given the first opportunity to describe in their own words what has brought them to the conference. We see this Wagga practice of temporally privileging the accounts of the young persons as a desirable way of seeking to empower them in the dialogue. For all parties, success is predicated upon a significant degree of agency. On the other hand, when agency is denied the ceremonies fail. Then there is the pretence of empowerment, with families and offenders being manipulated into agreements that are developed by the police or youth justice coordinators, an outcome that is not uncommon (Maxwell and Morris 1993, p. 112). There can be little real experience of shame when apology and remedial measures are forced on the offender and his family rather than initiated by them. Empowerment is crucial to reintegration, while manipulation makes instead for degradation.

6. *The perpetrator must be so defined by all the participants (particularly by the perpetrator himself) that he is located as a supporter of both the supra-personal values enshrined in the law and the private interests of victims.*

This condition of successful reintegration is accomplished by having the offender's responsible self disassociate itself from the irresponsible self. Apology is the standard device for accomplishing this, as Goffman (1971, p. 113) pointed out: "An apology is a gesture through which an individual splits himself into two parts, the part that is guilty of an offence and the part that disassociates itself from the delict and affirms a belief in the offended rule."

At all the conferences we attended, the offenders offered an apology.[6] Often they agreed to follow up with a letter of apology or a visit to apologize again to the victim and other members of the family. Often there was also apology to parents, teachers, even the police. A common feature of successful reintegration ceremonies can be a rallying of the support of loved ones behind the disassociation of self-created by a genuine apology.

After one moving and tearful statement by a Maori offender in Auckland, for example, elders offered congratulatory speeches on the fine apology he had given to his parents.

The verbal apology can be accompanied by physical acts. The most common physical accompaniment to apology is the handshake. Female victims sometimes hug young offenders, an especially moving gesture when it reaches across a racial divide. In Maori conferences,[7] kissing on the cheek, nose pressing, and hugging occur among various of the participants (even visiting sociologists!). Ritual bodily contact is not the only form of physical act to accompany apology. Other common acts include the handing over of compensation or the offer of a beverage. In a re-creation of the theme that commensalism celebrates solidarity, successful ceremonies have ended with victim and offender families arranging to have dinner together after the conference.

Despite the manifestly successful effect of apology, it is not something encouraged by courtrooms. Criminal trials tend to leave criminal identities untouched by attacks from responsible, law-abiding, or caring identities. Indeed, degradation tends to harden them. It is not a major challenge in identity management for a tough guy to sustain this identity during a criminal trial. The challenge is more difficult in an open dialogue among the different parties assembled for a community conference. Usually, there are some things that the police know about the offender's conduct that his parents do not know, and there are vulnerabilities the parents know that the police do not. The traditional criminal process enables the offender to sustain different kinds of stories and even different identities with parents and police. Conferences can expose these multiple selves to the partitioned audiences for which these selves are differentially displayed. Out of one conference, Wagga parents learned that their teenage son had punched a fourteen-year-old girl in the face; then the police learned that the boy had beat his mother before, once with a broom; then everyone learned that he had also hit other girls. There are some lies that the offender can live in the eyes of the police; others in the eyes of his parents; but many of them cannot stand in the face of a dialogue among all three that also enjoins victims.

All this is not to deny that apology, even the sincerest of apology, can be secured without challenging a delinquent identity that remains dominant over a law-abiding identity. In one case, a fourteen-year-old girl acknowledged that the effect of stealing a check from the mailbox of an elderly woman had been "awful" for the victim and she apologized with feeling. But when it came to the action plan, she was intransigently against the idea of returning to school: "No. I don't like school." Even a modest proposition from the group for community service work of twenty hours over four weeks was bitterly resisted: "It's too much time. I want to be a normal street kid and if you're a street kid you need time to be on the street. That would take up too much of my time." Nothing was going to interrupt her career path as a street kid! This is a familiar theme in literature on identity maintenance from writers associated with labeling and similar perspectives. There comes a point where a change which seems both possible and advantageous in the immediate context is resisted because of the degree of commitment to a path and the consequent "side bets" (Becker 1960) that an individual has made in following that path.

Interestingly, however, our empirical observations match the general case we made earlier: namely, that while such commitment to deviance is possible, it is also rare. The norm is strongly toward the reversibility rather than irreversibility of the deviant identity and, as in the case just described, in contrast to the labeling claim, irreversibility seems more connected to the individual commitment to an identity (agency) than to structural features that prevent reversion. No doubt, the matter of commitment is not exhausted by these brief comments. We might suppose that as adults get older, deviant identities might become more encrusted and harder to change (and hence shaming and reintegration less relevant). For some people such a process probably occurs. But as data on the relationship between age and deviance shows (Hirschi and Gottfredson 1983; Youth Justice Coalition 1990, pp. 22-23), reversion from deviant to mainstream identities is the norm with progressing age. Thus the idea that shaming and reintegration ceremonies are valuable only for the young is not well founded. Indeed, preliminary qualitative evidence indicates that it may be extremely valuable for individuals well into middle age.[8]

7. *Distance between each participant and the other participants must be closed; empathy among all participants must be enhanced; opportunities must be provided for perpetrators and victims to show (unexpected) generosity toward each other.*

At the start of conferences, victims and offenders, victim supporters, and offender supporters tend to work hard at avoiding eye contact. By contrast, at the end of a successful reintegration ceremony, participants are looking each other in the eye. Reintegration ceremonies succeed when one side makes an early gesture of self-blame or self-deprecation. In one case, an offender wrote a long letter of apology to the victim before the conference was convened. At another conference, a mix-up by the police resulted in the victim being advised of the wrong date for the conference. Despite this, she came within fifteen minutes of a "phone call at 6 P.M. in the middle of preparing for dinner guests." The conference coordinator said that she agreed to drop everything to come "if it would help the boys." "What do you think of that?" said the coordinator. "She's a nice lady," said one of the offenders. "And I bet you were frightened to go out from your own house after this," added the mother of another offender.

In many cases, the offender's family does not wait for their offspring to come under attack from the victim. They preemptively launch the attack themselves in terms so strong that the victim can be moved to enjoin that the family "[Not] be too hard on the boy. We all make mistakes." Self-deprecating gestures from either side can facilitate reintegration, which is powerfully facilitated by exchanges such as:

> Victim: "It was partly my fault. I shouldn't have left it unlocked."
> Offender: "No that's not your fault. You shouldn't have to lock it. We're the only ones who should be blamed."

A common strategy of all parties for seeking to elicit empathy from others is to refer to how they may suffer these problems themselves in another phase of their own life cycle.

> Offender's uncle to offender: "In a few years you will be a father and have to growl at your boys."
> Coordinator to victims: "You were once parents of teenagers yourselves."

One case we attended involved a father and son who had a stormy relationship. A Maori elder counseled the father that he should put his arm around his boy more often, advice the father conceded that he needed to take. The father was a harsh and tough man, once a famous rugby forward with a reputation as an enforcer. The attempt of a Maori police officer to elicit empathy in these difficult circumstances was both innovative and effective, since tears began to stream down the face of the young offender, who up to this point had managed the impression of being a young tough:

> Policeman: "Look what you have done to your father and mother. If your father hit you, you'd stay hit. You wouldn't be getting up. But he hasn't. [Offender gasps, his chest heaving with unnatural struggling for air.] I was always angry and bitter at my father. He was a hard man."

Uncle interjects: "Yes, he'd hit you first, then ask questions afterwards."
Policeman continues: "Then he died. Then I realized how I loved and
missed the old bastard. Don't wait till your father dies, Mark."

At this point the mother buried her head in her lap with quiet sobbing.
Then the father and then the son cried, by which point all in the room had
tears in our eyes. How impressive an accomplishment this was—eliciting
such empathy for a father about whom it was clearly difficult to say
anything laudatory. Taken out of context, it does not seem a very positive
thing to say about a father that he has refrained from ironing out his son.
But for a son who himself was enmeshed in the culture of rugby and who
knew his father's history of ironing out a great number of other human
beings, the tribute was deeply moving.

8. *The separation of denounced person must be terminated by rituals of
inclusion that place him, even physically, inside rather than outside.*

Already we have mentioned a number of rituals of inclusion: apology
and its acceptance, hand shaking, the putting of signatures side by side on
an agreement, and so on. In a traditional Samoan context, this is taken
further. Following an assault, the Matai, or head of the extended family
unit of the offender, will kneel on a mat outside the house of the victim
family until he is invited in and forgiven. Sometimes that will take days.
There may be something to learn from the Samoans here on the conditions
of successful reintegration ceremonies, namely the provision of a spatio-
temporal dimension to the imperative for reintegration. For how long
should I continue to avoid eye contact with this person who still kneels in
front of me? When do I conclude it by embracing him in forgiveness? The
sheer physicality of his remorse makes ignoring him indefinitely a rather
limited third option. The ceremony is driven by a spatial imperative.
Indeed, most successful ceremonies in our own society specify place (e.g.,
a church, a presentation dais) and a time when it is appropriate and fitting
to carry out that ceremony. Moreover, in moving individuals through
space and time, those movements are not haphazard—they fit the messages of transformation or reaffirmation that the ceremony seeks to
convey.
    In Wagga, the spatial arrangement that is employed to convey both
the unity of the community and yet the tension between victim and offender, is a horseshoe seating arrangement. At one end of the horseshoe
sits the offender(s) with her family(ies) sitting in the row behind. At the
other end sits the victim(s) with his family(ies) sitting in the row behind

him. The horseshoe symbolizes the tension of the meeting, part of one community but at widely separated points on this matter. Moreover, movements within the space can and do occur, such as when people cross the central space to shake hands at certain moments. These are culturally contingent matters; offending boys are commonly made to sit on the floor during Polynesian conferences, a temporary obeisance that seems culturally appropriate to them rather than debasing. Sometimes they are asked to come out and stand at the front for their formal apology, after which they return to their seat in a circle. In each of these, the physical space is used constructively to convey important messages. And, as we shall see later, the separation of the overall space into front and backstage areas also has its uses.

The symbolic meanings signified by space rarely surface in the discursive consciousness of the participants (or so we presume) but the successful use of space is not predicated upon that level of reflection. In all probability, more still could be done with the symbolic use of space in such ceremonies—one could take this even further by placing offenders alone in the center of the horseshoe for the first stage of the conference, though one might worry about this intimidating them into silence. These are matters that require more detailed exploration, but note here merely that there is a fine line between artifice and artificiality.

The temporal dimension of the ceremony is also important. The phases in a successful ceremony are clearly visible in the way that participants comport themselves and a "winding down" is often discernible. Indeed, the phased structure is not dissimilar to that described by Bales (1950) in his work on interaction process analysis. As Bales argued there, the social group that has formed to handle a particular task (in this case for the ceremony) comes to develop a bounded process of its own, marking its phases with different styles of comportment and mood. Although breaks in the meeting are rarely used in Wagga,[9] one could conceivably have a coffee break once there had been good progress toward a settlement during which the protagonists could physically mix; after the break, offender families could come back side by side with their children to present their plan of action. Certainly, such activities are used to mark the end of the formal ceremony and handle transitions back to the "outside world" and at such moments drinking together, whether coffee or—as might be appropriate in other contexts, alcohol—serves to mark that transition (Gusfield 1987. Cf. also Bott 1987; Hazan 1987).

It is also important to note here that the physical act of handing over money as compensation or a bunch of flowers (as happened in one case) creates a strong imperative for an apology-forgiveness interaction sequence. Most English-speaking people find it normal to cancel grudges at the moment of a physical act of compensating wrongdoing by uttering the word "sorry." Faced with such an utterance, only unusual victims resist the imperative to return a word of forgiveness, to "let bygones be bygones," or at least to show acceptance, thanks, or understanding.

Regrettably the common legal processes of a gesellschaft society sanitize such physical moments out of transactions. They are, in the Weberian sense, "disenchanted." With the loss of that enchantment they also lose powerful opportunities for transformations of self and context. Rational actor models of the world notwithstanding, successful practice of justice is not merely a technical-rational action. When restitution is reduced to "the check is in the mail" (likely put there by the clerk of the court) matters of deep moral concern have been reduced to mere money, to the ubiquitous question "how much?" (Simmel 1978). In contrast, successful reintegration ceremonies put reintegrative physicality back into the process. In so doing they transcend the merely rational to speak to vital concerns of human conscience.

9. The separation of the victim, any fear or shame experienced by victims, must be terminated by rituals of reintegration.

The objective of reintegrating offenders is advanced by reintegrating victims; the objective of reintegrating victims is advanced by reintegrating offenders.[10] Victims are invisible in Garfinkel's model, but our thesis is that effective reintegration ceremonies are victim-centered, a centrality described under conditions 3, 4, and 5. Victims often suffer from bypassed shame (Scheff and Retzinger 1991) and bypassed fear. The girl who is sexually assaulted by a young man often feels that the incident says something about the respect in which she is held by males. She feels devalued to have been treated with such disrespect (Murphy and Hampton 1989). One way to rehabilitate her self-respect is a ceremonial show of community respect for her. Apology from the man who disrespected her is the most powerful way of resuscitating this self-esteem and community shaming of the disrespecting behavior is also powerful affirmation of the respect for her as a person.

Victims often continue to be afraid after a crime and at an apparently irrational level. When a break-in causes a victim to feel insecure in her home, it is good for this fear to be openly expressed. For one thing, there is practical advice the police are usually able to give that can leave the victim both safer and feeling more assured of being safe.

In one Wagga conference involving teenage lads who inflicted a terrifying assault on a much younger boy and girl, the boys offered to come around to the home of the victim family to apologize more formally to all members of the family. The young girl looked afraid and said that she did not want them coming near her home. So it was decided they would apologize in writing. But from that point on in the conference, the cautioning sergeant highlighted the fact that there was no particular meaning to the choice of these two children as victims. It was a one-off incident that could have happened to anyone. At the end of the conference, the sergeant ushered the offenders and their supporters out, asking the victim family to stay behind. Then he asked the children if they now felt assured that these boys would not come after them again. He asked them what they thought of the boys and they said that the conference had put it all behind them now. They felt more sorry for the boys than afraid of them. The mother said later that she had come to see them as frightened little boys. This interpretation was confirmed by a minister of religion who met with the family immediately after the conference.

Note here the importance of two smaller backstage conferences after the formal conference—a further instance of the significance of space referred to earlier. Backstage conferences can do some reintegrative work for both offenders and victims that cannot be accomplished frontstage. Every conference we have attended broke up into some important little backstage meetings after the main conference. At times, the reintegrative work that happened after the conference was more significant than that transacted within it. A boy who maintained a defiant demeanor throughout the conference shed a tear when his uncle put his arm around him after the conference (his identity as nephew allows him to cry, but not the identity he must maintain in the face of his mates). A mother confesses that she does not believe she can get her daughter to attend the agreed community work and another uncle volunteers to "make sure she gets there." Backstage intimacy can allow some masks to be removed that actors feel impelled to sustain during the conference proper. A practical implication is not to rush the exit from the theater.

10. Means must be supplied to intervene against power imbalances that inhibit either shaming or reintegration, or both.

Of the various criticisms we have heard raised about the ceremonial process that we are describing in this chapter, one of the most common, concerns the imbalance of power in society and the way that this must spill over into, and hence structure in negative ways, the reintegration process. How, they ask, can this process disassociate itself from wider matters of class, race, patriarchy, and age stratification? If such dissociation does not occur, how can the ceremony act other than to reproduce that same patterning of ageism, class, race, and patriarchy? The risk is obvious. The etnomethodologists of the 1960s, among whom Garfinkel is counted, were rightly condemned by the Marxists of the 1970s (Taylor, Walton, and Young 1973) for inattentiveness to issues of power. By using Garfinkel's work as a starting point might we not fall into the same trap, blithely praising a ceremony whose deeper realities are much darker than we sense? Are the ceremonies of reintegration we are discussing capable of intervening against power imbalances in any serious way?

Our answer to this falls into several parts, and these parts relate to what we have seen in our observational work.

First, in no sense is intervention to deal with individual offences the most important thing we can do to respond constructively to the crime problem: attacking deeper structures of inequality is more important (Braithwaite 1991, 1993; Polk 1992). But let us not underestimate how important a basis of inequality criminal justice oppression is to (say) Aboriginal Australians. The structure of laws and the daily routines of the police and the courts contribute mightily to that oppression. Thus, to alter the police court process is an important step, even if it is not a sufficient step alone. Indeed the very history of the Antipodean conferences we are discussing here begins with Maori frustration with the way the Western state disempowered them through the criminal justice system (Report of the Ministerial Advisory Committee 1986). These reforms "came from below" and were explicitly understood by Maori protagonists to introduce communitarian reintegrative features into a system that lacked them and which stigmatized their young people in destructive ways. In this sense, if in no other, we advocate the reintegration ceremonies because they are valuable in the eyes of most of those who are involved in them.[11]

Our second point is more theoretical. At the core of the criticism about power imbalances undermining the ceremony is a failure to think through the precise nature of the ceremony. The current of mainstream sociology that has dealt with ritual and ceremony has principally been conservative and functionally oriented (Cheal 1988). As a result, the tendency has been to emphasize static, system integrative, and totaling aspects of rituals over dynamic aspects, multiple identities, and social change. But that shortcoming is a feature of the theory, not the ceremony. If commentators associate conservatism with ceremony for this reason, they do so out of habit rather than evidence. There are dynamic features to these ceremonies, which emphasize agency and social freedom (within obvious bounds) not merely totaling conformity. No doubt, there are meanings which ceremonies permit and others they do not and no doubt some of those privileging and silencing may be problematic. But we dispute that they can be "read off" in advance.

Third and last, the criticism implies that anyone who pursues the course we describe here is utopian—class, race, and patriarchy are so ingrained in "the system," it can be said, that the system can never transcend them. Perhaps. But our view is quite different. We see that the existing "system"—which is not particularly systemic in that it lacks unity, coherence, and direction—is racked with problems arising from differences in power which we can identify as "class, race, and patriarchy." But we go on to argue that if so this identifies the places where we need to work relentlessly for change. Moreover, we suggest that our observations of such ceremonies indicate that while power imbalances remain ineradicably within what we describe, they also provide a greater space in which people can be agents than the existing processes. More voices are heard, saying more things than in conventional courts and that is a positive thing. Concrete examples may help to make the point.

It is an empirical question whether powerful outside voices are likely to be raised in a conference or a court against a father who dominates his daughter. Here we observe that the condition of the successful reintegration ceremony is that the coordinator act on this fact of domination by asking the daughter *who she would like* to be there to stick up for her against her father.

The philosophy of the New Zealand reforms (*Children, Young Persons and Their Families Act 1989*) is that when families are in deep trouble, a social worker from the state is not likely to be the best person to straighten out their problems (Maxwell and Morris 1993). However big a mess the family is in, the best hope for solving the problems of families resides within the families themselves and their immediate communities of intimate support. What the state can do is empower families with resources: offer to pay to bring Auntie Edna from another city for the conference (as they do in New Zealand), offer to pay for a smorgasbord of life skills, job training, remedial education, anger control courses, but with *the power of choice from that smorgasbord resting entirely with the young offender and her support group.*[12] Processes like this do offer a redress of power imbalances centered upon race, albeit not completely. In New Zealand, where the Maori community contribute half the cases processed by the New Zealand juvenile justice system, conferences offer an important redress in a criminal justice system that is otherwise not a peripheral but a central source of their disempowerment. The same point can be made about racial minorities in all the English-speaking countries. It is a small blow against black oppression when the white father of the victim of a brutal assault offers to go with the family of the Aboriginal offender to argue the reversal of a decision to expel him from school because of the assault. Conferences will never usher in revolutionary changes; they do, however, give little people chances to strike little blows against oppression.

The possibilities for improving the position of women within criminal justice processes also seem to us to be quite promising. This is illustrated by the Wagga case mentioned earlier of the mother who was being beaten by her son. Court-based criminal justice systematically obscures the fact that in Australia we have a massive problem of son-mother violence. Domestic violence is constructed in the literature as spouse abuse because mothers keep the problems with their sons submerged, blaming themselves, refusing to complain against their own children. If the Wagga case discussed earlier had gone to court, it is most unlikely that the assault on the girl would have led on to a discussion of the wider problem of the assault on the mother and other females. The family group conference approach enabled community confrontation of this fifteen-year-old boy with the problem of his violence at an early enough age for such a confrontation to make a difference. But most mothers and sisters are unlikely to cooperate in a stigmatic or punitive vilification of their young son or brother. Ceremonies must be perceived as reintegrative, directed not only at getting the boy to take responsibility for his actions but also at supporting and helping him, before most mothers and sisters will break the silence.

We could add that the economic prospects of offenders, which are often very dim, are not always neglected in these conferences. While this is not a widespread feature, sometimes the unemployed are helped to find jobs; sometimes the homeless are found homes; often the school dropouts are assisted in getting back to school or into some alternative kind of technical training or educational development. Clearly there are many more important fronts on which to struggle for a more just economic system than through family group conferences, but these conferences are at worst not deepening the problems that the young offenders face.

In short, while the reintegration ceremonies we write of here do not overcome inequalities, they can be and are sensitive to them and do what they can to allow for and/or redress some of those inequalities. In so doing, they create spaces for agency and voice; they return conflicts that are "stolen" by state professionals to ordinary citizens (Christie 1977). This, we think, is a progressive move. The structural feature of successful conferences that we hypothesize to be most critical here is proactive empowerment of the most vulnerable participants—offenders and victims—with the choice of caring advocates, who may be more powerful than themselves, to exercise countervailing power against whoever they see as their oppressors.

11. Ceremony design must be flexible and culturally plural, so that participants exercise their process control constrained by only very broad procedural requirements.

We should be pluralist enough to see that a good process for Maoris will not necessarily be a good process for Europeans, or even for some Maoris who say they don't believe in "too much shit about the Maori way" (Maxwell and Morris 1993, p. 126).[13] At the same time, we should not be so culturally relativist as to reject the possibility of Europeans learning something worthwhile from Maori practice. Family group conferences are essentially a Maori idea, but the idea has been very favorably received by white communities in New Zealand and Australia, Australian Aboriginal communities, and Pacific Islander communities living in New Zealand. The reason is the flexibility built into the approach. Because Samoan participants have genuine process control, they can choose to encourage kneeling in front of the victim. Maori communities can choose to break the tension during proceedings by singing a song, something Westerners would find a rather odd thing to do on such an occasion. Maori conferences often signify the sacredness of the public interests involved (conditions 3 and 4) by opening and closing the conference with a (reintegrative) prayer.

Every conference we have attended has been completely different from every other conference. Indeed, flexibility and participant control of the process are the reasons why this strategy can succeed in a multicultural metropolis like Auckland. This is not a communitarian strategy for the nineteenth-century village, but for the twenty-first-century city. Flexible process, participant control—these are keys to delivering the legal plural-ism necessary for the metropolis. Another key is that this is an individual-centered communitarianism, giving it a practical edge for constructing community in an individualistic society. The authors of this chapter choose not to attend Neighborhood Watch meetings, because the appeal of community obligation is not sufficient to motivate our participation. In contrast, if one of us were asked to attend a family group conference on the basis that either a victim or an offender from our neighborhood or family had nominated us as a person who could lend support, we would go. We would be flattered to have been nominated by the individual. This is what we mean by the practical appeal of individual-centered communi-tarianism. Helping an individual is more motivating to citizens than abstractions such as "contributing to making your neighborhood safer."

While the reintegrative strategy is firmly grounded in the theory of le-gal pluralism, certain basic procedural rules cannot be trumped. The most important of these is that if the offender denies committing the alleged offences, she has the right to terminate the conference, demanding that the facts be tried in a court of law. She does not have to plead guilty. The conference can proceed only if she chooses "not to deny" charges made by the police. Some of the more informal ground rules that coordinators enforce, such as "no name calling" and "no badgering of the young person" have the effect of tipping the balance against degrading discourse in favor of reintegrative dialogue. What such basic procedural rules do is constitute a generally acceptable framework within which a plurality of dialogic forms can flourish (see Habermas 1986).

Given a commitment to flexibility and participant empowerment, one central concern is the prospect of standardization and routinization. It would be easy for ceremonies to be converted into Foucauldian "disci-pline," extending the net of state control. Disturbing signs of this as a future trend can be discerned, for example in the near-automatic tendency of some state officials at New Zealand conferences to suggest a curfew as part of the plan of action. Families can and do argue against their children being put on a rigid curfew, suggesting that a degree of participant control of the process is prevailing against pressures for standardized response, but the routinization of the suggestion without apparent consideration of case details implies a standardizing tendency. Similarly, after a training conference for coordinators in Wagga that we attended with Clifford Shearing and Jane Mugford, they expressed concern to us that some of the contributions to the training by local social workers and psychologists undercut the shifts away from stigmatization and toward community empowerment. The tendency there was to speak and reason in abstract categories such as "problem youth" in a way that, taken seriously, would erode the agency and voice of participants in favor of the imposition of control by "experts."

These tendencies notwithstanding, our view is that, at present, the family group conferences do not extend the net of state control (see also Moore 1992), but rather extend the net of community control, partly at the expense of state control, partly at the expense of doing something about problems that were previously ignored (such as mother bashing by sons).[14] Conferences can be used by communities to co-opt state power (formalism harnessed to empower informalism) (Braithwaite and Daly 1994); or they can be used by state authorities to expand their net of coercion by capturing informal community control (as in the net-widening critique). The contingent potential for both these developments and for the re-emergence of professionalism routinization need to be kept in mind in planning the expansion of such programs.

12. Reintegration agreements must be followed through to ensure that they are enacted.

In the early days of the family group conferences in both New Zealand and Wagga, there was poor follow-up to ensure that agreements reached at the conference were implemented. Now more systematic procedures are in place in New Zealand to ensure, for example, that where monetary compensation is involved, victims do receive it. For a sample of 203 family group conferences held in 1990, Maxwell and Morris (1993, p. 102) found that in 59 percent of cases agreements were completely implemented within three to four months and partly completed in a further 28 percent of cases, leaving only 13 percent of cases in which the tasks were largely uncompleted in this time frame—a very good result. At Wagga, young offenders and their families are invited to at least one follow-up workshop to close out the process. Families have an opportunity to swap notes at the workshop on the difficulties they have faced in implementing their plan of action. The Wagga police also see a reintegrative rationale for the workshop in helping families to overcome their shame by working with other families in the same situation. It is possible that this interpretation is right, as illustrated by the following passage from our fieldwork notes:

> Of the three offenders [in this particular case] George was the one who seemed totally unmoved by what the victim and his family said at the con-

ference. George's mother got together with mothers of George's friends who had also been in trouble, to talk about their problems. One of the mothers said that her boy had been sexually assaulted and that was one thing that upset him. Later George's mother said to George that he has not had it so tough as John, who had been sexually assaulted. George said nothing. Later, he called his mother back, broke down and said he had been sexually assaulted too (by the same person, we assume). George's mother now dates the assault as marking the time since which George had been getting into trouble. Her social construction of George is no longer as a boy who went bad. Now it is of a boy who was good, who went through a bad time as a result of a sexual assault, and who is now coming to terms with what happened to him and is coming out of it—a "good boy" again.

Implementation of agreements from family group conferences is more effective than with court-ordered compensation largely because the compensation is a collective obligation entered into by voluntary collective agreement.[15] Moreover, the coordinator will often secure the nomination of a relative who will be responsible for ensuring that the offender complies with the terms of the agreement. Dr. Gabrielle Maxwell has made the same point about completion of community work orders: "The community work projects that work are the ones the family comes up with itself."

13. When a single reintegration ceremony fails, ceremony after ceremony must be scheduled, never giving up, until success is achieved.

Traditional criminal justice processes paint themselves into a corner because of two imperatives: the desire to give kids another chance; notwithstanding this, the desire to signal that "the system is tough and next time you will not be so lucky." These two imperatives intersect with the empirical reality that young offenders offend a lot during their years of peak offending. Most will come through this peak period within two or three years if the criminal justice system does not make things worse by degradation ceremonies (such as institutionalization). The two imperatives and the empirical pattern of offending intersect to cause the criminal justice system to do exactly what its practitioners know is the worst thing to do, that is, set up a self-defeating chain of events:

Conviction 1: "Take this as a warning."
Conviction 2: "I'll give you a second chance. But this is your last chance."
Conviction 3: "With regret, I must say that you have already been given your last chance."

The policy in New Zealand is to avoid this slippery slope. While some cases in the juvenile justice system continue to slide down it, most do not and since 1988 the rate of institutionalization of young offenders has dropped by more than half (Maxwell and Morris 1993, p. 176), possibly by 75 percent (McDonald and Ireland 1990, p. 16). Now, most detected offences are judged not to warrant the cost of convening a family group conference, and informal warnings to juveniles on the spot or at the police station remain the predominant response for very minor offences (Maxwell and Morris 1993, p. 53). Taking no action beyond a formal letter of warning from the police is also common (Maxwell and Morris 1993, p. 59). Visits by the police to the offender's home to arrange informally for reparation and apology to the victim occur in a quarter of nonarrest cases (Maxwell and Morris 1993, p. 53). Only if these steps are insufficient is a full conference arranged.

In addition to these informal preconference measures, some New Zealand young offenders have been through six or seven formal conferences for different offences. The New Zealand Police Association, which strongly supports the family group conference strategy for most offenders, has reservations about repeated use of the approach on "hardened" offenders. They illustrated the problem with examples such as this:

> Ngaruawahia reports that a sixteen-year-old youth had a Family Group Conference on 26 June 1990 for three offences, another on 10 July for six offences, another on 20 July 1990 for two offences, Youth Court hearing on 24 July 1990, another Family Group Conference on 14 February 1991 for two offences. The youth committed suicide at Weymouth Boys Home in April 1991. (New Zealand Police Association 1991, p. 19)

Of course, such a case seems a "failure." But what kind of failure is it? We can think of three ways of categorizing it: (a) a failure of the family group conference; (b) the likely failure of any approach with the most difficult cases; or (c) the failure of giving up on the family group conference in favor of the court-institutionalization route. The implication of the passage is that this is a failure of type (a), but we suspect that it is better understood as type (b) and/or (c).

Of course, it would be naive to expect that a one- or two-hour conference can normally turn around the problems of a lifetime. In any case, the theory of the conference is not really that what is said at the conference will change lives in an instant and irreversible way—a conference is a social activity, not a genie from a bottle. Rather the hope for the conference is that it will be a catalyst for community problem-solving. Viewed in this way, when there is re-offending after a conference, it is to some extent the community that has failed. The failure of the conference was in not catalyzing the right sort of community support for the offender. If the failure is not inherent to the conference process, but is a failure in the community catalysis of the intervention, then one conference after another, each time seeking to catalyze community support in a different way, or with different invitees, makes sense.

To achieve a successful reintegration ceremony, then, it is necessary that coordinators must never give up, that they act as if there is always a reason for the failure of the last intervention *other than* the irretrievable badness of the offender. Even if the offender dies before the community succeeds in preventing his offending, by trying again and again with reintegrative approaches, the coordinator believes that she has at least refrained from accelerating his criminal career path during the time he lived. The typical criminal career is a useful touchstone here. Knowing the pattern typical of some offenders, it is *dis*abling to conceive success in terms of stopping offending. At the same time, it is *en*abling to define success as a downward shift in the slope of a criminal career path and failure as allowing an upward shift. Unless the offences are extreme,[16] it is always better to keep plugging away with a strategy that neither succeeds nor fails than to escalate to one that fails. At least the former does no harm.

Is there a practical way of implementing the attitude of never giving up? Below is an example of how the police might react to the first eight detected offences of a career criminal under a reintegrative strategy.

First offence: Boy warned by the police on the street for a minor offence. "If I catch you at this again, I'll be in touch with your parents about it."

Second offence: Same type of minor offence on the street results in a formal letter of warning and a visit to the family home to discuss the warning.

Third offence: Family group conference. Still a fairly minor offence, so no elaborate follow-up or detailed plan of action, just the reintegrative shaming of the offender and calling on the offender and the family to take responsibility for the problem in their own way. For the overwhelming majority of such minor offenders, this is the last the juvenile justice system will see of them, so any more detailed intervention is wasteful overkill.

Fourth offence: Second family group conference. More rigorous conference. What did the participants do, or fail to do, after the last conference? More detailed plan of action to respond to this analysis of the problem. Designation of offender supporters to monitor and report on implementation. Follow-up by coordinator to report back to participants on implementation. Modest quantum of community work.

Fifth offence: Third family group conference. Escalation of shaming of offender: "You gave undertakings to your family at the last conference that you have broken in the most thoughtless way. You breached the trust your parents put in you with that agreement." Redesign the plan of action. This time, secure a more solemn oath to the parents. Follow through. More community work.

Sixth offence: Fourth family group conference. New invitees. The smorgasbord of intervention options that the family group can choose (life skills or work skills courses, remedial education, church-run programs, anger control courses, regular meetings with the school counselor, outward bound, drug rehabilitation programs, etc.) is put before them in a different way. "We chose the wrong option before. That was our mistake. But we believe in the caring side of you that your family sees so often, so eventually you will find with them the right option to assist you to consider the hurt you cause to victims like Mrs. Smith and to consider your own future." Keep up the shaming, this time focused on the particular circumstances of Mrs. Smith. Work for Mrs. Smith.

Seventh offence: Fifth family group conference. Try again basic strategy of fourth conference with a different victim, different participants, and a different way of presenting the smorgasbord of intervention options.

Eighth offence: Sixth family group conference. Change tack. Eventually come back to the fact that the offender is still responsible for this particular criminal act, but lead off with collective self-blame: "As a group, your parents, your sister, grandfather and aunt, your teacher, Mrs. Brown, who has such a soft spot for you, and me as the coordinator of this conference, we all feel responsible that we have let you down. We haven't listened to you well enough to come up with the right ways to help you. We need you to tell us where we have gone wrong." Various other options can follow, such as one family member after another coming along prepared to give a speech on the mistakes they have made in the course of the saga. A search could be initiated by the family to find some new participants in the conference to add fresh perspectives, even asking another couple to become "godparents." An option on the coordinator's side could be to bring in a consultant professional of some sort with new ideas to participate in the conference.

Obviously, it gets very difficult to keep coming up with new angles, to keep projecting faith in the essential goodness of the offender, to persist with the never-give-up ideology. The relentless optimism that successful reintegration enjoins may eventually surrender in the face of a natural human pessimism. We saw one stigmatizing conference for an offender (his fourth) which exemplified this surrender. During this encounter, the exasperated coordinator described the offender as a "Yahoo." Before inviting the offender to give his side of the story, he turned to the family and asked them what they thought was wrong with the boy. He said: "The responsibility is the parents, not ours. I don't care. The Department doesn't care. We can just send it on to court." The youth advocate said that she saw the key question as being whether "his friends were bad or he was the bad one." She supported the interpretation of the police that escalation to institutionalization was the track the boy was heading down. The police, the coordinator, and the youth advocate had given up and everything they said gave the impression that they had given up on him. Even when the boy apologized, the coordinator evinced utter cynicism when he retorted dismissively, "That's what you said last time." This was a full-fledged degradation ceremony rather than an attempt at reintegration.

Pessimism is a natural human reaction to repeated misfortune and eventually the most determined commitment to "never giving up on the offender" may succumb to it. But a tenacious commitment to the ideology of never giving up will allow coordinators to cling to it for the fourth conference after the failure of the third. A slightly more tenacious commitment allows optimism to survive the fifth conference into the sixth. At each stage, more and more offenders drop off never to return, their criminal careers coming to an end without being inflicted with degradation ceremonies. Very few offenders indeed will make it through to a sixth conference. If we can hold out with optimism until then, the criminal justice system will have been transformed to a 99 percent reintegrative institution. That can hardly be a bad outcome.

True disciples of reintegration, including ourselves, take the injunction to never give up on offenders to the absolute extreme. Even when a criminal career has continued to the point of the offender being the most powerfully organized criminal in the country, the best hope for dealing with him is conceived as persuading him to convert his illegitimate capital into a legitimate business, giving his children a better future, a more respectable future, than the shame of his criminal empire. Going further still, as we have illustrated earlier (see note 8), we think even the top management of certain Australian insurance companies are best negotiated with reintegratively! In the extraordinary cases where offenders are such a danger to the community that incarceration is defensible, we should not give up on pushing for reintegration, even though the degradation ceremony of confinement makes this maximally difficult.

14. The ceremony must be justified by a politically resonant discourse.

Shaming and reintegration are terms that we think have merit (that we will not defend here) in the discourse of criminological theory. These days, they have surprising currency among the police and community of Wagga. But in New Zealand, the terms that have more currency are, respectively, young offenders and their families "taking responsibility" and "healing." The discourse of responsibility and healing may have more popular political appeal than that of shame and reintegration, as evidenced by the wide political support it has attracted in New Zealand and the growing support throughout Australia (Interim Report of the Select Committee on the Juvenile Justice System 1992; Tate 1992).

Much more crucial to this political and media support has been the marketing of this reintegration strategy as victim-centered and family-centered. It is a progressive reform that calls the hand of conservative politicians. They are forever claiming that victims are the forgotten people of the criminal justice system and bemoaning the declining importance of the family in contemporary society. Here is a reform that empowers victims and at the same time values and empowers families. Such a reform puts conservatives in a vulnerable position when they seek to oppose it.

Moreover, conservatives have also found in Australia and New Zealand that they cannot count on their allegedly "natural allies" in law and order campaigns, the police. The Australian and New Zealand Police Federation carried a resolution at its 1991 conference supporting the New Zealand juvenile justice reforms. In New Zealand, 91 percent of the time police report that they are satisfied with the outcomes of the conferences in which they participate, a higher level than for youth justice coordinators (86 percent), parents (85 percent), offenders (84 percent) and victims (48 percent) (Morris and Maxwell 1992). Perhaps this should not surprise us. The approach appeals to the common sense of police. On balance, it cuts their paperwork and economizes on criminal justice system resources; they often feel empowered by the capacity the conference gives them to make practical suggestions to the family on what might be done about the problem (an opportunity they are rarely given by courts); they like to treat victims with the decency that they believe courts deny them (in particular, they like to see victims actually getting compensation); and they find that the program builds goodwill toward the police in communities that are empowered through the process. Most critically, they find participation in community conferences more interesting, challenging, and satisfying work than typing up charges and sitting around in courthouses for cases that are rushed through in a matter of minutes. This is by no means a universal police reaction. But we can certainly say that the strongest support for these reintegrative programs in Australia has come from the police. While New Zealand reform was Maori-driven, the Australian reform is being police-driven.

Finally, the political appeal of the process is that it can be advocated in the discourse of fiscal restraint. In New Zealand, one of the most conservative governments in the Western world liked a reform that helped the budget deficit by allowing them to sell most of the institutions for juvenile offenders in the country. We were told that the Department of Social Welfare alone estimated that in 1991, they saved $6 million as a result of the reform. In this area of criminal justice, youth justice coordinators not only do the job more effectively that judges in court, they are cheaper than judges. By the same token, youth justice advocates are cheaper than prosecutors and public defenders. At all levels of the criminal justice system there are savings—not always massive savings, but rarely trivial.[17]

At the same time, reintegration ceremonies offer an attractive political package for a reforming politician. Presented properly, it can satisfy the otherwise incompatible imperatives of keeping the police and the finance ministry happy at the same time. It can even put the victims movement and liberally minded criminal justice reformers—who so often seem diametrically opposed—together on the same platform of support.

Conclusion

A useful way of thinking about ceremonies for dealing with rule breakers is in terms of the ratio of stigmatic to reintegrative meanings during the ceremony. When that ratio is high, we have a degradation ceremony; when low, a reintegration ceremony. There are few, if any, actors who are perfectly faithful to the theory of reintegrative shaming during such ceremonies. Typically, messages are mixed, as with the Maori participant quoted above: "You've got no brains, boy (stigmatization) . . . But I've got respect for you (reintegration) . . . " There are many actors like this one who communicate shame while also sustaining a high ratio of reintegrative to stigmatizing meanings. The subtleties in the ways shaming and reintegration are mixed by practical human communicators are myriad. We noted one police sergeant who addressed male offenders by their names whenever he was engaging them in responsibility talk, but who called them "mate" whenever he switched to reintegrative talk. When we pointed out this observation and asked him whether he was aware of the pattern, the sergeant told us it was a conscious communication strategy.

In Giddens's (1984) terms, many actors have practical but not discursive consciousness of the idea of reintegration; some actors, like this sergeant, have both. A feasible policy objective is to increase the proportion of actors who are conscious of the virtues of reintegration. This is not best achieved by lectures from theoretical criminology texts, but from telling stories (Shearing and Ericson 1991) and simple homilies such as that of one police constable: "just because we sometimes do stupid things; that does not mean we are a stupid person." It could be that if there is a key principle of successful reintegration ceremonies, it is that there should not be too many principles. Training of coordinators should be kept simple, leaving them wide discretion to implement flexibly a few broad principles.

Stigma cannot be rooted out of confrontations between people who are angry and affronted by acts of rule breaking. But the ratio of stigmatization to reintegration can be shifted substantially by story-based training methods that focus on a few core principles—empower the victim, respect and support the offender while condemning his act, engage the offender's supporters. Just by having a process that is more victim-centered, problem-centered, and community-oriented, rather than centered on the offender and his pathologies, we institute a logic that produces less stigmatization and more reintegration. Obversely, the offender-centered logic of the courtroom or the psychiatrist's couches institutionalizes stigmatization.

One of the inevitable problems is that the stigmatizing, disempowering professional knowledge of the court and consultancy rooms penetrates the reintegration ceremony. Most depressingly, this was observed in New Zealand with the role of certain youth advocates, private lawyers contracted by the state to watch out for the rights of young offenders during conferences. Sometimes they "earn their fee" by taking charge, telling the family what sort of action plan will satisfy the police and the courts. Or worse, we see "the practice of law as a confidence game" (Blumberg 1967) where advocate, coordinator, and police conspire to settle a practical deal among the professionals, then sell that deal to the conference participants, a deal that in at least one case seemed to us a sellout of both the offender and the victim.

We commented earlier about the observations made by Clifford Shearing and Jane Mugford after a Wagga training session. Their point was that the reform process must create a new knowledge, citizen knowledge, otherwise the old professional knowledge would colonize the spaces in the program. We agree—hence the importance of the simple principles outlined above and the importance of the central involvement of local police-citizen consultative committees and other community groups in guiding reform. At the same time, however, we think the professional knowledges also includes the seeds of their own reform. Reintegrative concepts have a major place in psychological and particularly social work discourse. These can be brought to the fore through reforms such as we are seeing in New Zealand and Wagga. While the youth advocates were criticized by a number of people we spoke to in New Zealand for importing professional control into family group conferences, some of these critics also pointed out how many advocates had changed their legalistic habits to accommodate the communitarian ideology of the conferences. Finally, there can be no doubt that these reforms are part of wider changes in police knowledge in Australia and New Zealand—away from "lock-'em-up" law enforcement and toward community policing. Nonetheless, at the crucial middle management levels, the old punitive knowledge of policing continues to predominate and must be confronted by reasoned cases based on the success of alternative practices. Reformers can't lock professional knowledge out of the process. Hence, reformers must be engaged with police education, counter-colonizing that area with reintegrative ideas.[18]

There are no criminal justice utopias to be found, just better and worse directions to head in.[19] The New Zealand Maori have shown a direction for making reintegration ceremonies work in multicultural metropolises such as Auckland, a city that faces deeper problems of recession, homelessness, and gang violence than many cities in Western Europe. Implementation of these ideas by the white New Zealand authorities has been riddled with imperfection—re-professionalization, patriarchy, ritualistic proceduralism that loses sight of objectives and inappropriate net-widening. The important thing, however, is that the general direction of change is away from these pathologies; it is deprofessionalizing, empowering of women, oriented to flexible community problem-solving and, for the most part, narrowing nets of state control (Maxwell and Morris 1993, pp. 25, 134, 136, but see 128, 176; on net-narrowing at Wagga see Moore 1992; O'Connell 1992). Most critically, it shows that the conditions of successful reintegration ceremonies that criminologists identify when in high theory mode can be given practical content for implementation by police and citizens.

As both Max Scheler and Garfinkel point out: "there is no society that does not provide in the very features of its organization the conditions sufficient for inducing shame" (Garfinkel 1956, p. 420). The question is what sort of balance societies will have between degradation ceremonies as a "secular form of communion" and reintegration ceremonies as a rather different communion. Garfinkel showed that there was a practical program of communication tactics that will get the work of status degradation done. We hope to have shown that equally there is a practical program of communication tactics that can accomplish reintegration.

Notes

This chapter originally appeared in the *British Journal of Criminology,* Volume 34, 1994, pp. 139-71. It is reprinted with permission.

    1. A common cynicism when we have spoken to American audiences about these ideas has been that it sounds like a good idea for sweet, sheep-loving New Zealanders, with their intact families, but that it could never work in the face of the family disintegration of American slums. This is an odd perspective, given the empirical reality in New Zealand that Youth Aid Officers saw "poor family support/background" as the most important factor *in favor of* opting for referral of a case to a family group conference rather than some other disposition (Maxwell and Morris 1993, pp. 60–61). Moreover, in practice, 14 percent of young people processed in family group conferences do not live with

their families, compared to 4 percent of those processed by informal police diversion (Maxwell and Morris 1993, pp. 64, 66).

2. See, however, the discussion of professionally manipulated consensus under point 5 and in the conclusion to this chapter.

3. The main reason for nonattendance for victims in New Zealand was simply their not being invited, followed by being invited at a time unsuitable to them (Maxwell and Morris 1993, p. 79), a result of poor understanding of the philosophy of the reform by conference coordinators, heavy workload, and practical difficulties, such as the police failing to pass on the victim's address. Only 6 percent of victims said they did not want to meet the offender (Morris et al. 1993).

4. An allusion to Rose (1990) and his discussion of "governing the soul."

5. This is not to downplay the wonderful successes with offender empowerment that can and do occur within the New Zealand process: "I felt safe because my whanau [extended family] were there with me. I would have felt like stink if I had to face it on my own. My auntie explained it so I understood. It was good that she allowed me to take a role" (young person quoted in Maxwell and Morris 1993, p. 78).

6. In this regard, we were somewhat surprised by Maxwell and Morris's (1993, p. 93) finding that an apology was formally recorded as offered in only 70 percent of their sample of conferences. We wondered if all of the more informal means of apology (including backstage apology) were counted in this result.

7. With Samoan conferences, it is common for offenders to apologize on their knees, a degrading form of apology in Western eyes, but perhaps not so when the cultural context is to quickly elevate the offender, embracing his restored identity. That is, for the Samoan, the kneeling may represent part of a reintegrative sequence rather than signifying degradation.

8. In Australia, we have been experimenting with reintegrative conferences with white-collar crime, cases that illustrate the problem of victim shame. A recent case has involved action by the Trade Practices Commission against a number of Australia's largest insurance companies in what have been the biggest consumer protection cases in Australian history. The victims were Aboriginals in remote communities who were sold (generally) useless insurance and investment policies as a result of a variety of shocking misrepresentations, even the misrepresentation that the Aboriginal would be sent to jail if he did not sign the policy. Victims sometimes escaped through the back door when the government man in the white shirt arrived to interview them, fearing that *they* had done something wrong. Many shook and cried throughout their interviews. They felt shame at losing the little money their families had. The apologies issued by company chief executives at highly publicized press conferences were about communicating the message that it was the company who had to face "the shame job" (as Aboriginals put it). Moreover, full compensation with 15 percent compound interest would acquit the shame victims felt as providers. In

addition, insurance company top management were required to attend negotiation conferences at Wujal Wujal, where they faced their victims, apologized to them and lived the life conditions of their victims, sleeping on mattresses on concrete floors, eating tinned food, during several days of negotiation. For more details on this and other cases of corporate shaming praxis, see Fisse and Braithwaite (1993) and Braithwaite (1992).

9. In New Zealand, it is usual to have a break in the proceedings during which the offender's family meets on its own to prepare a plan of action.

10. In practice, the Wagga process has been more oriented from the outset to reintegrating victims than the New Zealand process. Many New Zealand coordinators, interpreting literally a clause in the New Zealand *Children, Young Persons and Their Families Act*, have been reluctant to allow victim supporters to attend the conference. There has been a lot of learning in New Zealand on this question, but in some parts there is still a fear of the vindictiveness of victims and, more particularly, of victim supporters. If victims are to be reintegrated, however, caring supporters are a necessary ingredient. Our strongest criticism of the New Zealand reform effort has been the half-hearted commitment to victim reintegration in many quarters.

11. In New Zealand, 53 percent of the offenders processed through family group conferences are Maori (Maxwell and Morris 1993, p. 69). On Maori perceptions of the value of the reforms, see footnote 13.

12. With the weak welfare states that exist in both Australia and New Zealand, the range of such choices effectively available to young people, in most localities but particularly in rural localities, is very poor (Maxwell and Morris 1993, p. 180).

13. While it is easy to find Maoris who resist the notion that there is a lot of point in turning back the clock to a pre-European society and others who see family group conferences as a corruption and debasement of Maori traditions by the Western justice system, we suspect the predominant Maori reaction is as expressed by the Maori researchers on the Maxwell and Morris project in the following quote—accepting the need for mutual accommodation between Maori and Western justice systems, especially when victims and offenders come from different cultures:

We feel that the Act for the most part is an excellent piece of legislation which promises exciting possibilities for the future. When the processes outlined in the Act were observed, Maori families were indeed empowered and able to take an active part in decisions concerning their young people. It is not difficult to see the beneficial influences that the Act may eventually exert on wider Maori, Polynesian and Pakeha society. Maori society could gain immensely from legislation that acknowledges and strengthens the hapu and tribal structures and their place in decisions regarding the wellbeing of young people and [from legislation] that provides them with an opportunity to contribute to any reparation and to support those offended against. The same scenario would apply to Pacific Island peoples. Pakeha society would also benefit from a process which acknowledges the family and gives redress to victims (Maxwell and Morris 1993, p. 187).

14. Maxwell and Morris's (1993, p. 176) New Zealand data support this interpretation. They find that the result of the New Zealand reforms is fewer children going to court, fewer receiving custodial penalties, but more children whose delinquency was previously ignored altogether or discharged by the court experiencing moderate interventions such as formal apology, compensation, and community service decided through family group conferences or police diversion.

15. As an aside, it is worth noting here the implications for the justice model which provides a critique of family group conferences as inferior to courts. Courts, according to this critique, provide singular consistent justice, in contrast to the plural, inconsistent justice of conferences. It is an interesting empirical question whether in practice, as opposed to theory, courts do deliver more just sanctioning when compensation, fines, and community service ordered by the court are defied in the majority of cases. It is not inconceivable that even though there is greater inequity in the sanctions ordered by group conferences, in the sanctions actually implemented there is greater equity for the group conference than for the court process.

16. There will be rare cases where the offender is so dangerous that escalation to institutionalization is inevitable and necessary. We have no dispute with such a course of action in those cases.

17. Against this view, economists might say that we should cost the (considerable) time involved, by the attendance of victims and supporters, for example. If we calculated these costs, perhaps there would be no savings. But why should we make a negative entry for victims in the economic calculus when the fact is that the reform increases utility for victims? To enter the costs would make sense only if we could value the benefits. And if we did that, then no doubt the system we describe would again show a better balance sheet.

18. Something the senior author has been actively engaged with since 1986 as a member of the NSW Police Education Advisory Council.

19. There is no persuasive evidence that the reforms we have described actually work in reducing delinquency. That would require random allocation experiments. We can say that official statistics do not support the conclusion that they are failing. Crime rates in Wagga Wagga have fallen sharply since the juvenile justice reforms were introduced. In New Zealand, juvenile crime rates were falling slightly before the *Children, Young Persons and Their Families Act 1989* was passed, and continued to fall slightly after its introduction (Maxwell and Morris 1993, p. 45).

References

Ashworth, Andrew. 1986. "Punishment and Compensation: Victims, Offenders and the State." *Oxford Journal of Legal Studies* 6: 86-122.

Bales, Robert F. 1950. *Interaction Process Analysis.* Cambridge: Addison-Wesley.

Becker, Howard S. 1960. "Notes on the Concept of Commitment." *American Journal of Sociology* 66: 32-40.

———. 1963. *Outsiders: Studies in the Sociology of Deviance.* New York: Free Press.

Blagg, Harry. 1985. "Reparation and Justice for Juveniles: The Corby Experience." *British Journal of Criminology* 25: 267-79.

Blumberg, Abraham S. 1967. "The Practice of Law as a Confidence Game: Organizational Cooptation of a Profession." *Law and Society Review* 1: 15-39.

Bott, Elizabeth. 1987. "The Kava Ceremonial as a Dream Structure." In *Constructive Drinking: Perspectives on Drinking from Anthropology,* edited by M. Douglas, 182-204. Cambridge: Cambridge University Press.

Braithwaite, John. 1989. *Crime, Shame and Reintegration.* Cambridge: Cambridge University Press.

———. 1991. "Poverty, Power, White-Collar Crime and the Paradoxes of Criminological Theory." *Australian and New Zealand Journal of Criminology* 24: 40-58.

———. 1992. "Corporate Crime and Republican Criminological Praxis." Paper to Queens University Conference on Corporate Ethics, Law and the State, Kingston.

———. 1993. "Inequality and Republican Criminology." In *Crime and Inequality,* edited by John Hagan and Ruth Peterson. Stanford, CA: Stanford University Press.

Braithwaite, John, and Kathleen Daly. 1994. "Masculinities, Violence and Communitarian Control." In *Just Boys Doing Business? Men, Masculinity and Crime,* edited by T. Newburn and B. Stanko. London: Routledge.

Cheal, David. 1988. "The Postmodern Origins of Ritual," *Journal for the Theory of Social Behaviour* 18: 269-90.

Christie, Nils. 1977. "Conflict as Property." *British Journal of Criminology* 17: 1-26.

Cragg, Wesley. 1992. *The Practice of Punishment: Towards a Theory of Restorative Justice.* London: Routledge.

de Haan, Willem. 1990. *The Politics of Redress: Crime, Punishment and Penal Abolition.* London: Unwin Hyman.

Dignan, Jim. 1992. "Repairing the Damage: Can Reparation Work in the Service of Diversion?" *British Journal of Criminology* 32: 453-72.

Doob, Anthony, and Julian Roberts. 1983. *Sentencing: An Analysis of the Public's View of Sentencing. A Report to the Department of Justice, Canada.* Department of Justice, Canada.

———. 1988. "Public attitudes towards sentencing in Canada." In *Public Attitudes to Sentencing,* edited by N. Walker and M. Hough. Aldershot: Gower.

Erikson, Kai T. 1962. "Notes on the Sociology of Deviance." *Social Problems* 9: 307-14.

Fisse, Brent, and John Braithwaite. 1993. *Corporations, Crime and Accountability.* Cambridge: Cambridge University Press.

Galaway, Burt. 1985. "Victim-Participation in the Penal Corrective process." *Victimology* 10: 617-30.

Galaway, Burt, and Joe Hudson. 1975. "Issues in the Correctional Implementation of Restitution to Victims of Crime." In *Considering the Victim,* edited by Joe Hudson and Burt Galaway. Springfield, IL: Charles C. Thomas.

———. 1990. *Criminal Justice, Restitution and Reconciliation.* Monsey, NY: Criminal Justice Press.

Galaway, B., M. Henzel, G. Ramsey, and B. Wanyama. 1980. "Victims and Delinquents in the Tulsa Juvenile Court." *Federal Probation* 44: 42-48.

Garfinkel, Harold. 1956. "Conditions of Successful Degradation Ceremonies." *American Journal of Sociology* 61: 420-24.

Giddens, Anthony. 1984. *The Constitution of Society.* Berkeley, CA: University of California Press.

Goffman, Erving. 1971. *Relations in Public.* New York: Basic Books.

Gusfield, Joseph R. 1987. "Passage to Play: Rituals of Drink in American Society." In *Constructive Drinking: Perspectives on Drinking from Anthropology,* edited by M. Douglas, 73-90. Cambridge: Cambridge University Press.

Habermas, Jurgen. 1986. "Law as Medium and Law as Institution." In *Dilemmas of Law in the Welfare State,* edited by Gunther Teubner. Berlin: Walter de Gruyter.

Hazan, Haim. 1987. "Holding Time Still With Cups of Tea." In *Constructive Drinking: Perspectives on Drinking from Anthropology,* edited by M. Douglas, 205-19. Cambridge: Cambridge University Press.

Hazlehurst, Kayleen. 1985. "Community Care/Community Responsibility: Community Participation in Criminal Justice Administration in New Zealand." In *Justice Programs for Aboriginal and Other Indigenous Communities,* edited by K. Hazlehurst. Canberra: Australian Institute of Criminology.

Heinz, Ann, and Wayne Kerstetter. 1981. "Pretrial Settlement Conference: Evaluation of a Reform in Plea Bargaining." In *Perspectives on Crime Victims,* edited by Burt Galaway and Joe Hudson. St. Louis, MO: Mosby.

Hirschi, Travis, and Michael Gottfredson. 1983. "Age and the Explanation of Crime." *American Journal of Sociology* 89: 552-84.

Howard, Barbara, and Lee Purches. 1992. "A Discussion of the Police Family Group Conferences and the Follow-Up Program (Stage 2) in the Wagga Wagga Juvenile Cautioning Process." *Rural Society* 2: 20-23.

Interim Report of the Select Committee on the Juvenile Justice System. 1992. Adelaide: Parliament of South Australia.

Kigin, R., and S. Novack. 1980. "A Rural Restitution Program for Juvenile Offenders and Victims." In *Victims, Offenders and Alternative Sanctions*, edited by Joe Hudson and Burt Galaway. Lexington, MA: Lexington Books.

Marshall, Tony F. 1985. *Alternatives to Criminal Courts*. Aldershot: Gower.

Maxwell, Gabrielle M., and Allison Morris. 1993. *Family Participation Cultural Diversity and Victim Involvement in Youth Justice: A New Zealand Experiment*. Institute of Criminology, Victoria University of Wellington.

McDonald, John, and Steve Ireland. 1990. *Can It be Done Another Way?* Sydney: New South Wales Police Service.

Meima, M. 1990. "Sexual Violence, Criminal Law and Abolitionism." In *Gender, Sexuality and Social Control,* edited by B. Rolston and M. Tomlinson. Bristol: European Group for the Study of Deviance and Social Control.

Moore, David B. 1992. "Facing the Consequences. Conferences and Juvenile Justice." National Conference on Juvenile Justice, Canberra: Australian Institute of Criminology.

Morris, Allison, and Gabrielle Maxwell. 1992. "Juvenile Justice in New Zealand: A New Paradigm." *Australian and New Zealand Journal of Criminology* 26: 72-90.

Morris, Allison, Gabrielle Maxwell, and Jeremy P. Robertson. 1993. "Giving Victims a Voice: A New Zealand Experiment." *Howard Journal of Criminology* 32: 304-21.

Mugford, Jane, and Stephen Mugford. 1991. "Shame and Reintegration in the Punishment and Deterrence of Spouse Abuse." Paper presented to the American Society of Criminology Conference, San Francisco, November 20.

———. 1992. "Policing Domestic Violence." In *Policing Australia: Old Issues, New Perspectives*, edited by P. Moir and H. Eijckman, 321-83. Melbourne: Macmillan.

Murphy, Jeffrie G., and Jean Hampton. 1989. *Forgiveness and Mercy*. New York: Cambridge University Press.

New Zealand Police Association. 1991. Submission to the Review of the Children, Young Persons and Their Families Act 1989. Wellington: New Zealand Police Association.

Novack, S., B. Galaway, and J. Hudson. 1980. "Victim and Offender Perceptions of the Fairness of Restitution and Community-Service Sanctions." In

Victims, Offenders and Alternative Sanctions, edited by J. Hudson and B. Galaway. Lexington, MA: Lexington Books.

O'Connell, Terry. 1992. "It May Be the Way to Go." National Conference on Juvenile Justice, Canberra: Australian Institute of Criminology.

O'Connell, Terry, and David Moore. 1992. "Wagga Juvenile Cautioning Process: The General Applicability of Family Group Conferences for Juvenile Offenders and their Victims" *Rural Society* 2: 16-19.

O'Connor, Ian, and P. Sweetapple. 1988. *Children in Justice.* Sydney: Longman-Cheshire.

Pepinsky, Harold E., and Richard Quinney, eds. 1991. *Criminology as Peacemaking.* Bloomington, IN: Indiana University Press.

Polk, Kenneth. 1992. "Jobs Not Jails: A New Agenda for Youth." National Conference on Juvenile Justice, Canberra: Australian Institute of Criminology.

Report of the Ministerial Advisory Committee on a Maori Perspective for the Department of Social Welfare. 1986. *Puao-Te-Ata-Tu* (day break), Wellington, New Zealand: Department of Social Welfare.

Rose, Nikolas. 1990. *Governing the Soul: Shaping the Private Self.* London: Routledge and Kegan Paul.

Scheff, Thomas J., and Suzanne M. Retzinger. 1991. *Emotions and Violence: Shame and Rage in Destructive Conflicts.* Lexington, MA: Lexington Books.

Schur, Edwin M. 1973. *Radical Non-Intervention: Rethinking the Delinquency Problem.* Englewood Cliffs, NJ: Prentice-Hall.

Shapland, J., J. Willmore, and P. Duff. 1985. *Victims in the Criminal Justice System.* Cambridge Studies in Criminology. Brookfield, VT: Gower.

Shearing, Clifford D., and Richard V. Ericson. 1991. "Towards a Figurative Conception of Action." *British Journal of Sociology* 42: 481-506.

Simmel, Georg. 1978. *The Philosophy of Money.* London: Routledge.

Sykes, Gresham, and David Matza. 1957. "Techniques of Neutralization: A Theory of Delinquency." *American Sociological Review* 22: 664-70.

Tate, Senator Michael. 1992. Opening Address. National Conference on Juvenile Justice, Canberra: Australian Institute of Criminology.

Taylor, Ian, Paul Walton, and Jock Young. 1973. *The New Criminology: For a Social Theory of Deviance.* London: Routledge and Kegan Paul.

Umbreit, Mark. 1985. *Crime and Reconciliation: Creative Options for Victims and Offenders.* Nashville, TN: Abigdon Press.

Weitekamp, Elmar. 1989. "Restitution: An New Paradigm of Criminal Justice or a New Way to Widen the System of Social Control?" Unpublished Ph.D. dissertation, University of Pennsylvania.

Wright, Martin. 1982. *Making Good: Prisons, Punishment and Beyond.* London: Hutchinson.

Youth Justice Coalition. 1990. *Kids in Justice: A Blueprint for the 90s.* Sydney: Law Foundation of New South Wales.

Zehr, Howard. 1990. *Changing Lenses: A New Focus for Criminal Justice.* Scottdale, PA: Herald Press.

13

The "Community" in Community Justice: Issues, Themes, and Questions for the New Neighborhood Sanctioning Models

Gordon Bazemore

In the past few years, interest in "restorative justice," "community justice," and other alternatives to adversarial/retributive paradigms have captured the imagination of a number of criminal justice professionals and community members. But while much attention has been devoted to programs associated with these movements, such as restitution and community service, community policing, community courts, and community corrections, citizen involvement as decision makers in the sanctioning process remains unexplored. This chapter compares four neighborhood decision-making models now being used with some frequency in the United States and Canada. In doing so, I examine several questions about how each model defines the role of the community in the sanctioning process and consider the influence of three theoretical themes in establishing priorities and focal concerns of each model.

Model One: In cities and towns in the United States and Canada—as well as in Australia and New Zealand—family members and other citizens acquainted with a young offender or victim of a juvenile crime gather to determine what should be done in response to the offense. Often held in schools, churches, or other facilities, these family group conferences (FGCs) are facilitated by a community justice coordinator or police officer and are aimed at ensuring that offenders face up to community disapproval of their behavior, that an agreement is developed for repairing the damage to victim and community, and that community members recognize the need for reintegrating the offender once he or she has made amends. Based on the centuries-old sanctioning and dispute-resolution traditions of the Maori, a New Zealand aboriginal band, the modern FGC was adopted into national juvenile justice legislation in New Zealand in 1989. "Conferencing" is now widely used in modified form as a police-initiated diversion alternative in Australia and is being rapidly introduced in communities in Minnesota, Pennsylvania, Montana, and other American states and parts of Canada.[1]

Model Two: Throughout the state of Vermont, nonviolent offenders sentenced to reparative probation meet with a local citizen reparative board (RB), which recommends a plan that requires offenders to repair the harm to the victim, complete community service, and become involved in educational activities aimed at both increasing victim awareness and teaching ways to avoid reoffending. At the end of the session, an offender signs an agreement to complete the plan within ninety days. The boards, which became operational early in 1995 as part of a mandated separation of probation into community corrections service units (which provide supervision for more serious cases) and court and reparative service units (which coordinate and provide administrative support to the boards), are composed of five local citizens who make dispositional recommendations for eligible probation cases referred by the courts. If target goals of state correctional administrators are met, boards may soon be hearing up to 60 percent of these eligible cases (Dooley 1995; 1996a).

Model Three: In the city of Whitehorse (Yukon) and other Canadian towns and villages, members of the First Nation as well as other citizens sit sometimes for hours in a circle listening to offenders, victims, their advocates, and other community members speak about the impact of crimes. When the feather or "talking stick" is passed to them and it is their turn to speak without being interrupted, they may comment favorably on rehabilitative efforts already begun by the offender, who may be a chronic and sometimes violent perpetrator well known to the community. Speakers in these circle sentencing (CS) sessions also express concern for the victim or the continuing threat posed by the offender and, at the end of the session, attempt to come to consensus about a rehabilitative plan for the offender and an approach to healing the victim and the community. Circle sentencing is a recently updated version of ancient sanctioning and settlement practices adapted from the traditions of Canadian aboriginals (Stuart 1995b)—as well as those of indigenous people in the southwestern United States (Melton 1995)—and was resurrected in 1991 by supportive judges and community justice committees in the Yukon and other northern Canadian communities. These committees and communities are now working with police, justices of the peace, and other criminal justice officials to assume increasing responsibility for offender sentencing and supervision.[2]

Model Four: Throughout North America, as well as in many cities in Europe and other parts of the world, crime victims and offenders meet with trained mediators to allow the victim to tell his or her story to the offender, express feelings about the victimization, make the offender aware of the harm caused by his or her crime, and get information about the offender and the offense. At the conclusion of most of these victim-offender mediation (VOM) sessions, both victim and offender work with the mediator to develop a reparative plan that ensures that the offender provides appropriate restoration to the victim, the community, or both. Originally (and still frequently) referred to as victim offender reconciliation programs (VORPs), VOMs are still unfamiliar to some mainstream criminal justice audiences and marginal to the court process in many jurisdictions where they do operate. However, VOM programs now have a respectable twenty-five-year track record, and more than 300 programs now serve victims and offenders in Canada and the United States (Umbreit and Zehr 1996; Umbreit and Coates 1993).

Each paragraph above describes one model of informal, community-based sanctioning now being carried out in different parts of North America and the world. While citizen involvement in sanctioning is not new and these examples by no means exhaust the range of alternatives, the four models illustrate some of the diversity, as well as many of the common themes, in an emerging "new wave" of nonadversarial community alternatives to formal court sentencing.

The four models also represent one important component of a broader movement to bring less-formal justice processes and intervention practices to neighborhoods and local communities, increase responsiveness to citizens, and involve neighborhood residents and organizations. This broader movement, generally referred to as restorative justice (e.g., Bazemore and Umbreit 1995; Hudson and Galaway 1996; Zehr 1990), community justice (Barajas 1995; Griffiths and Hamilton 1996; Stuart

1995a), and restorative community justice (Bazemore and Schiff 1996; Young 1995), is becoming a topic of discussion and debate in the United States and Canada and has already had significant effects on state and local policies (Depew 1994; NIJ 1996a, 1996b).[3]

Restorative justice views crime primarily as harm to victims and the justice response as one that should, through restitution, community service, and victim offender dialogue and related processes, seek to repair this harm and actively involve victims and communities (Galaway and Hudson 1990; Van Ness 1993; Zehr 1990). Depending upon who is describing it, community justice may include a wide array of programs, and "community-based initiatives," including community policing, "weed and seed," neighborhood revitalization, drug courts, community corrections, community courts and neighborhood prosecution and defense units, prevention and diversion programs, restitution, community service, victim services, and dispute and conflict resolution efforts in schools and neighborhood organizations (NIJ 1996b). Agreeing upon what should and should not be included under the community justice "tent" is not an easy task.[4] As case studies in this broader community justice movement, the four community decision-making models are relevant to policymakers and court professionals because they address a critical, but frequently neglected, component of community justice programs and initiatives: providing citizens with a meaningful role in the sanctioning process. Specifically, these nonadversarial alternatives to court emphasize a more participatory approach to sanctioning, which allows for the expression of emotion and encourages problem-solving as part of the justice process.

This chapter has two primary objectives. First, I describe each of these models both in the context of previous efforts to engage citizens and community groups in the sanctioning process, and of the new broader international movement toward community justice. Second, it is important to more fully examine the interpretation given to the term "community" in each model. Hence, a second objective is to illustrate how community is defined in the practice of neighborhood sanctioning as practitioners attempt to identify the role of citizens vis-à-vis the role of the formal justice process and the role of crime victims relative to that of offenders in what is meant to be a restorative process. Because both quantitative and qualitative data on these models are in short supply, this discussion focuses on the assumptions, claims, and focal concerns of these approaches to community justice decision making. While no attempt is made to test hypotheses or to identify testable propositions, these questions are presented with the aim of developing agendas and benchmark criteria for future research into the effectiveness of community justice decision making. After outlining three theoretical themes or perspectives that have significantly influenced each of these models, I then describe how each addresses key questions about the role of the community in community justice.

What's "New" about the New Community Justice Decision-Making Models?

While the four models share a nonadversarial, community-based sanctioning focus, there are substantial differences between them (see Table 1). Eligibility ranges from minor first offenders to serious repeat offenders (in the case of circle sentencing), and the models differ in point of referral and staffing.

Although a few judges in Yukon, Canada, have held circle sentencing sessions inside their courtrooms, for the most part, each of these informal sanctioning processes takes place in community centers, schools, churches, and other neighborhood settings. With the exception of the Vermont reparative boards, decision making in each model is by consensus, but process and protocol vary substantially—ranging from ancient rituals in the case of circle sentencing (Stuart 1995b); to the "script" of family group conferencing, which ensures that offender, victim, and intimates of each are given an opportunity to speak (McDonald et al. 1995); to the nondirective approach used in victim-offender mediation sessions (Umbreit 1994); to the more deliberative agenda followed by community boards (Dooley 1995). The time needed to complete the process may range from a half-hour, in the case of some reparative board hearings, to seven hours or more in the case of some circle sentencing conferences. Although police may participate in each model, only the Australian model of family group conferencing gives the police a formal role. Finally, the models operate at different levels of integration with the formal system. The new Reparative Boards in Vermont have been adopted by statewide statute and policy as the preferred option for nonviolent felons. New Zealand has required since 1989 that all but the most violent and serious delinquency cases be resolved through a family group conference (Alder and Wundersitz 1994; Maxwell and Morris 1993; McElrae 1993); this appears to be the most systemically institutionalized of the four models.

While the importance of administrative and process differences should not be underestimated (see Table 1), it should also be emphasized that, except for victim-offender mediation, the other models are relatively new—at least to the modern Western world (McElrae 1993; Melton 1995)—and will continue to evolve. Hence, more important than

Table 1

Community Decision-Making Models: Administration and Process

	Circle Sentencing	Family Group Conferencing	Reparative Probation	Victim/Offender Mediation
Time in Operation	Since approximately 1992	New Zealand—1989; Australia—1991	Since 1995	Since mid-1970s
Where Used	Primarily in the Yukon; sporadically in other parts of Canada	Australia; New Zealand; cities and towns in Montana; Minnesota; and Pennsylvania	Vermont	Throughout North America and Europe
Point in System	Used at various stages—may be diversion or alternative to formal court hearings and correctional process for indictable offenses	New Zealand—throughout juvenile justice system; Australia Wagga-Wagga model—police diversion	One of several probation options	Mostly diversion and probation options, but some use in residential facilities for more serious cases
Eligibility and Target Group	Offenders who admit guilt and express willingness to change; entire range of offenses and offenders eligible; chronic offenders targeted	New Zealand—all juvenile offenders eligible except murder and manslaughter charges; Wagga-Wagga model—determined by police discretion or diversion criteria	Target group is nonviolent offenders; eligibility limited to offenders given probation and assigned to the boards (some boards have been given discretion to accept violent offenders)	Varies but primarily diversion cases and property offenders; in some locations, used with serious and violent offenders (at victim's request)

Table 1 (Continued)

	Circle Sentencing	Family Group Conferencing	Reparative Probation	Victim/Offender Mediation
Staffing	Community justice coordinator	Community justice coordinator	Reparative coordinator (probation staff)	Mediation coordinator—other positions vary; volunteers and staff mediators
Setting	Community center, school, or public building	Social welfare office, school, community building, occasionally police facility	Public building or community center	Neutral setting such as meeting room in library, church, or community center, occasionally in victim's home if approved by other parties
Nature and Order of Process	After judge, justice of the peace, or keeper opens session, each participant allowed to speak when feather or "talking stick" is passed to them; victim(s) generally speak first; consensus decision making	Coordinator follows "script" in which offender speaks first followed by victim and other participants; consensus decision making	Mostly private deliberation by board after questioning offender and hearing statements, some variation emerging	Victims often speak first followed by offender, mediator facilitates but encourages victim and offender to speak, encouraged to use nondirective style to facilitate dialogue; does not adhere to script or force consensus

these current differences are common elements that distinguish these "new wave" models as a group from other community justice practices and processes.[5] What appears to be most new and significant about these models is that in defining distinctive roles for citizens in determining sanctions, as well as how sanctions may be carried out, they add an important new dimension to ongoing efforts to "devolve" justice decision making to the neighborhood level.

Community Justice and Citizen Decision Making: Old and New

Efforts to increase community participation in sanctioning and dispositional decision making are nothing new. In the late 1970s, the Law Enforcement Assistance Administration (LEAA) of the U.S. Department of Justice supported "neighborhood justice centers," also referred to as "dispute-resolution centers," in several cities (Garafalo and Connelly 1980; McGillis and Mullen 1977). Although their history is not entirely clear, and only a few outlasted federal funding, neighborhood justice centers did provide a faster alternative to the formal court process and more satisfactory resolution of disputes ranging from tenant-landlord to neighborhood and business conflicts to domestic disturbances (McGillis and Mullen 1977). The four new models should also be viewed in the context of a more recent effort to bring courts, prosecution units, and defense teams to local neighborhoods. A recent publication of the National Institute of Justice, for example, describes a variety of initiatives to locate prosecution and defense services—as well as entire courts—in neighborhoods and to adapt their services to the needs of local citizens (NIJ 1996b).

What dispute-resolution centers, community courts, and court units have in common with the new wave decision-making models is an attempt to respond to citizen frustration with limited access to courts or, more broadly, to the justice decision-making process. Both new and old approaches have increased the accessibility of justice processes in communities. Specifically, they have (1) moved decision-making forums to decentralized, neighborhood locations; (2) adapted work hours, staffing patterns, and services to increase the flexibility and relevance of the justice process (Rottman 1996; Stone 1996); and (3) limited formal legalistic barriers, which alienate many citizens from courts, and offered a wide array of "user friendly" and informal approaches for resolving disputes and solving problems (NIJ 1996b; Zehr 1990).[6] But while improved access may increase citizen satisfaction with justice services, it does not change the essential role of the citizen from service recipient to decision maker with a stake in what services are provided and how they are delivered. Rottman suggests, for example, that simply making programs and professional positions more accessible to neighborhoods is a somewhat one-dimensional approach that is insufficient to meet the needs underlying the demand for community justice:

> The demand (of citizens for personal involvement) is not met by adding more legal aide centers and more pro bono work by attorneys. What people want challenges the professionalization of the court and their dominance by lawyers—forces that originally contributed to the drift from community ties. Court and community collaboration today consequently depends on balancing . . . the formalism (lawyers) bring against the influence of extra-legal factors on the one hand and public expectations for user-friendly, problem-solving courts on the other. (Rottman 1996, pp. 50-51)

It is the intention to increase community involvement and ownership that appears to most clearly distinguish the four new decision-making models from other approaches. While not the only important dimension of community justice, citizen input into the nature of sanctions may be necessary for implementing a more systemic community justice reform agenda. Such an agenda would assume the need for change in both the content and the context of justice intervention based on different values, clients, and role definitions, which more clearly distinguish the new restorative community justice from more traditional community-based criminal justice (Bazemore 1997). As key components of this more systemic agenda, the new decision-making models share several common influences.

Restoring, Shaming, and Healing: Theoretical and Ideological Influences in the New Community Decision Making

In contrast to the earlier manifestations of community decision making, the new wave of community justice models came on the scene during a unique period of convergence between diverse justice philosophies and political, social, and cultural movements. Hence, they appear to have been directly influenced by new developments in the victims' rights movement and an expanded role for victims in community justice (Young 1995); the community and problem-oriented policing philosophy and movement (Moore and Trojanowicz 1988; Sparrow, Moore, and Kennedy 1990); and renewed interest in indigenous dispute resolution, settlement processes, and associated political efforts (especially in Canada) to transfer criminal justice responsibilities to local communities (Griffiths and Hamilton 1996; Melton 1995).[7] In addition, the women's movement and feminist critique of patriarchal justice (Bowman 1994; Harris 1991) and the growing critique of both "just deserts" and rights-based, adversarial perspectives, as well as social welfare models, in criminal and juvenile justice (Bazemore and Umbreit 1995; Braithwaite and Petit 1992; Walgrave 1995) have also influenced the evolution of the new community justice movement.

More specifically, in contrast to both earlier dispute-resolution approaches and the new community courts, the new decision-making models have been directly influenced philosophically and theoretically by the restorative justice and community justice perspectives (Bazemore and Schiff 1996; Van Ness 1993; Young 1995; Zehr 1990).[8] The distinct concerns and priorities of each of the four models have been shaped by three "sensitizing concepts," which constitute distinguishable themes within the restorative and community justice literature. Each of these themes emerges from a slightly different ideological or theoretical critique of the adversarial/retributive justice process and, in turn, puts forward a somewhat different hierarchy of concerns and objectives in the community justice process.

First, the four decision-making models share one primary goal: that justice should not be punishment or treatment of the offender but reparation of harm to victims. This restorative theme focuses its critique of current criminal justice practices, as well as of some community justice alternatives, on the lack of attention to victim needs, the lack of concern with protecting victims from abuse, and the tendency to view victims merely as means to an end (e.g., increasing prosecution, increasing diversion) rather than as active participants in justice decision making (Umbreit 1994; Bazemore 1994). The three-dimensional focus on community, offender, and victim in some restorative justice literature notwithstanding (e.g., Bazemore 1996; Van Ness 1993), most practices labeled as "restorative justice," and much written commentary (e.g., Messmer and Otto 1992; Umbreit 1994; Wright 1991), emphasize three general bottom-line objectives of sanctioning and intervention: (1) meeting victims' needs for physical, material, and emotional reparation and healing; (2) holding offenders accountable to their victims; and (3) maximizing victim involvement in the system. A fourth goal, communicating to offenders through victims' voices the harm caused by their crimes, is also assigned a great deal of importance in most statements of restorative justice, but appears to have been getting less emphasis in recent years.[9]

Second, each model is concerned with sending offenders a personalized and emphatic message of disapproval about the impact of crime. Each is, therefore, consistent with a newer theme in restorative justice based on an emerging theory of crime and social control known as reintegrative shaming (Braithwaite 1989; Moore and O'Connell 1994; Makkai and Braithwaite 1994). Reintegrative shaming challenges any process that does not maximize the role of community members— especially those closest to the crime and those most intimate with the offender, such as family and extended family and the victim—in expressing disapproval of the offense and in imposing consequences. It would be equally critical of "stigmatizing shaming" (Moore and O'Connell 1994) that did not provide for reacceptance of and support for the offender following the shaming ceremony. Reintegrative shaming is also broadly concerned with the larger sociological issue of the absence of a sense of common purpose and of mutual relationships between citizens necessary to set tolerance limits in "high-crime" societies or communities (Braithwaite 1989). The bottom-line objective of the sanctioning process, however, is to make the offender experience feelings of nonstigmatizing, "discretion shame," which will make it easier for the offender to be accepted back into the community (Moore and O'Connell 1994).[10]

Third, each approach challenges the traditional boundaries of the criminal justice process. Drawing upon a worldview common among indigenous peoples, the new models share a more holistic understanding of the justice process that blurs Western distinctions between community development, quality-of-life, spirituality, social justice, and criminal justice issues (Griffiths and Hamilton 1996; Melton 1995; Yazzie 1993). This understanding moves beyond changing the offender to focusing on interventions and outcome standards for the justice process that give equal emphasis to community change; this focus implies a vision of justice as "transformative," as well as ameliorative or restorative (Belgrave 1995; Morris 1994). What will be referred to here as community healing (Griffiths and Belleau 1993; Griffiths and Hamilton 1996) focuses its critique on weaknesses in the breadth and depth of community participation in most formal, as well as many alternative, decision-making processes. The bottom line in the community-healing perspective is, therefore, an insistence on meaningful community participation not only in the "justice" process but also in solving problems, resolving conflicts, and building or rebuilding damaged relationships. Breakdowns in these community relationships are argued to be the primary source of crime. Constructive citizen participation in maintaining and repairing these relationships and in resolving conflicts is viewed as key to strengthening the capacity of communities to control crime (Morris 1994; Stuart 1995a).

Mediating, Conferencing, Hearings, and Circle Sentencing: Three Questions for Community Justice Decision Making

While idiosyncrasies of historical coincidence, local community dynamics, cultural preferences, leadership, and bureaucratic and political constraints have no doubt played major roles in shaping the new decision-making models, the three theoretical themes in restorative justice continue to influence the evolution of these models in important ways. Specifically, despite the common influence of the restorative, reintegrative shaming, and community-healing themes, each model has been influenced differently by each perspective. Most important, although the precise nature and scope of this influence is not entirely clear at this time, the focal concerns of each perspective appear to have significant implications for how advocates of each model envision the community's role. In an important sense, the four models also provide an important context for closer examination of how each of these themes is put into operation.

Several important questions about community justice decision making provide useful points of comparison between each model (see Table 2). First, how is the "community" defined in each intervention (Rottman 1996): how many and which citizens and professionals participate in the process, and what is the nature of their involvement? Second, what is the role of the victim relative to the offender and community in the process? Third, what is the mandate of the decision-making process, and how does it relate to the formal system? These questions should raise issues for research aimed at achieving a more thorough understanding of both the implementation and effect of neighborhood decision making on the justice process.

In making these comparisons, my sources of data are primarily secondary—based on program descriptions and literature review. This information was supplemented by limited telephone interviews with program directors and staff and brief observations of three of the four models (RBs were the exception). Finally, it is important to note that my use of certain somewhat "loaded" terms, such as empower, participation, or even neighborhood, is not necessarily a reflection of empirical reality as much as an indication of the intent and beliefs of advocates of the various models. Notably, these terms also reflect the ideological concerns of one or more of the three sensitizing themes.

Table 2
Community Decision-Making Models: Community Role and Involvement

	Circle Sentencing	Family Group Conferencing	Reparative Probation	Victim/Offender Mediation
Who Participates? ("The Community")	Judges, prosecutor, defense counsel participate in serious cases; victim(s), offender(s), service providers, support group present; open to entire community; justice committee ensures participation of key residents	Coordinator identifies key people; close kin of victim and offender targeted, as well as police, social services	Reparative coordinator (probation employee); community reparative board	Mediator, victim, offender are standard participants; family and others allowed on occasion
Victim Role	Participates in circle and decision making; gives input into eligibility of offender; chooses support group	Victim expresses feelings about crime; gives input into reparative plan	Input into plan sought by some boards; inclusion of victims currently rare but being encouraged and considered	Major role in decision about offender obligation and content of reparative plan; express feelings regarding crime and impact

Table 2 (Continued)

	Circle Sentencing	Family Group Conferencing	Reparative Probation	Victim/Offender Mediation
Gatekeepers	Community justice committee	New Zealand—court and criminal justice coordinator; Australia and United States—law enforcement and school officials	Judge	Victim has ultimate right of refusal; consent is essential
Role and Relationship to System	Judge, prosecution, court officials share power with community (i.e., selection, sanctioning, follow-up); currently minimal impact on court caseloads	New Zealand—primary process for juvenile cases, required ceding of disposition power, major impact on court caseloads; Australia— police driven; variable impact on caseloads; concern regarding netwidening	One of several probation options for eligible low-risk offenders with minimal services needs; plans to expand; some impact on caseloads anticipated	Varies on continuum from core process in diversion and disposition to marginal programs with minimal impact on court caseloads
Preparation	Extensive work with offender and victim before circle; explain process and rules of circle	Phone contact with all parties to encourage participation and explain process; New Zealand model requires offender and family have face-to-face visits	Preservice training provided by boards; no advance preparation for individual hearings	Typically face-to-face with victim and offender to explain process; some programs use phone contact

Table 2 (Continued)

	Circle Sentencing	Family Group Conferencing	Reparative Probation	Victim/Offender Mediation
Enforcement and Monitoring	Community justice committee; judge may hold jail sentence as incentive for offender to comply with plan	Unclear; police in Australian Wagga-Wagga model; coordinator in New Zealand model	Condition of probation; coordinator monitors and brings petition of revocation to board, if necessary	Varies; mediator may follow-up; probation and or other program staff may be responsible
Primary Outcome Sought	Increase community strength and capacity to resolve disputes and prevent crime; develop reparative and rehabilitative plan; address victim(s) concerns and public safety issues; assign victim and offender support group responsibilities and identify resources	Clarify facts of case; shame/denounce crime while affirming and supporting offender; restore victim loss; encourage offender reintegration; focus on "deed not need"	Engage and involve citizens in decision-making process; decide appropriate reparative plan for offender; require victim awareness education and other activities, which address ways to avoid re-offending	Victim—relay impact of crime to offender; express feelings and needs (victim satisfied with process); offender—increase awareness of harm; gain empathy; agree on reparative plan

What Is the "Community" in Community Decision Making?

> Offender-based control strategies are incomplete, since they take a closed
> system view of correctional interventions: change the offender and not the
> community.
> —James Byrne

Community is an amorphous concept that is unfortunately often used
to obfuscate, rather than clarify, issues of citizen involvement in government-sponsored processes. Criminal justice discussions of community
are certainly a case in point. Although I will not attempt to impose a
definition here, it is possible, as Gardner (1990) points out, to be more
specific in breaking down "the community" into component parts for
discussion of citizen involvement and participation in civic life. Community may be defined, for example, as a neighborhood, church, school,
labor union, civic or fraternal organization, extended family, aboriginal
band or tribe, support group, or other entity.

How community is defined in justice decision making affects the
nature and extent of citizen involvement and ownership (see Table 2).
While each model claims to increase the level of this involvement and
ownership, practical agendas for doing so vary because conceptualiza-
tions of the "community" differ. As has been true of corrections, and
most recently community policing (Byrne 1989; Clear 1996; Mastrosfski
and Ritti 1995), the community and restorative justice movement has
achieved little consensus on this issue. There is a tendency to talk about
community in the macro or societal sense for some purposes, while
defining community as those who "show up" at a community sanctioning
process for others.

In victim-offender mediation (VOM), the "community" is limited to
the essential parties in the offense: victim, offender, and a neutral mediator. This focus—at least in the vast majority of cases (Umbreit
1994)—on the victim-offender dyad is understandable based on the
restorative directive to give victims a primary role in the justice process
and, above all else, to do no further harm to them (e.g., Bazemore 1994;
Umbreit 1994). Theoretically, the advantages in allowing only victim,
offender, and mediator to participate are that more time is allowed for
victim input and that victims who might feel intimidated in a larger
group may feel empowered to speak (Umbreit and Stacy 1996). Advocates of VOM have argued that family participation, for example, may
confuse the issue of offender accountability for the crime, that interpersonal dynamics between young offenders and their parents may cause the
offender to be less honest and forthcoming, and that the presence of other
parties diminishes the impact of the victim's statement. Moreover, the
bottom-line objectives of involving the victim, gaining reparation, and

holding the offender accountable for his or her crime do not necessarily require the larger community. Though it is at times argued that citizens who volunteer as mediators represent the larger community (e.g., Galaway 1989; Umbreit 1994), such participation assigns a decidedly restricted role to citizens and, as Harris (1989, p. 35) has observed: "[L]aying out ways to operationalize the admirable notion of eliciting more active community involvement in the reconciliation process remains an elusive task."

Family group conferencing (FGC), which is informed most explicitly by the reintegrative shaming perspective (e.g., Braithwaite and Mugford 1994), attempts to maximize participation of those citizens most intimate with the offender and victim in the sanctioning process (Moore and O'Connell 1994). In contrast to VOM, involvement of the offender's family and this broader community of intimates is viewed as essential in achieving the objective of shaming the offender. The coordinator is charged with ensuring the participation of the offender and his or her family or kin, the victim, intimate acquaintances (e.g., a teacher or coach), and other community residents directly affected by the crime. These participants are viewed as the essential "personal community" most likely to induce shame in offenders (Braithwaite and Mugford 1994), but conferences are open to any citizens who may wish to participate.

Increasing community involvement in the decision-making process was a major motivation behind the Vermont reparative community boards, or RBs (Dooley 1995). Statewide surveys indicated that a majority of the public would be interested in such involvement in criminal justice decision making; therefore, policy directives for the reparative probation program required nomination and designation of a five-member standing board chosen from a pool of volunteers to ensure citizen participation in RBs. Administrators appear to have been influenced by a communitarian concern to maximize citizen involvement at the neighborhood level. However, by emphasizing the restorative theme and focusing primarily on achieving reparation for the victim and offender accountability, administrators showed less concern, at least initially, with victim involvement (Dooley 1996b). Because shaming is not at issue in RBs, intimacy with the offender is also not a concern in identifying participants for the hearings; hence, the board members conducting the hearings and the offender constitute "the community."

As in FGCs, the number of participants in circle sentencing is apparently limited only by the size of the facility available (and to those citizens who do not present a disruptive influence by drinking or drug use). Circle sentencing is most directly influenced by the community-healing theme, and maximum citizen participation is essential to resolving conflict and improving broader social conditions. Hence, circles both encourage and demand extensive community participation, and proponents of circle sentencing articulate what is perhaps the broadest conceptualization of "the community." Intimates and supporters of the victim and offender are at the core of this definition, but a range of responsibilities (e.g., interviewing and screening offenders, requesting a hearing from the circle, assigning support groups for victims and offenders) demands participation from a broader segment of citizens as well as government officials. In the Canadian Northwest, Royal Canadian Mounted Police (RCMP) also function as part of the community, participating in some circles as interested citizens as well as law enforcement officers.

Despite these differences in the concept of community, there are signs of growing consensus between advocates of each model that the central component of the community for purposes of neighborhood sanctioning must include the victim, offender, and those supportive of each. Differences in practice remain regarding the importance attached to victim participation relative to that of other citizens—and to a lesser extent the appropriateness of participation by community members beyond these core actors (see Table 2).

The definition of community is also, in part, a function of the respective roles assumed by court and criminal justice professionals. While these roles vary somewhat across the four models, these professionals are generally regarded as facilitators of citizen participation rather than direct service providers or primary decision makers (e.g., Dooley 1995; Pranis 1996b; Stuart 1995b). Specifically, paid staff help to organize, coor-dinate, and support citizens in the sanctioning process by assuming more or less responsibility (depending on the model) for such tasks as preparation of participants before each session and sanction enforcement (see Table 2). The staff role in each model (with the possible exception of VOM) should be viewed as emerging, however, and there remains a great deal of ambivalence about how much responsibility professionals should (or must) assume. Although the mandate assumed by the community in each model defines a clear role for court decision makers and law enforcement, some advocates initially argued that the involvement of any paid support staff in the process itself (including preparation and enforcement) would exert a corrupting influence (Stuart 1995b).

The Participants: What Is the Role of the Victim in Relation to Offender and Community in the Process?

> Victims frequently want longer time for offenders because we haven't given them anything else. Or because we don't ask, we don't know what they

want. So [the system] gives them Doors Number One, Two or Three, when what they really want is behind Door Number 4.
—Mary Achilles, Crime Victims' Advocate.

In the formal justice system, the bulk of attention is directed toward the offender, first with regard to guilt or innocence, and second with regard to appropriate punishment, treatment, or monitoring. The community and the victim have been, at best, distant concerns (e.g., Barajas 1995; Clear 1996; Zehr 1990). Hence, perhaps the most important rationale, and also one of the most critical standards for gauging success, in any community justice initiative is the extent to which the process identifies and meets the needs of citizens and crime victims as primary "clients" (Bazemore and Schiff 1996). Because victims have been so neglected as clients of both formal and community justice approaches, each of the four models has attempted to focus attention on their needs for reparation and involvement. Each model differs, however, in the priority given to these objectives and in the importance given to the role of the victim vis-à-vis the role of community and offender (see Table 2).

VOM gives first priority to meeting the needs of crime victims (Umbreit 1994). Specifically, victims are given maximum input into the sanction; referred for needed help and assistance; allowed to tell the offender how the crime has affected them and to request information about the crime; and, to the greatest extent possible, repaid for their losses. To ensure that the victim feels empowered, or at a minimum is not more abused or overwhelmed by the process, victims often speak first in mediation sessions (see Table 1). While both victim and offender needs receive priority over the needs of other potential players (parents, relatives, other citizens), the victim is the primary client. The victim must, after all, consent to the process, while the offender is often a less-than-willing participant (Belgrave 1995). Hence, in contrast to other models, victim satisfaction with VOM has been uniformly high (e.g., Belgrave 1995; Umbreit and Coates 1993).

Like VOM, proponents of the circle sentencing (CS) process are concerned with protecting the victim, providing support, and hearing the victim's story. In the circle, victims or their advocates generally speak first to avoid an "imbalanced focus on the offender's issues," which may cause the victim to withdraw or challenge the offender (Stuart 1995b, p.7). The telling of the victim's story is important, not only for the victim, the offender, and their supporters, but also for the community as a whole, and CS facilitators emphasize the value of residents hearing the victim's story firsthand whenever possible (Stuart 1995b). Because the process is so open and community driven, however, the importance given to the victim's needs and point of view in circle sentencing may vary widely. The seriousness of offender needs may slant the focus of the group to execution of the rehabilitative and offender service/support plan rather than toward meeting the reparative and other needs of the victim, which also occurs sometimes in FGCs (Maxwell and Morris 1993; Umbreit and Stacy 1996). In addition, the effort required on the part of the offender before the event itself may result in circles stacked with offender supporters who have little relationship to victims. Achieving appropriate balance is a task left to the community justice committee, which relies heavily on an innovation not apparent in any of the other processes, a victim support group (Stuart 1995a). This group is formed by the community justice committee, generally at the time the offender petitions for admission to the circle, but may develop or be enhanced at any time, including during the circle ceremony itself.

The complexity of the challenge of victim protection and empowerment when one moves beyond the small group to the larger community is even more apparent in FGCs. FGCs are perhaps the strongest of all the models in their potential for educating offenders about the harm their behavior causes to victims. From a restorative perspective, however, the concern is that the priority given to offender education through the reintegrative shaming process will—as appears to be the case when conferences are held with little or no victim involvement (Alder and Wundersitz 1994; Maxwell and Morris 1993)—overshadow or trivialize the concern with meeting the victim's needs (Belgrave 1995; Umbreit and Zehr 1996). In direct contrast to both VOM and CS, FGCs require that offenders speak first. This is believed to increase the chance that young offenders will speak at all in the presence of family and other adults. In addition, speaking first is said by FGC supporters to help offenders "own" their behavior early in the session, to let their support group know what happened, to give the victim a different perspective on the crime and on the offender, and to put the victim at ease (McDonald et al. 1995).[11]

The central concern in FGCs with shaming and reintegrating offenders, however, may lead to some interesting twists in how positive victim outcomes are achieved. As one recent Australian attempt to evaluate victim outcomes illustrates, even objective observers may become vulnerable to giving primary focus to offender outcomes:

> Conferencing engenders in the offenders and their supporters a sense of shame, through providing the victims with a forum to explain directly to all experienced in the process. [Such an explanation] is sufficient for the expression of a sincere apology for the harm flowing from the offence. In a successful conference, the shame [experienced by] offenders—in turn, gives rise to the expression of forgiveness by victims, while the outcome can provide for material restitution. (Strang 1995, p. 3; emphasis mine)

As suggested in this explanation, the essential business of the conference appears to be getting offenders to experience shame (Alder and Wunderstiz 1994). The "benefit" to the victim is an apology and perhaps material restitution. While either may meet the primary needs of many victims, other concerns may be neglected or not even considered. Moreover, if the ultimate motive is forgiveness for the offender, the process may be slanted in the direction of eliciting an apology from the offender, and victims may feel pressured to forgive the offender, or become so resentful at the implication that they should, that they refuse to participate (Umbreit and Stacy 1996). Others have questions about FGCs and their apparent lack of concern with victim empowerment and protection against abuse or retaliation, as well as their use of victims as "props" to meet offender needs (Umbreit and Zehr 1996).

While victim participation and victim satisfaction has been an ongoing problem in FGCs (Maxwell and Morris 1993), it is unfair to conclude that most FGC advocates are not concerned with victims' needs (see Braithwaite and Mugford 1994; Moore and O'Connell 1994). Moreover, like all such criticisms of alternative community models, the critique of FGC from the victim's perspective should be made first with reference to the extent of reparation, empowerment, and support available within the current formal system (Stuart 1995a). However, as FGC models evolve, it will be important to examine the extent to which concern with offender shaming and reintegration may diminish the capacity of FGCs to attend to the needs of crime victims.[12]

In the early months of operation, victim involvement in most Vermont RBs has been difficult (Dooley 1996b). While victim participation has recently been strongly encouraged by state officials who developed and now monitor the programs, and referral to victim-offender mediation is an option for some boards, it remains to be seen whether citizen board members will want to take on the at-times demanding task of engaging crime victims in the justice process. Although program administrators have strongly embraced the restorative theme, the commitment to local control has made them reluctant to push local boards in this direction (Dooley 1995, 1996b). However, the strong commitment on the part of some local boards to seeing that offenders repay victims may ultimately provide greater motivation for increasing victims' involvement, especially if the positive effect of VOM on restitution completion rates becomes more clear (Umbreit and Coates 1993; see also note 5). Boards have also been encouraged by administrators to refer offenders to victim-offender mediation, and some have done so in communities where mediation programs are available.

What Is the Mandate Assigned and What Is the Relationship of the Model to the Formal Justice System?

> When community people have input into who is accepted into a community sentencing process, they don't just pick the "cream puffs" . . . they pick the guys who have been wreaking the most havoc on them for years.
> —Barry Stuart

Does collaboration with formal justice agencies inevitably lead to cooptation of community justice models? Does independence from the formal system, on the other hand, equate to irrelevance? Is the court the "enemy" of communities and community justice processes, or a vital participant in those processes? Such questions are not easily answered and are part of an ongoing debate that certainly precedes the rise in popularity of the four models discussed here (e.g., Harrington and Merry 1988).

This section directly addresses one of the most practical concerns in community decision making: how the mandate and responsibility assigned to the community in each decision-making model may influence the nature and extent of citizen participation.

The amount of discretion granted to local residents by the formal system can hinder or facilitate the community's involvement and may indicate the extent to which a government is either sharing power with neighborhoods or simply allowing the community to supplement and extend government power in response to crime (Griffiths and Hamilton 1996). For example, while each model seems capable of claiming some discretion for the community in the sanctioning decision (see Table 1), offender eligibility varies widely from relatively minor offenders to those convicted of very serious crimes. Citizens may have little or no voice in admission decision making, or may claim significant input into decisions about offender eligibility or the selection process itself (see Table 2).

Most victim-offender mediation programs depend on the formal system for referrals. Hence, their primary restorative mandate to respond to victims and offenders as clients often varies based on the extent to which programs operate as part of courts or probation departments or as part of independent, community-based organizations (Belgrave 1995). In the former case, VOM programs are often responsible for processing cases as quickly as possible to reduce court workload, minimize costs, or increase diversion. In the latter case, programs may survive almost completely outside the system based on referrals from community groups or victim requests (Belgrave 1995). Such programs may be more responsive to genuine client needs and better able to maintain their integrity as alternative processes truly serving victims and offenders (Van Ness 1993). However, their potential for sharing power or changing the nature of the court process is minimal.

Based in part on this structural variation, eligibility for and admission to VOM programs may differ significantly between jurisdictions, ranging from those in which courts or intake departments refer only first offenders to those programs in which crime victims themselves make a direct request for mediation to program staff. On the one hand, the victim as primary gatekeeper can always limit offender eligibility and use of mediation by refusing to participate. On the other hand, it is also possible for victims to alter the admission process and broaden the scope of cases traditionally heard in community justice settings by requesting mediation in violent and even homicide cases (Umbreit 1994). While the victim's ultimate right of refusal is a primary restriction on the number of cases eligible for VOM, recent research indicating high rates of victim involvement and willingness to participate in well-managed programs suggests that limits on eligibility are at least equally a function of policy, statute, or customs, which, for example, may exclude all but nonviolent felonies and misdemeanors referred by courts or through a diversion process (Belgrave 1995; Umbreit and Coates 1993).

From a community justice perspective, the biggest challenge to RBs may be that they have been implemented in the system itself. As one of several options for nonviolent offenders in Vermont who represent a "relatively lower risk to re-offend" (Dooley 1995, p. 185), RBs are perhaps the most closely linked to the formal system of the four alternative models. Hence, although RBs encourage citizen participation, the community is actually assigned a relatively narrow decision-making mandate: to choose reparative activities from four program goal areas, including restitution or other action to "restore and make whole the victims of crime"; making amends to the community through community work service; learning about the impact of crime through victim awareness or empathy panels; and "learning ways to avoid the offense" through educational programs (Dooley 1995, p. 187). Although the scope of the community role is clearly greater than in VOM, the court and probation administrators exert control as primary gatekeepers, and judicial discretion and probation policy guidelines are the primary factors in decisions about offender eligibility.

On the one hand, as a creation of the corrections bureaucracy, RBs may be at the center on an ongoing struggle between efforts to give greater power and autonomy to citizens and the needs of the system to maintain control or ensure system accountability. Ultimately, board members may also be challenged to decide the extent to which their primary client is the community or the probation and court system. On the other hand, RBs may exert the greatest influence on the response of the formal system to nonviolent crimes. Moreover, the commitment of administrators to local control may also result in the community assuming and demanding a broader mandate. For example, although the number of cases referred to RBs in Vermont has been relatively small, the strong policy commitment to the RBs seems to open the doors to wider community demands for deeper and more meaningful involvement and for judges to refer more cases. In fact, in recent months, some boards have elected to hear a few violent offense cases (the statute defines the target group as nonviolent offenders but does not specifically forbid boards from hearing personal offense cases).

The mandate of FGCs is to confront the offender with the consequences of the crime, develop a reparative plan, and, in more serious cases (in the New Zealand model), determine the need for more restrictive supervision, custody, or both. While the community mandate is somewhat broader than that of VOM or RBs, advocates of FGCs appear reluctant to extend the reach of the reintegrative shaming focus of conferences beyond the response to the offense as a discrete event (see Braithwaite and Mugford 1994). This restriction thus discourages conference participants from addressing underlying offender socialization and service needs, on the one hand, or community issues and community building, on the other. In fact, a focus on what some FGC advocates call the "deed not the need" (Hakiaha 1995) both circumscribes the agenda of conferences and limits the responsibility of the community to addressing the harm caused by the offense at hand.[13]

With the exception of New Zealand—which by statute requires conferencing for all youths who are found delinquent or admit guilt for all offenses, excluding homicide, rape, and aggravated assault—FGCs restrict offender eligibility by policy limits on offender and offense seriousness or by police discretion. In the Wagga-Wagga model, practiced most frequently in Australia and the United States, police officers generally serve as primary gatekeepers (McDonald et al. 1995; Umbreit and Stacy 1996).[14] Hence, any decision about whether to expand or minimize community vs. system power is limited to the front-end of the system. As some critics of the Wagga-Wagga model point out, this limitation would seem to make the process more vulnerable to net-widening by bringing more youth under the jurisdiction of social control authorities (Polk 1994). In New Zealand, however, FGCs appear to have taken over, rather than extended, the dispositional function of the juvenile court. While they have clearly met a system need to reduce court workload, they have also apparently limited the role of government in juvenile justice by replacing a formal decision-making process with an informal one (Belgrave 1995; Maxwell and Morris 1993; McElrae 1993). But while the community plays a major role in the sanctioning decision and reintegrative process, citizens have little if any control over the admission decision.

Viewed through the lens of the community-healing perspective, and the worldview of many participants involved in CS, the only limit on the citizens' mandate to shape and reshape the justice process should be the needs of the community. Moreover, the effort to blur the distinction between crime and more general problems in social relationships, social justice, and spirituality provides a philosophical justification for this openness to citizen participation (Griffiths and Hamilton 1996; Melton 1995). As a leading advocate of circles suggests, the ideology underlying the circle is that representatives of the legal system clearly lack the knowledge of communities needed to make appropriate decisions in the response to crime:

> Crime should never be the sole, or even primary business of the state if real *differences* are sought in the well-being of individuals, families and communities. The structure, procedures, and evidentiary rules of the formal criminal justice process coupled with most justice officials' lack of knowledge and connection to (the parties) affected by crime, preclude the state from acting alone to achieve transformative changes. (Stuart 1995a, p. 8; emphasis in original)

Only by listening to and supporting the involvement of the community can the legal system play a meaningful role in the response to crime. From a community-healing perspective, the government (justice system) is responsible for preserving *order*, but the community is responsible for establishing *peace* (Van Ness et al. 1989). Since the root of crime is community conflict and disharmony, "justice" cannot be achieved by a government "war on crime." Rather, justice is best achieved by *peacemaking, dispute-resolution,* and *rebuilding right relationships.*

Of the four models, circle sentencing provides the most complete example of neighborhood residents as gatekeepers (see Table 2). Acting through the community justice committee, the community is clearly the "driver" in determining which offenders will be admitted to the circle. Eligibility in circles is apparently limited only by the ability of the offender to demonstrate to the community justice committee his or her sincerity and willingness to change. Surprisingly, the lesson of circle sentencing has been that when given decision-making power, neighborhood residents often choose to include the most, rather than the least, serious offenders in community justice processes (Griffiths and Hamilton 1996; Stuart 1995a). As a result, courts and other agencies in Canadian communities experimenting with circle sentencing have experienced ongoing tension over the extent to which power sharing with the community should be limited and whether statutes are being violated.

Where, then, does this leave the formal justice system? Circle sentencing also provides an interesting case example of the principle that it is not necessary, or desirable, to eliminate the involvement of court officials and system professionals in community justice decision making. While legal representatives of the formal system are often invisible in traditional court diversion and other alternative decision-making processes, this is primarily because participants have little control or authority over cases or input into any decisions viewed as important by system decision makers. Hence, the extent to which a community decision-making process changes the nature of the involvement of judges, prosecutors, and defense attorneys, rather than limiting their participation by limiting the seriousness of the cases being heard, may be a primary indicator of the significance of the citizens' role in the justice decision-making process.

Sentencing circles considering disposition of indictable cases include prosecutors, defense counsel, police officers, and judges. However, even in the most serious cases, the bulk of discussion and primary decision-making responsibility remains in the hands of the citizen participants in the circle. While prosecutors read the charges and make recommendations to the court, and judges are asked for legal input on what is required by statute, criminal justice officials for the most part play the role of members of the circle, expressing their personal views of the offense, offender, and victim when it is their turn to speak. Most important, they listen to the ideas of citizens participating in the circles, make suggestions to ensure that legal criteria are met, and assist circle participants in forming and carrying out their sanctioning plan. Frequently, this professional assistance takes a form consistent with one of the primary modalities of the circle process, "problem-solving." In a recent session in the Yukon attended by this writer, for example, the local RCMP officer, after explaining the circumstances in a stolen vehicle and drunken driving offense that caused extensive damage and investment of police time, volunteered to act as a mentor for the young offender involved in this incident. In another session, an officer (supported by the crown prosecutor and defense attorney) asked the presiding judge to allow another offender to meet with him regularly for counseling and community service at the local RCMP outpost in lieu of statutorily mandated jail time. Judges may also facilitate citizen involvement in problem-solving by assigning a participant to serve as a support or as a mentor for an offender, to assist a victim, or to provide a job or service opportunity for the offender.

Another important mandate that may be assigned to or assumed by neighborhood residents in each community decision-making model is the responsibility for up-front case preparation and for postsession monitoring, enforcement, and follow-up (see Table 2). While contrasting the models on this mandate is beyond the scope of this chapter, the ability of community members to carry out these preparation and enforcement responsibilities may be critical for the survival of these informal processes. The fact that both enforcement/monitoring and preparatory tasks demand collaboration with other parts of the system—e.g., corrections and law enforcement—may, for example, protect programs that follow through on these responsibilities from becoming isolated and irrelevant. Similarly, the preparation stage of the community decision-making process provides perhaps the greatest opportunity to ensure meaningful citizen participation (Stuart 1995a; Umbreit 1994). Given the importance of these issues to the credibility and viability of the models, it is somewhat surprising that proponents have not specifically addressed these concerns. Monitoring and enforcement appear to range from highly informal to relatively formal, and preparation from extensive to none at all. Allocation of responsibilities for these tasks varies widely and appears to be ambiguous in some models (see Table 2).

Discussion

> So we make mistakes—can you say—you (the current system) don't make mistakes. . . . If you don't think you do, walk through our community, every family will have something to teach you. . . . By getting involved, by all of us taking responsibility, it is not that we won't make mistakes. . . . But we would be doing it together, as a community instead of having it done to us. We need to find peace within our lives . . . in our communities. We need to make real differences in the way people act and the way we treat others. . . . Only if we empower them and support them can they break out of this trap.
> —Rose Couch, Community Justice Coordinator, Kwalin Dun First Nations, Yukon, Canada (as quoted in Stuart 1995b)

This chapter has described four alternative justice community decision-making models and contrasted the way each defines the roles of citizens and community groups in the sanctioning process. The four models have been informed by three increasingly influential perspectives in restorative and community justice: reintegrative shaming, community healing, and the restorative theme.

It is, of course, possible to raise a variety of criticisms and questions about the extent to which each model truly meets the objective of meaningful citizen involvement and empowerment in the decision-making process. I have suggested, however, that these efforts have more potential for doing so than many of the other programs and components that make up a new community justice or community restorative justice movement in North America (e.g., National Institute of Justice 1996a; Young 1995). This movement is uniting a growing number of justice professionals and community leaders around what appears to be an emerging consensus that neither punitive nor rehabilitation-focused models of sanctioning and intervention have met the needs of communities, victims, and offenders (e.g., Barajas 1995; Bazemore and Schiff 1996). As some justice systems and agencies begin to "reinvent" themselves to better serve the needs of these new clients, the implementation struggles of what may appear to be rather marginal initiatives to devolve decision making and "ownership" of justice processes should, therefore, assume greater significance and relevance to criminal justice decision makers.

There are several policy and practice issues associated with expanded use and effective implementation of community justice decision-making models. In addition, a number of theoretical and research issues need to be addressed if there is to be fair and meaningful evaluation of the implementation and effectiveness of these models.

Theory and Research Issues

Research and theory in community justice decision making is in its infancy. Despite a few recent and ongoing studies of family group conferencing (see Hudson et al. 1996) and a number of studies of victim-offender mediation (e.g., Umbreit 1994), empirical findings concerning the role of citizens in decision making are in short supply. There is not only a scarcity of data, but also a shortage of concepts and benchmark criteria that can be used to form testable propositions.

Initially, basic implementation concerns suggest essential empirical questions. For example, a fundamental question, which requires baseline data before court and other system decision makers decide to support community justice decision making, is whether citizens really want these alternatives and are willing to be involved in neighborhood sanctioning processes. Alternatively, citizens may simply want more accessible, or "user-friendly," courts.[15] A similar question comes from detractors of community justice options, who often ask about both the practical difficulty of operationalizing and implementing these approaches and the specific challenges associated with mobilizing what are often viewed as apathetic and overextended community groups and residents. The surprisingly high level of citizen participation in some models, especially FGCs and RBs, provides some evidence that residents are willing to participate in justice decision making, especially when they have a personal stake in a particular case (Braithwaite and Mugford 1994).

Theory and concepts are badly needed, however, to account for differential participation and variation in the success of justice decision making in different communities. Why, for example, have some Aboriginal communities—devastated by violence, alcoholism, and crime—apparently been able to "heal" themselves while others seem incapable of implementing dispute-resolution processes, such as circle sentencing, and others use the processes to extend patterns of oppression and abuse of power (Griffiths and Hamilton 1996)? Similarly, what might account for the success of processes such as mediation or family group conferencing in some crime-ridden urban areas and their failure in others?

As one anonymous reviewer of this chapter proposed, theorists and researchers attempting to understand the dynamics of community decision making might do well to turn to the literature concerning the social ecology of crime and community (e.g., Reiss and Tonry 1986). Other criminological theories may also provide useful concepts that can be creatively adapted to develop propositions about community decision making and its impact that flow from assumptions of the three theoretical themes described in this chapter. The community-healing perspective, for example, in suggesting that crime is a result of weak or "broken" community relationships and an absence of community capacity to resolve disputes peacefully (e.g., Stuart 1995a; Van Ness et al. 1989) is consistent with assumptions of social control theory (e.g., Hirshi 1969) about the centrality of the "bond" to community groups and conventional adults in preventing crime. Community healing is also consistent with learning theories because it implies that the capacity to settle disputes peacefully can be learned in the same way that violent behavior is learned.

Notably, the reintegrative shaming, community-healing, and restorative perspectives also have their own theoretical logic that can be used to develop propositions about the effect of community decision-making processes on offenders, victims, and communities. Thus far, each perspective has exerted a more dominant influence on some models than others, influencing the way in which the community is defined, the role assigned to the victim vis-à-vis the offender and other citizens in the process, and the unique mandate assumed by or granted to the community for such tasks as gatekeeping. It was suggested that the strong influence of the restorative theme in victim-offender mediation, for example, gave highest priority to victim needs and empowerment, while the influence of the community-healing perspective on circle sentencing was in part responsible for its more fully developed focus on active roles for citizens in a more holistic healing process. Each perspective is associated with a different hierarchy of possible community justice objectives (see Table 3).

Hence, even as proponents of each model continue to adapt and borrow insights from practitioners of other approaches, the contrasting priorities of each approach suggest that some general empirical propositions are inherent in each perspective. The influence of these priorities on each decision-making model and on its relative capacity to achieve victim satisfaction, community involvement, offender sanctioning and reintegration, and other community justice objectives is thus an important topic for future empirical research.

However, the scarcity of prior research and the limitations of the descriptive data presented here greatly limit our ability to generalize about these models. Initially, exploratory research will need to examine the extent to which the three perspectives continue to accentuate practical differences or blur distinctions between the models as practitioners borrow insights from each perspective. Such initial investigation can also explore the extent to which the assumptions of reintegrative shaming, restoration, and healing are compatible. Then, as one anonymous reviewer of this chapter suggests, researchers can address what may soon become the most salient question of many policymakers and administrators: whether the most effective community decision-making approach might in fact integrate aspects of all three models as part of a comprehensive restorative justice approach. Following this exploratory research, a second agenda could focus on the relative importance of public denunciation of the offender ("shaming"), vs. repaying the victim or meeting with the victim, vs. "community problem-solving" or "healing" in the community sanctioning process.

It is clear that the three perspectives and the concrete objectives of the four models will challenge the narrow parameters placed on criminal justice performance objectives (e.g., recidivism, just punishment, treatment) and promote a distinctive and broader set of standards for evaluating success. As Judge Stuart observes, justice system effectiveness must not be gauged simply in terms of standard offender-based criteria:

> Communities should not measure the success of any (community-based initiative) based upon what happens to the offenders. The impact of community based initiatives upon victims, upon the self-esteem of others working (in the community justice process) on strengthening family, building connections within the community, on enforcing community values, on mobilizing community action to reduce factors causing crime—and ultimately to make the community safer—while not readily visible, these impacts are, in the long run, significantly more important than the immediate impact on an offender's habits. (1995b, p. 6)

Table 3
Models, Theories, and Outcomes in Community Justice

(Objectives)	(Models)			
	Circle Sentencing	Family Group Conferencing	Reparative Probation	Victim Offender Mediation
Victim Restoration	I	HI-I	I	HI
Shame/Denounce Offender	NA	HI	NA-SI	NA-SI
Citizen Involvement	HI	I-HI	HI	NA-SI
Sharing Power	HI	SI-I	I	NA
Meet Victim's Needs	I-SI	SI-I	SI-I	HI
Protect Victim	I	I	NA-SI	HI
Community Empowerment	HI	NA-SI	HI	NA
Victim Involvement	SI-I	I	NA-SI	HI
(Primary Theoretical Base)	Community Healing	Reintegrative Shaming	Restorative Justice	Restorative Justice

Key:
HI = Highly Important
I = Important
SI = Somewhat Important
NA = Not Applicable

Further focus on community involvement and ownership, a unifying concern of the four decision-making models, may ultimately help in establishing common standards for evaluating community justice approaches. While most observers are reluctant to impose restrictive definitions on what is clearly an evolving movement, lack of agreement on key components and dimensions has led to indiscriminate, all-inclusive, groupings of programs and practices under the community justice umbrella. Unless there is an effort to distinguish what should and should not be included, and to further define success in these interven-

tions, theory, research, and implementation in community justice decision-making are unlikely to move forward.

Policy and Practices Issues

Among the most critical policy issues associated with community
involvement in justice decision making is the role of political power and
the question of who controls the agenda. A related concern is determining which activities to include within the community justice process vs.
the formal system and process.

Implicit in some of the rhetoric of community and restorative justice
is the notion of courts and formal criminal justice agencies as the "enemy
of communities," or as, at best, an alien force. Although there is actually
little support among proponents of the four decision-making models for
abolishing formal criminal justice agencies, each model suggests that the
role of these agencies must be reexamined. In fact, the viability of
community justice decision making depends in part on defining the
responsibilities of the government and community and ensuring that the
two justice processes work in relative harmony. If formal agencies and
paid professionals are not enemies, however, what is their role in community justice?

There are no easy answers to this critical question, and some proponents of community justice appear to be grappling with this issue. Pranis
(1996a), for example, proposed an intriguing "role reversal" in which the
community provides the primary response to crime, with the formal
justice system providing backup and support. From this perspective, the
question of the appropriate role of the formal system is in part addressed
by conceptualizing the community as the source of "moral authority"
and, hence, the "center of decision making and action." Government, on
the other hand, is viewed as the source of "legal authority" (Pranis
1996a, p. 4). In this framework, each model in theory allows citizens and
community groups to establish the terms of accountability and to exercise moral authority by participating in the sanctioning process, while the
court gives legal weight to those obligations and provides enforcement
backup.

A different policy issue related to power and ultimately to government accountability is the extent to which certain communities can
implement and practice neighborhood decision making without great risk
of allowing the triumph of the tyranny of the majority. Dramatic and
dysfunctional power differentials within communities may make true
participatory justice difficult to achieve and may produce harmful side
effects. In some Aboriginal communities in Canada, for example, elders
and kinship networks that have practiced sexual abuse and other forms of

oppression against political foes have at times gained power over justice and social services decision making (Griffiths and Hamilton 1996).

Hence, the somewhat optimistic portrayal of community justice decision making in this chapter should in no way lead readers to conclude that any of these models have resolved the difficult problem of increasing citizen participation and protecting the interests and needs of participants in the process. Generalizations should therefore be viewed as reflecting the intent and not necessarily the reality of each approach. At this stage in their development, in the absence of standards and evaluation criteria, the relative importance one assigns to community and victim involvement, offender shaming, reparation to victims, dispute-resolution, and healing will determine the value and effectiveness of each model.

At the most practical level, other issues not addressed or only touched on in this chapter may also be of critical importance. The issue of decision-making power and discretion, for example, obviously influences both implementation and effectiveness in community decision making. The inability or unwillingness of formal decision makers to share power with communities seems likely to result in netwidening, rather than in more effective alternative decision-making processes (Blomberg 1983; Polk 1994). In addition, although some degree of institutionalization is critical if these models are to avoid the marginalization experienced by previous community sanctioning approaches, institutionalization and collaborative relationships with criminal justice agencies are no guarantee of the long-term impact of community justice or on the quality of life in communities of the type envisioned in the community and restorative justice literature. Of greater concern is the prospect that such institutionalization may result in cooptation of these approaches to meet the demands of retributive/adversarial justice (Van Ness 1993).

Ultimately, it would appear that the advocates of any model of community justice decision making will need to work with sympathetic justice professionals who are committed to systemic change in what they also perceive to be intransigent, top-down, rule-driven criminal justice bureaucracies. Such change must not begin and end with new programs or staff positions, but with new values that articulate new roles for victims, offenders, and communities as both clients and participants in the justice process. Accordingly, acknowledging these key parties in the crime as clients will create and perpetuate new decision-making models, which will provide the means for their meaningful involvement. The most challenging aspect of this vision for systemic change will be the change in the role of judges, prosecutors, and other court professionals from decision maker and point of referral to community justice processes to facilitator of community involvement and resource to the community (Bazemore and Schiff 1996).

Ultimately, as advocates of restorative justice suggest, the capacity of these models to affect and even transform formal justice decision making seems to lie in their commitment to the potential power of victim, offender, and community as fully engaged partners. If citizens increase participation in community justice processes that use restoration, reintegrative shaming, or community-healing principles and that actually achieve sanctioning, rehabilitative, and public safety objectives, they may begin to demand more involvement in decision making. As they assume this authority over the terms of accountability in sanctioning, they may also challenge key premises of the retributive/adversarial model (Bazemore and Umbreit 1995; Zehr 1990). If, on the other hand, citizens and community groups do not participate as full partners in developing and implementing those decision-making models, the "community" in community justice may be lost.

Notes

This chapter originally appeared in *Justice System Journal,* Volume 19, 1997, pp. 193-228. It is reprinted here with permission.

1. Differences between approaches to family group conferencing based upon the police role, as well as the exclusion of more serious offenders, have led some to discuss the New Zealand and Australian "Wagga-Wagga" models as distinct approaches (Alder and Wundersitz 1994; Pranis 1995; Umbreit and Stacy 1996). A Pennsylvania project based primarily on the Wagga-Wagga model is now being evaluated with funding from the National Institute of Justice, U.S. Department of Justice.

2. Experiments with circle sentencing are currently being carried out in the United States in small towns and on reservations in rural Minnesota. The parallels between circle sentencing and the widely discussed Navajo peacemaker court models are also obvious (Melton 1995; Yazzie 1993). The decision to focus here on circle sentencing is its more frequent implementation, its growing popularity among indigenous and nonaboriginal peoples, and its link in Canada to the larger devolution movement (Griffiths and Hamilton 1996; Stuart 1995b).

3. The most visible impact in the United States can be seen in Vermont where reparative boards based on the restorative justice perspective are now state policy. Other states that have adopted restorative justice as the mission for their corrections departments include Minnesota and Maine. State juvenile justice systems in Pennsylvania, New Mexico, and Montana, among others, have adopted restorative justice principles in policy or statute. A series of high-level discussion work group meetings have recently been held within the Office of Justice Programs at the request of the attorney general. These have, in turn,

sparked several national and cross-national forums on community and restorative justice (NIJ 1996a; Robinson 1996).

4. For the remainder of this chapter, the generic term community justice describes this overall movement and set of philosophies. However, the terms restorative justice and restorative community justice more accurately characterize the specific theoretical and philosophical influences on the four decision-making models and are used for this more focused part of the discussion. Community justice is also frequently associated in Canada with a political transfer of justice decision-making power to local communities or indigenous groups (Depew 1994; Griffiths and Hamilton 1996). I use the term community decision-making model to refer to an approach that defines an explicit role for unpaid citizens in sanctioning and occurs outside the formal court process. The concept of "community" is discussed later, and the restorative justice perspective is described in more detail. Finally, the term adversarial refers to the formal (if often idealized) court model in which decisions about sanctions are made by judges after receiving input from representatives of the state and of the defendant, who "do battle" according to predefined rules and procedures to determine disposition.

5. There is already evidence of hybridization—for example, in efforts to incorporate mediation principles into family group conferencing and efforts to encourage Vermont community boards to increase victim involvement in hearings (Dooley 1995; Umbreit and Stacy 1996). Indeed, as one anonymous reviewer of this chapter suggested, describing each of these approaches as "models" may imply a distinction that is somewhat artificial. Victim-offender mediation programs were recently targeted for experimental and quasi-experimental evaluations, which have documented their success in achieving a variety of offender and victim outcomes (Belgrave 1995; Marshall and Merry 1990; Umbreit and Coates 1993).

6. Neighborhood dispute-resolution centers differed from the new decision-making models in that they generally dealt with a more narrow range of cases, focusing primarily on domestic and neighborhood disputes rather than crimes per se, and appear to have been motivated primarily by an attempt to relieve overcrowded court dockets (Garafalo and Connelly 1980). Regarding the currency of community sanctioning, as an anonymous reviewer pointed out, New Jersey has had a statutorily mandated system of juvenile conference committees in place since 1948.

7. The victims' movement for example, has altered thinking about the role and needs of crime victims, as has the related but somewhat distinct movement in support of victim-offender mediation (Umbreit 1994). In addition, community policing as a model for changing the role of the police and the nature of the policing may serve as an exemplar for how one component of the justice system may redefine its own role and boundaries (Travis 1996); community and problem-oriented probation seems to aspire to a similar effect (Barajas 1995). Several of the ideological influences on earlier neighborhood dispute-resolution approaches (Harrington and Merry 1988) also appear to have shaped the current

community justice movement. Other less widely acknowledged influences include the "peacemaking" focus in criminology (Pepinsky and Quinney 1991) and interest in communitarianism and its application in a justice context (Etzioni 1993; Moore and O'Connell 1994).

8. Although some of the neighborhood justice centers, such as the San Francisco community boards, appear to be an exception, there appears to have been only a minor focus on reparation and meeting victim needs in most centers (Garafalo and Connelly 1980), and there was certainly little sense of a restorative philosophy as a guiding approach in most of the original centers. "Reintegrative shaming" and holding offenders accountable to victims and the community were also not concepts that informed the process of response to crime and disputes. Despite the neighborhood focus, the earlier centers also did not appear to share the deliberate pursuit of a vision of a more holistic (and ambitious) community justice process alternative that is a central concern in the community-healing perspective (Griffiths and Hamilton 1996). Some neighborhood courts and community justice centers, such as the Midtown Manhattan Community Court and the Redhook Community Justice Center in New York City, appear to be currently adapting some elements of a restorative justice model, but they are focusing primarily on civil disputes and quality-of-life misdemeanors (Rottman 1996).

9. In response to criticism from the victims' movements that VOM itself was often much too "offender-driven" (e.g., giving priority to the need to divert offenders from incarceration), a traditional goal in mediation emphasized in the VORP programs, "reconciling" victim and offender (e.g., Messmer and Otto 1992; Umbreit 1994; Wright 1991), also appears to be getting less direct emphasis in restorative writings in recent years. Rather, a growing focus in mediation training and practice is on the victim's need to regain control, get information, and feel empowered, and on their need (and the system's need) for meaningful involvement in the justice process (e.g., Center for Restorative Justice and Mediation 1996). Additionally, a growing range of victim-focused interventions, including victim services, victim awareness education, victim panels, and victim-offender dialogue, are now included in restorative justice writings (Bazemore and Umbreit 1995; Umbreit 1994). So strong is the victim focus that restorative justice is still often equated with victim-offender mediation. This elevation of the victim's role is not, however, associated with promoting victim rights as the absence of offender rights or with seeking to help victims by hurting offenders. Rather, restorative justice seeks to bring balance to an offender-driven system in which victim needs are addressed only after the needs of judges, prosecutors, probation officers, treatment providers, and even offenders have been considered (Bazemore and Umbreit 1995). In this increasingly mainstream statement of restorative justice, the offender is viewed first and foremost as someone with an obligation to make it right with the victim and who may benefit personally by increasing his or her own awareness of and understanding of the harm his or her behavior has caused to a real person (Umbreit 1994; Wright 1991). Likewise, the community, when mentioned at all,

is viewed in much of this writing as providing either support for victims or volunteer mediators (Umbreit 1994), rather than as an entity with its own independent needs for intervention to strengthen its resources and capacity.

10. In this sense, reintegrative shaming departs both from retributive approaches, which, in condemning the act, also condemn the actor and the welfare model, which views unacceptable acts as symptoms of deeper problems that should invoke sympathy for the offender rather than condemnation. Communities should neither excuse nor condone the unacceptable act, but also should not condemn the actor (Hyndman, Moore, and Thorsborne 1994). As some have suggested, differences between reintegrative shaming and stigmatization (or disintegrative shaming) resulting in "disgrace shame" may be subtle in implementation, and even completely blurred when police officers (rather than family and intimate adults) take the primary role in the shaming ceremony (Adler and Wundersitz 1994). It is these differences that have concerned some critics of FGCs. Although in recent statements of the reintegrative shaming perspective there is much overlap with the concerns of the restorative perspective, Braithwaite's (1989) classic work *Crime, Shame, and Reintegration*, for example, actually said little about the victim and referred to reparative obligations only in passing remarks affirming the value of restitution. Overall, there has been little focus in reintegrative shaming on the nature of the sanction, and the sanctioning process apparently can (and does) sometimes take place without the victim (Belgrave 1995).

11. Critics of this approach suggest that it is symbolically important that the victim speak first, and one compromise that has been proposed gives the victim a choice of whether to precede or follow the offender (Umbreit and Stacy 1996). FGC advocates argue that the facilitator can avoid situations in which an offender speaking first might anger a victim by a less-than-repentant, or less-than-accurate, portrayal of the incident by coaching the offender and possibly challenging aspects of his or her story in advance. Facilitators are also encouraged to prepare the victim for what he or she may feel is an unfair account of the incident by the offender (McDonald, et al. 1995).

12. To the extent that getting restitution to victims or having work provided for them is an important measure of the effect on victims, FGCs have yet to prove their effectiveness. According to early evaluations, FGCs were ineffective both in initiating victim-oriented reparative agreements and in ensuring collection of restitution for victims (Maxwell and Morris 1993). In response to early evaluations in New Zealand, which found low rates of victim satisfaction and participation, several efforts were made to improve what has been viewed as the weakest link in conferencing. Recently, more conscientious and systematic personal phone calls to victims are reported to have dramatically increased participation at least in New Zealand conferences (Hakiaha 1995).

13. While lines between healing and justice functions may blur to some degree in FGCs, and advocates of reintegrative shaming hope to build community capacity to manage sanctioning efforts, a concern is to avoid an overly ambitious effort to accomplish these functions in the context of administering

community justice (Hakiaha 1995). Thus, Braithwaite's concern with excessive separation between sanctioning and reintegration notwithstanding, he also does not wish to complicate the sanctioning function with a focus on the broader needs of young offenders (Braithwaite and Mugford 1994). He also hopes to avoid the excessive reach of "reintegrative institutions": "The criminal justice system should settle for communicating disapproval and securing compensation for harm done. There is hope that this ceremony of disapproval will be enough . . . then it must be hoped that the developmental institutions will do a better job with the terrible life circumstances that this young person has been dealt" (1994, p. 210).

Finally, despite pressure from the New Zealand Maori to restore traditional conflict resolution processes (Belgrave 1995), there appears to have been little emphasis among FGC advocates on the community-healing concern with "giving justice back to communities."

14. While there is relatively little data on compliance in the Australian model, the national evaluation of FGCs in New Zealand reported rates of compliance with reparative orders (59 percent full completion; 28 percent partial completion) that would not be considered high—at least by the standards of juvenile restitution programs in the United States (Butts and Snyder 1990; Schneider 1986). It would not be low, however, by standards of restitution collection and enforcement in most criminal justice systems where responsibilities are allocated across agencies and individuals so as to diffuse accountability, and collection and enforcement of restitution is a low priority. One evaluation of VOM suggests a significant increase in the rate of successful completion of restitution for juvenile offenders randomly assigned to VOM programs (Umbreit and Coates 1993).

15. I am grateful to an anonymous reviewer for raising this essential, and generally unanswered, empirical question. The state of Vermont is an interesting case study in how system decision makers (in this case, corrections administrators) can actually survey citizens before implementing a community sanctioning process to determine if public support exists, what offenders would be deemed appropriate for these processes, and the degree of citizen willingness to participate. The Vermont findings suggest that, in that state, the question of the desire for community sanctioning and willingness to participate was answered in the affirmative (Dooley 1995).

References

Alder, C., and J. Wundersitz, eds. 1994. *Family Group Conferencing and Juvenile Justice: The Way Forward or Misplaced Optimism?* Canberra: Australian Institute of Criminology.

Barajas, E., Jr. 1995. "Moving Toward Community Justice." In *Topics in Community Corrections*, 1-7. Washington, DC: National Institute of Corrections.

Bazemore, G. 1991. "New Concepts and Alternative Practice in the Community Supervision of Juvenile Offenders: Rediscovering Work Experience and Competency Development." *Journal of Crime and Justice* 14: 27-50.

————. 1994. "Developing a Victim Orientation for Community Corrections: A Restorative Justice Paradigm and a Balanced Mission." *Perspectives* 18: 19-24.

————. 1996. "Three Paradigms for Juvenile Justice," In *Restorative Justice: International Perspectives*, edited by J. Hudson and B. Galaway, 37-68. Monsey, NY: Criminal Justice Press.

————. 1997. "What's New About the Balanced Approach?" *Juvenile and Family Court Journal* 48: 1-23.

Bazemore, G., and M. Schiff. 1996. "Community Justice/Restorative Justice: Prospects for a New Social Ecology for Community Corrections." *International Journal of Comparative and Applied Criminal Justice* 20: 311-35.

Bazemore, G., and M. Umbreit. 1995. "Rethinking the Sanctioning Function in Juvenile Court: Retributive or Restorative Responses to Youth Crime." *Crime and Delinquency* 41: 296-316.

Belgrave, J. 1995. "Restorative Justice." Discussion paper. Wellington: New Zealand Ministry of Justice.

Blomberg, T. 1983. "Diversions, Disparate Results, and Unresolved Questions: An Integrative Evaluation Perspective." *Journal of Research in Crime and Delinquency* 20: 24-38.

Bowman, C. G. 1994. "The Arrest Experiments: A Feminist Critique." In *Taking Sides: Clashing Views on Controversial Issues in Crime and Criminology*, edited by R. Monk, 186-91. Gilford, CT: Dushkin Publishing Group.

Braithwaite, J. 1989. *Crime, Shame, and Reintegration.* Cambridge: Cambridge University Press.

Braithwaite, J., and S. Mugford. 1994. "Conditions of Successful Reintegration Ceremonies." *British Journal of Criminology* 34: 139-71.

Braithwaite, J., and P. Petit. 1992. *Not Just Deserts: A Republican Theory of Criminal Justice.* Oxford: Clarendon Press.

Butts, J., and H. Snyder. 1991. *Restitution and Juvenile Recidivism.* Pittsburgh, PA: National Center for Juvenile Justice.

Byrne, J. M. 1989. "Reintegrating the Concept of Community into Community-Based Corrections." *Crime and Delinquency* 35: 471-99.

Center for Restorative Justice. 1996. *What Is Restorative Justice?* St. Paul: Center for Restorative Justice, School of Social Work, University of Minnesota.

Clear, T. R. 1996. "Toward a Corrections of 'Place': The Challenge of 'Community' in Corrections." *National Institute of Justice Journal* 231: 52-56.

Depew, R. C. 1994. *Popular Justice in Aboriginal Communities.* Ottawa: Aboriginal Justice Division, Ottawa Department of Justice.

Dooley, M. J. 1995. *Reparative Probation Program.* Vermont: Department of Corrections.

———. 1996a. "Reparative Probation Boards." In *Restoring Hope Through Community Partnerships: The Real Deal in Crime Control,* 1-12. Lexington, KY: American Probation and Parole Association.

———. 1996b. "Personal communication." March 14.

Eglash, A. 1975. "Beyond Restitution: Creative Restitution." In *Restitution in Criminal Justice,* edited by J. Hudson and B. Galaway, 91-101. Lexington, PA: Lexington Books.

Etzioni, A. 1993. *The Spirit of Community: Rights, Responsibilities and the Communitarian Agenda.* New York: Crown Publishers.

Fund for City of New York. 1996. "Red Hook Community Justice Center." Concept paper.

Galaway, B. 1989. "Informal Justice: Mediation Between Offenders and Victims." In *Crime Prevention and Intervention: Legal and Ethical Problems,* edited by P. Albrecht and O. Backes, 30-43. New York: Walter de Gruyter.

Galaway, B., and J. Hudson, eds. 1990. *Criminal Justice, Restitution, and Reconcilation.* Monsey, NY: Criminal Justice Press.

Garafalo, J., and K. J. Connelly. 1980. "Dispute-resolution Centers Part I: Major Features and Processes." *Criminal Justice Abstracts* 12: 416.

Gardner, J. W. 1990. *On Leadership.* New York: Free Press.

Goldstein, H. 1987. "Toward Community-Oriented Policing: Potential, Basic Requirements and Threshold Questions." *Crime and Delinquency* 33: 6-30.

Griffiths, C. T., and C. Belleau. 1993. "Restoration, Reconcilement and Healing— The Revitalization of Culture and Tradition in Addressing Crime and Victimization in Aboriginal Communities." Paper presented at the meeting of the eleventh International Congress on Criminology, Budapest, Hungary.

Griffiths, C. T., and R. Hamilton. 1996. "Spiritual Renewal, Community Revitalization and Healing: Experience in Traditional Aboriginal Justice in Canada." *International Journal of Comparative and Applied Criminal Justice* 20: 289-311.

Hakiaha, M. 1995. "New Zealand Youth Family Conference Coordinator." Presentation in Whitehorse, Yukon.

Harrington, C., and S. Merry. 1988. "Ideological Production: The Making of Community Mediation." *Law and Society Review* 22: 709-35.

Harris, M. K. 1989. "Alternative Visions in the Context of Contemporary Realties." In *Justice: The Restorative Vision. New Perspective on Crime and Justice,* edited by P. Arthur, 1-25. Akron, PA: Mennonite Central Committee.

———. 1991. "Moving into the New Millennium: Toward a Feminist Vision of Justice." In *Criminology as Peacemaking,* edited by H. Pepinsky and R. Quinney, 83-97. Bloomington: Indiana University Press.

Hirschi, T. 1969. *Causes of Delinquency.* Berkeley, CA: University of California Press.

Hudson, J., and B. Galaway, eds. 1996. *Restorative Justice: International Perspectives*. Monsey, NY: Criminal Justice Press.

Hudson, J., B. Galaway, A. Morris, and G. Maxwell. 1996. "Research on Family Group Conferencing in Child Welfare in New Zealand," In *Family Group Conferences: Perspectives on Policy and Practice*, edited by J. Hudson, B. Galaway, A. Morris, and G. Maxwell, 1-16. Monsey, NY: Criminal Justice Press.

Hyndman, M., D. B. Moore, and M. Thorsborne. 1994. "Family and Community Conferences in Schools." In *Preventive Criminology*, edited by R. Homel, 16-29. Brisbane, Australia: Griffith University.

Klien, A. 1995. "Community Probation: Acknowledging Probation's Multiple Clients." In *Topics in Community Corrections*, 23-29. Washington, DC: National Institute of Corrections.

Laprairie, C. 1994. "Community Justice or Just Communities? Aboriginal Communities in Search of Justice." Unpublished paper, Ottawa Department of Justice.

Makkai, T. and J. Braithwaite. 1994. "Reintegrative Shaming and Compliance with Regulatory Standards." *Criminology* 31: 361-85.

Marshall, T. and S. Merry. 1990. *Crime and Accountability*. London: Home Office.

Mastrofsky, S. and R. Ritti. 1995. "Making Sense of Community-Policing: A Theory-Based Analysis." Paper presented at the annual meeting of the American Society of Criminology, November.

Maxwell, G. and A. Morris. 1993. *Family Participation, Cultural Diversity and Victim Involvement in Youth Justice: A New Zealand Experiment*. Wellington, New Zealand: Victoria University.

McCold, P. 1996. "Restorative Justice and the Role of Community." In *Restorative Justice: International Perspectives*, edited by J. Hudson and B. Galaway, 85-102. Monsey, NY: Criminal Justice Press.

McDonald, J., M. Thorsborne, D. Moore, M. Hyndman, and T. O'Connell. 1995. *Real Justice Training Manual: Coordinating Family Group Conferences*. Pipersville, PA: Piper's Press.

McElrae, F. W. M. 1993. "A New Model of Justice." In *The Youth Court in New Zealand: A New Model of Justice*, edited by B. J. Brown, 1-15. Auckland, New Zealand: Legal Research Foundation.

McGillis, D., and J. Mullen. 1977. *Neighborhood Justice Centers: An Analysis of Potential Models*. Washington, DC: National Institute of Law Enforcement and Criminal Justice.

Melton, A. 1995. "Indigenous Justice Systems and Tribal Society." *Judicature* 70: 126-33.

Messmer, H., and H. U. Otto. 1992. "Restorative Justice: Steps on the Way Toward a Good Idea." In *Restorative Justice on Trial*, edited by H. Messmer and H. U. Otto, 28-31. Netherlands: Kluwer Academic Publishers.

Moore, D. B., and T. O'connell. 1994. "Family Conferencing in Wagga-Wagga: A Communitarian Model of Justice." In *Family Conferencing and Juvenile*

Justice: The Way Forward or Misplaced Optimism? edited by C. Adler and J. Wundersitz, 45-86. Canberra: Australian Institute of Criminology.

Moore, M., and R. Trojanowicz. 1988. "Policing and the Fear of Crime." *Perspectives on Policing.* Washington, DC: National Institute of Justice.

Morris, D. B. 1994. "Evaluating Family Group Conferences," In *National Conference on Juvenile Justice Conference Proceedings.* Canberra: Australian Institute of Criminology.

National Institute of Justice. 1996a. *National Symposium on Restorative Justice Proceedings.* Washington, DC: National Institute of Justice.

————. 1996b. *Communities: Mobilizing Against Crime: Making Partnerships Work.* Washington, DC: National Institute of Justice.

Pepinsky, H. E., and R. Quinney, eds. 1991. *Criminology as Peacemaking.* Bloomington: Indiana University Press.

Polk, K. 1994. "Family Conferencing: Theoretical and Evaluative Questions." In *Family Conferencing and Juvenile Justice: The Way Forward or Misplaced Optimism?,* edited by C. Alder and J. Wundersitz, 155-68. Canberra: Australian Institute of Criminology.

Pranis, K. 1995. "Building Community Support for Restorative Justice: Principles and Strategies." Unpublished paper, Minnesota Department of Corrections.

————. 1996a. "Communities and the Justice System—Turning the Relationship Upside Down." Paper presented before the Office of Justice Programs, U.S. Department of Justice, Washington, DC.

————. 1996b. "A State Initiative Toward Restorative Justice: The Minnesota Experience." In *Restorative Justice: International Perspectives,* edited by J. Hudson and B. Galaway, 493-504. Monsey, NY: Criminal Justice Press.

Reiss, A. J., and M. Tonry, eds. 1986. *Communities and Crime.* Chicago: University of Chicago Press.

Robinson, J. 1996. "Research on Family Group Conferencing in Child Welfare in New Zealand." In *Family Group Conferences: Perspectives on Policy and Practice,* edited by J. Hudson, B. Galaway, A. Morris, and G. Maxwell, 49-64. Monsey, NY: Criminal Justice Press.

Rottman, D. 1996. "Community Courts: Prospects and Limits." *National Institute of Justice Journal* 231: 46-51.

Schneider, A. 1985. *Guide to Juvenile Restitution.* Washington, DC: Office of Juvenile Justice and Delinquency Prevention.

————. 1986. "Restitution and Recidivism Rates of Juvenile Offenders: Results from Four Experimental Studies." *Criminology* 24: 533-52.

Sparrow, M. K., M. H. Moore, and D. M. Kennedy. 1990. *Beyond 911: A New Era for Policing.* New York: Basic Books.

Stone, C. 1996. "Community Defense and the Challenge of Community Justice." *National Institute of Justice Journal* 231: 41-45.

Strang, H. 1995. "Family Group Conferencing: The Victims' Perspective." Paper presented at the American Society of Criminology annual meeting, Boston, November.

Stuart, B. 1995a. "Circle Sentencing, Mediation, and Consensus—Turning Swords into Ploughshares." Unpublished paper, Territorial Court of the Yukon.

———. 1995b. "Sentencing Circles—Making 'Real' Differences." Unpublished paper, Territorial Court of the Yukon.

Travis, J. 1996. "Lessons for the Criminal Justice System from Twenty Years of Policing Reform." Keynote address at the First Annual Conference of the New York Campaign for Effective Crime Policy, New York.

Umbreit, M. 1990. "The Meaning of Fairness to Burglary Victims." In *Criminal Justice, Restitution, and Reconciliation,* edited by B. Galaway and J. Hudson, 47-57. Monsey, NY: Criminal Justice Press.

———. 1994. *Victim Meets Offender: The Impact of Restorative Justice in Mediation.* Monsey, NY: Criminal Justice Press.

Umbreit, M., and R. Coates. 1993. "Cross-site Analysis of Victim-Offender Conflict: An Analysis of Programs in These Three States." *Juvenile and Family Court Journal* 43: 21-28.

Umbreit, M., and S. Stacy. 1996. "Family Group Conferencing Comes to the U.S.: A Comparison with Victim Offender Mediation." *Juvenile and Family Court Journal* 47: 29-39.

Umbreit, M., and H. Zehr. 1996. "Restorative Family Group Conferences: Differing Models and Guidelines for Practice." *Federal Probation* 60: 24-29.

Van Ness, D. 1993. "New Wine and Old Wineskins: Four Challenges of Restorative Justice." *Criminal Law Forum* 4: 251-76.

Van Ness, D., D. Carlson, T. Crawford, and K. H. Strong. 1989. "Restorative Justice Practice." Monograph. Washington, DC: Justice Fellowship.

Vermont Department of Corrections. 1995. *Reparative Probation, Program Design.* Unpublished report. Waterbury, VT.

Walgrave, L. 1993. "Beyond Retribution and Rehabilitation: Restoration as the Dominant Paradigm in Judicial Interpretation in Juvenile Crime." Paper presented at International Congress on Criminology, Budapest, Hungary.

———. 1995. "The Restorative Proportionality of Community Service for Juveniles: Just a Technique or a Fully-Fledged Alternative?" *Howard Journal of Criminal Justice* 34: 228-49.

Wright, M. 1991. *Justice for Victims and Offenders: A Restorative Response to Crime.* Philadelphia: Open University Press.

Yazzie, R. 1993. "Life Comes from It: Navajo Justice Concepts." *New Mexico Law Review* 24: 175-90.

Young, M. 1995. "Restorative Community Justice: A Call to Action." Report for National Organization for Victim Assistance, Washington DC.

Zehr, H. 1990. *Changing Lenses: A New Focus for Crime and Justice.* Scottsdale, PA: Herald Press.

VI. Conclusion

14

Community Justice
in a Communitarian Perspective

Amitai Etzioni

A key element of the new and rising field of community justice is that it is as important as it is elementary: it builds on the recognition of the significance of the third realm, the social one. Public policy discussions of alternative approaches to crime in the past have often focused on the ideological opposition of punishment versus jobs. Conservatives tend to focus on the state as a source of punitive measures. As has been often noted, they have increasingly stressed the importance of longer sentences, curtailment of probation, the death penalty, the building of more prisons, and the hiring of more police. Liberals tend to focus on the economy. They stress the importance of jobs, secure jobs, well-paying jobs, and jobs that are meaningful, have a future, lead to a career (in contrast to "dead end" jobs). Providing more education and overcoming discrimination have also been stressed as factors that prevent crime. Decriminalizing (that is, further reducing the role of the state) has also been championed. Rehabilitation is to be relied upon when all these preventive measures fail and crimes are committed.

Lost in this debate, as in so many others, is that the social reality contains more than the state and the private sector. The core third element is the social fabric, the elementary but crucial fact that people are social animals, deeply in need of the support of others (Wrong 1994). Hence, the specific nature of the social bonds available or formed by a given group of people matters a great deal to the question whether or not crimes will be committed, which kind, and how one best deals with them.

Social bonds can make rehabilitation nearly impossible, as we see when they make inmates into tightly knit antisocial groups. And social bonds can tie police officers into a conspiracy of silence, that often effectively prevents the rehabilitation of the police. But, given different kinds of social bonds, they can serve to strongly uphold the pro-social values of communities that abhor crime and work a great deal to minimize it, as studies indicate (Bursik and Grasmick 1993; Sampson, Raudenbush, and Earls 1997). I have shown elsewhere that social cohesion is like a pipeline; if properly laid it greatly eases the flow of whatever is "sent" through the pipe, but the pipe does not predict the nature of the content (Etzioni 1975, Chapter 11). Bonds can make either a Mafia or a kibbutz stronger; they strengthen a militia or the Amish.

There has been considerable confusion when terms such as community and social groups are used (Fowler 1991). I suggest that communities have two defining elements: people who are members of communities have an affective criss-crossing web of relationship with one another (not just one-on-one relationships as friends do) and have a set of shared moral understanding (values and mores) (Etzioni 1996, Chapter 4). When social entities score low on both of these variables, we have social aggregates or groups but not communities. When social entities score higher, they form a variety of communities, depending on the score. When the scores are very high, we have overpowering communities, of the kind we had in traditional villages; communities that are able to suppress their members. When the scores are middle to high, there is an ability to uphold the mores the community undergirds, but also to allow for a considerable amount of variations in behavior, within the given confines.

The connection of these considerations to community justice is as elementary as it is often overlooked. They suggest, as chapters in this book show again and again, that social bonds, values (and social norms derived from them but much closer to behavior), can be a major factor in effectively preventing crime and in dealing with criminals. Better yet, community justice provides a rather profoundly new way of thinking about criminals not as individuals that must be handled but as persons who, together with their victims, are members of one community, and to view crime as a communitarian incident. Once approached in that manner, one gains a wholly new outlook about the processes at work and what might be done.

We learn that isolating and segregating criminals, that keeping the victims and the offenders apart, is often a poor way to prevent and punish crime, or to make the victims whole. In contrast, we learn about the merit of using the dealing with a crime as an opportunity to activate the communal processes; to help shore up bonds that may have been frayed; to assist both the offender and the victim in finding ways to deal with their past and to be restored to full membership in the community. Much about this is found in the body of this volume and hence not repeated here. I should, though, call attention to a factor that is not always sufficiently considered. Arguments in favor, and claims for community justice, as has often happened when enthusiasm runs high following the discovery of a new field and approach, are insufficiently qualified. I predict that in the next phase of the development of this important new field more attention will be paid to the following considerations, which speak to the questions—which criminals? which communities?

- Not all criminals can or should be subject to community justice. There are some psychopaths, serial murderers, and hard core sex offenders who will not respond well to communal processes, and some of their victims may not be ready to be "reintegrated" with them.
- Community justice works best for first time offenders and for non-violent ones.
- Community justice works best for communities that have accepted the moral values of reconciliation and forgiveness, and the nonpunitive approach.
- Community justice is going to be hampered when one seeks to implement it in social entities in which there are no or only very weak communal bonds or where the community is divided into two or more groups along racial, ethnic, religious, class, or sexual preference lines. Here community building will have to precede, or at least accompany, community justice.

We must realize that the very idea of community justice, as compelling as it is, is endangered when it is being overhyped and oversold. To guard against this tendency, we should seek to know much more about the conditions under which community justice works. And we should not equate all programs that do not entail incarceration with community justice, less the concept becomes so diffuse and deluded it will lose its intellectual and normative power.

Individual Rights and the Communal Good

Earlier communitarians, such as Ferdinand Tonnies and Robert Nisbet, who were on the rather conservative end of this school, focused on the loss of community and authority. Communitarians in the 1980s, on the left or liberal side, focused on the rediscovery of the social, showing that individuals are not free standing agents but socially "encumbered" selves. Responsive communitarians, who arose as of 1990, stressed the need to balance the social and the personal, the public and the private, individual rights and social responsibilities (Communitarian Network 1991; Etzioni 1993; Selznick 1992; for an additional discussion, see various articles in *The Responsive Community Quarterly).*

The concept of balance helps highlight the danger of tilting too far in either the direction of too much state control and social pressures, of the kind one sees in Singapore, China, and even Japan (and historically in Salem and Calvinistic Geneva), or in the direction of excessive individualism as in the United States of the 1980s (Bellah et al. 1985). The concept of balance also suggests that societies in different time periods and places need to move in *opposing* directions to arrive at the same place—the zone (not point) of balance between individual rights and the common good. Thus many Asian societies need more room for individual expression, minority's rights, women's rights, and so on, while the American society needed more attention to social responsibility.

The concept of balance between liberty and the social order, which has proven to be rather germane, does tend to distract attention from a major point on which community justice builds, from the existence of important areas of human behavior that constitute not a zero-sum relationship but are win-win situations from the viewpoint of the issue at hand. A community that succeeds in implementing and nurturing a full program of community justice will succeed in enhancing both individual rights and the common good, a much desired outcome.

The common good will be strengthened as more offenders come to realize the damage their acts have inflicted on other members of the community and on the community itself and truly accept the obligation to refrain from offending others and the community in the future. This may entail driving at a slower speed, refraining from drinking and driving, attending better to their children, paying taxes due, and numerous other social responsibilities. Moreover, members of the community that did not offend, but who participate or are aware of the proceedings (or "conferences") through which community justice is affected, will find their own sense of social responsibility enhanced. This will occur both because the members of the community will witness that those who evade their social responsibilities will be subject to communal censure, and that other members of the community will work to ensure that justice is done.

The special merit of community justice, if properly introduced, is that individual rights are *not* diminished in order to attain a higher level of social responsibility; on the contrary, these rights themselves may in the process become better guarded. This may not necessarily be the case if one thinks about community justice in legalistic terms. For instance, a victim of a crime who agrees to participate in a reconciliation process, to accept the results of mediation or some other such community justice process, may have in the process to yield some legal rights she or he would have otherwise. The same may be said about an offender who agrees to come clean, express remorse for a crime he or she committed, and thus at least technically incriminate him- or herself. If, however, one examines the matter in a broader normative perspective, community justice respects the individual a great deal. It treats each offender and victim as a whole person rather than as a legal entry in some formal proceeding. It tailors the response of the community to each situation and person, drawing on intimate knowledge of the case at hand and those involved. And it serves to ensure that in the future, rights that were endangered by the crime will be much better respected, a result it seems less often achieved by court proceedings and the jail sentences meted out by them.

All this is not to suggest that individual rights and social responsibilities never come into conflict even when community justice is working to perfection. It is only to suggest that one should realize that these two facets of the good society are not necessarily always oppositional, and that community justice is a new social approach that promises often to lift both facets to a higher level of realization and respect.

References

Bellah, Robert, Richard Madsen, William M. Sullivan, Ann Swidler, and Steven M. Tipton. 1985. *Habits of the Heart: Individualism and Commitment in American Life.* Berkeley: University of California Press.
Bursik, Robert J., and Harold G. Grasmick. 1993. *Neighborhoods and Crime: The Dimensions of Effective Community Control.* New York: Lexington

Books.

Communitarian Network. 1991. *The Responsive Communitarian Platform: Rights and Responsibilities.* Policy paper. Washington, DC: The Communitarian Network.

Etzioni, Amitai. 1975. *A Comparative Analysis of Complex Organizations.* Rev. ed. New York: Free Press.

———. 1993. *The Spirit of Community.* New York: Simon Schuster.

———. 1996. *The New Golden Rule.* New York: Basic Books.

Fowler, Robert Booth. 1991. *The Dance with Community: The Contemporary Debate in American Political Thought.* Lawrence, KS: University Press of Kansas.

Selznick, Philip. 1992. *The Moral Commonwealth: Social Theory and the Promise of Community.* Los Angeles: University of California Press.

Sampson, Robert J., Stephen W. Raudenbush, and Felton Earls. 1997. "Neighborhoods and Violent Crime: A Multilevel Analysis of Collective Efficacy." *Science* 277 (August): 918-24.

Wrong, Dennis. 1994. *The Problem of Order: What Unites and Divides Society.* New York: Free Press.

Index

ACLU *see* American Civil
　　Liberties Union
aggressive enforcement, 129,
　　186, 203
Alexandria, VA, 211
Alinsky, S., 141, 151, 153, 156
American Civil Liberties Union
　　(ACLU), 211, 215, 233
Anderson, D., 9
Anderson, E., 111
Antidrug Abuse Act of 1986, 205
apology, 11, 280, 294-95, 298-
　　300, 309, 346
asset forfeiture, 205, 211, 212
Atlanta, GA, 103
Australia, 281, 304-5, 313, 328,
　　346, 350

Baltimore, MD, 101, 107
Baum, A., 236
Bayley, D., 171
beat officer, 178, 187, 193-94
beat probation, 3, 19
Berkeley, CA, 211
BIDs, *see* business improvement
　　districts
BJA, *see* Bureau of Justice
　　Assistance
black homicide, 97, 101
block watch, *see* neighborhood
　　watch

block-busting, 109, 150
Boston, 19
Bradley, B., 119-20
broken homes, *see* family
　　disruption
broken windows hypothesis,
　　146, 157, 238, 260
Buffalo, NY, 210
Bureau of Justice Assistance
　　(BJA), 168
Burnes, D., 236
Bursik, R., 106, 109, 148, 150
Bush, G., 120
business improvement districts,
　　12

capacity-building, 15, 81
CCIs, *see* comprehensive
　　community initiatives
CDCs, *see* community
　　development corporations
Center for Social and
　　Community Development,
　　81, 88
Center for Substance Abuse
　　Prevention (CSAP), 88
CHA, *see* Chicago Housing
　　Authority
Chicago, 97, 101, 109-11, 211,
　　215, 218-23

Chicago Housing Authority (CHA), 211

Chicago School, 99, 109, 149

churches, 12, 21, 103, 158, 161

circle sentencing, 328, 331, 337, 343, 351

citizen driven search warrant, 271

citizen patrols, 6, 148, 153, 205, 264

civic organizations, *see* community organizations

civil liberties, 203

Clean Car Program, 18

coalitions, 10, 48, 81, 257

communitarian, 291, 294, 297, 336, 373

community corrections, 9-11, 327-28, 330

community development corporations, 32

community organizations: and accountability, 19; and antidrug activities, 204-5, 212; and coalitions, 83-84; and community capacity, 12, 90, 92, 157; and crime prevention, 31, 138-39, 155; and informal control, 152; and policing, 21, 171, 191

Community Partnership Program, 88

community patrols, *see* citizen patrols

Community Response to Drug Abuse (CRDA), 204

community service, 9, 11, 16, 292, 296, 327, 330, 352

comprehensive community initiatives (CCIs), 12, 88

concentrated poverty, 101, 104, 110, 112, 114

Constitution, U.S., 203, 206, 210

Covington, J., 151

crack, 254, 256, 270

CRDA, *see* Community Response

to Drug Abuse

Crenson, M., 41-42

Crime Stoppers, 212

CSAP, *see* Center for Substance Abuse Prevention

DEA, *see* Drug Enforcement Administration

Denver, CO, 152

disorder: and community courts, 16; and community justice ideal, 5; and fear, 130, 151, 178, 238; and policing, 6, 171, 233; and problem-solving, 17; and prosecution, 8-9, 253, 260

diversion from court, 8, 328, 330, 348, 351

drug courts, 9, 330

Drug Enforcement Administration (DEA), 213, 210

drug war, *see* war on drugs

drug-free school zones, 143, 205

family disruption, 100-102, 115

family group conferences, 3, 281, 327, 331, 342, 354

fear of crime, 5, 11, 40, 119, 139, 151, 177, 238, 261, 300

First Amendment, 215, 234-35, 246, 248-50

Fish, S., 247

Flint, MI, 142

foot patrols, 141, 179, 240, 258, 260

Fourteenth Amendment, 234

gangs, 108, 110, 207, 215, 227, 253, 258

Garfinkel, H., 280, 282-83, 289, 317

General Social Survey, 121
Glendon, M., 274
Glensor, R., 5
Goldstein, H., 187, 191, 240
Grasmick, H., 148, 150
Groves, B., 107-8

Hacker, A., 132
Hannerz, U., 112
Harlem, NY, 8
Hayward, CA, 168
Hirsch, A., 109
Horton, W., 120, 132
hot spots, 204, 205, 207
Housing and Urban Development
    (HUD), Department of, 211
Houston, TX, 168
HUD, *see* Housing and Urban
    Development

inequality, 24, 97, 121
informal social control: and
    community capacity, 15,
    107; complementing formal
    control, 11, 228, 307; and
    crime prevention, 40, 108,
    151, 156, 170; increasing,
    154, 178; and social
    disorganization, 152
intensive enforcement, *see*
    aggressive enforcement
*International Society for Krishna
    Consciousness v. Lee,* 249

Jackson, P., 120
joblessness, 100, 103
Joliet, IL, 243

Kelling, G., 233, 260-62
Kolender v. Lawson, 234
Kornhauser, R., 106, 110
Kuykendall, M., 257, 269-72

labeling theory, 282-83, 296

Land, K., 107
Lane, V., 211
Lauritsen, J., 106
Lawrence, MA, 214
learning community, 85
liberalism, 373, 376
Liska, A., 126
Loper v. NYCPD, 237, 244,
    248
Los Angeles, CA, 211, 214,
    215, 217, 225
Louisville, KY, 168

Maori, 280, 288, 295, 302, 305,
    328
Mapp v. Ohio, 241
Marshall, T., 229
McKay, H., 99-101, 103, 106,
    110
mediation, see victim-offender
    mediation
Merry, S., 129-30
Miami, FL, 214
Midtown Community Court, 9,
    15-16
Miranda v. Arizona, 241
Moeller, G., 128
Monkkonen, E., 242-43
Multnomah County, OR, *see*
    Portland

neighborhood organizations,
    see community
    organizations
neighborhood watch, 138, 143,
    205
New York City, 3, 15, 101,
    233, 246
New Zealand, 281, 286, 289,
    291, 294, 303, 309, 313,
    327, 331, 350
Norfolk, VA, 168
normative standards, 14
nuisance abatement, 205, 271

O'Neill, T., 151
offender reintegration, 10, 20, 279, 283, 347, 355
offender risk, 11, 22, 349
Office of National Drug Control Policy, 205
Operation Clean Sweep, 211
Operation Night Light, 19

Papachristou v. City of Jacksonville, 234
peacemaking criminology, 280
Peak, K., 5
Pearson, W., 255, 257-59, 264-65
Philadelphia, 97
Police Activity Leagues (PAL), 141
police discretion, 240-41
Police Foundation, 260
Portland, OR, 253, 255
prevention, 12-13, 31-32, 35, 81-82, 137, 154, 156, 171
Prince George's County, MD, 168
problem-solving, 14, 16-18; and community crime prevention, 34-35, 41, 156, 170; and policing, 5-7, 38, 141, 170, 188; and prosecution, 273-74; and sanctioning, 309, 317, 330, 335, 352, 356
public housing, 103-4, 109, 174, 211
public order, 253-55, 267

quality of life, 4, 8, 12, 18, 253, 255

reasonable suspicion, 209-10, 212
reconciliation, 3, 280, 293, 342
redlining, 109, 150, 154
redress, 280
reintegrative shaming, *see* shame
reparation, 291, 309, 328-29, 331, 336, 344, 347

reparative probation, 328, 343
restitution, 3, 7, 8, 11, 16, 300, 327, 330, 346, 349
restorative justice, 279, 327, 329, 330, 335-38, 359
retribution, 327, 336,
Rosenbaum, D., 34, 139, 154, 156, 203
Rottman, D., 334-35

schools, 12, 21, 25, 34, 89, 103, 123, 131-32, 141
Schrunk, M., 255-57, 269
segregation, 103-4, 110, 114-15, 124, 126, 128
Seminole County, FL, 215
shame, 280-81, 283, 289, 300, 337, 343, 346
Shaw, C., 99-101, 103, 106, 110
Shuttlesworth v. City of Birmingham, 234
situational crime prevention, 12
Sixth Amendment, 214
Skogan, W., 119, 139, 156, 138, 152, 239, 246, 260-62
Skolnick, J., 171
social disorder, *see* disorder
social disorganization theory, 105-10, 140, 152-53
social isolation, 98, 105, 110, 151, 157
socialization, 103, 106, 345
Stinchcombe, A., 121
Strang, H., 346
Stuart, B., 347, 351, 357
subculture of violence, 98, 101
surveillance, 6, 22, 32, 139, 153, 272
Suttles, G., 110

take back the night rallies, 143
Taylor, R., 107, 151
teen courts, 9
Tempe, AZ, 168

Terry v. Ohio, 208
Tribe, L., 212

U.S. v. Rhodesian Stone Statutes,
    212
UCDP, *see* Urban Community
    Development Program
unemployment, *see* joblessness
Urban Community Development
    Program (UCDP), 88
urban renewal, 103, 110

Vera Institute, 168
Vermont, 3, 10, 328, 331, 343,
    349
victim impact statements, 7

victim-offender mediation, 7, 8,
    291, 329, 331
voluntary organizations, *see*
    community organizations
Volusia County, FL, 209

Wacquant, L., 109, 113
war on drugs, 97, 203
Washington, DC, 47, 238, 255
Weed and Seed, 205
Wilson, J. Q., 15, 238, 260-62
Wisconsin, 3, 19

Young v. NYCTA, 247

zero tolerance, 179

About the Contributors

Gordon Bazemore is currently an associate professor of criminal justice at Florida Atlantic University. His primary research interests include juvenile justice, youth policy, community policing, corrections and victims issues. He is editing a book entitled: *Restoring Juvenile Justice: Changing the Context of the Youth Crime Response* (Criminal Justice Press). Dr. Bazemore currently is the principal investigator of a national action research project funded by the Office of Juvenile Justice and Delinquency Prevention to pilot restorative justice reform in several jurisdictions and is completing a project funded by the Office for Victims of Crime (U.S. Department of Justice) to study judges' and crime victims' attitudes toward victim involvement in juvenile court.

Susan F. Bennett is associate professor of the public services graduate program at DePaul University and is currently a teaching fellow for the social sciences curriculum development program at the Institute of Sociology, University of Warsaw. Her current research focuses on the nature of civil society in contemporary Poland. Recent publications include "Police, Crime and Crime Prevention," in R. K. Vogel, ed., *Handbook of Research on Urban Politics and Policy* and *Community Policing in Chicago: Year Four* by the Chicago Community Policing Evaluation Consortium.

Barbara Boland, a Washington-based crime policy analyst, is presently a visiting fellow at the National Institute of Justice where she is conducting a series of case studies of community prosecution. A study of the Manhattan District Attorney's initiative will be published by NIJ in 1998.

John Braithwaite is head of the Law Program, Research School of Social Sciences, Australian National University. He is currently working on the globalization of business regulation and restorative justice. Recent books include *Corporations, Crime and Accountability* (with Brent Fisse) and *Responsive Regulation: Transcending the Deregulation Debate* (with Ian Ayres).

385

Michael E. Buerger has recently joined Northeastern University's College of Criminal Justice in Boston, Massachusetts, as an associate professor, following a stint as research director for the Jersey City (NJ) Police Department. A former police officer, his current interests include police organizational change; police response to domestic violence; improving the pre-service education for prospective police officers and better integration of education and training; and the evolution of police-community dynamics. He has published articles on street-level drug markets, police problem-solving efforts, and the limits of community policing, and is working on a book about the community policing movement.

David M. Chavis, Ph.D., is president of the Association for the Study and Development of Community, a network of leading community development scientists and consultants in the United States and Europe. His current research includes evaluations of the Comprehensive Strategies Program sponsored by the Office of Juvenile Justice and Delinquency Prevention, the Safe Havens and Community Policing Initiative of the Milton S. Eisenhower Foundation, and several community building initiatives. His current publications include articles on community capacity-building, coalitions, and comprehensive community initiatives.

Todd R. Clear is professor and associate dean, School of Criminology and Criminal Justice, at The Florida State University. His most recent book is *Harm in American Penology*, published by SUNY Press. Previous books include *Controlling the Offender in the Community* and *American Corrections*. Other published research covers the topics of correctional classification, prediction methods in correctional programming, community-based correctional methods, intermediate sanctions, and sentencing policy. His current research includes religion and crime, the correctional implications of "place," and the concept of "community justice."

Catherine M. Coles is a research associate in the Program in Criminal Justice, John F. Kennedy School of Government, Harvard University. An anthropologist and attorney, she has conducted research on community-oriented prosecution and community policing in the United States, as well as studies of social change in African urban centers. She is co-author (with George Kelling) of *Fixing Broken Windows*, and has published articles on community prosecution, as well as *Hausa Women in the Twentieth Century*.

Amitai Etzioni is the first university professor of The George Washington University and director of the Institute for Communitarian Policy Studies. In 1991, he founded the Communitarian Network, and in 1995, he was president of the American Sociological Association. He is the author of numerous books, including *The Active Society* (1968), *The Spirit of Community: Rights, Responsibilities, and the Communitarian Agenda* (1993), and *The New Golden Rule: Community and Morality in a Democratic Society* (1996).

Suzanne Goldsmith-Hirsch is the editor and publisher of *Dig: People Growing Strong Communities*, a newsletter about community service and community-building initiatives based in Columbus, Ohio. Her book, *A City Year: On the Streets and in the Neighborhoods With Twelve Young Community Service Volunteers* (The New Press: 1993) was recently issued in paperback by Transaction Publishers in New Brunswick, NJ.

Randolph M. Grinc is an assistant professor of Sociology and Criminal Justice at Caldwell College. His current research interests include community resident and line-level officers' perceptions of community policing programs. From 1989 to 1994, he was a research associate at the Vera Institute of Justice where he served as deputy director for Vera's National Institute of Justice-funded evaluation of the Bureau of Justice Assistance's "Innovative Neighborhood Oriented Policing" (INOP) project.

David R. Karp is an assistant professor of Sociology at Skidmore College in Saratoga Springs, New York. He was previously a research scientist at the George Washington University Institute for Communitarian Policy Studies. His current research interests focus on the identification and synthesis of community justice as a field of inquiry. He has published most recently in *Crime & Delinquency*, *The Responsive Community*, and *Correctional Management Quarterly*, and has recently completed with Todd Clear a report to the National Institute of Justice on community justice.

George L. Kelling is a professor in the School of Criminal Justice at Rutgers University, a research fellow in the Kennedy School of Government at Harvard University, and an adjunct fellow at the Manhattan Institute. He conducted the Kansas City Preventive Patrol Experiment, the Newark Foot Patrol Experiment, and, with James Q. Wilson, published "Broken Windows" in the *Atlantic Monthly*. His most recent work is *Fixing Broken Windows: Restoring Order in Our Communities*, with his wife, Catherine M. Coles.

Stephen Mugford is managing director of Qualitative and Quantitative Social Research and visiting fellow in Law at Australian National University (formerly associate professor, sociology, ANU) in Canberra, Australia. His research interests include the sociology of crime and deviance and organizational change. He is currently working on a review of sexual harassment and assault at the Australian Defence Force Academy and several evaluation projects.

Dennis P. Rosenbaum is professor and head of the department of criminal justice at the University of Illinois at Chicago. He has conducted studies of community policing, community mobilization, comprehensive interagency partnerships, media-based crime prevention, school-based drug education, and crime prevention in public housing. His books include *Community Crime Prevention: Does it Work?* (1986), *The Social Construction of Reform: Crime Prevention and Community Organizations* (1988), *Drugs and Communities* (1993), *The Challenge of Community Policing: Testing the Promises* (1994), and *Preventing Crime* (1997).

Robert J. Sampson is a fellow for 1997-98 at the Center for Advanced Study in the Behavioral Sciences, Lucy Flower professor of sociology at the University of Chicago, and research fellow at the American Bar Foundation. He is currently studying the natural history of crime among 500 men followed from adolescence to age 70 and conducting a long-term study of the social organization of Chicago neighborhoods. His most recent book, written with John Laub, is *Crime in the Making: Pathways and Turning Points Through Life*.

Wesley G. Skogan is a professor at Northwestern University's Institute for Policy Research. During the 1990s his research has focused on community policing issues. His latest book is *Community Policing, Chicago Style* (with Susan Hartnett, from the Oxford University Press).

William Julius Wilson is the Malcolm Wiener professor of social policy at the Malcolm Wiener Center for Social Policy in the Kennedy School of Government where he is director of the Joblessness and Urban Poverty Research Center. He is also a professor in the department of Afro-American studies at Harvard University. He is the author of numerous publications, including *The Truly Disadvantaged* (1987) and *When Work Disappears: The World of the New Urban Poor* (1996).